*To my wife, Elida,
and my parents, Charles and Marjorie,
who stood by me
through the twenty-three years
it took to complete this book*

CONTENTS

TODAY'S TECHNOLOGY IN BIBLE PROPHECY

TODAY'S TECHNOLOGY IN BIBLE PROPHECY

CHARLES W. MILLER

TIP

P. O. BOX 21113

LANSING, MI 48909-1113

Printed in the United States of America

Second Printing November 1994
94 95 96 97 98 99 / 10 9 8 7 6 5 4 3 2

The photographs and illustrations on the following pages are used by permission: front cover, 22 (Comstock Inc.); 78 (*The San Francisco Examiner*); 79 (Hugh Haynie, copyright, The *Courier-Journal* and *Louisville Times* Co.); 82, 128 (Culver Pictures); 407 (Ranan R. Lurie, Cartoonews International).

Unless otherwise noted, Scripture quotations are from the King James Version of the Bible. Other translations are identified as follows:

IGENT	*Interlinear Greek-English New Testament*
NASB	*New American Standard Bible*
NIV	*New International Version*
RSV	*Revised Standard Version*
THS	*The Holy Scriptures*
TSVGE	*The Septuagint Version: Greek and English*

ACKNOWLEDGMENTS

In preparing the manuscript for *Today's Technology in Bible Prophecy* I have had the assistance of my family and several friends. My wife, Elida, and parents, Charles and Marjorie Miller, provided support and many useful suggestions as they read successive versions of the manuscript.

Glen Van Antwerp, a layman Bible scholar with a discriminating eye for detail, spotted and corrected subtle flaws in some of my initial explanations of Daniel's prophetic imagery.

Dr. Andrew E. Hill, Associate Professor of Old Testament Studies, Wheaton College, Wheaton Illinois, carefully assisted me in comparing the differences between the various English translations of passages describing today's technology with the original Hebrew, Aramaic, or Greek texts. It was also Dr. Hill's relentless persistence that eventually found a way to actually get the book into print.

My mother, Marjorie Miller, and my sister, Tamsen Jane Blackwell, improved the book significantly by condensing over one hundred pages from the original manuscript. My sister, Shannon Elizabeth Parnofielleo and her husband Paul, also offered suggestions for improvement as they read and edited the later draft.

Dr. Chester Trahan, a computer scientist and educator with broad insight into many of the scientific issues of our time, made a major contribution to the project by offering a number of constructive suggestions on how to improve and simplify the readability of the scientific content of the book.

I am also blessed with another sister, Hollis Ann Crumback, who captured the central theme of many of the prophecies on technology with her illustrations and maps.

INTRODUCTION

The Bible's unabridged report on today's technology was written in ancient times to the inhabitants of the modern world. It begins with a series of feature for feature descriptions of the twentieth century's most distinguished engineering achievements. The startling accuracy and completeness of these writings are thought provoking. And that is precisely what these ancient texts are designed to do—make people think. They challenge people to seriously examine what the God of all creation has to say about modern man's inventions, the influence these advances will have on the milestone events of the future, and the final destiny of mankind's unguided experiment with modern technology.

Those who find it hard to accept the idea that centuries-old prophecies explain future events in terms of present-day inventions should consider the methods Jesus Christ used to teach spiritual concepts. Jesus repeatedly selected the familiar earthly objects of that day to better instruct His listeners. During His ministry, Jesus also answered a number of questions about the events leading up to the end of the world.

In view of Christ's teaching style, it is reasonable to assume that He would explain time of the end events in terms of the unique cultural surroundings of that future civilization. Those who look will find that Christ's forewarnings often included descriptions of present-day inventions. Those who look further will find that many Old Testament prophecies also spelled out end time events in terms of modern advances in technology. Isaiah noted that God alone has the authority to explain "what is still to come" (Isa. 46:10, NIV) in terms of future inventions.

9 I am God, and there is no one like Me (Isa. 46:9, NASB), 10 I make known the end from the beginning, from ancient times, what is still to come (Isa. 46:10, NIV). 6 "From now on I will tell you of new things, of hidden things unknown to you. 7 They are created now, and not long ago; you have not heard of them before today. So you cannot say, 'Yes, I knew of them.' (Isa. 48:6–7, NIV).

True to His statement, God "created now" (in ancient times), the biblical blueprints for a broad range of the inventions even-

11

tually spawned by the twentieth century's knowledge explosion. These "new things"—from superdams, to atomic missile-firing submarines, to air-burst nuclear bombs, to satellites in space—were "unknown" to men in Bible days. Yet they were obviously not hidden from God. The Bible's meticulous documentation of every aspect of these man-made objects, including the role they will play in shaping the events of the technological age, makes it impossible for even the most determined critic to dismiss God's knowledge, "from ancient times," of future inventions.

The presence of God's statement: "I declare new things; before they spring forth I proclaim them to you" (Isa. 42:9, NASB), immediately raises the next question: Why did God announce today's achievements in technology in advance? The answer to this question comes down to God's promise that He "is long-suffering to us-ward, not willing that any should perish, but that all should come to repentance" (2 Pet. 3:9). Thus, God, seeing from afar the certain destruction astride the path of man's mindless pursuit of sensational technology, backed up His stated objective to rescue a doomed race with a plan of action. That plan spells out how the twentieth century's rapid establishment of precedent-breaking change will erase previous ways of living. What emerges from the Bible is a chronological list of the significant events of the technological age, including Christ's timely rescue of the human race from the brink of annihilation. This plan of action is a living testament to God's commitment to re-establish an everlasting relationship with a fallen race.

The Bible's list of end time prophecies begins with a series of prelude signpost events, which, in turn, are followed by seven major milestone events. The fulfillment of the signpost events provides the visible evidence necessary to convince the people living at that time that they are, indeed, living during the biblically defined last days of the age. Examples of the fulfillment of signpost events in our time include the return of the dispersed nation of Israel to their original homeland for the second time in their history, the 1960s construction of Egypt's Aswan High Dam, modern Israel's conquest of adjacent territory as a result of her decisive, 1967 Arab-Israeli Six-Day War victory, and the first manned space flight around the earth, on April 12, 1961.

The seven major milestones are the final countdown events leading up to Christ's promised return and establishment of His earthly kingdom of peace at the end of the age. The first milestone on the Bible's list of final announcement events is a global nuclear war. The threat of extinction by nuclear war which has hung over planet Earth since the advent of atomic weapons, is a familiar subject in our time. We live in a world with over 60,000 nuclear warheads—a few hundred of which could destroy Western civilization for decades to come. These facts underscore the central question of our unsettled age: How can the risk of a nuclear catastrophe be reduced?

The search for an answer has polarized policymakers of all nations as well as their increasingly impatient citizenry. Strategic arms limitations treaties, stronger national defense, maintenance of stable relations between nations, and every other strategy have failed to guarantee survival. This leaves people with the frustration of not knowing what the future holds, or even worse, wondering if they have a future.

Are there any answers? Is anyone in control? Is there a God? If so, does He care about all this? Fortunately, the human race is not alone. There is a God who knows and cares about the problems of our time. In fact, He cared enough to share with us the outcome of the nuclear age in which we live. He accomplishes this feat with His remarkable descriptions of nuclear weapons, the before and after events of the wars that will be waged with them, and most important of all, His promise to put the affairs of this world on a just footing directly following man's final atomic war. Herein lies the value of a reliable list of events preceding Christ's return, namely, the guarantee that there is a tomorrow, despite the ominous threats of the nuclear age.

One other point to keep in mind is that prior to the advent of the technological era, Bible prophecies detailing modern man's inventions were simply beyond the reach of human understanding. (In fact, after the detonation of the world's first atomic bomb, it took almost forty more years to gather the scientific knowledge base necessary to understand the prophesied aftermath events of the world's first atomic war.) This situation changed suddenly in the early 1980s, thanks in large part to a new generation of supercomputers. Operating at blinding speeds, these high-performance machines opened up areas of science that had previously been completely overlooked. The ability of these superpowered "number crunchers" to perform 1.2 billion mathematical operations per second enabled them to make short work of the vexing computations required to simulate meaningful nuclear war scenarios. The results of these nuclear war simulation studies revealed how large scale nuclear war could plunge the world into a "nuclear winter" lasting for several months. This fact, along with other recent scientific findings, just as suddenly opened heretofore closed Bible prophecies foretelling the sequence of events surrounding the world's first nuclear war.

The knowledge gained from the research efforts of the '80s enables today's generation to understand the Bible's account of a coming atomic war and the chaotic events of its aftermath, including the extent of the environmental damages that will be caused by the ensuing nuclear winter. In fact, the insights gained from these findings are so extensive that the Bible's once perplexing portrait of the future can now be viewed with surprising clarity. Moreover, where the supercomputer projections end, it is now possible to determine the intended meaning of Bible prophecies describing a post-atomic war world government and the rest of the events leading up to Christ's second coming.

Today's technology is the key to the long-standing mysteries of Bible prophecies concerning the last days. God's message of the hour is addressed to today's generation. Incredible chaos will shortly engulf the technically advanced world we have created. We need to be prepared for the coming battles of our time, both physical and spiritual. Contained within this book is a review of the Bible's impressive prophecies on these vital issues.

PART
1

THE PROPHECTIC SIGNIFICANCE OF EGYPT'S ASWAN HIGH DAM

1 Egypt's Wandering Idols

The story of today's technology in Bible prophecy begins in Egypt, a modern day nation in an ancient land. In many ways Egypt is an unusual setting for a prophesied twentieth century achievement to take place. For much of Egypt, little has changed in the 4,500 years since Pharaoh Cheops raised his Great Pyramid at Giza. In harmony with their forebearers of past millenniums, farm workers more often than not continue to work the fertile land along the Nile Valley by hand. Here, women in flowing black, balance on their heads great clay water jugs, the shapes of which are unchanged from biblical days. Yet, silently taking place in the midst of these pastoral surroundings is the fulfillment of a prophecy foretelling the unexpected side effects of a modern engineering achievement, one which will inexorably end the ageless cycles of Egyptian rural life.

Super dams are monuments to modern technology, the Great Pyramids of our time. The Aswan High Dam of Egypt is one of the grandest of its kind. It can generate 10 billion kilowatts of power a year; it forms a lake nearly 2,000 miles square; it hobbles the mighty 4,160-mile-long Nile River that spans half of Africa en route from the equator to the Mediterranean; the dam's construction was foretold by Isaiah the prophet over twenty-six centuries before engineers ever completed the dam's blueprints.

Man, the restless builder, constantly shapes and changes the face of the planet. In modern times some of his best-laid plans have gone completely awry. According to Isaiah 19, such will be the fate of the Aswan High Dam.

In 1960, above the town of Aswan, Egypt started building the dam that would fulfill Isaiah's prophecy of the utter ruin of Egypt in the latter days of man's reign upon the earth. Four years later the High Dam began harnessing the Nile, but it also broke the cycle of flood and drought, radically altering the rhythm of agriculture in ways not yet fully understood. The dam's initiators, the late President Gamal Abdel Nasser and his government planners, failed to foresee the negative effects the dam would bring upon Egypt. Today, Egyptian experts continue to debate the long-term changes the dam is bringing to the country.

The foretold construction of the High Dam provides a classic example of how God speaks to today's generation through the fulfillment of a technological prophecy. He often begins with a description of the technology in terms of its disruptive effects on the lives of people and their environment. Once the relationship between the physical object and the changes it will bring is established, God then spells out spiritual lessons to be learned from the situation. These instructive lessons invite today's technologically minded generation to seriously consider their shortcomings and return to God's instruction. This teaching pattern is used in the prophetic texts foretelling the blocking of the Nile by the High Dam.

WANDERING IDOLS

1 The burden of Egypt. Behold, the Lord rideth upon a swift cloud, and shall come into Egypt: and the idols of Egypt shall be moved at his presence, and the heart of Egypt shall melt in the midst of it (Isa. 19:1).

The burden of Egypt is the prophecy's title. The word burden declares the message to be of considerable importance to the nation of Egypt.

"Behold, the Lord" establishes God as the author of the message. God is often represented as riding on a cloud: "who maketh the clouds his chariot: who walketh upon the wings of the wind" (Ps. 104:3b). This is a bold introduction, used by Isaiah to inform the reader that he is simply the recorder of the matter. Isaiah does not claim to have the ability to see into the future; instead he acknowledges God to be the one speaking with authority about the things to come upon the land of Egypt.

The narrative begins with the first event to look for in the prophecy's fulfillment—"the idols of Egypt shall be moved."

In the early 1960s Egypt was straining to build the Aswan High Dam across the Nile. Upon completion, 310 mile long Lake Nasser would eventually form behind the 364 foot high structure. Towns, ancient cities, temples, and prehistoric sites would be flooded, once the lake began creeping southward and expanding towards its average six mile width. This fact prompted Egypt to appeal to experts around the world to help save the idols and temples of Nubian Upper Egypt from sinking beneath the rising waters.

For a time it appeared certain that the archeological treasures along the waters path would be swallowed. For Nubia was a gigantic outdoor museum, where temples, fortresses and cemeteries along the Nile contained the legacy of a parade of cultures going back to the dawn of history.

In all, some two dozen salvageable monuments and hundreds of other antiquities, survived in the threatened part of Nubia. Hoping to save them from the encroaching waters, Egypt and Sudan turned to UNESCO (the United Nations Educational, Scientific and Cultural Organization) for help. UNESCO appealed to all member states, and to private organizations and individuals as well, to assist in saving these mighty mementos of man's past. As a result, at least 23 of Nubia's major historical sites were rescued from the waters. Many of the shrines were relocated on the shores of the new storage lake.

ASCENT OF TEMPLES

The huge temples at Abu Simbel, 180 miles upstream from Aswan, were the largest monuments dismantled and saved. Hewn out of a rock bluff 3,200 years ago, they pay perpetual homage to Ramesses II and his wife, Queen Nefertari. Four seated colossi of Ramesses, each 67 feet high and weighing 1,200 tons, guard the entrance to the cavernous Great Temple behind them. The Great Temple honored the sun god Re-Haraklte and Ramesses himself (like all Pharaohs a god in the eyes of his contemporaries). A smaller temple nearby was dedicated to

Cliff-cut temples of Ramesses II at Abu Simbel, Egypt.

Hathor, goddess of love, music, the dance, and to Queen Nefertari.

Abu Simbel turned out to be the most challenging salvage operation of them all. Engineers throughout the world proposed ingenious schemes to rescue the huge sandstone masterpiece from drowning.

All but one plan, however, proved unsatisfactory or prohibitively expensive. The plan finally accepted, submitted by Swedish consulting engineers, called for dismantling Abu Simbel's temples and rebuilding them on the desert plateau 212 feet above the old site. The project, officially launched on November 16, 1963, involved engineers from five countries and eventually cost nearly $40,000,000.

One of the first steps in the salvage operation involved removal of 330,000 tons of rock surrounding the temples. Just to reach the innermost rooms of the shrines, engineers had to excavate nearly 190 feet down through the cliff above them. Ramesses' workmen had carved the temples into the mountain on a precise angle so that twice a year the rising sun's rays would strike 200 feet back into the Sanctuary to illuminate the side-by-side statues of the god Amun and the god-king himself. As a precautionary measure, engineers shored up the temples' interiors with 156 tons of steel girders. Without these supports the ceilings and walls might have collapsed.

The second phase of the removal called for cutting the two monuments and the rock that frame them into 7,520 pieces. Under the supervision of the West German firm of Hochtief, stonecutters used electric drills and saws to cut the massive figures into manageable blocks, some of which weighed as much as 33 tons each.

Relocating Abu Simbel's ancient temples ranks as one of the most spectacular moving jobs ever achieved by man. The relocation of Ramesses and numerous other idols and temples of Upper Egypt also marks the beginning of the fulfillment of an ancient prophecy of great importance to today's generation. Its significance will come into sharper focus in the rest of Isaiah's prophecy foretelling the negative effects the High Dam will bring upon Egypt.

For centuries Bible translators have had great difficulty translating Isaiah 19. According to the Interpreter's Bible Commentary the passage contains a number of obscure words and debatable references subject to numerous interpretations and disagreements. For example, some English translations render: "the idols of Egypt shall be moved at his presence," as: "the idols of Egypt will tremble at His presence." The following excerpt from Barnes' Notes, written in 1838, points this out: "Shall be moved. That is, shall tremble, be agitated, alarmed; or shall be removed from their place. The word will bear either construction."

Yet, even though the idols trembled while being dismantled and relocated, the word *tremble* does not even begin to describe the unprecedented international salvage operation that moved them to safety above the rising waters. For example, the exact same Hebrew word translated here as "move," also appears in several other Old Testament verses where it is translated into English as "wandered off" (e.g., Lam. 4:14, Amos 4:8). This rendering of the original Hebrew word describes the journey and final destination of five of Upper Egypt's temples perfectly. Egypt designated the temples of Dandur, Dabud, Tifa, El Dirr, and Ellesiya as gifts to countries making donations for the salvage work. Stone by stone, these temples and the idols they housed were dismantled and collected in storage areas on Elephantine Island, opposite Aswan. There they remained for several months awaiting shipment to nations, which at the time were as yet unnamed. While they were being moved to the storage areas, neither the movers, Egyptian government, donor

Truck moving head of Ramesses II from storage yard to assembly site.

nations, nor the gods, knew how far they were going, or where their final wanderings would end.

In retrospect, the fulfillment of the initial portion of Isaiah's prophecy provides a good example of how modern technology is providing the context for determining the intended meaning of an ancient word. As Bible prophecies about today's technology continue to come to pass, Bible language scholars will have a unique opportunity to establish the correct translation of many debatable prophetic passages.

TAMING THE FLOODS

Isaiah 19:1 ends with the statement: "and the heart of Egypt shall melt in the midst of it." "The heart" refers to the foundation on which the Egyptian nation based its life. The Nile has long been recognized as Egypt's source of strength, vigour, and health. "Egypt," wrote the Greek historian Herodotus, "is the gift of the river." No other country is so dependent on a single lifeline. Egypt's very soil was born in the Nile's annual flood; with the flood came the life-giving mud that made Egypt the granary of the ancient world. It was along this fertile green line, running 750 miles from the Sudanese border to the Mediterranean Sea, where early civilizations took root. The Nile valley's average width is seven miles. Through countless centuries the river carved a vast canyon or trench, bounded on either side by cliffs ranging in height from a few hundred to a thousand feet. Beyond the cliffs on either side of the river, there is nothing but scorching hot, trackless desert. Not surprisingly, Egypt's early inhabitants lived along the river. Even today, 96 percent of Egypt's 51 million people crowd the Nile Delta and narrow Nile Valley to the south, which make up only 3 percent of this desert land.

Isaiah's prophecy foretells the Egyptian heartland melting away in the days following the moving of Egypt's idols. *Barnes' Notes on Isaiah* states that the word melt as used in this passage denotes "dissolve." (This same word "masas" occurs in Psalm 97:5; Isaiah 34:3; and Micah 1:4 in reference to land melting). Interestingly, in the mid-1960s, the distinctive mud houses of some 50,000 Nubians, their walls gaudily painted with symbols ranging from scorpions to colorful steamboats, dissolved and collapsed as the rising Nile waters lapped among them. So also went the farms, villages, and towns in the 310-mile stretch of river where Lake Nasser formed.

The drowning of Nubia did not affect greater Egypt, however, since most of the country's heartland lies north of the dam. Isaiah's prophecy, on the other hand, does not predict partial heart failure, but rather, total destruction of Egypt's arable heartland. Therefore the final fulfillment of Egypt's complete destruction by a melting process can be expected to take place gradually over time.

Erosion of the Nile Valley increased dramatically following the successful blocking of the river by the High Dam. Silt-free water flowing downstream much faster was the primary cause, both around the Delta and along the Nile's banks. Before the dam's intrusion, the river's annual load of silt replaced what was lost by erosion. Today this treasury of silt is trapped behind the dam in the southern 100-mile third of the reservoir. In former times this sediment added a little more to the rich Delta land it had formed in the first place and helped shield the sand dunes serving as dikes along the Mediterranean shore from the full force of marine currents.

By 1971, just six years after the building of the Aswan High Dam, some parts of the coast were receding several yards a year. This unrelenting negative effect of the High Dam continues to

The growing disaster described in 1971 continues to this day. The Egyptians are becoming more and more discouraged with the passage of time. Eventually the situation will become so bleak that according to Isaiah 19 they will resort to seeking answers to their dilemma from idols, ghosts of the dead, and from mediums and spiritists.

It may seem improbable that twentieth century Egyptians will seek solutions for their man-made environmental and economic problems through occult practices. Yet evidence exists which indicates Egyptian government officials in recent times may have done so. In 1971, Al Ahram Editor Mohammed Hassanein Heikal claimed in his weekly column that members of President Anwar Sadat's Cabinet had relied on the occult while plotting an unsuccessful coup against the president. Citing taped evidence, Heikal said that during one seance a university professor acted as their medium and consulted the spirit of a departed sheik for a favorable date on which to attack Israel.

ANARCHY AND CHAOS

4 And the Egyptians will I give over into the hand of a cruel lord; and a fierce king shall rule over them, saith the Lord, the LORD of hosts (Isa. 19:4).

According to Isaiah's prophecy, Egypt's total collapse will end in a state of anarchy. A preliminary sample of the coming civil chaos erupted in January of 1977 when the Egyptian government cut food subsidies as an economy measure. Cairo's and Alexandria's poor responded by rampaging through the streets in the worst riots since the nationalist upheavals of 1952. The subsidies were quickly restored.

Once the negative effects caused by the intrusion of the High Dam have completely destroyed Egypt's crops and land, food subsidies will not help the starving Egyptians. Isaiah prophesied that a brutal dictatorship will check the ensuing civil chaos generated by this coming famine.

The demoralizing poverty that grips the world's most populous Arab nation was already gnawing steadily away at Egyptian President, Hosni Mubarak's pro-U.S. government in the mid-1980s. The extent of Egypt's worsening economic woes and the vulnerability of its government surfaced abruptly in late February of 1986 when about 8,000 ill-paid security police conscripts mutinied. Mobs of civilian troublemakers and looters, including Muslim fundamentalists and leftist students, joined the rioting policemen. It took the superior firepower of the Egyptian army two days to put down the mutiny.

Many diplomatic observers in Cairo believed the security police rebellion was symptomatic of Egypt's economic downturn and warned that it might foreshadow a wider revolt as the country's economic picture continues to darken. Conditions are already so bad that without U.S. aid, Egypt could not feed even half its 51 million people, let alone the additional million born every 10 months. Its $500 per capita income, one of the world's lowest, has been depressed further in recent times by soft Mideast oil prices and plummeting tourism hurt by fears of terrorism.

These troubles only fuel the hopes of the nation's Islamic fundamentalists who blame the West for Egypt's woes. With living standards falling, some Egyptians maintain the nation can be saved only by embracing Islamic fundamentalism.

A religious revival, led by fanatical mullahs, is gaining momentum. The mullahs' alternative religious solution will probably continue to "stir up Egyptians against Egyptians." According to Isaiah's forewarning, spreading discontent will eventually lead to open fighting and anarchy, which in turn will usher in "a fierce king [who] shall rule over the Egyptians."

DROUGHT AND FAMINE

5 And the waters shall fail from the sea, and the river shall be wasted and dried up (Isa. 19:5).

Here Isaiah begins to expand his initial description of the ecological damage that is coming upon the land of Egypt in our time. The Aswan High Dam began storing water in 1964; effectively ending the Nile's history of fluctuating floods. Termination of the annual rise of the river marked the fulfillment of Isaiah's forewarning: "and the waters shall fail from the sea."

In 1838, Albert Barnes wrote, "to this day in Egypt, the Nile is named el-Bahr, the sea." In former times its waters at the time of overflow resembled a sea.

never rains above the Delta. Thus, despite countermeasures being taken, farming areas that were formerly well drained and highly productive are gradually being ruined.

STREAMS OF DUST

In concert with the Nile's canal system becoming polluted, "the branches of Egypt's Nile will diminish and dry up." The branches of the Nile refers to the network of canals and ditches that make up the country's irrigation system. "Dry up" predicts a major decrease in the amount of water reaching Egypt's fields. Isaiah's warning, therefore, identifies pollution of the nation's irrigation system followed by a severe shortage of Nile waters, eventually bringing about the complete destruction of Egypt's agricultural system.

A limitless water supply was the foremost benefit expected from the High Dam. Instead, the dam has squandered the very water it was meant to save. Egypt engineered Lake Nasser to store 163 billion cubic meters of water and expected this capacity to be reached by 1970; however, by 1971 the lake was less than half full. The three-hundred-mile western bank of the lake was one of the reasons for the delay. The entire bank is composed of porus Nubian sandstone, part of a million-square-kilometer aquifer underlying the Libyan Desert, which can absorb endless quantities of water. Directly under the High Dam the Nile channel cuts across a water-bearing bed nearly half a mile deep through which water may flow either in from the Libyan aquifer or out. Before any dams were built in the area the predominant flow was into the Nile, adding about three billion cubic meters annually. But after the first Aswan Dam was built in 1902, pressure from its reservoir pushed all this water the other way and as much besides. Six billion cubic meters of Nile waters were lost through this flow reversal before the High Dam even got started. The far larger Aswan High Dam increased the amount of water escaping under the river. Water losses from the water-bearing bed, the sandstone banks, and fifteen billion cubic meters evaporating from Lake Nasser's surface, comes to more than a third of the water flowing into the lake, thirty billion cubic meters yearly. This seepage and evaporation has reduced Egypt's annual water supply 10 billion cubic meters below what the celebrated nilologist, Dr. H.

E. Herst, said it needed in 1970 for irrigation, river transport and the High Dam's turbines.

The High Dam's negative effects are bringing to pass the portion of Isaiah's prophecy foretelling that "the reeds and rushes will rot away." Although previously only 12 percent of the silt brought by the annual flood of the Nile reached the land, as much as 20 million tons of the rich alluvial mud was deposited on the fields along the river. As the flood receded, the water draining through the soil leached out the salts that would otherwise choke the life out of growing plants and carried them off to the Mediterranean. It was a natural system of replenishment and cleansing. Today this treasury of silt is trapped behind the dam, and there is no effective natural drainage system. To keep Egypt's soil fertile, millions of tons of expensive chemical fertilizer must be used. Even so, the crops are less. By 1975, increased salinity had reduced agricultural productivity by as much as 50 percent on much of 1.2 million waterlogged acres below the dam.

In the not-too-distant future Egypt's entire agricultural system will be reduced to the desolate description given in Isaiah's prophecy: "The bulrushes by the Nile, by the edge of the Nile and all the sown fields by the Nile will become dry, be driven away, and be no more" (Isa. 19:7, NASB).

DISCOURAGED FISHERMEN

In conjunction with Egypt's crops withering and the topsoil blowing away, the nation's fishing industry will be destroyed.

> 8 The fishers also shall lament, And all they that cast angle into the Nile shall mourn, And they that spread nets upon the waters shall languish (Isa. 19:8, THS).

Just six years after the Nile was dammed, the aquatic food chain had been broken in the eastern Mediterranean along a continental shelf 12 miles wide and 600 miles long. The lack of Nile sediment reduced plankton and organic carbons to a third of what they had been before the river was blocked. Deprived of an adequate food supply, the sardines, scombroids, and other crustaceans either died or migrated elsewhere.

Loss of silt translating into loss of fish was an unexpected side effect of the dam. Much of the fishing industry was wiped out with startling speed. By 1973, the sardine harvest around the mouth of the Nile had dropped from about 300,000 tons each year to under 100,000 tons. Other seafood—the famous Nile shrimp, for instance—completely disappeared. By 1981 *Environment* magazine reported that damming the river had effectively killed off the seasonal sardine industry.

Runoff of chemical wastes from agricultural modernization and industrial development have also contributed to the dramatic drop in fish takes in Egyptian waters.

TEXTILE INDUSTRIES CLOSE THEIR DOORS

9 The workers in combed flax will be in despair, and the weavers of white cotton (Isa. 19:9, RSV).

Egyptian's have been known throughout history as producers of fine linen and cotton products. Quality Egyptian cotton continues to be well received in today's world markets. Workers in this industry will also suffer the hardships of unemployment when the cotton crop withers and dies along with all the other vegetation in the Nile Valley.

There are probably more variations in the reading of Isaiah 19:10 than any other verse in the book of Isaiah. In 1838, Albert Barnes made the following comments about the marked difference of opinion on the interpretation of the reference. "There has been a great variety of opinion in regard to the interpretation of this verse, and much difficulty in the construction of the Hebrew words. This variety of reading arises chiefly from the different modes of pointing the Hebrew words." Here again it has become much easier for today's generation to derive the intended interpretation of the texts containing these obscure ancient words, simply because the larger context of prophetic passages centering around modern technical advances can now be understood.

The Holy Scriptures, according to the Masoretic Text, printed in 1917 by the Jewish Publication Society of America, will be used to begin the analysis of verse ten. Some other renderings of this text will also be reviewed along the way.

CRUMBLING FOUNDATIONS

10 And her foundations shall be crushed, All they that make dams shall be grieved in soul (Isa. 19:10, THS).

Riverbed erosion became an immediate problem following the blocking of the Nile by the High Dam's structure. The silt-free water began flowing downstream much faster, carrying off not just fringes of the banks but a quantity of the riverbed. By 1971, experts reported that this scouring process was undermining the foundations of three old barrier dams and 550 bridges built since 1952. To slow the current and so prevent their collapse, the Ministry of the High Dam proposed the construction of 10 new barrier dams between Aswan and the sea.

Erosion is also eating away at the Delta's coastline. Silt used to protect the Mediterranean coast between Alexandria and Port Said, where there are two large lagoons with narrow land spits. These fragile sand barriers have kept the sea back through the ages by serving as dikes along the shore. Effectively, they are the foundations upon which the rich Delta land rests. Now unreplenished by silt, much beach and Delta land are being lost to the sea's powerful currents.

Changes in the water table caused by the High Dam have brought another unanticipated problem. In 1966 temples that would have been flooded out by Lake Nasser were moved, but no one considered temples below the reservoir to be in any danger from the dam. Today the rising water table is undermining temple foundations more than 100 miles downstream. The 3,500-year-old Karnak temple at Luxor, separated from the river by only 20 meters, is one example. Dark stains in the lower portions of temple walls were the first indication of salt damage. The higher water table created by the dam causes water to migrate to the surface of the sandstone from which the monuments were built. The water evaporates, but the salts are left. They crystallize, blistering the surface and crumbling the stone.

Even the Great Sphinx, which has guarded the Pyramids for some 4,000 years, is being threatened at its foundation indirectly by the High Dam's presence. As Egypt's agricultural fortunes continue to decline, farm workers are thrown out of employment. Many head for a big city such as the nation's capital, Cairo, where more than 1,000 peasants were arriving every day by 1978. Swarming with 8-million people then, the numbers swelled to 14-million by 1985, turning Cairo into a municipal disaster. Public utilities did not keep pace with the exploding population which quickly stretched the suburbs to the edge of the Pyramids, 9 miles from the central city. One innocent by-stander, the Sphinx, is becoming a casualty from all this, as seepage from substandard sewers undermine its foundation.

As the adverse effects of Aswan's High Dam relentlessly bring to pass the foretold physical collapse of Egypt, the people are beginning to grieve over the sickening destruction taking place before their eyes. Dedicated Egyptian experts hired to find solutions to the proliferating problems were some of the first to become heavyhearted over the wrenching environmental reverses. A remark made by one development planner in 1970 to Claire Sterling, a free-lance journalist, reveals the growing distress shared by many of his countrymen. "I'd give my soul to turn it muddy brown again," he said, as he pointed to the translucent green Nile.

The agronomist probably understood better than anyone else at the time, the magnitude of the unfolding environmental catastrophe being wrought upon Egypt by the dam. Quite remarkably, his words echoed the same pronouncement foretold by Isaiah, "all they that make dams shall be grieved in soul."

WHERE ARE THE FISH?

Despite the striking parallels between the translation of this verse and the actual crumbling of Egypt's land and man-made structures, some may feel less than comfortable with the Jewish Publication Society of America's interpretation of the passage. Certainly the King James rendering appears quite different. "And they shall be broken in the purposes thereof, all that make sluices and ponds for fish" (Isa. 19:10).

Barnes' points out that the word "purposes" is found only in the plural, and is translated in Ps. 11:3 as "foundations," from the Hebrew word "foundation" or "pillar." According to this, it would mean all the pillars or foundations would be trodden down. The NASB rendered the passage this way, "and the pillars of Egypt will be crushed." Thus, all three translations are in complete agreement regarding the idea that something will be broken or crushed.

The variation in the texts as to what is being broken—them, pillars, or foundations—arises chiefly from the original language's occasional lack of clarification in the use of nouns and pronouns, and the different modes of pointing the vowels in the Hebrew consonantal text. The differences, nevertheless, leave the meaning essentially the same, since all three translations are actually coming to pass. For instance, as the foundations of Egypt's land, river, cotton industry, bridges, ancient temple pillars, etc., are broken, so also are the lives of the people being broken and crushed.

Barnes in his analysis of the phrase, "all that make sluices and ponds for fish," made the following comment. "There has been quite as great a variety in the interpretation of this passage as the former." Barnes goes on to say that the most probable interpretation is that fish ponds would be built, by confining the Nile's waters behind artificially made banks, for the purpose of earning a livelihood. These efforts would fail to succeed, or in other words the designers original purpose would be trodden down and broken.

Another interesting analysis was made in Jamieson, Fausset and Brown's commentary: "All that make sluices, etc.—'makers of dams,' made to confine the waters which overflow from the Nile in artificial fishponds (Horsley)." Here again there is no great need to prove that the King James translation is better, or less accurate, (depending on one's point of view) than the first presented rendering, "all they that make dams shall be grieved in soul," since both interpretations are coming to pass.

Without a doubt, nearly 2,000-square-mile Lake Nasser is the largest Egyptian fish pond ever built. The fish harvest was expected to reach fifty-to-a-hundred-thousand tons each year. Egypt's development planners listed the new lake's fishing industry as another one of those nice economic fringe benefits that would come to be realized from the construction of the dam. However, six years after the reservoir began filling with water, less than five thousand tons were coming out of its waters. Nevertheless, Lake Nasser Development Center officials remained optimistic in 1970 about the lakes future fish takes. Yet, by 1981, the following quote appearing in the May issue of *Environment* magazine still left one question unanswered, "Egypt hopes to build up the Lake Nasser fishing industry into an economically important resource, but this is still in the early stages." After seventeen years, where are the fish?

THE EVIDENCE DEMANDS A VERDICT

Setting aside the difficulties interpreting verse 10, the larger context of this prophecy reveals that the described physical collapse of Egypt can only be a reference to the side effects caused from blocking the natural flow of the river. The obstruction doing the blocking today is a dam, and not just any one of many dams the Egyptian's have built over the past 4,700 years, but specifically the Aswan High Dam.

The old Aswan Dam, begun in 1898 and completed in 1902, is the first exhibit supporting this position. The dam, located five miles downriver from the High Dam, was improved by making it higher in 1912, and again in 1933. Built to control the Nile's floods and reserve water, it is a substantial structure with a height of 174 feet. However, the old dam did not create Egypt's present ecological grief, since its much smaller reservoir was emptied each year during the dry season. This fact allowed the silt to reach the lower Nile, where it continued to maintain the balance of nature.

The primary evidence fixing the High Dam as the focal point for the fulfillment of this prophecy was established when the idols and temples of Egypt were moved, during and directly following its construction. The 30-million dollars spent on the Philae salvage program to remove and reassemble some 40,000 original blocks of the temple of the goddess Isis, underscores the significance of this statement. Prior to its relocation in 1972, few travelers ever set foot in the Temple of Isis. For Philae was an island in the Nile, and most of the year it used to be covered almost entirely by the waters held by the old Aswan Dam. Only when the summer dry season reached its peak did Philae and the temples's mud-covered colonnades emerge from the flood. But summer's end would bring rising waters, and once again Philae would sink beneath the Nile.

Contingent upon a six-million-dollar contribution from the United States, the original proposal to save Philae's temples called for the construction of three dikes to protect the monuments. Curiously, instead, the temples were relocated on loftier Agilkia Island in keeping with the letter of the prophecy, "the idols of Egypt shall be moved at his presence."

POOR COUNSEL YIELDS POOR RESULTS

11 The princes of Zoan are utterly foolish; the wise counselors of Pharaoh give stupid counsel. How can you say to Pharaoh, "I am a son of the wise, a son of ancient kings"? (Isa. 19:11, RSV). **12** Where are they? where are thy wise men? and let them tell thee now, and let them know what the Lord of hosts hath purposed upon Egypt (v. 12). **13** The princes of Zoan have acted foolishly, The princes of Memphis are deluded; Those who are the cornerstone of her tribes Have led Egypt astray. **14** The LORD has mixed within her a spirit of distortion; They have led Egypt astray in all that it does, As a drunken man staggers in his vomit (vv. 13–14, NASB).

According to the text all of Egypt's "princes" and "wise counselors," or government authorities and development planners, would enthusiastically promote the foolish decision to build the High Dam of the Nasser era. The reference to the ancient Egyptian capitals—Zoan, which was located on the southeastern coast of the Delta, and Memphis which was on the Nile above the Delta near today's Cairo,—emphasizes the fact that there was general support from the political leaders of Egypt's two principal geographical areas to proceed with the dam's construction.

Raising the High Dam across the Nile fired the imagination of Egyptians everywhere. The sheer size of the dam, larger than the Great Pyramid of Cheops by a factor of 17, sharpened the nation's sense of history. It reminded them of the fact that they are the sons of the wise, the sons of ancient kings, the offspring of the ancient pyramid builders who gave the art of grand construction to the world.

The late President Nasser and his government looked upon the Aswan project as a panacea for most of Egypt's ills. A man of energy and enthusiasm, Nasser proceeded to unofficially approve the project by word and action, long before any meaningful official evaluation could be presented. Not surprisingly, the engineers, limnologists, agronomists, and other experts, became excited about the proposed dam.

Isaiah listed the principal source of their "stupid counsel" as a "spirit of distortion." Gripped by the emotional appeal of the grandeur of the project, there was a tendency to distort the potential benefits of the dam, or at the very least lean toward

the positive viewpoint. The natural order of the Egyptian ap-
proval process amplified the overly optimistic expectations of
the dam's supporters, by shutting out all critical views. Thus,
Egypt's technical experts and political leaders, "the cornerstones of her tribes," "foolishly led Egypt astray."

A brief look at some of the original benefits expected from
the dam compared against its unprofitable side effects, will
serve to show just how far "the cornerstones of her tribes have
led Egypt astray in all that it does."

Egypt's original plan envisioned 1.3 million acres of desert
land reclaimed for agriculture. But soil studies made before the
dam was completed, showed that only 750,000 acres were
suitable. Nevertheless, by 1980 about 950,000 acres had been
reclaimed. Unfortunately, much of the new land is of inferior
quality and yields poor crops. Marginal crop performance coupled with extremely high reclamation cost, ranging from $600
to $1,200 an acre, resulted in suspension of some reclamation
projects by the mid 1970s.

One initially undisputed merit of the dam's stored water
was its use in the conversion of 2.5 million acres from seasonal
flood to year-round canal irrigation. This permits double and
sometimes triple-cropping, adding half again to the yearly
production of these lands. But, by 1970, nearly all of Egypt's
land was becoming dangerously waterlogged and salty. Egypt
responded to the problem by installing expensive closed underground drains on a million acres in the Delta and in some areas
of upper Egypt. This was the most ambitious drainage project
on earth at the time, costing $147 million. Experts estimated the
cost of installing closed drains and the pumps to go with them
on Egypt's remaining land at well over a billion dollars, a
quarter of the country's income. Despite these efforts, by 1975
poor drainage and increased soil salinity had reduced productivity on most of 1.2 million acres below the dam by as much as
50 percent. This fact essentially cut crop production yields back
to former pre-dam levels, but doubled planting, harvest and
labor costs.

Another staggering cost affecting the profitability of Egyptian farms comes from the necessity to buy artificial fertilizers
to replace the fertile silt, which nature in the past provided free.
By 1970 experts estimated the yearly cost of the extra fertilizer
to be upwards of a hundred million dollars.

After declaring Egypt's political leaders "utterly foolish" and the counsel of their development planners "stupid," Isaiah asked a rhetorical question. "Where are they? where are thy wise men?" Isaiah's reason for asking this question goes beyond exposing the learned Egyptian scientists for not having viable solutions to the nations proliferating problems. Instead, he challenges Egypt's experts to diligently research the problems, and "know what the Lord of hosts hath purposed upon Egypt." The dedicated experts who have studied the science of the dam's ill effects have found that there are no simple solutions to the problems caused by man's tinkering with nature. Their studies also confirm Isaiah's grim forewarnings.

Interestingly, one descendant of ancient Egyptian kings has been found in America, living in the university town of Ann Arbor, Michigan. Khalil H. Mancy, now a naturalized U.S. citizen, is an environmental chemist at the University of Michigan School of Public Health. In 1975 Professor Mancy was instrumental in establishing and coordinating a multidisciplinary research team of U.S. and Egyptian scientists to study the side effects introduced by the High Dam. The U.S. Environmental Protection Agency and the Ford Foundation helped pay for the study which was called the "U.S.-Egyptian Lake Nasser-River Nile Project."

After seven years of effort the conclusions from the Nile Project findings were less than encouraging. For instance, commenting on costly chemical fertilizer imports to correct reduced soil fertility from loss of silt, Mancy said that Egypt will at least have the hydroelectric power to run its new fertilizer plants. It is true, new fertilizer plants have cut import costs, however, consumption of huge quantities of electricity by these plants represents a less than auspicious use of the nation's precious power.

One of the big payoffs expected from the Aswan complex was an abundant supply of cheap power. But power installed is not necessarily power consumed; nor is it cheap, unless every kilowatt-hour is consumed from the start, over a span of many years. By 1970, Egypt was unable to use even a third of the High Dam's 10-billion-kilowatt-a-year capacity. By the mid seventies only 7 or 8 of the 12 giant turbines were being used. The reason: The Ministry of Irrigation, not the Ministry of Power, controls the complex, and water is released to meet irrigation rather than power requirements. Because of past periods of drought, irrigation officials hoard as much water as possible, especially during winter when the fields need less water. Since industry needs power throughout the year, the number of plants that can be built is limited by the amount of energy available at the lowest level of monthly output.

Perhaps better than any other example, the proposed solutions for stemming erosion damage resulting from loss of silt, exposes the emptiness of today's scientific counsel. Consider Egypt's early 1970's plan to build 10 new barrier dams between Aswan and the sea. These structures would prevent the river's scouring process from undermining 3 old barrier dams and 550 bridges by slowing the Nile's much faster silt-free flow. The project was expected to cost a quarter of a billion dollars—a quarter of what the High Dam itself cost.

Reports coming out of Egypt in 1975 indicated the proposed barrier dams were still in the planning stage, but the number had been scaled back to "about half a dozen." Six years later an updated report recommended the construction of check dams and bridges to accommodate the new bed scoured out by the Nile below the dam. The same report recommended shore reinforcement to counteract the continuing erosion of the Delta coastline. As he was finishing up the Nile Research Project, Professor Mancy pointed out that many shorelines, including those of the American Great Lakes, are reinforced routinely.

Somehow, all these recommendations have a hollow ring. Years have gone by while the erosion continues unabated. What good does it do to identify the same problems and recommend the same solutions, over and over again? Obviously, Egypt simply does not have the massive amount of money it would take to implement the proposed solutions. As Egypt's leadership helplessly watches the vastness of the silent destruction stalking the land, Isaiah's pronouncement rests upon them. "They have led Egypt astray in all that it does, As a drunken man staggers in his vomit" (Isa. 19:14, NASB).

TOTAL ECONOMIC COLLAPSE

15 Neither shall there be any work for Egypt, which the head or tail, branch or rush, may do (Isa. 19:15).

Unable to solve the nation's mounting problems, the Egyptians will eventually find their economy grinding to a complete halt. Employees in high positions, literally the heads of companies, will become unemployed along with the workers at the tail end of the economic ladder. The proverbial expression, "branch or rush," compares the lofty palm branch at the top of the palm tree with the lowly reeds that grow in the marshes. The expression is used for emphasis—the highest and lowest classes will be unemployed together.

Egypt's present terrible poverty already makes it a ward of wealthier nations. The nation was technically bankrupt in 1977. It has only been kept alive since by massive handouts and loans from abroad, mostly from Saudi Arabia, Kuwait, and the United States. Much of the outside aid is needed just to feed the growing population. The country went from a position of food exporter in 1976 to importing half its food a decade later at a cost of 10 million a day.

Egypt's poverty was compounded further during the 1980s, by plummeting demand for oil in the world marketplace. The 8-billion dollars a year the nation had received from Egyptians overseas fell sharply as tens of thousands lost their jobs in Libya and the Persian Gulf countries.

The situation is already grim for the estimated 250,000 to 900,000 living in the City of the Dead—a cemetery of crumbling vaults near downtown Cairo. However, the tomb dwellers are luckier than tens of thousands elsewhere in the city. In the worst slums, where the population density is almost 250,000 per square mile, the squalor and degradation match Calcutta's. Vast numbers of displaced farm workers spend their lives in one room, sleeping on the floor, taking their water from a public faucet and using the street as a toilet. Infants who play in garbage and excrement are themselves covered with flies, and they suffer from chronic dysentery, as well as lung diseases.

The worst off are the thousands who live in the filth, smoke, and stench of Cairo's seven garbage dumps. They share their hovels with donkeys and pigs, plus mounds of refuse and clouds of insects.

Once Egypt's agricultural system collapses, the people will find the days of Isaiah's prophecy upon them when there shall not be "any work for Egypt, which the head or tail, branch or rush, may do."

FEAR AND DOOM GRIP THE NATION

The next five events to look for in the prophecy's fulfillment begin with the expression "in that day." The meaning seems to be that during the days when Egypt's accelerating agricultural misfortunes are systematically destroying the nation's economy, the next five events can be expected to come to pass in rapid succession. Since the last of the five describes an unprecedented age of peace, "in that day" implies that the generation witnessing the dramatic decline of Egypt's agricultural system will also see the establishment of Christ's promised age of peace.

16 In that day shall Egypt be like unto women: and it shall be afraid and fear because of the shaking of the hand of the LORD of hosts, which he shaketh over it. 17 And the land of Judah shall be a terror unto Egypt, every one that maketh mention thereof shall be afraid in himself, because of the counsel of the LORD of hosts, which he hath determined against it (Isa. 19:16–17).

Isaiah explained the meaning of "the shaking of the hand of the Lord of hosts" over Egypt in chapter eleven's introductory overview of the ecological collapse of Egypt. "And with his mighty wind shall he shake his hand over the river" (Isa. 11:15b). Isaiah named wind as the instrument contained in God's hand which He shakes over the land of Egypt. Also, Isaiah 19:7 forewarned: "Every sown field along the Nile will become parched, will blow away and be no more" (NIV). Thus, as the Egyptian's watch their crops blow away on their worn out parched soil, they will become filled with fear, "because of the counsel of the LORD of hosts, which he hath determined against it." Since Isaiah was a prophet who lived in the land of Judah 2,700 years ago, the Egyptian's initial reaction to his prophecy will be sheer terror. They will stand in awe and fear of the God of the Israelites whose predictions of Egypt's destruction originated in the land of Judah. As the prophesied wind blows and the famine intensifies, the people will fear for their lives.

EGYPT'S FORETOLD CONVERSION
TO CHRISTIANITY

18 In that day there will be five cities in the land of Egypt which speak the language of Canaan and swear allegiance to the LORD of hosts. One of these will be called the City of the Sun (Isa. 19:18, RSV).

Speaking "the language of Canaan" is an expression used to describe the conversion of Egyptians to the worship of the true God of Israel. This is evident from the stated fact that they will not only "speak the language of Canaan," but will also "swear allegiance to the LORD of hosts."

A similar expression, to denote conversion to the true God, occurs in Zephaniah 3:9: "For then will I turn to the people a pure language, that they may all call upon the name of the LORD, to serve him with one consent."

Five cities are foretold to become major centers for the worship of the true God of Israel. "One of these will be called the City of the Sun." There has been a great variety of interpretation in regard to which city this expression represents. In the past, Bible scholars have suggested several cities as candidates. Among the cities proposed prior to the twentieth century only the fashionable Cairo suburb of Heliopolis still remains. Heliopolis is a Greek name which means city of the sun. If Heliopolis becomes a major center for the worship of the true God of Israel, as the larger prophecy concerning Egypt comes to pass, then the question will be settled.

19 In that day there will be an altar to the LORD in the midst of the land of Egypt, and a pillar to the LORD near its border (Isa. 19:19, NASB). 20 It will be a sign and a witness to the LORD of hosts in the land of Egypt; when they cry to the LORD because of oppressors he will send them a saviour, and will defend and deliver them (Isa. 19:20 RSV). 21 And the LORD shall be known to Egypt, and the Egyptians shall know the LORD in that day, and shall do sacrifice and oblation; yea, they shall vow a vow unto the LORD, and perform it. 22 And the LORD shall smite Egypt: he shall smite and heal it: and they shall return even to the LORD, and he shall be intreated of them, and shall heal them (Isa. 19:21–22).

The word *altar* as used here designates a place of worship. It means the worship of the true God will be established in the midst of Egypt.

Also, there will be a pillar to the Lord "near" Egypt's border which will be erected for a sign and for a witness unto the Lord of hosts in the land of Egypt. The Bible records how Israel's founding father Jacob set up a pillar of stone as a memorial to God, to mark the place where God talked with him (Gen. 35:14). In recent times modern technology has enabled man to construct pillars of concrete and steel to God, which also mark the place where God speaks to men over the air via radio waves.

According to the text, the pillar will be located on the soil of one of the nations bordering Egypt. Today there is at least one radio tower dedicated to broadcasting religious programs into Egypt and other Middle Eastern countries which meets the described requirements for the fulfillment of this prophecy. It is located on Cyprus, an island nation that shares a common international border with Egypt's northern coastal waters. This medium wave AM broadcasting facility is owned and operated by Trans World Radio. The station witnesses to the Egyptians daily, declaring the Lord God of Israel to be the Savior of all mankind. The very existence of the radio station properly fulfills another "sign" of Isaiah's prophecies coming to pass in Egypt today.

With the exception of the 6-million member Coptic Christian minority, Egypt's 51-million people are practicing Moslems. Since the larger context of Isaiah's prophecy is coming to pass, then it must be true that the Egyptians "shall return even to the Lord" in the near future. To do so the majority of the people will have to depart from the Moslem religion. Therefore, since the only non-Moslem stations dedicated to broadcasting religious programs into Egypt are religious broadcasters such as Trans World Radio, then it also follows that Trans World Radio properly fulfills Isaiah's description of the witnessing pillar to the Lord. Moreover, it must be presenting God's true message to the Egyptians, since God foretold these events concerning Egypt in the first place.

The statement: they "shall do sacrifice and oblation" does not necessarily mean that the Egyptians will set up animal sacrifice since by the law of Moses there was to be no altar for sacrifice except for the one at Jerusalem. Rather, the sense more likely meant here is that they will be sincere worshippers of God in keeping with Samuel the prophets teaching: "to obey is better than sacrifice" (1 Sam. 15:22).

The passage closes with a summary explanation as to why the Egyptian nation will turn to God. "The Lord shall smite Egypt," refers to the foretold calamities previously described in this prophecy. "He shall smite and heal it," promises restoration of the broken country to health and prosperity. And because of what happened following the High Dam's construction, the Egyptian people "shall return even to the Lord, and he shall be intreated of them, and shall heal them." For instance, they will learn, from Christian radio broadcasts, about Isaiah's prophecy foretelling the destruction the dam's side effects would bring upon Egypt. At first these facts will fill them with fear and doom; but, they will also hear about a Savior who loved them enough to die for their sins–a Savior who will, in addition to helping them out of their present dilemma, also save their souls. The Egyptians will know the radio station's witness about the Savior is true because of the prophecies coming to pass in their land. A widespread conversion to Christianity will follow.

A PROMISE OF PEACE

> **23** In that day there will be a highway from Egypt to Assyria, and the Assyrians will come into Egypt and the Egyptians into Assyria, and the Egyptians will worship with the Assyrians. **24** In that day Israel will be the third party with Egypt and Assyria, a blessing in the midst of the earth, **25** whom the LORD of hosts has blessed, saying, "Blessed is Egypt My people, and Assyria the work of My hands, and Israel My inheritance" (Isa. 19:23–25, NASB).

Once the preceding prophesied events are fulfilled, a lasting peace will be established between Israel, Egypt and the neighboring Arab States, referred to here as Assyria. Moreover, in addition to the Egyptians turning to God, Israel and her Arab neighbors will also become Christian nations. The three historically contending groups of people will freely travel back and forth on a highway connecting their territories. They will not only visit one another but will worship the same God together as friends.

The reason Assyria is used to represent today's Arab States in this passage can be found in the history of Isaiah's day. The Assyrian people as early as 3,000 B.C. had founded a tiny kingdom on the plateau of Assur some 500 miles up the Tigris River. About 1,300 B.C. these people began to expand northward, and eventually they came to be called Assyrians. Their empire was reaching its height in the eighth and seventh centuries B.C., when Isaiah was writing these prophecies down. It came to encompass nearly all of the civilized world of that time, including: Syria, Phoenicia, the kingdom of Israel, Babylonia, and Egypt. Only the little kingdom of Judah, where Isaiah lived, retained its independence. Today, the modern Arab states of Iraq, Syria, Lebanon, and Jordan occupy the lands once ruled by Assyria.

In summary, Isaiah's prophecy defines the negative consequences resulting from the construction of a dam across the Nile—e.g., the systematic destruction of Egypt's entire agricultural and economic system—as prelude events to a lasting peace in the Middle East.

2 Egypt— A Prophetic Hourglass

Isaiah 11 lists a series of three events that will occur before a new age of peace is set up on the earth. These three events are tied to the prophecies concerning modern Egypt in such a way that together they provide considerable insight into when this coming age of peace can be expected to arrive.

Isaiah begins this prophecy by introducing the person who will establish this coming period of peace.

> **1** There shall come forth a shoot from the stump of Jesse, and a branch shall grow out of his roots (Isa. 11:1, RSV).

Jesse was the father of King David. "The stump of Jesse," describes the ancient ruling family of David that fell into decay after the Babylonians conquered and destroyed their country. The shoot coming forth from the stump and growing into a branch, out of the roots of the kingly line of Jesse, promises the reestablishment of the throne of David by one of his obscure descendants.

According to the biblical record the last person to be born into the house of David was Jesus Christ (Matt. 1). True to the words of this prophecy, when Jesus was born, the ancient family of David had fallen into obscurity. In fact, Christ's mother, though a direct descendant of David, was poor, obscure, and unknown.

vided Israel with more defensible borders, which has helped insure her continuing existence as a nation. Even more important, the Israeli army was able to eventually cut off the constant harassment from Arab saboteurs who were based on these lands. In fact, Israel's occupation army completely "cut off those who harassed Judah" from the former guerrilla strongholds based on Arab lands surrounding southern Israel.

The Israeli army also cut off those who formerly harassed its northeastern border from Syria's Golan Heights. The Golan area was once part of the ancient northern kingdom of Israel. Yet, Isaiah does not say those who harass Ephraim shall also be cut off. The reason for this omission rests upon the fact that part of the ancient kingdom of Israel has since become modern Israel's northern border with Lebanon. In the years following the Six-Day War, the Palestinian Liberation Organization (PLO) made southern Lebanon a virtual "state within a state." From mountain redoubts, the PLO continued to harass northern Israel for the next 15 years until Israel invaded Lebanon in 1982 and drove them out of the area.

In retrospect, only the southern half of modern Israel, encompassing the ancient territory of the kingdom of Judah, gained secure borders from the Six-Day War victory. Had the intent of the prophecy been to foretell the eventual cutting off of all those who would harass the entire restored nation, then a reference would have also been made to Ephraim in such a way as to include the elimination of the PLO's last infiltration route across Israel's northern border in 1982. Because of these related historical facts, it follows that the main purpose of the prophecy is to define the Six-Day War to be the second major signpost event to occur just prior to Christ's Second Coming.

The passage ends with a positive identification of the modern nation of Jordan and foretells the political relationship that would be established between Israel and Jordan after the war.

OBEDIENCE OF AMMON

"They shall put forth their hand upon Edom and Moab; And the children of Ammon shall obey them" (Isa. 11:14, THS).

Edom was an ancient country that was south of Judea and extended from the Dead Sea to the Gulf of Aqaba. Today much of Edom's former territory is part of southern Jordan. Moab and Ammon were also ancient countries. Moab lay north of Edom on the east side of the Dead Sea. Ammon was north of Moab. The lands of both Moab and Ammon were within Jordan's present boundaries. Thus, Isaiah was very precise in pinpointing Jordan as the nation to the east which would come to obey Israel.

All Monday morning, at the outbreak of the Six-Day War, the Israeli government, through local agencies of the United Nations, had sent messages to King Hussein of Jordan asking him to hold fire. If he would keep his peace, so too would they. The Israelis were convinced the messages were received; but they believe that by Monday the Egyptians so completely controlled the Jordanian army that Hussein could not reply. So instead of taking Israel's sensible advice to keep the peace, the Jordanians obeyed the Egyptian orders to attack and opened up a second battle front.

Entering the war was a suicidal action on the Jordanians' part. With their air force already smoldering in ruins from the Israeli's dawn attack, they could not even hope to successfully defend their own territory. Four days later the inevitable outcome was complete; the entire West Bank of Jordan and the sacred city of Jerusalem was in Israeli hands.

After the war, the number of Palestinian refugees in Jordan swelled to over half a million. The guerrillas eventually came to run "a state within a state" inside Jordan. They set up training camps wherever they chose, issued arms to sympathizers, built up their own intelligence and security organizations, and established their own checkpoints. Swaggering commandos carried their guns openly in city streets, commandeered passing taxi-cabs, and raised funds at gunpoint.

By the fall of 1970 the Palestinian commandos were engaged in open warfare against Jordan's regular army troops. For a time they were in command of the ravaged capital of Amman itself.

Fighting for his life and the survival of his kingdom, Hussein finally decided to throw his entire 55,000 man Army and his Air Force into a fight to the finish. By late July of 1971, the King's tough Bedouin troops had killed, captured, or scattered virtually all of the guerrillas. The fighting was so fierce that some of the dedicated Palestinian terrorists fled into Israel, where they surrendered to their enemies, rather than face captivity in Jordan.

The net effect of the Israeli conquest of Jordan's West Bank coupled with the crushing defeat of the PLO by King Hussein's army, effectively resulted in the Israelis "putting forth their hand upon Edom and Moab." In other words, Israel's occupation of Jordan's West Bank precipitated a massive exodus of Palestinians into east Jordan. The PLO subsequently attempted to take over the country by military force but failed; thus, even though the Israelis did not carry the Six-Day War across the Jordan River into the Hashemite Kingdom, their initial military action influenced events in Jordan in the postwar period. Instead of the Israelis having to fight the PLO saboteurs in Jordan, Hussein's army did it for them.

Two years after Hussein crushed the PLO in Jordan, the Yom Kippur War of 1973 erupted. Suddenly the extension of Israel's hand of influence over the international affairs of Jordan became even more apparent. Instead of acquiescing to Egyptian, Syrian, and PLO pressure to open another front against Israel, the Jordanian capital of Amman accepted Israel's sensible advice to hold fire. Thus, since Jordan's defeat in the Six-Day War, the "children of Ammon have come to obey Israel" instead of their more powerful Arab neighbors.

STREAMS OF DUST

15 And the LORD shall utterly destroy the tongue of the Egyptian sea; and with his mighty wind shall he shake his hand over the river, and shall smite it in the seven streams, and make men go over dryshod (Isa. 11:15).

This verse summarizes the ecological collapse of Egypt. Isaiah declared it to be the third major signpost event to occur prior to Christ's Second Coming.

The utter destruction of "the tongue of the Egyptian sea" will complete the foretold desolation of Egypt's entire agricultural system as detailed in Isaiah 19. The Hebrews applied the word "tongue" to anything that resembled a tongue—to a bar of gold: "When I saw among the spoils a goodly Babylonish garment, and two hundred shekels of silver, and a wedge [tongue] of gold of fifty shekels weight, then I coveted them" (Josh. 7:21); to a flame of fire: "Therefore as a tongue of fire consumes stubble" (Isa. 5:24, NASB); to a bay of the sea: "And their south border was from the shore of the salt sea, from the bay [tongue] that looketh southward (Josh. 15:2). In this passage it refers to the tongue of land that makes up the 8,500-square-mile Nile Delta between Cairo and the Mediterranean coast. As mentioned earlier the Egyptians often called the Nile *el-Bahr*, the sea, because before the blocking of the river by the Aswan High Dam its waters at the time of overflow resembled a sea. The "Egyptian sea" therefore further identifies the tongue to be the fertile delta land that was formed by the annual flooding of the Nile over the ages.

"And with his mighty wind shall he shake his hand over the river, and shall smite it in the seven streams." God's wind blowing over the river is named as the primary force which will cause the delta to be utterly destroyed. *The Interpreter's Bible* (IB) notes that "the river usually refers to the Euphrates, but here as in Isaiah 19:5 it almost certainly means the Nile." The larger context of Isaiah's prophecies concerning the desolation of Egypt in the latter days (e.g., the river drying up, vegetation dying, fish dying), coupled with the measurable wind damage taking place in Egypt today, confirms the commentary's interpretation.

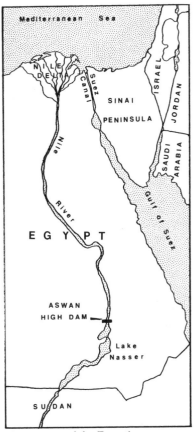

The tongue of the Egyptian sea.

As mentioned in the previous chapter a number of unsettling reports concerning the adverse effects of wind on the Nile Valley's ecosystem began surfacing in the years following the blocking of the Nile by the High Dam. Driven by prevailing winds, the Mediterranean's west-to-east currents were eating away several yards of delta coastline each year by 1971. Since 1971 the pace of delta coastal erosion has accelerated. Robert

Caputo filed the following update on the extent of damages in 1985 for *National Geographic* magazine:

> Standing on a sandy beach at the mouth of the Rosetta branch of the Nile, I was puzzled by what seemed a ghost town—a sad vista of crumbling buildings, smashed windows, and broken wires dangling from utility poles. One house teetered drunkenly, half in, half out of the sea.
>
> "Last summer, people stayed in those rooms—this was a summer resort," said a voice behind me. The speaker was a young Egyptian named Muhammad, member of a team from Alexandria that had come to this abandoned village to study coastal erosion. "Now the sea is moving in," Muhammad said. He pointed to a lighthouse perched on a tiny island a couple of miles offshore: "That lighthouse used to be on land. About six years ago it became an island. Day by day the sea is eating the land—the dam has stopped the sediment of the Nile from replenishing the shoreline."
>
> "If all this can happen in 25 years, what will happen after 50 years, or 100 or 200?' asked Muhammad."

What will happen to the Nile Delta has already been answered over 26 centuries ago in Isaiah's prophecy: "And the LORD shall utterly destroy the tongue of the Egyptian sea." What "utterly destroyed" means is that even as "every sown field along the Nile will become parched, will blow away and be no more" (Isa. 19:7, NIV); so also will every sown delta field become parched, blow away and be no more. It is also becoming increasingly apparent, as mile after mile of coastal sand dunes and whole villages collapse into the sea, that "utterly destroyed" means the curve of the delta's tongue, between Alexandria and Port Said, will continue to suffer substantial loss of land to marine erosion.

Six years after the High Dam began storing water, experts were warning that erosion of coastal dunes and sandbars would eventually endanger cities such as Alexandria and the delta's fertile farmland. They also warned that the situation could become extremely dangerous if the fragile sand barriers separating the northern delta's freshwater lakes from the sea were breached.

According to Isaiah's prophecy these barriers will be breached. Once that occurs the curve of the delta's tongue will be exposed to the full force of marine currents. This will, in turn, lead to groundwater intrusion and increased soil salinity. Even without a breach, by 1978 salt water pushing inland from the Mediterranean was already destroying some of Egypt's precious few acres of fertile delta land. Here again the blame can be placed squarely on the High Dam. Its presence has lowered the water level downstream, allowing salt water to back farther up into the river.

Isaiah 11:15 emphatically names the wind blowing over the Nile, which God formed in "His hand," as the instrument He will use to smite the river "in the seven streams, and make men go over dryshod." It is hard to imagine the world's longest river drying up to the point where people will cross it dryshod—that is, without getting their shoes wet. Yet, in recent years, winds over the Nile and changing wind patterns over the many African rivers and lakes that feed the Nile, have dramatically reduced the amount of water flowing downstream into Egypt.

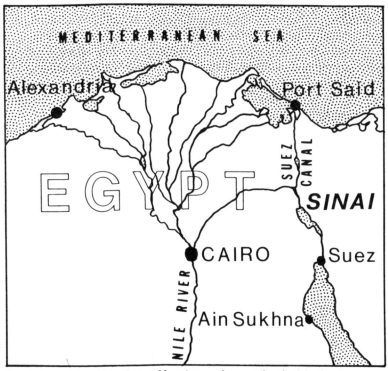

Coastal erosion of fragile sand barriers endangers fertile delta land.

represented by the four beasts were not given to Daniel. Because of this fact, the attachment of the wrong name to even one of these unnamed beasts could easily result in the incorrect rendering of the intended prophetic message.

The basis for explaining the meaning of Daniel's prophecy has to begin with the selection of the nations that the four beasts symbolize. A collection of writings by the early church fathers down to A.D. 325, titled the Ante-Nicene Fathers, affixed the nation of Babylon to the lion, Medio-Persia to the bear and Greece to the leopard. This standard assignment of names to the first three beasts has since been published essentially unchanged in countless religious books, including today's best sellers such as Hal Lindsey's *The Late Great Planet Earth*.

Yet, simple inspection reveals a glaring flaw in this view. For instance, why would God explicitly define the ram to be Medio-Persia and the he-goat to be Greece, in one prophecy, and then use a bear and a leopard as the emblems for these same nations in another prophecy? The unequivocal answer is found in 1 Cor. 14:33, "God is not the author of confusion."

A search of the historical record yields the same verdict—a complete lack of facts upon which to base this interpretation. For both archaeological artifacts and ancient documents fail to provide any connection, whatsoever, between Medio-Persia and the bear emblem, or Greece and the leopard emblem.

In direct contrast, history confirms that the two beasts in the ram-goat vision were recognized national emblems of Persia and Greece, respectively. The Persian monarchs, for example, wore a jewelled ram's head of gold instead of a diadem, such as are seen on the pillars at Persepolis. Moreover, the Grecian goat symbol originated in Macedon where Caranus, the first king of Macedonia, was said to have been led by goats to Edessa, which he made the seat of his kingdom, in 814 B.C., and renamed AEge, i.e., "goat-city." Nearly three hundred years after Caranus, during the reign of Amyntas the First, the Macedonians, upon being threatened with an invasion, became tributary to the Persians.

Albert Barnes reported that "in one of the pilasters of Persepolis, this very event seems to be recorded in a manner that throws considerable light on this subject. A goat is represented with an immense horn growing out of the middle of his forehead, and a man in Persian dress is seen by his side, holding the horn with his left hand, by which is signified the subjection of

Macedon. Also, in the reign of Archelaus of Macedon, 413 B.C., there occurs on the reverse side of a coin of that king the head of a goat having only one horn."

These initial biblical and historical facts demonstrate why Medio-Persia and Greece cannot be the nations symbolized by the bear and leopard. Obviously, the selection of the wrong nations to represent the bear and leopard symbols voids the rest of the presentation of this long accepted interpretation of the vision of the four beasts. An awareness of these inherited misconceptions provides a first step towards establishing the correct interpretation of Daniel's vision of the four beasts.

One-horned goat from pilaster at Persepolis.

DANIEL'S VISION OF THE FOUR BEASTS

During the days when the Babylonian Empire was at the height of its power, a panoramic vision of the future rise and development of the world's last four major powers was given to the prophet Daniel. God used beasts to portray, in order, the consecutive rise to prominence of these coming modern nations. Daniel's vision is an essential key to understanding the whole of Bible prophecy concerning the last days of man's reign upon the earth. This key reveals what will happen in the future with considerable certainty. Moreover, Daniel's vision promises that God has established a future for mankind on this planet despite the nuclear age.

1 In the first year of Belshazzar king of Babylon Daniel had a dream and visions of his head upon his bed: then he wrote the dream, and told the sum of the matters (Dan. 7:1).

General George Washington becoming king of the new nation, a constitution was drawn up establishing the office of an elected president for a four year term. Thus, standing on its feet as a man and being given a man's heart is a picture of American democracy with an elected president representing the heartbeat of the nation.

Standing on its feet as a man is also a picture of Uncle Sam who symbolically represents the government elected by the people of the United States. This imagery clearly demonstrates how the United States established a democratic government that responds to the hearts and minds of the people through its elected representatives.

The cartoon below shows the people of the United States in the caricature of Uncle Sam trying to decide between two alternatives: namely; evil, which will result in his falling on his face; or good, which will result in his getting on his feet. Thus, U.S. citizens readily recognize that their nation stands on its feet as a man or falls on its face as a direct result of the actions taken

by their elected government symbolized in this cartoon as Uncle Sam.

In the years following the American Revolution the world would see many kings replaced by democratic forms of government. Quite interestingly, the British monarchy was among those removed in favor of a democracy. Although the decline of Britain's monarchy evolved over a lengthy period of time, the British people eventually succeeded in lifting up a democratic form of government that stands upon the feet of the men and women who elect its governing officials. The British people also elect a Prime Minister to officiate over the heart of their nation's business.

Here again, "standing on its feet as a man" has come to be personified in British cartoons in the caricature of John Bull who symbolically represents the English people.

Note also how the British lion symbol is used to portray Anglo-American history in today's political cartoons. Curiously, modern man continues to use the ancient practice of referring to nations in terms of animal symbols.

THE FOUR BEASTS' ISRAELI CONNECTION

It is important to note that Daniel was an Israelite whose dream pertained to the shape of things to come when Israel would again be an established nation in her original homeland. The four power structures in his vision would be directly involved with the restored nation of Israel. For instance, Britain was largely responsible for laying the ground-work for the eventual establishment of the twentieth century nation of Israel. This process began during World War I when the British drove the Ottoman Turks out of Palestine. In 1917, to gain Jewish support in the war, Britain issued the Balfour Declaration, which backed the Zionist ideal of establishing a Jewish homeland in Palestine under a League of Nations Mandate. Thousands of Jews returned to their ancient homeland during the Mandate years. Finally, in 1948 they became an official nation, recognized by the nations of the world.

Since becoming a nation Israel has not been able to get along without the United States, their protector, banker and armorer. If they had not received billions in U.S. military aid and economic support, it is questionable whether Israel could have survived as a nation. The other three beasts will also affect the course of Israel's future history.

The parallels drawn from the picture of the first beast show why God chose to reveal these power structures in the form of beasts. Symbols are memorable ways of communicating truth. Today we are quick to draw a cartoon or sketch to tell a story. Take the U.S. Eisenhower dollar for an example. One side of the

Eisenhower dollar.

coin displays an eagle landing on a pock-marked surface with a sphere in the background. This picture, of course, depicts the U.S. successful moon landing of Apollo 11 with the earth watching in the background.

DEMOCRATIC CAPITALISM— THE FIRST WIND OF CHANGE

In summary, the first wind of revolutionary change successfully altered the thoughts and lives of large numbers of people on the earth by establishing the ideology of democratic capitalism. The lion with attached eagle's wings aptly represents the initiators of this form of government. Great Britain and the United States, though separated over two hundred years ago, remain united as standard bearers of democracy and the free enterprise economic system. Both nations still stand upon the feet of the men and women who elect the officials who, in turn, run their governing instruments. Britain and the United States also continue to be the chief proponents of this way of life.

THE BEAR

5 And behold another beast, a second, like to a bear, and it raised up itself on one side, and it had three ribs in the mouth of it between the teeth of it: and they said thus unto it, Arise, devour much flesh (Dan. 7:5).

The bear represents Russia, which has the bear as her national emblem. Ivan III (Ivan the Great), Grand-Duke of Muscovy, put an end to Mongol domination in the late fifteenth century and began to lay the foundations for a Russian national monarchy by uniting the adjacent tribal states. However, Russia's Bolshevik Revolution in 1917 marked her beginning as a great world power. The Bolshevists claimed a government that would embody a dictatorship of the proletariat by the sea of people from whence their revolution sprang. Lenin, as the head of the new government, soon proved that in practice the dictatorship was exercised by one man. Nevertheless, the Bolshevik Revolution introduced the ideology of socialistic communism to the masses, the second major wind of change.

At Lastki!

By Sykes

RUSSIA

RECOGNITION

1933 *New York Evening Post* cartoon marking U.S. recognition of Russia's communist government.

WORLD WAR II IN PERSPECTIVE

The Russian bear began to raise itself up on one side with the signing of a ten-year nonaggression pact between the Soviets and the Nazis on August 23, 1939. The pact pledged the contracting parties to refrain from acts of aggression against one another for a period of ten years. A secret protocol signed at the same time divided Eastern Europe into Russian and German spheres. All territory east of a line drawn from the Baltic to the Black Sea was to be in the Russian sphere and everything west of the line was to be left to the Germans. This gave Russia a free hand in Finland, Estonia, Latvia, Bessarabia, and the eastern half of Poland.

On September 1, 1939, the German blitzkrieg struck into western Poland. Sixteen days later Russia moved into hapless Poland from the east. The Russian bear had the first rib in its mouth "between the teeth of it," in the form of eastern Poland.

The second rib followed the same fate when Russian troops went into eastern Finland on November 30, 1939. The Finns' resistance surprised the world but after two months they gave way before tremendous numbers and superior equipment. The terms of the ensuing peace gave Russia the entire Karelian Isthmus in addition to other pieces of Finnish territory.

The following May, Russia quietly annexed her former Baltic provinces, Estonia, Latvia, and Lithuania. These provinces are not considered one of the ribs since a rib signifies a part of a country and not a complete country. Unlike the imagery of a "rib between the teeth" that represents a country being partially dismembered by Russia, these three tiny nations were swallowed whole by the Soviet bear.

The Russian bear sank her teeth into the third country when she moved into the two Rumanian provinces of Bessarabia and Bucovina, in June of 1940.

It is important to note that all three of the invaded countries and the Soviet's three former Baltic provinces were to the west of greater Russia or "on one side." The world quickly discovered in the closing days of World War II that this was only a beginning.

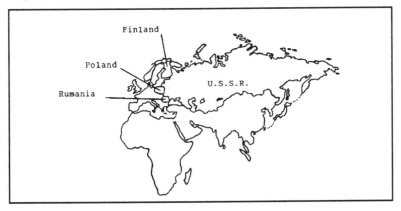

"And the bear raised up itself on one side, and it had three ribs in the mouth of it between the teeth of it (Dan. 7:5)."

Given the large number of members in the Arab League, it is not surprising to find the leopard beast caricature to be more complex than the previous two beasts. Since no one animal could possibly be the national emblem of all the League's member nations, one might wonder why God selected a leopard to represent this four-headed third beast. The answer lies in the fact that the League designated the Egyptian capital of Cairo as its headquarters.

If you were to go back three or four thousand years in time and watch a royal Egyptian investiture you would hear a new pharaoh state: "my leopard skin is on my arm." Thus with this statement a pharaoh assumed his role as high priest. Today we can look at the sculpture of a deity wearing the priestly leopard mantle in the tomb of King Seti I at Thebes. The leopard-head ornament on his chest resembles the golden one from the tomb of King Tutankhamen.

God knew Egypt's pharaohs of old used the leopard as their symbol for power and authority. God also knew the initial seven signatories of the Arab League would select Egypt's capital as its central headquarters. Thus, Egypt's ancient leopard symbol of authority was chosen to represent the leopard beast's body.

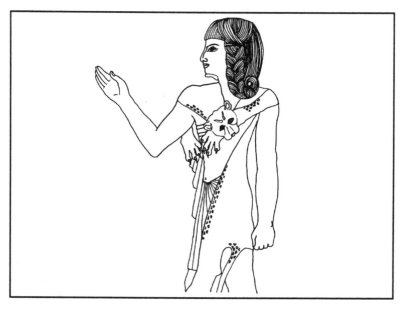

Pharaoh wearing priestly leopard mantle of authority.

THE ARAB LEAGUE'S MOST BINDING FORCE

The Arab League charter promotes political cooperation and collaboration in economics, culture, social affairs, and other matters through the work of specialized committees. The success or failure of these functions aside, the League of Arab States' most binding force is its hatred of Israel over the problem of a Palestinian homeland and control of the Moslem holy city of Jerusalem. As a result of these ongoing issues the world soon found these loosely linked Arab nations to be an unquenchable catalyst for major world confrontation.

RESURGENT ISLAMIC FUNDAMENTALISM—
THE THIRD WIND OF CHANGE

Furthermore, the League's semiannual council meetings provide the communications base for establishing anti-Israeli strategy. An example is the general Arab economic boycott of trade with Israel. In 1981, the 37 Muslim nations represented at the Third Islamic Summit in Saudi Arabia expanded this economic boycott of Israel. They passed a so-called Mecca Declaration, named for Islam's holiest city, which declared a jihad, or holy war, against Israel, using their combined "military, economic, and political resources—including oil." The proclamation proposed broad new economic sanctions against Israel, along the lines of the Arab League boycott. Thus, establishment of scheduled League meetings has helped fuel the flames of resurgent Islamic Fundamentalism, the third wind of change.

The idea of a modern day Islamic Empire has fired the imagination of Moslems everywhere and especially the leaders of Libya, Iran, Iraq and Syria. Libya's march into Chad, Syria's into Lebanon, and Iraq's into Iran and Kuwait are recent examples of attempts by these nations' leaders to build a grand Islamic Empire, governed under the laws of Mohammed.

CAN THE LEOPARD CHANGE HIS SPOTS?

The prophet Jeremiah noted the leopard as a symbol of unchangeableness when he wrote: "can the Ethiopian change his skin, or the leopard his spots?" (Jer. 13:23). Unchangeableness is certainly the Arab League's most outstanding characteristic. In 1967, after three disastrous wars with Israel in two decades, the Arab World refused to acknowledge Israel's right to exist as a nation. Most of the world's 150 million Arabs have shown time and again a total inflexibility in this matter. In fact, the greater their humiliation the more unbending they seem to become. For example, one month after the Arab defeat to Israel in the Six-Day War in June, 1967, Cairo's semiofficial newspaper Al Ahram had some extraordinary news for its readers, "the battle is still going on," it proclaimed. "Victory is ours." Even today many seemingly rational and well-informed Arabs continue to cry for a perpetual war with Israel until she is destroyed.

FOUR WINGS OF A FOWL

Notice how the leopard is similar to the lion in the sense that both have attached wings. Like the lion's wings, the leopard's wings represent a people who are dependent on an established political power structure for many of their essential needs. The American people, represented by the eagle's wings, had the desire of a young bird to fly away and be free and independent. The leopard's wings also have the same objective: namely, to become an independent Palestinian nation.

The Palestinians have lived in the troubled land of Palestine for most of their history. In Arabic the word is Filastin; it derives from the name of the home of the ancient Philistines. The region was ruled by the Hebrews, Assyrians, Babylonians, Persians, Greeks, Maccabeans, Romans, Byzantines, Arabs, Egyptians, Crusaders, Mamelukes and finally Ottoman Turks, who indifferently governed the backward, neglected territory from the sixteenth century until the British drove them out in World War I. The British ruled the area until the establishment of the nation of Israel in 1948.

Under the British Mandate the population mix and land ownership shifted in favor of Jewish immigrants. As a result fighting broke out between Jews and Palestinians. The Israelis won time after time and eventually controlled all of Palestine. Consequently, the Palestinian's hope of establishing a nation was never realized.

Because of their frustration the Palestinian's have enlisted the Arab League nations in their attempts to wrest Palestine from the Jews. Yasser Arafat, Chairman of the Palestine Liberation Organization, summed up the relationship between Palestinians a٦d the Arab League states with the following remark: "Palestine is the cement that holds the Arab World together, or it is the explosive that blows it apart."

Fortunately, closer inspection of the initial description, "like a leopard, which had upon the back of it four wings of a fowl," reveals enough information to secure the significance and intended meaning of the number "four." The location of the four symbolic wings shows their attachment to be precisely where the Palestinian people have come to rest as a burden "upon the back" of the Arab League nations. More specifically, the actual confrontation Arab states, who have suffered the most for the Palestinian cause, in terms of lost land, men and material over the course of past Arab wars with Israel, are the states who have borne the brunt of the Palestinian burden. Thus, the number "four" refers to the four Arab nations of Egypt, Jordan, Syria and Lebanon, which share a common border with Israel. These border states are where the four symbolic wings of the displaced Palestinian nation physically attach to the Arab League leopard beast. Moreover, since the establishment of the renewed nation of Israel, in 1948, it is the lands of these four nations upon which the Palestinian refugees and fighters have come and built their camps, in the aftermath of the various Arab-Israeli wars.

UNUSUAL GIFTS

Before discussing the four heads, in the picture of the leopard, the phrase, "and dominion was given to it," needs to be examined. One meaning for dominion is the power or right of governing a territory.

Going back to the period following World War I, the British largely controlled vast stretches of former Turkish territory, although the French commanded a smaller area which eventually became the states of Syria and Lebanon. A noteworthy feature of the Arab people living on these lands was their complete lack of any forcible means to drive the superior British and French from the area, which would have enabled them to set up independent states of their own. Yet, in a very short span of time after World War I a number of independent states were created in the Middle East with the "dominion" of these states literally "given" to a few of the upper class Arabs. The British, for instance, brought King Hussein's family from Saudi Arabia to govern heavily Palestinian Jordan. Other states created at the time were Egypt, Iraq, Saudi Arabia, Lebanon, and Yemen.

Even the idea of a league of Arab states was approved in advance by the British. Britain, hoping to make friends with the pro-axis Arabs during World War II, decided to help them realize their dreams of unity. In London, on May 29, 1941, Foreign Secretary, Anthony Eden, said that his Majesty's government would give "full support to any scheme" designed to strengthen cultural, economic, and political ties between Arab countries. The product was the Arab League, founded in 1945, with headquarters in Cairo.

THE "BIG FOUR"

One interesting aspect of the Arab League is the provision giving each state one vote with decisions to be binding only if unanimously reached by all members. This policy has helped to keep any one Arab state from assuming the dominant role as head of the Arab World. Consequently the four heads of the leopard which the Arab countries have looked to for economic and military help and leadership in times of crisis are those nations which were commonly referred to after World War II as the "Big Four" (the United States, Russia, Britain and France).

The "Big Four" were the world's dominant powers after World War II and were the first nations to build atomic weapons. Quite naturally the Arab League states have always received the bulk of their military hardware from the "Big Four" powers since they were the world's leading arms merchants during the decades following World War II.

The Arab states have used the "Big Four's" abundant arms supplies to initiate violent wars with Israel and with each other through the years. On more than one occasion Arab-initiated wars have brought the world to the very edge of World War III. The first crisis of this magnitude took place in 1956 when Egypt nationalized the Suez Canal. Egypt's action prompted Britain and France to form an alliance with Israel in an effort to topple Egypt's dynamic young leader, Gamal Abdel Nasser. Their objective was to make secure their oil deliveries through the canal. More than two hundred British and French warships assembled to back the main Anglo-French invasion force that landed at Port Said and Port Fuad.

Russia, which had been arming Egypt, threatened to intervene in the Suez and hinted at missile attacks against London and Paris. In a message to U.S. President Eisenhower the Russians urged that America and Russia "crush the aggressors." Eisenhower warned that if any outside troops moved into the Middle East they would be opposed by the United States. At the same time Eisenhower opposed the Anglo-French invasion and worked to get them and Israel out of Egyptian territory. All three countries resisted mightily but eventually withdrew.

Thus, although the four heads averted a nuclear catastrophe, the Suez Crisis proved to be a hinge point in history: It spelled the end of Western colonialism in the Arab World; it brought the entry of America as the major Western power in the Middle East, and it also secured a Russian presence in that area that continues to this day.

FOUR COMPETING INFLUENCES

Egyptian President Nasser's proposal to build the Aswan High Dam in the 1950s provides a typical example of the Arab states dependency on the four heads. Egypt, lacking everything except the river the dam would span, turned to one of the heads, namely the United States, for the necessary technology and money needed for the project. However, the United States refused to help build the dam when Egypt refused to guarantee the pursuit of peaceful policies in the Middle East. A second head, Britain, also withdrew support over political differences. Straightway Egypt turned to Russia, another head, which then granted the aid for the project without attaching any immediate conditions on Egyptian foreign policy.

It is also interesting to note that the Arabs have turned to the four heads to bail them out after their disastrous wars with Israel. For example, three and one half years after the Six-Day War with Israel the Arabs were still looking to the four heads to resolve the problems of the war's aftermath. In January of 1971 Egypt handed the United Nations special Mideast mediator, Gunnar Jarring, a memorandum stating their general conditions for a peace settlement. The memorandum went a slight step beyond generalities by calling for guaranteed security in the area. This was to be accomplished by establishing demilitarized zones on both the Arab and Israeli sides of the frontier, zones that could be policed by a U.N. peace-keeping force made

Taiwan in the United Nations. When China had become powerful enough to demand a seat in the United Nations it was also
able to demand that Taiwan be uprooted from the organization.
In the same way, "the little horn" will be able to force the
restructuring of the "ten horned" organization.

The statement: "In this horn were eyes like the eyes of man,"
shows that the eleventh country will have a leader who will
engineer its rise to power. From the description of "a mouth
speaking great things," it can be surmised that this super politician will rise to power via his ability to sell his solutions to the
problems at hand.

JUDGMENT OF THE FOUR BEASTS

> **9** I beheld till the thrones were cast down, and the Ancient of
> days did sit, whose garment was white as snow, and the hair
> of his head like the pure wool: his throne was like the fiery
> flame, and his wheels as burning fire. **10** A fiery stream issued
> and came forth from before him: thousand thousands minis-
> tered unto him, and ten thousand times ten thousand stood
> before him: the judgment was set, and the books were opened
> (Dan. 7:9–10).

Here the Fourth Beast is foretold to be man's last power
structure to rule the earth since all the thrones were cast down
by the Ancient of days, or God, who will terminate man's reign
on earth. A vast multitude will accompany God's return and
man will be judged for his flagrant rebellion against God.

> 11 I beheld then because of the voice of the great words which
> the horn spake: I beheld even till the beast was slain, and his
> body destroyed, and given to the burning flame. 12 As con-
> cerning the rest of the beasts, they had their dominion taken
> away: yet their lives were prolonged for a season and time
> (Dan. 7:11-12).

God emphatically states again that the fourth power structure will be destroyed. At the same time the first beasts will not
be permitted to retain their authority; however, their countries
will continue to exist for some period of time. For instance,
England, the United States, Russia, and the various Arab states

will still be referred to by their respective names but God will not allow them to govern themselves.

> **13** I saw in the night visions, and, behold, one like the Son of man came with the clouds of heaven, and came to the Ancient of days, and they brought him near before him. **14** And there was given him dominion, and glory, and a kingdom, that all people, nations, and languages, should serve him: his dominion is an everlasting dominion, which shall not pass away, and his kingdom that which shall not be destroyed (Dan. 7:13–14).

At this point God gives a kingdom to a man, referred to as the Son of man, which will include all the different people and nations. Furthermore this kingdom will be an everlasting kingdom that shall never be destroyed. Other passages in the Bible, which will be covered throughout this book, firmly establish the Son of Man and Jesus Christ to be one and the same person.

In view of the foretold return of the King of kings to rule the earth, it behooves everyone to listen carefully to the prophecies foretelling the events leading up to His arrival. Like the prophets of old we too should be preparing the way of the Lord because "the glory of the Lord shall be revealed and all flesh shall see it" (Isa. 40:5).

DANIEL'S PROPHETIC QUESTION

> **15** I Daniel was grieved in my spirit in the midst of my body, and the visions of my head troubled me. **16** I came near unto one of them that stood by, and asked him the truth of all this. So he told me, and made me know the interpretation of the things (Dan. 7:15–16).

During the vision Daniel became troubled since he did not grasp the meaning of it. He then asked one that stood by the significance of the vision and received additional facts.

SHALL ARISE MEANS SHALL ARISE

> **17** These great beasts, which are four, are four kings, which shall arise out of the earth (Dan. 7:17).

The answer Daniel received provides two important keys to the interpretation of the vision. The first being that each great beast symbolically represents a king or power structure. The second key lies in the two words "shall arise," which places these power structures in the distant future. It is certain that the Babylon of Daniel's day could not be one of the four beasts since Daniel states at the beginning of the vision that Belshazzar, who was the last king to rule Babylon, is on the throne.

Here again, a glaring flaw emerges in the long accepted inherited interpretation of Daniel's vision of the four beasts. For if "shall arise" can be made to mean the Babylonian Empire, which was being ruled by its last king in Daniel's day, then grammar would seem to have lost all force.

THE EVERLASTING KINGDOM

18 But the saints of the most High shall take the kingdom, and possess the kingdom for ever, even for ever and ever (Dan. 7:18).

The saints are the people in the past and those living today who believe in God and His promises. One of the promises is that the saints will be part of the everlasting kingdom.

DANIEL'S RECAPITULATION OF THE VISION

19 Then I would know the truth of the fourth beast, which was diverse from all the others, exceeding dreadful, whose teeth were of iron, and his nails of brass; which devoured, brake in pieces, and stamped the residue with his feet; **20** And of the ten horns that were in his head, and of the other which came up, and before whom three fell; even of that horn that had eyes, and a mouth that spake very great things, whose look was more stout than his fellows (Dan. 7:19–20).

Daniel then retold the vision of the Fourth Beast and sought more understanding. He mentioned that the Fourth Beast also had "nails of brass." Injuries inflicted by deeply penetrating sharp nails help a ferocious beast immobilize and weaken its prey. This is a picture of wiretapping and sophisticated space-based electronic surveillance satellite systems that will be used by the Fourth Beast to get a better grip on the common man. Other prophecies describe how these high-tech electronic "nails of brass" will literally penetrate the lives of the people at the end of the age: ripping, tearing, and shredding the very fabric of their existence.

> 21 I beheld, and the same horn made war with the saints, and prevailed against them; 22 Until the Ancient of days came, and judgment was given to the saints of the most High; and the time came that the saints possessed the kingdom (Dan. 7:21–22).

Daniel then saw the little horn whose look was more stout than his fellows making war against the saints, or those people who believe in God. This dictator will triumph in his war against the saints until God intervenes on their behalf. God will then destroy the fourth power structure and give His saints the authority to judge and reign over the earth under the leadership of the Son of Man.

> 23 Thus he said, The fourth beast shall be the fourth kingdom upon earth, which shall be diverse from all kingdoms, and shall devour the whole earth, and shall tread it down, and break it in pieces (Dan. 7:23).

The main difference between the Fourth Beast and the previous three is the stated fact that it will control the entire world. This power structure will use its vast control to wreak havoc from one end of the planet to the other, leaving the earth literally broken in pieces the day God terminates man's reign on the earth.

> 24 And the ten horns out of this kingdom are ten kings that shall arise: and another shall rise after them; and he shall be diverse from the first, and he shall subdue three kings (Dan. 7:24).

Here the ten horns are defined to be ten kings or countries. These countries will be tied together in some form of a confederation. According to the Book of Revelation, they will eventually become the most powerful component of the fourth power structure. Again the two words "shall arise," explicitly places these ten countries in the future.

Notice that the ten countries are not the beast but only a part of it. The second half of this verse restates the fact that after the ten countries establish their confederation an eleventh country will become powerful enough to uproot three of its members from their previous positions of power.

TIMES AND LAWS WILL CHANGE

25 And he shall speak great words against the most High, and shall wear out the saints of the most High, and think to change times and laws: and they shall be given into his hand until a time and times and the dividing of time (Dan. 7:25).

Upon gaining control over the nations this dictator will launch a massive propaganda campaign against God that will seek to discredit and destroy God's faithful followers on the earth. The dictator will put "iron teeth" into this campaign by replacing the existing laws of the various nations with a new set of all encompassing laws. These laws will enable the global government to establish better control over the common man.

The first dictator of the world will also "think to change times." Exactly what is meant by this phrase is not explained here, but more than likely, Christmas, Easter and various other religious holidays will be abolished. As a matter of fact, a world dictator who is actively speaking out against God, will more than likely do away with today's calendar. After all, a calendar based upon the birth of a man who claimed to be the Son of God, certainly would not fit into the dictator's newly generated philosophy. At any rate, setting up a new calendar should not cause any problems since the majority of the people on the earth do not believe Jesus Christ was the Son of God, including the Jewish nation into which Christ was born.

"Given into his hand," implies that this dictator will receive his authority by popular demand. It also attaches a definite period of time to the Fourth Beast's reign. A prophecy covered later in this book defines this period of time to be three-and-one half years.

WORLD UNITY—THE FOURTH WIND OF CHANGE

The fourth wind of revolutionary change will usher in the ideology of world unity. Using the guise of world peace through unity, the fourth power structure will install a new set of laws, a new calendar, new holidays, and a universal religion under which everyone will supposedly live together in peace. The politician with the "mouth speaking great things" will fire the imagination of people around the globe with these lofty ideas of world unity.

26 But the judgment shall sit, and they shall take away his dominion, to consume and to destroy it unto the end. 27 And the kingdom and dominion, and the greatness of the kingdom under the whole heaven, shall be given to the people of the saints of the most High, whose kingdom is an everlasting kingdom, and all dominions shall serve and obey him (Dan. 7:26–27).

Three-and-one-half years after the dictator comes to power "the judgment shall sit," and man's last government will be completely destroyed. God will then give His saints a part in His everlasting kingdom.

REFLECTIONS

Stop and reflect a moment on the winds of change sweeping over the world. In recent times the eastern European nations have cast aside socialistic communism in favor of democratic capitalism. The original champion of communism, the Soviet Union, is also moving toward democracy and free enterprise in the hope of building a better future and a safer world. Unfortunately, Daniel's prophecy teaches that these efforts will not succeed. Instead of correcting the wrongs of the past, today's international penchant for change will fuel a movement clamoring for peace and prosperity through the formation of a world government. Yet once installed, the Fourth Beast's heavy-handed attempt to establish lasting peace through global unity will also come to nothing. According to Daniel's vision, man's last four great power structures will fail miserably and cease to function.

SUMMARY OF THE FOUR BEASTS IMAGERY

PHRASE	EXPLANATION
Daniel 7:4	
The first was like a lion, and had eagle's wings:	The lion symbol represents Great Britain.
I beheld till the wings thereof were plucked,	A picture of the Thirteen Colonies abrupt separation from Brtain to establish the United States.
and it was lifted up from the earth, and made stand upon the feet as a man, and man's heart was given to it.	Imagery outlines how the United States established a democratic form of government that responds to the hearts and will of the people through its elected representatives.
Daniel 7:5	
And behold another beast, a second, like to a bear,	The bear represents Russia.
and it raised up itself on one side,	Prophetically notes that the Soviet's territorial conquests would all occur to the west of greater Russia during World War II.
and it had three ribs in the mouth of it between the teeth of it:	Symbolically represents Russian seizure of part of Poland, Finland and Rumania during World War II.
and they said thus unto it, Arise, devour much flesh.	Refers to the United States and Britain's acquiescence to Soviet expansionist demands after World War II that allowed the Kremlin to extend its sway over 100 million people.
Daniel 7:6	
After this I beheld, and lo another, like a leopard,	The leopard represents the Arab League.
which had upon the back of it four wings of a fowl;	The four wings represent the displaced Palestinian people who have come to rest as a burden "upon the back" of the four Arab League states that share a common border with Israel.

Daniel 7:6 (continued)	

PHRASE	EXPLANATION
the beast had also four heads;	The world's "Big Four" dominant powers properly fulfilled the leadership role of the Arab League leopard beast after World War II.
and dominion was given to it.	Refers to the unprecedented act of Britain and France creating several independent Arab states after World War I.

Daniel 7:7	

PHRASE	EXPLANATION
a fourth beast, dreadful and terrible, and strong exceedingly;	A picture of the eventual arrival of a powerful world government that will rule over the nations.
and it had great iron teeth:	Great iron teeth represent rigid laws and oppressive totalitarian enforcement of those laws.
it devoured and brake in pieces, and stamped the residue with the feet of it:	A description of the world government's ruthless rule and its total disregard for the rights and lives of the common man.
and it was diverse from all the beasts that were before it;	Declares that the coming world government will not be a replica of any previously established form of government.
and it had ten horns.	The ten horns represent an international body of ten powerful nations.

Daniel 7:8	

PHRASE	EXPLANATION
I considered the horns, and, behold, there came up among them another little horn,	Predicts the rise of an eleventh nation to a position of prominence.
before whom there were three of the first horns plucked up by the roots:	Describes the eleventh nation's decisive reorganization of the ten nation group.

Thus, the sum of the governments, confederations, and various international alliances formed by men through the ages, have not, and will not bring peace to the nuclear age. God's people need to realize that their allegiance is to God and His everlasting kingdom. This kingdom will usher in true change that will allow truth, justice, peace, safety and plenty for everyone.

> **28** Hitherto is the end of the matter. As for me Daniel, my cogitations much troubled me, and my countenance changed in me: but I kept the matter in my heart (Dan. 7:28).

After considerable thought Daniel could not decipher the meaning of the dream. This is not surprising since the nations about whom Daniel wrote did not exist in his day. Unable to find a clue in the identical monarchial kingdoms of Babylon, Persia and Greece, he kept the matter in his heart. The correct interpretation waited for the future, and for the radically diverse ideologies of democratic capitalism, socialistic communism, resurgent Islamic fundamentalism, and world unity to appear on the world scene.

In Daniel's vision of the four beasts God has given man a definite benchmark as to when the last power structure can be expected to gain control of the earth, and God has also given man a formal proof of His existence by foretelling these events over 2,500 years before they actually came into view for man's inspection.

Daniel's prophecy provides a panoramic view of the rise and fall of the four most significant power structures of the latter days. God has provided further information about the fourth power structure and the events surrounding its future arrival in the Book of Revelation. In later chapters of this book, the Revelation text, coupled with other important technological prophecies found elsewhere in scripture, will be used to shed more light on the role of the Fourth Beast.

PART
3

ATOMIC WORLD WAR I

4 Russia Invades Israel

Ezekiel's account of a Russian invasion of Israel in the latter days is one of the Bible's most written about prophecies. The alignment of the nations and the course of the battle have been documented in great detail; e.g., *The Late Great Planet Earth*, by Hal Lindsey. Many writers correctly support the view that this event will not be missed by anyone, since the invasion escalates into a global thermonuclear war. Those who are familiar with current literature on this subject are probably of the opinion that there is nothing further to discuss. Yet, the Bible emphatically warns that the arrival of the nuclear age will be a time of widespread misinterpretation of the prophecies pertaining to the end times.

JEREMIAH'S INDICTMENT

One such warning is found in a blistering indictment written against the religious leaders of the twentieth century by Jeremiah the prophet just before the Babylonians destroyed Jerusalem and conquered his native kingdom of Judah. It is a curious prophecy in that Jeremiah issued a proclamation to twentieth century pastors in the midst of a message condemning the false prophets of his day. In essence, he applied his words to the pastors of the nuclear age by inserting a vivid description of a nuclear explosion in the middle of his message. This is a profound condemnation of prophetic interpretations

105

being preached by the religious leaders of the nuclear age. All who are preaching and writing about Bible prophecy concerning the last days of the age should seek to determine, from Jeremiah's text, what is wrong with today's prevailing prophetic teachings.

> **16** Thus saith the LORD of hosts, Hearken not unto the words of the prophets that prophesy unto you: they make you vain: they speak a vision of their own heart, and not out of the mouth of the LORD. **17** They say still unto them that despise me, The LORD hath said, Ye shall have peace; and they say unto every one that walketh after the imagination of his own heart, No evil shall come upon you. **18** For who hath stood in the counsel of the LORD, and hath perceived and heard his word? who hath marked his word, and heard it? **19** Behold, a whirlwind of the LORD is gone forth in fury, even a grievous whirlwind: it shall fall grievously upon the head of the wicked. **20** The anger of the LORD shall not return, until he have executed, and till he have performed the thoughts of his heart: in the latter days ye shall consider it perfectly. **21** I have not sent these prophets, yet they ran: I have not spoken to them, yet they prophesied. **22** But if they had stood in my counsel, and had caused my people to hear my words, then they should have turned them from their evil way, and from the evil of their doings (Jer. 23:16–22).

Here Jeremiah pauses in the midst of his message against the false prophets of his day to interject a graphic description of a nuclear explosion as "a whirlwind of the LORD gone forth in fury, even a grievous whirlwind," which "shall fall grievously upon the head of the wicked." Jamieson, Fausset and Brown note that "a grievous whirlwind" literally means "eddying, whirling itself about, a tornado." They further render, "it shall fall grievously" as, "it shall be hurled on" the head of the wicked.

Two other English translations of this verse amplify this striking description of an air-burst nuclear bomb.

> "Behold, the storm of the LORD has gone forth in wrath, Even a whirling tempest; It will swirl down on the head of the wicked (Jer. 23:19, NASB).

Behold, the storm of the LORD! Wrath has gone forth, a whirling tempest; it will burst upon the head of the wicked (Jer. 23:19, RSV).

Twenty-five centuries ago the false prophets who listened to Jeremiah's description of an atomic explosion did not understand what they heard. Today it can be understood "perfectly." Air-burst atomic explosions are similar in appearance to naturally occurring whirlwinds and both destroy on a large scale. Furthermore, Jeremiah's declaration that the prophecy could not be understood until the "latter days" categorically eliminates naturally occurring whirlwinds as candidates for the prophecy's fulfillment.

JEREMIAH'S DEFINITION OF THE "LATTER DAYS"

Jeremiah's description of a devastating nuclear war declares the days when atomic weapons come into use to be "the latter days" of mankind's reign upon the earth. He also pronounces the prophetic interpretations being preached at the onset of the nuclear age to be every bit as worthless as the unfounded reports delivered by the false prophets of his day.

HISTORY JUSTIFIED JEREMIAH'S INDICTMENT

In Jeremiah's day the Judahites dwelling in the kingdom of Judah were living under the unsettling shadow of the powerful Babylonian Empire. They knew their civilization could end abruptly if the Babylonians invaded since they had seen the Babylonian's pagan armies systematically conquer their neighbors. Nevertheless, the Jews were not overly concerned; thanks in large part to their prophets who continually told them: "The LORD hath said, Ye shall have peace; and No evil shall come upon you" (Jer. 23:17).

Jeremiah spoke out against the prophets forecasting peace and safety and warned people not to listen to their message. History proved Jeremiah's indictment of these false prophets to be justified. Instead of peace, the Babylonians destroyed the nation according to the words of Jeremiah's prophecy. They invaded Judah, burned Jerusalem, and also brought much evil

upon the kingdom's inhabitants, who were either killed or
carried off to Babylon as slaves.

Just as Jeremiah said they would, more than forty years after
the first atomic explosion, Christian pastors are preaching the
same message that was prevalent in his day: "The LORD hath
said, Ye shall have peace; and No evil shall come upon you."
Central to today's message of "no evil shall come upon you" is
the idea that before a terrible period of war and tribulation sets
in upon the world, Christ will return and remove all Christians
from the earth. This event is commonly referred to as the
Rapture. The message is a pleasant one and church-goers never
tire of hearing it, but according to the words of Jeremiah and
the Bible's other technological prophecies, this view is not valid.

The Bible's prophetic texts foretelling the technical inventions of the present age shed new light on such prophecies as
the Russian invasion of Israel, the Great Tribulation and the
Second Coming of Christ. They also provide the additional
information needed to determine the sequence in which these
events will occur. Once one gains an understanding of the
Bible's technological connection, the import of Jeremiah's blistering indictment against today's prevailing prophetic teachings will become clear.

FALSE TEACHINGS WILL FALL

Laying aside for the moment the larger issues associated
with this prophecy, it should be pointed out that although
Jeremiah's warning to today's keepers of the faith may seem
subtle, its primary message is not difficult to understand. Since
Bible scholars in former times could not possibly comprehend
the complexities of the present era, they also could not understand the Bible's prophecies foretelling the technical inventions
of the modern world. Because of this barrier, prophecies directed to the nuclear age became mired in misconceptions,
which in turn introduced distortions in the interpretation of the
events leading up to the Second Coming of Christ. Jeremiah's
prophecy bears witness against these mistaken teachings. Even
as the peace forecasts in his day were found wanting, so also
will be those in the latter days. The placement of a description
of an atomic blast in the middle of Jeremiah's indictment underscores the certainty of the message.

TRUTH WILL STAND

Jeremiah concluded his message with a reminder that following false teachings will not alter the truth.

> **30** Therefore, behold, I am against the prophets, saith the LORD, that steal my words every one from his neighbour. **31** Behold, I am against the prophets, saith the LORD, that use their tongues, and say, He saith. **32** Behold, I am against them that prophesy false dreams, saith the LORD, and do tell them, and cause my people to err by their lies, and by their lightness; yet I sent them not, nor commanded them: therefore they shall not profit this people at all, saith the LORD (Jer. 23:30–32).

ISRAEL'S INTERNAL POLITICS

Ezekiel begins his account of the Russian invasion of Israel by foretelling a dramatic replacement of Israel's long-standing political leadership by a former minority. According to Ezekiel, this political power switch will take place sometime after the modern nation of Israel is established, but prior to the actual Russian invasion of Palestine. The passing of the reins of government into the hands of the nation's former minority will serve to trumpet the impending arrival of the invading Russian army. Since this invasion will escalate into a global thermonuclear war, the fulfillment of Israel's internal political power switch is of great importance to us.

TWO UNITED STICKS

> **15** The word of the LORD came again unto me, saying, **16** Moreover, thou son of man, take thee one stick, and write upon it, For Judah, and for the children of Israel his companions: then take another stick, and write upon it, For Joseph, the stick of Ephraim, and for all the house of Israel his companions: **17** And join them one to another into one stick; and they shall become one in thine hand (Ezek. 37:15–17).

Ezekiel opens this prophecy by noting that the returning Jews will not be divided into two contending kingdoms of Judah and Israel again, but rather, the people will be united into one stick, or nation. The first stick named is Judah, which was the ruling tribe over the ancient southern kingdom of Judah. "Judah and the children of Israel his companions" refers to the tribes of Benjamin, Levi, part of Simeon, and individual members of various other tribes that lived in the southern kingdom (2 Chron. 11:12–16, 15:9). Joseph is the general name given here for the ten tribes which comprised the northern kingdom of Israel (Ps. 78:67). The northern kingdom is referred to as "the stick of Ephraim" (cf. Hos. 5:5), because Ephraim was the ruling tribe of "his companion" tribes.

Modern Israel is composed of two ethnically distinct Jewish communities; the Ashkenazic Jews of European descent and the Sephardic (Oriental) Jews whose forebearers lived mainly in the Arab lands of North Africa and Asia. The Ashkenazim ("Germans," in Old Hebrew), many of them descendants of the Polish and Russian Jews who founded Israel, originally were a tiny community on the Rhine. They are the fair-skinned, generally better-educated, high culture Europeans whose Western ideas shaped Israel's beginnings at the time of independence in 1948. The original Sephardim (literally "Spaniards") were the powerful Jews of Moorish Spain, who were expelled from the country in 1492 and dispersed to North Africa, the eastern Mediterranean and Asia. The darker Sephardim came to Israel mainly as poor cousins from Arab North Africa and the Middle East. As a group they inherited many cultural shortcomings, tend to live in small towns where they raise large families, and still earn 40 percent less than the Ashkenazim.

Today's two differing cultures of Ashkenazic and Sephardic Jews have fulfilled Ezekiel's prophecy of the two sticks by joining together to form the modern state of Israel. The European Ashkenazic Jews, who made up 85 percent of the population in 1948, dominated the new nation's leadership. They fulfilled the leadership role symbolized in Ezekiel's first stick. The sometimes scorned and culturally disadvantaged Sephardic Jews fulfilled the less prominent role in building the nation. They are symbolized in Ezekiel's second stick.

REVERSED ROLES

18 And when the children of thy people shall speak unto thee, saying, Wilt thou not shew us what thou meanest by these?

19 Say unto them, Thus saith the Lord GOD; behold, I will
take the stick of Joseph, which is in the hand of Ephraim, and
the tribes of Israel his fellows, and will put them with him,
even with the stick of Judah, and make them one stick, and
they shall be one in mine hand (Ezek. 37:18–19).

Notice how Ezekiel introduces one slight change when he
retells the prophecy of the two sticks being joined together into
one nation by naming the stick of Ephraim first. The meaning
seems to be that the politically entrenched Ashkenazim and
their Labor party—which ruled Israel without a break from
1948 to 1977—will eventually be displaced from their historical
hold on the nation's governing helm by the Sephardic Jews.

Interpretation, in this case, awaits tomorrow's developments; however, fundamental changes in Israel's electorate
reveal that a role reversal of Sephardi over Ashkenazi is already
well under way. As the Sephardim's numbers increased from
15 percent of Israel's Jewish population in 1948 to 60 percent by
the early 1980s, so also did the number of votes they cast at the
ballot box. In 1977, after Labor Prime Minister Yitzhak Rabin
was caught keeping an illegal bank account in the United States,
the Sephardic vote put the Likud block candidate, Manachem
Begin, into office. The fact that the Likud was dominated by
Ashkenazim, including Begin, did not bother the intensely
nationalistic Sephardim, who liked his hard-nosed attitude
toward the Arabs and his rejection of the idea of a Palestinian
homeland on the West Bank.

The Sephardim's increasing political role was evident in the
1984 Israeli national elections. Although the Sephardi backed
Likud block candidate, Yitzhak Shamir, did not win; neither did
Labor's candidate, Shimon Peres, since both sides failed to
muster a majority in the 120-member Knesset. After seven
weeks of political deadlock, the country finally got a new
government when the two contending parties agreed to rotate
the prime ministership. Under the deal, Peres was sworn in as
Prime Minister for the first twenty-five months, with Shamir
filling the posts of Foreign Minister and acting Prime Minister;
for the following twenty-five months, starting October 1, 1986,
the two men agreed to switch jobs.

This unusual Labor-Likud "national unity" coalition shows
the position of Ezekiel's two joined sticks to be at the midpoint
of a gradual replacement of Israel's original ruling Askenazic

nounce the timing of Christ's return. That is, the descendants of the ancient contending kingdoms of Judah and Israel will return to their original homeland; they will join together under one government to rebuild the nation; and also the destiny of the restored nation of Israel will apparently be firmly in the hands of the Sephardic branch of the Jewish family, symbolized here as "the stick of Joseph, that is in the hand of Ephraim," before Christ returns.

This prophecy regarding Christ's reign is followed by a reference to the Jews dwelling in the land of their forefathers, "even they, and their children, and their children's children for ever." This additional information shows that Christ's reign will begin as a literal earthly one that will go on for several generations. The everlasting character of Christ's reign is also spelled out with: "and my servant David shall be their prince for ever."

An earthly sanctuary, or temple for worship, is also mentioned. This temple will be used to worship Jesus Christ, the God of Israel and all mankind. The message going forth from this earthly temple will inform the world's heathen nations "that I the LORD do sanctify Israel, when my sanctuary shall be in the midst of them for evermore" (Ezek. 37:28).

In order to fully understand the significance of the two-joined sticks, it is necessary to see how this prophecy relates to Ezekiel's greater message concerning the Second Coming of Christ. The next two chapters of Ezekiel cover the Russian invasion of Israel. This topic is followed by nine concluding chapters detailing Christ's return and the establishment of His earthly kingdom. These nine chapters greatly expand the concluding remarks announcing Christ's Second Coming at the end of Ezekiel's two-joined sticks prophecy. They serve to reassure God's people that Christ will return and establish His earthly kingdom following the massive Russian-led attempt to destroy the renewed nation of Israel. Thus, the sequence of events presented in Ezekiel's prophecy match the same order in which these events will be fulfilled. For example, the placement of the Russian-led invasion against Israel, directly after the Scriptures's description of the political demise of modern Israel's original Ashkenazic nation builders at the hands of the more numerous Sephardic Jews, provides a visible signpost to look for prior to the arrival of the Russian-led confederated army into the Middle East.

GOD AGAINST GOG

1 And the word of the Lord came unto me, saying, 2 Son of
man, set thy face against Gog, the land of Magog, the chief
prince of Meshech and Tubal, and prophesy against him, 3
And say, Thus saith the Lord God; Behold, I am against thee,
O Gog, the Chief Prince of Meshech and Tubal (Ezek. 38:1–3):
4 And I will turn you about, and put hooks into your jaws,
and I will bring you out, and all your army, horses and
horsemen, all of them splendidly attired, a great company
with buckler and shield, all of them wielding swords (v. 4,
NASB).

Here, Ezekiel stated that Gog, the ruler of a nation located
in the land of Magog, will assemble a well-equipped army for
a future invasion. Magog is named in the Book of Genesis as the
second son of Japheth. Japheth was Noah's third son. The
Genesis account also names Tubal and Meshech as sons of
Japheth.

During the first century the Jewish writer Josephus wrote
about the origins of nations from their first inhabitants. Josephus stated that "Magog founded those that from him were
named Magogites, but who are by the Greeks called Scythians."

The Greek historian Herodotus devoted more than half a
volume to the Scythians. The Scythians were known for their
ferocity in battle and their great troves of gold. In the early 1970s
Russian archaeologists unearthed an unlooted royal Scythian
tomb north of the Black Sea. The dig provided new evidence of
Scythian ferociousness, lending credence to the Herodotus account which claims the Scythians beheaded their fallen enemies
and brought their skulls back to camp to use as wine goblets.
Lances and bows and arrows found in graves along with female
skeletons and ornaments suggest that the Scythian women
fought beside their men. The Russian archaeologists' findings
provided additional evidence that the Scythians, or Magogites,
roamed and ruled great areas of the Russian heartland more
than 2,000 years ago.

In like manner scholars of history who have examined
Josephus and other ancient texts have found that the tribes of
Meshech and Tubal also settled in Russia. According to *A Survey
of Bible Prophecy,* by Raymond Ludwigson, some have traced
the source name for the city of Moscow to the Hebrew name

be put in the Russians' jaws will be forged in the form of Russian friendship treaties with other nations. Some of the Arab states that will quite likely join Russia's future invasion force, have already established formal treaties with Russia. For example, Syria signed such a treaty in 1980 that contains a hook that fits the prophesied description given in this passage. Under the terms of the Syrian-Soviet treaty Moscow has pledged to provide military assistance in the event that Syria becomes engaged in battle with Israel on the Golan Heights.

Interestingly, during the Israeli invasion of Lebanon in 1982, the PLO's leaders urged Syrian President Hafez Assad to attack Israeli forces on the Golan as a means of forcing the Soviets to come into the fray. Assad declined, probably due in part to 93 Soviet-made Syrian fighter-jets having been shot down in air-to-air combat compared to zero for Israel. Undoubtedly another factor was the inopportune timing for the Soviets. They were preoccupied with the Polish crisis and had already committed about 100,000 troops to the military takeover of Afghanistan. They were simply not in a good position to open a third major front.

PREREQUISITES TO RUSSIA'S INVASION

8 After many days you will be summoned; in the latter years you will come into the land that is restored from the sword, whose inhabitants have been gathered from many nations to the mountains of Israel which had been a continual waste; but its people were brought out from the nations, and they are living securely, all of them (Ezek. 38:8, NASB).

RETURN OF JEWS TO PALESTINE

In 70 A.D. the Roman general Titus destroyed Jerusalem and proceeded to sell the Jews as slaves on the world market. From that time on the Jews were dispersed around the world. Israel became a barren wasteland and remained so until the Jews began returning from the various nations of their dispersion in the twentieth century.

Ezekiel sets the timing of the Russian invasion in the "latter years" of mankind's reign upon the earth. Here again, the beginning of the "latter years" is defined to be the time when the Jews return to the ancient land of Israel.

DEFENSIBLE BORDERS

Israel was engulfed in a war with the Palestinians the day she officially became a nation on May 14, 1948. Israel won the 1948 war, but her hostile neighbors tested again and again her ability to survive in the following decades. However, she also won three major conflicts with her Arab and Palestinian neighbors in 1956, 1967, and 1973. As a result of these wars Israel inexorably gained control of adjoining Arab lands, which enabled her to establish more defensible borders.

Finally, in 1982 Israel invaded Lebanon for the purpose of establishing a 25-mile buffer zone in southern Lebanon. The buffer zone would put northern Israel out of range of the Palestinian Liberation Organization's Soviet-made Katyusha rockets. Again Israel won the ensuing war with Syria and the PLO. As a result of this action Israel's northern border settlements were no longer within range of PLO artillery. For the first time, Israelis throughout Israel, were "living securely, all of them."

The Israeli capture of Beaufort Castle in southern Lebanon provides memorable insight into the relief felt by all Israelis following their successful military action against the PLO's last border stronghold. Some 50 Palestinians had dug into caves and shelters around Beaufort Castle, built in the twelfth-century atop a 1,500-foot-high granite mountain. From this vantage point they lobbed 57-mm artillery and mortar shells on northern Israel. A small unit of Israel's Golani Brigade, an elite commando unit, advanced under cover of night while artillery blasted the guerrilla hide-out, sending parts of the old fortress tumbling into the Litani river. After successful capture of the castle an aide woke Israel's Prime Minister, Menachem Begin, at 2 A.M., and declared: "Mr. Prime Minister, the Beaufort is in our hands." "Wonderful!" exclaimed Begin. "Go to Arik [General Sharon], give him a hug for me and tell him that from now on I will be able to sleep in peace."

In summary: the Jews have returned from many nations to a land that had been wasted and desolate for centuries; they have regained their ancient territory and are presently dwelling safely in that land. Although the surrounding Arab states are far greater in numbers, the Israelis are superior in raw military might. Today the Arabs cannot hope to prevail against Israel without outside help. This is the same situation that will exist the day the Russian military machine moves into the Middle East to assist the Arab states in a war against Israel.

RUSSIAN AIRLIFT KICKS OFF INVASION

9 Thou shalt ascend and come like a storm, thou shalt be like a cloud to cover the land, thou, and all thy bands, and many people with thee (Ezek. 38:9).

"Ascending", "coming like a storm" and "like a cloud to cover the land," describes a massive airlift of troops and equipment, supporting the invasion force on the ground.

VISIONS OF BOOTY

10 "'Thus says the Lord God, "It will come about on that day, that thoughts will come into your mind, and you will devise an evil plan, **11** and you will say, 'I will go up against the land of unwalled villages. I will go against those who are at rest, that live securely, all of them living without walls, and having no bars or gates; **12** to capture spoil and to seize plunder, to turn your hand against the waste places which are now inhabited, and against the people who are gathered from the nations, who have acquired cattle and goods, who live at the center of the world.' **13** Sheba, and Dedan, and the merchants of Tarshish, with all its villages, will say to you, 'Have you come to capture spoil? Have you assembled your company to seize plunder, to carry away silver and gold, to take away cattle and goods, to capture great spoil?'"'" (Ezek. 38:10–13, NASB).

In Ezekiel's day walls were essential defense systems for a nation's principal cities. Yet, Ezekiel emphatically states that the Israelis will be "dwelling safely," in cities that are not walled, when this invasion takes place. Twentieth century Jews have built unwalled major cities for the first time in their history. Actually building a principal city without a protective encircling wall was hard to imagine in Ezekiel's day; therefore, this fact was recorded in order to certify that this prophecy refers to the twentieth-century restored nation of Israel.

ISRAEL'S SECURE POSITION EMPHASIZED

Here again Ezekiel points out that the Israelis will be living securely before the Russian confederacy invades. Some may take exception with the position that the fulfillment of this portion of the prophecy has already been established as a result of Israel's successful military campaign into Lebanon in 1982. Indeed, this view may seem premature. After all, in recent times terrorists have blown up Israeli airline offices and randomly killed Jews in Israel and around the world. Certainly the Israeli citizens victimized by these terrorists attacks were confronted with a life-and-death situation. Yet, terrorists' strikes against individual Israeli citizens cannot be classified as a life-and-death threat to Israel's national survival, anymore than terrorists' attacks against individual Americans can be considered a serious threat against the national security of the United States. Accordingly, the meaning of "living securely" seems to be that the surrounding Arab states will not be militarily strong enough to mount a successful surgical strike against the restored nation of Israel prior to the arrival of the Russian invasion force. Israel gained this position of strength for the first time in 1982, as a result of her iron-fisted invasion that smashed Lebanon and scattered the Palestinian Liberation Army. That victory transformed Israel from the underdog to the overlord in the Middle East. Since gaining this position of strength in 1982, all Israel has been able to live without fear of being destroyed by a sudden surprise attack from a superior Arab invasion force.

Yet, the 1982 establishment of secure Israeli borders does not mean the Arabs will not continue to build up their military forces; nor does it imply that Israel will not be attacked by Arab armies in the future. Indeed, according to Ezekiel's prophecy, Israel will be engaged in combat with at least one Arab army immediately before Russia's invasion force comes into Palestine. This position is in keeping with the initial reason Ezekiel gave for the coming Russian thrust into the Middle East: "and I will turn you about, and put hooks into your jaws, and I will bring you out, and all your army" (Ezek. 38:4, NASB). As noted earlier in this chapter, the hooks put into the Russians' jaws stand for Russian friendship treaties with Arab states. These Soviet-Arab treaties will obligate Russia to come to the assistance of the Arab states in the event that they become engaged in battle with Israel in a future war.

Syria is already in the process of making advance preparations for the coming Russian war with Israel, in keeping with Ezekiel's blueprint. Syria has systematically refurbished its military machine since the Israelis crushed its Air Force and antiaircraft defenses during the 1982 invasion of Lebanon. In an effort to achieve "strategic parity" with Israel, Syrian President Hafez Assad has enlarged his standing army to as many as 500,000 troops. Russia has assisted the Syrian buildup by providing Syria with heavy armaments and antiaircraft-missile batteries, including surface-to-surface missiles capable of reaching every sizable Israeli city. The bulk of Syria's new military might is concentrated hard by the cease-fire line on the Golan. Naturally this massing of Syrian forces haunts Israeli strategists. Yet, even though Syria's military buildup appears to give it rough parity with Israel, in the final analysis Israel has a clear advantage in technological superiority, combat experience, and expertise. The reality of these factors continues to translate into secure living conditions for the citizens of Israel.

In spite of these facts some may still find it hard to apply "living securely" to Israel's present wary relationship with her Arab neighbors. The ongoing shipment to Syria of Russian-built surface-to-surface missiles that can reach virtually every sizable city in Israel certainly does not speak of a more secure Israeli future. But this is precisely what Ezekiel's prophecy is about—a less secure Israeli future that will culminate in a massive invasion by the Russian giant. Moreover, in a world containing thousands of nuclear missiles poised to be launched at almost every sizable city in America, Western Europe, and Russia, the citizens of Israel's cities can be looked upon with envy. After all, who wouldn't trade a nuclear missile aimed at their city for one carrying a mere conventional bomb? In other words, there are degrees of "living securely" in the nuclear age. Hence, the meaning of "living securely" as used in this passage compares the precarious uncertain early days of the fledgling restored nation to the expanded military might and defendable borders enjoyed by the mature nation prior to Russia's move into the Middle East.

Putting Ezekiel's prophecy in perspective with recent Middle Eastern events provides the following picture of what will lead up to the Russian invasion of Israel. Israel will be the dominant military power in the Middle East. Israel's position of strength will enable its citizens to "live securely, all of them." Russian-Arab treaties pledging Russian military support in the event of a future Arab-Israeli war will be in place. Neighboring Arab states will continue to build up their military forces. Eventually a war between Israel and one or more of the Arab states will occur. Israel will undoubtedly prevail in the ensuing war that will in turn activate the Russian-Arab treaty "hooks." The very words of those binding treaties, which proceeded out of the "jaws" of the Russians' mouths, will make it virtually impossible for the Russians not to come to the aid of their Arab allies. Not wanting to lose credibility in the Arab World, the Russian bear will be pulled into the Middle East conflict. Unfortunately, according to God's Word, the subsequent invasion will escalate into the world's first atomic war.

OIL AT THE CENTER OF THE WORLD

Ezekiel stated again that Russia will invade at a time when the Jews have returned "out of the nations" to settle "desolate places that are now inhabited." Ezekiel listed the taking of cattle, goods, and other wealth as part of Russia's motive for invading Israel. At first glance, this phrase sounds absurd to the modern mind. Israel isn't especially rich and is very small. Why would the Russian giant come to plunder Israel, a tiny country? Actually Russia would gain greatly by subjugating Israel. If Russia were to attack and conquer Israel, nothing could stop the Soviet bear from completely devouring the Middle East and controlling its vast oil reserves. Once such control was established, Russia could easily force advantageous trade agreements on Japan, Western Europe, and even the United States. Suddenly Russia would be in a position to provide its citizens with more of the consumer goods they want. A solution to her greatest domestic problem would finally be within the nation's reach. Thus, if Russia could conquer the Israelis "who live at the center of the world," the Russians could control the world from that central vantage point.

Oil is the single most important resource needed to run the modern industrial world. It is a vital basic commodity without which a modern military industrial complex cannot be maintained. Oil is at the center of a modern nation's strength; and, as it turns out, the majority of the world's long-term oil supplies happen to be in the Middle East. This geological fact places Israel and the surrounding oil-rich region, strategically, "at the center of the world."

DIPLOMATIC EFFORTS WILL FAIL

As Russia and her confederates move in to attack Israel, protests will be made by Sheba, Dedan, and the merchants of Tarshish. Although it is not entirely clear as to where the ancient lands of Sheba and Dedan resided geographically, traditionally they have been located in the southwest part of the Arabian peninsula. Tarshish, on the other hand, is generally identified with the lands of the far west of Europe, including perhaps a part of Spain, but very definitely Great Britain. It was from Tarshish of old that the Phoenicians obtained tin, and the word Britannia means the "land of tin."

Naturally the Western nations and even conservative Arab states such as Saudi Arabia will see through Russia's scheme and protest strongly. However, according to Ezekiel's prophecy, diplomatic protests will not persuade the Russians to halt their plans for conquest in the Middle East.

MODERN ARMIES RIDING ON HORSES?

14 "Therefore, prophesy, son of man, and say to Gog, 'Thus says the Lord God, "On that day when my people Israel are living securely, will you not know it? **15** "And you will come from your place out of the remote parts of the north, you and many peoples with you, all of them riding on horses, a great assembly and a mighty army"'" (Ezek. 38:14–15, NASB).

The description of this army: "all of them riding on horses," is curious. On the one hand Ezekiel describes part of the invaders "ascending" and "like a cloud covering the land;" an obvious aerial assault, but on the other hand he describes the ground forces, "riding on horses," "all of them."

In order to bring this seemingly contradictory description into focus, one has to step back a hundred years or so to the days of the old puffer-belly steam engines when the railroads were first being built. In those days men who had used horses all of their lives as their primary means of transportation, called the steam engines that pulled the first trains the "Iron Horse."

Now consider the man Ezekiel. He walked this earth over 2,500 years ago, when horses, camels, and donkeys were used for transportation of people and goods. Then one day Ezekiel viewed a divine vision of a modern army invading Israel in the latter days. His panoramic view of this invasion included modern aircraft, trucks, tanks, self-propelled rocket launchers, etc., but when he proceeded to write the vision down he did not have any suitable words in his vocabulary to describe these modern machines of war. So he simply referred to the ground forces as horsemen riding on horses, "all of them splendidly attired" (Ezek. 38:4, NASB). Ezekiel was really impressed. He lets us know this by inserting the fact that "all" the members of this army will be riding on horses—amazing to Ezekiel since most soldiers walked to battle in his day.

Thus the Russians can be expected to invade Israel in the same way they stormed into Afghanistan in late 1979; all of them riding on trucks, tanks and various armored personnel carriers. (Prophecies presented later in this book reveal that some of God's prophets were very descriptive in detailing today's modern machines of war.)

GOD'S DISTINCT INTERVENTION

16 "and you will come up against My people Israel like a cloud to cover the land. It will come about in the last days that I shall bring you against My land, in order that the nations may know Me when I shall be sanctified through you before their eyes, O Gog." **17** Thus says the Lord God, "Are you the one of whom I spoke in former days through My servants the prophets of Israel, who prophesied in those days for many years that I would bring you against them?"" (Ezek. 38:16–17, NASB).

This passage again describes the awesome army Russia will assemble against Israel in the latter days. The army will be so massive that no other nation will try to match Russia's conventional force. Israel will be alone. This is the situation into which

God will step to intervene on Israel's behalf. In fact, God will move in such a distinct manner that the nations will know He is God.

A GREAT EARTHQUAKE

18 "And it will come about on that day, when Gog comes against the land of Israel," declares the Lord God, "that My fury will mount up in My anger. **19** "And in My zeal and in My blazing wrath I declare that on that day there will surely be a great earthquake in the land of Israel. **20** "And the fish of the sea, the birds of the heavens, the beasts of the field, all the creeping things that creep on the earth, and all the men who are on the face of the earth will shake at My presence; the mountains also will be thrown down, the steep pathways will collapse, and every wall will fall to the ground" (Ezek. 38:18–20, NASB).

BROTHER AGAINST BROTHER

21 "And I shall call for a sword against him on all My mountains," declares the Lord God. "Every man's sword will be against his brother" (Ezek. 38:21, NASB).

Due to God's tremendous earthquake, Russia's army will think they are under attack and begin returning fire. Quick escalation will follow, resulting in Russia's confederate army annihilating each other.

According to the text, Russia's overwhelming forces will overrun Israel's defenders all along the country's mountainous border areas. This is clear from Ezekiel's battlefront observation that at the moment of the earthquake's impact the "sword" will be unleashed "against him on all My mountains." In other words, the invaders will be driving through Israel's rugged mountainous border areas toward the nation's less defendable lowlands when the earthquake occurs. (From the information provided here, a major Russian invasion force can be expected to come down through Israel's mountainous northern Highland region. This region includes the strategic Golan Heights that Israel and Syria have fought over on more than one occasion in recent times.)

AN OUTBREAK OF PESTILENCE

22 "And with pestilence and with blood I shall enter into judgment with him; and I shall rain on him, and on his troops, and on the many peoples who are with him, a torrential rain, with hailstones, fire, and brimstone. **23** And I shall magnify Myself, sanctify Myself, and make Myself, known in the sight of many nations; and they will know that I am the LORD" (Ezek. 38:22–23, NASB).

The potential to lose more soldiers to an outbreak of pestilence than to the enemy has always been an ever present threat to armies on the march. According to Ezekiel's prophecy, rapidly spreading plagues will eliminate significant numbers of the Russian-led invasion force.

JUDGMENT OF THE GOG OF THE NORTH

1 "And you, son of man, prophesy against Gog, and say, 'Thus says the Lord God: "Behold, I am against you, O Gog, chief prince of Meshech and Tubal; **2** and I will turn you about and drive you forward, and bring you up from the uttermost parts of the north, and lead you against the mountains of Israel; **3** then I will strike your bow from your left hand, and will make your arrows drop out of your right hand. **4** You shall fall upon the mountains of Israel, you and all your hordes, and the peoples that are with you; I will give you to birds of prey of every sort and to the wild beasts to be devoured. **5** You shall fall in the open field; for I have spoken," says the Lord God'" (Ezek. 39:1–5, RSV).

Verse two states, for the third time in this prophecy, that the invader will come from the "uttermost parts of the north." This further identifies the location of Russia and Magog's capital as Moscow, the last major city on earth due north of Israel.

RUNAWAY NUCLEAR ESCALATION

6 "And I shall send fire upon Magog and those who inhabit the coastlands in safety; and they will know that I am the Lord" (Ezek. 39:6, NASB).

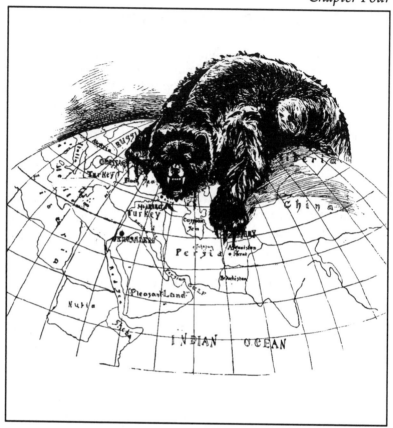

View of Russian threat appearing in an 1890 edition of Frank Leslie's
Illustrated Newspaper.

In addition to the destruction of Russia's confederated armies, fire will be sent on the Russian heartland. Fire will also be sent upon those who "inhabit the coastlands in safety." This statement implies an equal sending of fire between two groups of people. In the nuclear age, an equal sending of fire on two groups of people means a nuclear exchange of fire.

When God's earthquake hits Israel, fear, confusion, and general chaos will cause exchanges of fire within the Russian forces. Escalation will ensue. The Russians may well think the West has attacked. Most likely a nuclear exchange will begin inadvertently—not as a result of a grand design. Ezekiel didn't say who will start the nuclear exchange; only that it would happen. Ezekiel also does not identify the people inhabiting the coastlands in safety; but he does say that they will also be on the receiving end of this nuclear war. For the foreseeable future, the U.S.-led Western Alliance is the only group of nations capable of engaging the Russians in a major nuclear war.

GOD'S HAND REVEALED

Verse six ends with one remaining fact: "and they will know that I am the Lord." This additional comment declares that the two nuclear combatants will survive this nuclear exchange and that the survivors will know that God moved against the Russian confederacy on Israel's behalf.

> 7 And My holy name I shall make known in the midst of My people Israel; and I shall not let my holy name be profaned any more. And the nations will know that I am the Lord, the holy one in Israel. 8 "Behold, it is coming and it shall be done," declares the Lord God. "That is the day of which I have spoken" (Ezek. 39:7–8, NASB).

God will also make His holy name known to His people Israel. Furthermore, they will change their attitude from irreverence and indifference towards God to one of proper respect. All nations (including those that deny there is a God) will know there is a God, "the holy one in Israel."

The nation of Israel crediting God for destroying the Russian army is a reasonable national response; after all, the Israelis will be the ones who will be rescued from certain destruction. What is not as easy to understand is why other nations will come to realize there is a God and give Him the credit for delivering Israel. How this will come about is not given in this passage. However, Scriptures presented in later chapters of this book will describe this coming worldwide evangelistic effort in more detail.

THE SPOILS OF WAR

> 9 "Then those who inhabit the cities of Israel will go out, and make fires with the weapons and burn them, both shields and bucklers, bows and arrows, war clubs and spears and for seven years they will make fires of them. 10 And they will not

take wood from the field or gather firewood from the forests,
for they will make fires with the weapons; and they will take
the spoil of those who despoiled them, and seize the plunder
of those who plundered them," declares the Lord God. (Ezek.
39:9–10, NASB).

For centuries Russian Jews were killed, persecuted, and
often driven from the country. In recent times Nazi Germany
and many of the Arab states have mistreated Jews in like
manner. They have confiscated Jewish lands and goods. Following the defeat of Russia and her allies on the hills of Palestine the Israelis are going to "seize the plunder of those who
plundered them."

Among the goods and weapons left behind by the defeated
Soviet forces, the most useful commodity mentioned is enough
fuel to supply Israel's needs for seven years. Ezekiel explains
the great value of the large amount of fuel collected by pointing
out that the Israelis "will not have to take wood from the field
or gather firewood from the forests for seven years." Since
wood was used for heating and cooking in Ezekiel's day he was
impressed prophetically by the fact that the Russians will leave
enough fuel behind to supply Israel's needs for seven years.
Note here that Ezekiel did not say that the Russian weapons
will be made of wood, but rather that Israel will make fires with
the weapons. Again, an ancient man did not have words to
describe gasoline, diesel fuel, etc.

Enough leftover Russian fuel to supply Israel's needs for
seven years also emphasizes the massive size of the invading
army. This fact indicates that Russia's huge invasion force will
apparently be massed for the purpose of conquering not only
Israel but probably much of the entire oil-rich Middle East as
well.

GOG'S GRAVEYARD

11 "And it will come about on that day that I shall give Gog
a burial ground there in Israel, the valley of those who pass
by east of the sea, and it will block off the passers-by. So they
will bury Gog there with all his multitude, and they will call
it the valley of Hamon-gog. 12 For seven months the house
of Israel will be burying them in order to cleanse the land. 13

Even all the people of the land will bury them; and it will be
to their renown on the day that I glorify Myself," declares the
Lord God. **14** "And they will set apart men who will constantly pass through the land, burying those who were passing through, even those left on the surface of the ground, in
order to cleanse it. At the end of seven months they will make
a search. **15** And as those who pass through the land pass
through and anyone sees a man's bone, then he will set up a
marker by it until the buriers have buried it in the valley of
Hamon-gog. **16** And even the name of the city will be
Hamonah. So they will cleanse the land" (Ezek. 39:11–16,
NASB).

Israel will hire full-time employees to bury the dead soldiers "left on the surface of the ground" by the decimated
Russian invasion force. The task will take seven months to
complete. This fact gives a good indication of the vast numbers
of troops killed in the fighting.

DIRECTIONS

The primary objective of this book hereafter is to present the
prophesied events leading up to the Second Coming of Christ
in the same sequence in which they will come to pass. In some
instances it will not always be entirely possible to do so, since
a number of events will actually occur simultaneously. The
reader will find this to be the case during the period of upheaval
following the world's first nuclear war. Nevertheless, with the
additional insight gained from the Bible's technological
prophecies, the milestone events leading up to the Second
Coming of Christ can now be ordered in their proper sequence.
These same prophecies will also lay to rest many of the inherited misconceptions surrounding the Russian-led invasion of
Israel in the latter days.

ious places: **8** all this is but the beginning of the birth-pangs (Matt. 24:6–8, RSV).

Despite Christ's plainly spoken instructions: "see that you are not alarmed; for this must take place, but the end is not yet," Christians have consistently taken the view during times of violent wars and natural disasters that these calamaties are signs of the final countdown to the end of man's reign on the earth and Christ's imminent return. This persistent misunderstanding among Christians through the centuries is the central theme of the fifth seal prophecy.

THE FIFTH SEAL

9 When he opened the fifth seal, I saw under the altar the souls of those who had been slain because of the word of God and the testimony they had maintained. **10** They called out in a loud voice, "How long, Sovereign Lord, holy and true, until you judge the inhabitants of the earth and avenge our blood?" **11** Then each of them was given a white robe, and they were told to wait a little longer, until the number of their fellow servants and brothers who were to be killed as they had been was completed (Rev. 6:9–11, NIV).

Here, the Christians in heaven who suffered persecution, hardship and death, "because of the word of God and the testimony they had maintained," ask: "how long" will it be before God judges the inhabitants of the earth who inflicted these injustices upon us? The answer they receive instructs them "to wait a little longer" until their Christian brothers on earth have had time to carry out their mission of preaching the Word of God to a lost and dying world. They are told further that their fellow Christians will also suffer trials, persecution and death over the course of the spiritual battle for lost souls, until their mission has been completed. Then, God will intervene and vindicate His name.

THE SIXTH SEAL

Therefore the message of the fifth seal is that Christians will go through the sixth seal events. The opening sixth seal event, the world's first nuclear war, defines the outbreak of that war to be the first day of what is biblically called "the Great Tribulation."

> **12** I watched as he opened the sixth seal. There was a great earthquake. The sun turned black like sackcloth made of goat hair, the whole moon turned blood red (Rev. 6:12, NIV).

John, like Ezekiel before him, predicts that an unexpected great earthquake will trigger the world's first atomic war. It is also important to note that Ezekiel named a great earthquake as the first significant event to occur once a Russian-led confederated army commences its invasion of Israel.

> **18** "And it will come about on that day, when Gog comes against the land of Israel," declares the Lord God, "that My fury will mount up in My anger. **19** And in My zeal and in My blazing wrath I declare that on that day there will surely be a great earthquake in the land of Israel" (Ezek. 38:18–19, NASB).

John's systematic presentation of fact after fact about the world's first global nuclear war makes it clear that John and Ezekiel were talking about the same great earthquake and the same all-out atomic war.

John then listed the diminished visibility of the sun and moon as the most damaging consequence of that unexpected great earthquake. John did not say why this will be the case here; however, he eventually provided a full explanation of every aspect of the First Atomic War, directly following his sixth seal introductory remarks.

STARS FALLING TO THE EARTH

> **13** and the stars of the sky fell to the earth, as a fig tree casts its unripe figs when shaken by a great wind (Rev. 6:13, NASB).

The emphatic pronouncement: "and the stars of the sky fell to the earth," could not be fulfilled by stars literally falling to the earth, since even a star as small as the sun would incinerate the planet in a collision. Furthermore, the possibility that the falling stars represent meteor showers was categorically eliminated by John in a later chapter.

An investigation of John's reference to falling stars logically leads to man-made, air-borne inventions. John compared what he saw in the vision to falling stars, simply because they most closely resembled the action of the man-made objects he was viewing.

Falling stars and air-borne atomic weapons have a number of observable features in common. For example, the fiery streak of a falling star is similiar in appearance to the rocket exhaust of a nuclear-tipped missile as it hurtles through the heavens at speeds up to 8,000 miles per hour. Then, like a free-falling star, once the intercontinental ballistic missile's (ICBM) rockets burn out, the warhead continues its ballistic trajectory under the influence of gravity as it falls toward the target. Also, even as a meteor ignites with a burst of bright light during the course of its fall to the earth, so does an air-borne nuclear warhead explode into brilliant light in the midst of its fall to the earth.

WIND-SHAKEN UNRIPE FIGS

John compared the unexpected arrival of this nuclear war to a sudden violent windstorm shaking unripe figs from a tree. That is, even as people do not plan for, or expect, a sudden violent windstorm to shake unripe figs from a tree, so likewise will they not be expecting the unleashing of large numbers of nuclear weapons on the day the atomic war breaks forth on the earth.

John's comparison certainly fits man's precarious position in the nuclear age. Thousands of nuclear weapons are poised to be unleashed in a matter of seconds upon targets around the world, if an international controversy precipitates a conflict that gets out of hand. Hence, the point of the comparison is to show the suddenness of the escalation from a conventional to a nuclear war in a future armed conflict.

According to the rest of John's Revelation account and Ezekiel's companion prophecy on the Russian-led invasion of Palestine, this very situation will occur when an unexpected earthquake jars the Middle East in the midst of the Russian invasion of Israel. The ensuing unplanned nuclear exchange, in turn, will quickly engulf the world in its first atomic war; "like a fig tree casting its unripe 'nuclear' figs when shaken by a great wind."

THE FANTASTIC POWER OF THE BOMB

At this point in the vision, John described the fantastic power of these falling star-like nuclear bombs.

14 And the heaven departed as a scroll when it is rolled together; and every mountain and island were moved out of their places (Rev. 6:14).

The heavens, that is, the clouds and colorless gases of the atmosphere, departed, or moved from where they were to some other place. Anyone who has viewed films of atomic bomb tests can testify to the accuracy of John's description. The films show how the continuing force of a one-megaton bomb's nuclear blast wave literally splits the heavens asunder, as the thermonuclear reaction drives everything away from its boiling, superheated center, with winds up to 400 miles per hour. After a few seconds, the nuclear reaction plays itself out and the winds die down and reverse their direction. This wind reversal phenomenon is called the negative (or suction) phase. There is a partial vacuum left where the heavens resided before the bomb went off. Hence, the air, dust and smoke rush back to fill the void, in the reverse direction, with winds of diminished intensity. These inflowing winds, called "afterwinds," produce a strong updraft in the immediate vicinity some seconds after the explosion and are sustained by cooler surface air being drawn up into the hot cloud. A column of fiery dust and smoke-filled air promptly forms, like "a scroll being rolled up" (IGENT). The entire superheated gaseous mixture then proceeds to abruptly "depart," (at an average speed of nearly 300 miles per hour in the first minute for a 1-megaton air burst), as it rises several miles into the darkening sky. John equated the visual effects of this wind reversal phenomenon to the suddeness of a fully extended scroll rolling itself up upon being released.

Interestingly, people do not think of the radioactive cloud from a nuclear explosion in terms of a scroll being rolled up, even though the gaseous stem retains a scroll-like appearance. This is because typical photographs of atomic explosions show a gigantic mushroom shaped cloud. These pictures present the

An atomic explosion.

most dramatic view of the visible cloud, which is fully formed some minutes after the toroidal circulatory motions of its hot gases have risen near their maximum height. What aftermath photographs invariably fail to capture is the radioactive cloud's early ascent to a height of several miles before the hot gases abruptly spread out into a mushroom shape. Thus, the first phase of the rapidly ascending cloud creates a momentary visual impression of "the heavens departing" into open space as the escaping "sky rolls up like a scroll."

Although the rising radioactive cloud does not actually escape into open space, the heavens do depart, or leave, their normal place of residence in the troposphere. The troposphere is the stratum of the atmosphere where clouds form, convective disturbances occur, and the temperature decreases with the altitude. In short, it is where the planet's weather resides. Above the troposphere is the relatively stable air of the stratosphere. The height at which the stratosphere begins varies with season and latitude, ranging from about 5 miles near the poles to approximately 10 miles in equatorial regions. Now since a typical low air burst, 1-megaton explosion lifts its superheated gases to a height of 12 miles in less than four minutes, the heaven—that is, the clouds and colorless gases of the troposphere—literally "departs" from its natural dwelling place as the heat from the atomic explosion carries the gaseous mixture well into the alien stable air of the stratosphere.

ISAIAH'S REPORT ON
THE DEPARTING HEAVENS

Some seven hundred years before the Apostle John was born, Isaiah wrote about nuclear wars between the nations in the latter days. On this subject John used many of the symbols Isaiah originated, not because he was at a loss for words to describe his visions, but rather because symbolism in prophetic writing was a recognized language in its own right.

The following excerpt from one of Isaiah's complementary prophecies illustrates this consistancy of symbolic description.

> 4 All the stars of the heavens will be dissolved and the sky rolled up like a scroll; all the starry host will fall like withered leaves from the vine, like shriveled figs from the fig tree. 5 My sword has drunk its fill in the heavens; (Isa. 34:4–5, NIV).

Isaiah, in addition to reporting that all these star-like nuclear bombs will fall from the heavens: "like withered leaves from the vine and shriveled figs from the fig tree;" noted that the star-like bombs themselves will actually "dissolve" at some point in the course of their fall. This is precisely what happens to a hydrogen bomb at the appointed in-flight detonation time. For at the moment of the explosion, boiling and surging atomic particles reach superstellar temperatures that instantly gasify, or "dissolve," the bomb. If the bomb is detonated at a nominal height of one mile, the thermal pulse from the growing fireball vaporizes people below within two seconds. The fiery updrafts subsequently carry the victims gaseous remains miles into the heavens. When it's over, the star-like 'nuclear' "sword has drunk its fill in the heavens."

THE BIBLE'S TECHNOLOGICAL ACCURACY

The significance of the Bible's impeccably accurate descriptions of modern man's technological achievements cannot be overstated. The considerable effort put forth by the U.S. Department of Defense and the Energy Research and Development Administration to document and jointly publish the book, *The Effects of Nuclear Weapons*, underscores the point. Since the deadly effects of radiation, blinding light, intense heat, etc., do not allow men to observe atomic explosions at close range, elaborate scientific instruments and special cameras have to be developed and deployed to do the task for them. Hence, when *The Effects of Nuclear Weapons* records the obscure fact: "The radioactive cloud ascends several miles before spreading out abruptly into a mushroom shape," about a fleeting observable feature of a nuclear explosion, it represents a tremendous expenditure in terms of time and money. In direct contrast, the Bible compresses all of that effort into nine words: "the heaven departed as a scroll being rolled up," without so much as one ancient shekel invested.

All things considered, the biblical image of the transient initial stage of a radioactive cloud's formation, "like a scroll being rolled up," is so flawless that it voids all attempts to slough off the Bible's greater prophetic statement foretelling the final destiny of the nuclear age. The presence of God's prophetic descriptions of modern man's inventions and their workings likewise eliminate any sound reason for doubting the Bible's most important message—namely, the proclamation that Jesus Christ is the only One who can save a man's eternal soul.

MOUNTAINS AND ISLANDS MOVED

"And every mountain and island were moved out of their places." This does not mean that every mountain and island on the planet will be moved, but rather, when these star-like bombs go off in the vicinity of a mountain, or an island, the targeted mountains and islands will be severely moved and shaken by the intense heat and violent forces of the nuclear blast's concussion wave.

Both the United States and Russia maintain super warheads for the purpose of knocking out top-priority targets such as command and control centers located deep in mountain redoubts and hardened, well-fortified, air and naval bases located on islands. These multi-megaton warheads are designed to literally move substantial portions of mountains and islands "out of their places." Further, the nuclear war plans of these nations often call for two or more warheads to be aimed at significant targets, to ensure that one gets through. Needless to say, when the war comes, there is a nontrivial probability that in some instances, all the missiles assigned to a target will arrive at their shared destination. If 10-to-60-megaton behemoths are used, (warheads of this size have already been built and tested), mountains and islands would not only be badly broken up, but also literally moved out of their places.

Taking the position that nuclear blasts will physically move fair-sized mountains and islands out of their places may sound speculative. Yet the 15-megaton thermonuclear bomb tested near the surface of a coral island at Bikini Atoll on March 1, 1954—the BRAVO shot of Operation Castle—demonstrated that at least one island on the planet has already been "moved out of its place." For when the atomic fire, dust and smoke cleared, observers found that the island had literally vanished from the sea.

THE PLIGHT OF THE VICTIMS

John followed his documentary on the startling extent of damages inflicted on the planet by the nuclear war with a report on the plight of the victims.

> **15** Then the kings of the earth and the great men and the generals and the rich and the strong, and every one, slave and free, hid in the caves and among the rocks of the mountains (Rev. 6:15, RSV).

John noted that everyone will be subjected to the horrors of this nuclear war. Unlike former conventional wars where the privileged people—"the generals, the rich and the strong"— often managed to avoid personal hardships, all classes of people in the target zones will be exposed to the devastation wrought by the world's First Atomic War. Everyone surviving on the perimeter of the radioactive bombed-out areas will head for the hills, literally, since staying near the blast areas would invite death by severe radiation poisoning.

> **16** and they said to the mountains and to the rocks, "Fall on us and hide us from the presence of Him who sits on the throne, and from the wrath of the Lamb; **17** for the great day of their wrath has come; and who is able to stand?" (Rev. 6:16–17, NASB).

All the survivors, including military commanders, will be in a state of extreme shock when the smoke clears. The overwhelming scene of destruction and death will fill them with sheer terror and foreboding. The statement: "and they said to the mountains and to the rocks, 'Fall on us,'" reveals the victims numbed state of mind; namely, one of utter hopelessness. When they take stock of their injuries, exposure to radiation, lack of adequate food, water, shelter, and medical support, they will consider death from a falling rock a better fate than the calamities engulfing them.

The language "and hide us from the presence of Him who sits on the throne, and from the wrath of the Lamb; for the great day of their wrath has come" shows that the survivors will believe that God and the Son of God, Jesus Christ "the Lamb," are about to return at that very moment and judge them. The calamity will be so awful that they will suppose the end of the world is upon them. This assumption will be incorrect. John did not say God would return immediately after this atomic war, but rather, "they said" (the uninformed survivors) "the great day of their wrath has come."

Despite many books and graphic films documenting the horrors of nuclear war, the Bible teaches that people will be unprepared to cope with the aftermath of the world's first atomic war. The survivors' initial reaction of sheer terror also points out a very real shortcoming of knowledge gained from written and visual media; i.e., informative literature and realistic films cannot transmit pain nor the impact of uncontrolled violence, only a faint echo of the real thing.

THE WINDS WILL CEASE TO BLOW

1 After this I saw four angels standing at the four corners of the earth, holding back the four winds of the earth, so that no wind should blow on the earth or on the sea or on any tree (Rev. 7:1, NASB).

The statement, "After this I saw," establishes the end of the atomic war as the beginning of the next chronologically ordered series of events. Accordingly, the first event in the list will find fulfillment in what the four angels and winds symbolically represent.

By biblical precedent, angels have often been sent by God to deliver messages about the future to members of the human race. In this fashion, much of the contents of the Book of Revelation was delivered to the Apostle John. Hence, the four-angel team in this passage was sent to facilitate the process of explaining the most important event that will occur directly after the atomic war ends.

Unlike the "stars, falling from the sky to the earth," which were presented in a video-like vision, this portion of the prophecy could not be shown with a video-like medium because it had to do with the literal stopping of the winds. Blowing winds, of course, are not something that can be seen, especially if they are not blowing at all. Imagine trying to detect winds that are not blowing, and the greater significance of that, simply by viewing a film strip showing shots of the land, the sea, and some trees. It would not be within the realm of reason to assume anyone could do so.

For these reasons the four-angel team stationed themselves "at the four corners of the earth." Their mission was to overcome the technical difficulties of conveying this unprecedented irregularity in the global weather patterns to a future generation. They accomplished this task by physically locating themselves at the four points of the compass and by assuming bodily positions that would project to the beholder the idea of holding the earth's four winds. Thus, both their location and their body language serve to demonstrate the interjection of some dramatic atmospheric change that will physically bring global wind movement to a standstill. Since this event will occur after the global atomic war, it follows that this major climatic disruption will be a direct consequence of the massive stress imposed on the Earth's biosphere by that war.

The statement, "so that no wind should blow on the earth or on the sea or on any tree," is added to drive home the point that even as the land and the sea constitute the entire surface of the globe, so also will the cessation of all wind movement on land and sea be absolute, after the atomic war. The universal calm will be so complete that the wind will not blow "on any tree." This language indicates a state of profound quiet, such as would be found on a day when the leaves on the trees do not even rustle.

THE ANGEL FROM THE EAST

A fifth angel, who arrived after the four-angel team had already established the fact that the world's winds will cease to blow after the atomic war, led the whole operation with expert dispatch. His instructions help explain the technical complexities surrounding the subject matter—that is, why the winds will stop after the nuclear war and why the halting of their normal motions will be a blessing in disguise for the earth and its inhabitants.

21 For the prophecy came not in old time by the will of man: but holy men of God spake as they were moved by the Holy Ghost (2 Peter 1:21).

In the second instance, prophecy is eventually correctly interpreteted through diligent prayerful study, research, and reasoning.

15 Study to shew thyself approved unto God, a workman that needeth not to be ashamed, rightly dividing the word of truth (2 Tim. 2:15).

Clearly, according to the procedure outlined in this verse, finding the correct interpretation of Bible prophecy begins with study—a decidedly different process than a divine interruption, by which the transmission of a prophecy from God to a member of the human race begins. The combination of Bible study and careful examination of historical events led to the correct interpretation of a number of Bible prophecies foretelling the rise and fall of various nations. Yet this same approach failed to unravel the mysteries of Bible prophecies concerning latter day inventions. In fact, none of the opinions about the Bible's technological prophecies written before the inventions and science of the nuclear age came into view are valid. For example, there was not even a remote possibility that the four angels holding the four winds could have been interpreted as a nuclear war-induced temperature inversion prior to the invention of the atomic bomb. The point here is that studying the science of the technological era turns out to be a prerequisite to finding the correct interpretation of the Bible's technological prophecies.

Due to the immense complexities of the global ecosystem, sizing the infinite number of environmental interactions introduced by the effects of nuclear war is extremely complicated. Though the study of the environmental consequences of nuclear war is interesting, it is beyond the scope of this book to delve deeply into all the intricate factors that will contribute to the planet's winds coming to a standstill after AWWI. Therefore, the explanation that follows will simply summarize the main features of the process that will bring this unprecedented event to pass.

First, all scientific nuclear war studies begin with the fact that nuclear bombs burn cities and surrounding fields and forests to the ground. The firestorms quickly loft vast quantities of smoke miles high into the atmosphere. In a global nuclear war 1,000 or more large cities would be burning simultaneously. Since war planners generally target cities only in the final, all-out phases of a nation's war plans, 10 to 20 thousand other targets would likely already be on fire as well. Several hundred million tons of smoke are expected to be produced by all the fires—the atmosphere will be turned on its head. Day will quickly be transformed into night over vast continental areas.

Computer studies reveal several important features resulting from all this atomic smoke and dust being introduced into the atmosphere. At the highest layers of the upper atmosphere, sunlight will raise the temperature of the smoke-ladened air between 30 and 80 degrees C. Meanwhile, the ground below, deprived of up to 95 percent of its daily ration of solar energy, will cool in darkness. The hot clouds, like hot-air balloons, would not remain stationary, but would rise and expand.

According to a three-dimensional smoke simulation model developed at Colorado State University, almost half of the smoke generated by a computerized firestorm was driven into the stagnant, weatherless stratosphere (above 12 kilometers), where it could reside for years. Other smoke simulation studies predict that as this vast quantity of high altitude smoke continues to be warmed by sunlight, it will spread out horizontally and move briskly around the globe. One study, christened TTAPS, by Richard P. Turco, Owen B. Toon, Thomas P. Ackerman, James B. Pollack and Carl Sagan, warns that a high altitude sooty pall of smoke will absorb most of the incoming incident sunlight and keep all but a small fraction from being scattered back into space or down toward the surface. The entire troposphere over land is expected to be thermally brought to a standstill as it continues to be deprived of its daily ration of heat by the thick smoke clouds above it. Thus, the rapid interhemispheric transport of high altitude, continent-size smoke clouds will effectively seal off the layers of air below, creating an alien, motionless, low altitude atmosphere.

By definition a temperature inversion is a layer of cool air held in place by a layer of warm air above it. When such a condition is introduced as a direct consequence of a global nuclear war, the lower level "four winds of the earth" will be and the subject of "the seal." In regard to the seal it can be said here that no information, as to the form of the seal, is supplied. This is because the seal is a spiritual seal between the believer and God. The Scripture says "Ye were sealed with that holy Spirit of promise" (Eph. 1:13). A physical seal will never exist— only the everlasting seal of salvation between Christ and His servants.

THE 144,000 SEALED JEWS

4 Then I heard the number of those who were sealed: 144,000 from all the tribes of Israel. 5 From the tribe of Judah 12,000 were sealed, from the tribe of Reuben 12,000, from the tribe of Gad 12,000, 6 from the tribe of Asher 12,000, from the tribe of Naphtali 12,000, from the tribe of Manasseh 12,000, 7 from the tribe of Simeon 12,000, from the tribe of Levi 12,000, from the tribe of Issachar 12,000, 8 from the tribe of Zebulun 12,000, from the tribe of Joseph 12,000, from the tribe of Benjamin 12,000 (Rev. 7:4–8, NIV).

John reported that he "heard the number of those who were sealed;" he did not see it done. The way John received this information is in keeping with how one person learns of another's sealed commitment to Christ—namely by the individual's personal testimony of salvation and new life found in Christ.

John then reported that 144,000 were sealed and that they would be members of the twelve tribes of Israel. The fact that he did not say the 144,000 will be from the nation of Israel, but rather, that they will be from the twelve tribes, indicates that the majority of these Jews will not be citizens of the restored nation of modern Israel. That is, they will not necessarily be the visible Jews of the world, like those living in the renewed nation of Israel, but Jews who are tucked in among the populations of other nations around the globe. Zechariah's prophecy (Zech. 12:9–10—covered in chapter 2), which declares that the majority of the Jews living in the restored nation of Israel will not worship Christ until the day He returns and sets up His earthly kingdom, confirms the position that most of the members of this specific group of sealed Jews will not be citizens of the renewed nation of Israel. Hence, John did not see these Jews grouped together in one location, but only heard the number of them which would be sealed after AWWI.

In modern times the typical Jew does not identify himself as a member of one of the original twelve tribes of Israel. Common sense dictates that today's larger Jewish community is the polygenetic product of all the original twelve tribes. With these facts in view the meaning of the specific assignment of the number 12,000 to each tribe seems to be that the 144,000 will simply be an identifiable group of Jews from the world's greater Jewish community.

THE GREAT MULTITUDE

9 After these things I looked, and behold, a great multitude, which no one could count, from every nation and all tribes and peoples and tongues, standing before the throne and before the Lamb, clothed in white robes, and palm branches were in their hands; 10 and they cry out with a loud voice, saying, "Salvation to our God who sits on the throne, and to the Lamb." 11 And all the angels were standing around the throne and around the elders and the four living creatures; and they fell on their faces before the throne and worshiped God, 12 saying, "Amen, blessing and glory and wisdom and thanksgiving and honor and power and might, be to our God forever and ever. Amen" (Rev. 7:9–12, NASB).

The statement, "After these things," establishes the completion of 144,000 Jews making a firm commitment to Christ as the beginning of the next chronologically ordered series of events. The setting for this series of events will take place in heaven since the great multitude from every tribe and nation and tongue appeared "before the throne and before the Lamb;" that is, before the throne of God in heaven.

"The Lamb" is a reference to God's Son, Jesus Christ. John the Baptist identified Jesus Christ as "the Lamb of God, which taketh away the sin of the world" (John 1:29). Thus, the "great multitude, which no one could count," ascribed their salvation to "our God who sits on the throne," as the author of their salvation, "and to the Lamb," as the finisher of their salvation. The rescued multitude's acknowledgment of both God and Christ is scripturally correct since Paul spoke of "looking unto

Jesus the author and finisher of our faith (Heb. 12:2); and Christ plainly said, "I and my Father are one (John 10:30). The language of the entire passage teaches that God and Christ are one and entitled to equal praise.

At this point in the vision John did not have enough information about the great multitude to come to any definite conclusions concerning their specific importance with respect to the greater context of the sixth seal prophecy. He did know, however, from the palm branches in their hands (which were commonly carried by the Greeks and Romans in triumphal processions), that the great multitude was celebrating a victory. While John was undoubtedly contemplating the multitude's significance, one of the heavenly elders asked him a rhetorical question.

THE DEFINITION OF THE GREAT TRIBULATION

> **13** Then one of the elders asked me, "These in white robes—who are they, and where did they come from?" **14** I answered, "Sir, you know." And he said, "These are they who have come out of the great tribulation; they have washed their robes and made them white in the blood of the Lamb" (Rev. 7:13–14, NIV).

The elder answered the second half of his two-part question first because it was the main reason he posed the question. Note that "have come out" is incorrectly translated here, since in the original Greek the elder's answer reads: "These are the ones coming out of the great affliction" (IGENT). Although slight, the difference turns out to be important since "have come out" could be interpreted to mean that the Great Tribulation had already come to an end at this point in the prophetic flow of sixth seal events. This is quite contrary to the intended meaning of the prophecy. For "these are the ones coming out" not only implies that the great multitude just came out of the Great Tribulation, but also implies that there will be many more Christians coming out of this Great Tribulation, which will continue for some unspecified period of time.

"These are the ones coming out of the great affliction" also serves to separate this group of Christians from the ones under the altar in the fifth seal prophecy, who were already in heaven before the sixth seal event arrived in the prophesied course of human history. In other words, "the ones coming out of the Great Tribulation" are singled out as a distinct group from the Christians who had suffered and died before the opening, or arrival, of the sixth seal, which marks the start of the world's First Atomic War. This deliberate division between pre-AWWI Christians and post-AWWI Christians is by design. The objectives behind the design are twofold. First, the split defines the great earthquake, which will trigger AWWI, to be the beginning of the time period biblically referred to as the Great Tribulation. Second, the setting apart of Christians "coming out of the great affliction" into a second, well-defined group, eliminates a commonly held notion that there will be a wholesale Rapture of all Christians before the Great Tribulation begins. The fact that the answer to the elder's question—"where did these in white robes come from?"—plainly states: "These are the ones coming out of the great affliction" (IGENT) emphasizes the point.

THE IDENTITY OF THE
GREAT MULTITUDE REVEALED

The elder then proceeds to address the other half of his two part question: "Who are they?" His answer: "They have washed their robes and made them white in the blood of the Lamb," serves to positively identify the multitude as Christians. Washing robes in the blood of the Lamb would not be expected to literally turn robes white; therefore the statement has to refer to God's acceptance of Christ's death on the cross as the means by which the multitude in heaven were cleansed of all their sins and unrighteousness. The course of thought here is that they were not made holy by their own great deeds, sufferings, and trials but by the blood of the Lamb that had been shed for their sins. "All our righteousnesses are as filthy rags" (Isa. 64:6). Christ is our righteousness (1 Cor. 1:30).

Clearly then, the focus of the great Christian multitude's triumphant celebration is Christ. For Christ is the one who paid the ransom for their eternal souls by shedding his blood and dying on the cross.

THE 144,000 SEALED JEWS' MISSION

Now since the "sealed Jews" were announced immediately before the introduction of "the great multitude, which no one could count," it follows that the 144,000 will be a group of Jewish Christian evangelists who will join forces with those already engaged in leading the great multitude to Christ during the closing days of the tribulation epoch. Later chapters of this book will confirm this position.

The informative comment: "which no one could count," is a very encouraging statement. It reveals that vast numbers of people will be led to Christ during the Great Tribulation. It also discards a commonly held opinion that only a few people will be saved.

> **15** "For this reason, they are before the throne of God; and they serve Him day and night in His temple; and He who sits on the throne shall spread His tabernacle over them. **16** They shall hunger no more, neither thirst any more; neither shall the sun beat down on them, nor any heat; **17** for the Lamb in the center of the throne shall be their shepherd, and shall guide them to springs of the water of life; and God shall wipe every tear from their eyes" (Rev. 7:15–17, NASB).

They are before the throne of God solely because Christ made full payment for their sins when He died on the cross. Christians will be gratefully happy to serve Christ throughout eternity, for He will not only rescue them from a dying planet and eternal death, but will establish a new dwelling place for them, where there will no longer be misery and sorrow.

THE OPENING OF THE SEVENTH SEAL

> **1** When he opened the seventh seal, there was silence in heaven for about half an hour (Rev. 8:1, NIV).

When the seventh seal is opened, the full prophetic communication of the Book of Revelation is suddenly available for everyone's inspection. Viewing the opened book left those in heaven in a state of stunned silence. For the opened book immediately delegates the sixth seal overview of the world's

First Atomic War to a mere glimpse of an infinitely greater, and still unfolding, catastrophy.

In order to understand why "there was silence in heaven for about half an hour," the question asked by the Christians under the altar in the fifth seal prophecy—that is, "How long, Sovereign Lord, holy and true, until you judge the inhabitants of the earth?" (Rev. 6:10, NIV)—needs to be revisted. Their question, posed in the form of a request for divine intervention on behalf of their fellow Christians still suffering persecution on the earth, reveals their grief over the world's rampant injustice. They could see no reason for God to allow the misery to continue. After all, Scripture plainly teaches that God will eventually step in and halt man's senseless violence. Why not now instead of later? The answer revealed to them, when the Book of Revelation was opened to their understanding, left them speechless. For the unprecedented post-AWWI horrors prophesied in the rest of the Revelation will continue for a much longer time than anyone anticipated. The point made here is that stunned silence will be the same emotional reaction of today's Christians when they finally learn from the opened Book of Revelation that the Sixth Seal Atomic War (AWWI) and its violent aftermath is about to engulf the world.

saw the seven angels which stood before God; and to them
were given seven trumpets (v. 2).

According to Revelation chapter 5, Jesus Christ opened the
seven seals binding the Book of Revelation. Hence, the pronoun
"He" refers directly to Christ. The word "whenever," as used
here, means "at whatever time" Christ determines the right
time to be, He will open the seventh seal and thus the full
prophetic contents of His Revelation message for the world's
inspection. In practical terms, the prophecy places this "opening" prior to the arrival of the first trumpet event.

ANOTHER ANGEL'S PROPHETIC INTERRUPTION

Each angel was given a trumpet. The angels used their
respective trumpets to successively sound, or announce, the
seven most important milestone events leading up to the establishment of Christ's earthly kingdom of peace. However, before
the seven angels could sound their trumpets, they were inter-
rupted by the arrival of another angel.

> 3 And another angel came and stood at the altar, having a
> golden censer; and there was given unto him much incense,
> that he should offer it with the prayers of all saints upon the
> golden altar which was before the throne (Rev. 8:3). 4 And the
> smoke of the incense, with the prayers of the saints, went up
> before God out of the angel's hand (v. 4, NASB).

This unnamed angel is one of many employed throughout
the Revelation to present various future events to the human
race. Since Christ opened the Book of Revelation, it follows that
Christ also directed the communication of its contents. Hence,
it was Christ who dispatched this unnamed angel to make a
timely instructive presentation before the first of the seven
trumpets sounded.

The incense symbolizes Christ's death on the cross which
renders the saints' prayers acceptable to God. The angel's role
in this prophetic presentation is not to receive the prayers of the
saints unto himself, but only to facilitate the delivery of their
prayers to God. "For there is one God, and one mediator
between God and men, the man Christ Jesus" (1 Tim. 2:5). The
angel carries out his assignment "and the smoke of the incense,

with the prayers of the saints, went up before God out of the angel's hand." (The reason for the angel's symbolic action comes to light in the next verse.)

When the Christian Church recovers from the shocking news that a prophesied global nuclear war will shortly engulf "their" world, they will look to God in prayer. They will return to the basics: to the altar where Christ paid for their souls with His death at the cross and to a fundamental prayer—God help us!

WAR BREAKS FORTH ON THE EARTH

5 Then the angel took the censer, filled it with fire from the altar, and hurled it on the earth; and there came peals of thunder, rumblings, flashes of lightning and an earthquake (Rev. 8:5, NIV).

The angel filled the censer, or fire-pan, "with fire from the altar, and hurled it on the earth." The sounds of war immediately broke forth on the earth. That is, the thunder of tank and artillery fire, the rumblings of exploding shells and small arms' fire mingled in with the screams of the injured and dying, and lightning-like flashes of exploding rockets and combat planes hit by anti-aircraft fire.

CORROBORANT FACTS

Note that the last entry in John's list of destructive items is an earthquake. This means that once this future battle is fully joined, an unexpected earthquake will occur. The earthquake's position between this description of a conventional war and the first trumpet angel's report on the nuclear war (directly following this text), matches Ezekiel's same prophetic footprints of the events leading up to the outbreak of AWWI: "I declare that on that day there will surely be a great earthquake in the land of Israel" (Ezek. 38:19, NASB). Likewise, John's Sixth Seal Atomic War prophecy also lists a great earthquake as the spark that will touch off the world's First Atomic War: "I watched as he opened the sixth seal. There was a great earthquake" (Rev. 6:12, NIV). Thus, since all three passages prophetically document the same great earthquake as the catalyst that will ignite an unprece-

Nuclear explosions at or near the earth's surface produce substantial amounts of atomic hail. Atomic hail is formed when large quantities of earth or water, sucked into the fireball at an early stage, become vaporized. Vaporized fission products subsequently become incorporated with the earth particles as a result of condensation and gradually descend to earth. This phenomenon is referred to as "fallout," and the same name is applied to the particles themselves when they reach the ground. Quite naturally, John described this atomic fallout as hail since it looks much the same as ordinary hailstones. In test blasts these particles have generally been the size of a marble, i.e., roughly 1 cm (0.4 inch) in diameter, and even larger close to the burst point. Atomic hail in this size arrives on the ground within one day after the explosion. Lighter particles, approximately 100 micrometers in diameter or smaller, continued to fall like dusty snow (and eventually invisibly) for days to weeks afterwards.

Atomic hail, the main source of residual nuclear radiation on the ground, remains radioactive over a long period of time (30.2 years for cesium). The area within a few hundred miles of the shot, where the larger visible hail falls, is subjected to the most severe radioactive contamination. U.S. nuclear-weapons tests on Bikini Atoll provide some idea of the magnitude of the hazard from lingering radioactive hail. Radiological tests by American technicians reveal that the main island of Bikini will remain too "hot" for human habitation for at least 60 and maybe as long as 90 years.

Here again John's prophetic description of AWWI is scientifically correct. Radioactive hail is far more destructive to the land than fire. If one-third of the earth was burned by fire, crops could still be planted and harvested within a year's time. By contrast, food crops cannot be harvested from land subjected to severe contamination from radioactive hail for decades.

THE EXTENT OF AWWI'S FIRE DAMAGE

A war that will leave one-third of the Earth reduced to ashes could not be fathomed in the Apostle John's day. In direct contrast, members of the nuclear generation are often surprised to learn that this prophesied atomic war will burn only one-third of the Earth. An examination of the fantastic power of the bomb—a megaton explosion can set ninety-five square miles or so on fire at the same time—helps explain why many people doubt that earth has a future in the aftermath of a global nuclear war.

A typical nuclear explosion sends out a surge of heat far hotter than the breath of a blast furnace, moving outwards in all directions with the speed of light. Based on known incendiary effects of the nuclear explosions over Hiroshima and Nagasaki in 1945, it can be projected that the fires likely to be caused by just one of the far more powerful strategic nuclear weapons available today would extend over an area from tens to hundreds of square kilometers.

Also, one-third of the trees and all green grass will be burned up. The meaning seems to be that the holocaust will not be confined to a contiguous third of the planet's land mass, but rather, the nuclear war will spread to cities and military bases around the world, and that wherever these nuclear bombs go off, a third of the trees and all the grass will be burnt up. Thus understood, this sweeping world-wide atomic war will reduce most combustible materials in the targeted third of the earth to ashes.

CLOUDS OF BLOOD CAST TO THE EARTH

John stated further that blood, mixed with hail and fire, will also be cast to the earth. The blood is a reference to the vaporized remains of people falling back to the earth, out of the atomic clouds, after the blast. A moment after an air-burst nuclear explosion, people on the ground would be instantly reduced to super-heated gases. Their gaseous remains would then be raised miles above the earth by the fiery atomic whirlwind. Once the shock waves and ferocious updrafts quieted down, the forces of gravity would eventually return the atomic hail, burning debris, and vaporized blood of the dead to the earth.

The actual number of deaths expected from the major nuclear war described in the first trumpet prophecy has been recently quantified by a group of forty scientists who met in Cambridge, Massachusetts, in April of 1983, to discuss the Long-Term Worldwide Biological Consequences of Nuclear War. Their studies of large-scale nuclear war (5,000- to 10,000-megaton yields) estimate that there would be 750 million immediate deaths from blast alone; a total of about 1.1 billion deaths from the combined effects of blast, fire, and radiation;

and approximately an additional 1.1 billion injuries requiring medical attention. Thus, 30 to 50 percent of the total human population could be immediate casualties of a nuclear war. They expect the vast majority of casualaties to be in the northern hemisphere, especially in the United States, the U.S.S.R., Europe, and Japan.

In summary, the first trumpet prophecy lists the most deadly effects of nuclear weapons and the overall extent of the war's damages to the Earth and its inhabitants.

JOHN DID NOT KNOW

A question naturally surfaces here: How could John, born over 1900 years before the nuclear age, possibly have known enough to deliberately list radioactive hail first, in front of fire damage, as the most powerfully lethal of the local effects of nuclear weapons? After all, radiation contamination can not be seen by the human eye. There is only one answer to the question—John did not know. Obviously, without the guiding hand of Jesus Christ it would have been impossible for anyone in the pre-atomic bomb world to unerringly describe the observable features of nuclear explosions, let alone sequence the severity of damages from nuclear war correctly.

Common sense reveals that ancient men could not and did not compose the Bible's prophecies about the nuclear age—God did. That means every word in the Bible's technological prophecies are loaded with meaningful information, and often, even the order of items and events are necessary to the process of determining the correct interpretation of a prophecy's greater message. The testimonies of the prophets themselves attest to the source of the profound information contained in their prophetic documents: "And the word of the Lord came unto me saying, . . . (Ezek. 38:1, NASB).

PARALLEL ACCOUNTS

Ezekiel's account of the events that will touch off AWWI also includes a list of the most powerful killing effects of nuclear weapons. As mentioned earlier, Ezekiel began his report with a description of the unexpected earthquake that will start AWWI (Ezek. 38:19). Ezekiel then captured the intensity of the total chaos that will break out in the ranks of Russia's confederated forces:

> **21** "And I shall call for a sword against him on all My mountains," declares the Lord God. "Every man's sword will be against his brother. **22** And with pestilence and with blood I shall enter into judgment with him; and I shall rain on him, and on his troops, and on the many peoples who are with him, a torrential rain, with hailstones, fire, and brimstone" (Ezek. 38:21–22, NASB).

The great earthquake's violent shaking of the earth will fill the Russian-led troops with such sheer terror that "every man's sword will be against his brother." Ezekiel's description—"and I shall rain on him, and on his troops, and on the many peoples who are with him, a torrential rain, with hailstones, fire, and brimstone"—matches the first trumpet angel's graphic description of the deadly local effects of nuclear explosions: "and there occurred hail and fire having been mixed in with blood" (Rev. 8:7, IGENT).

Thus, Ezekiel's prophecy also deliberately lists radioactive hail first, in front of nuclear fire, as the most powerfully lethal of the local effects of nuclear weapons. Furthermore, since the text plainly states that the Russian "brothers" will unleash their swords on each other, it follows that some of the "swords" the Russian "brothers" will use against each other "on all My mountains" of Israel will be "nuclear swords" in the form of battlefield nuclear weapons.

It should be pointed out here that the lethal local effects of radiation will kill more soldiers on the battlefield than the intense heat from the atomic fireball. Although most troops within a 6-mile radius of an air-burst, 1-megaton blast would be killed from blast or burns, shifting winds would extend lethal doses of deadly radiation to far greater numbers of troops fighting in areas miles beyond the relatively short range of the nuclear fireball's flames. All things considered, visible hailstones were the best means Ezekiel had to convey to posterity the most deadly aspect of a nuclear explosion—the awesome invisible killing effects of its radiation emissions.

EZEKIEL'S DESCRIPTION OF
CONVENTIAL WEAPONS

The brimstone part of the destructive rain, on the other hand, is a reference to the less destructive effects of conventional weapons. Brimstone in its naturally occurring state has a yellow hue due to its high sulfur content. The NIV uses "burning sulfur" here instead of brimstone. Sulfur is a component of gunpowder that is used to detonate shells and conventional bombs. Hence, part of the killing power of the "overflowing rain" will come from bullets, exploding shells and other conventional projectiles that use gunpowder to propell them to their targets.

The First Trumpet Atomic War will dwarf all wars previously waged in human history. Revelation and other Scriptures describe the massive repercussions in its aftermath. Much attention is focused on the disruption of the world's balance of nature and the effect the atomic war will have on the global ecosystem. The next two trumpet events detail the successive stages of the war and the mounting destruction that will follow the opening atomic exchanges.

THE SECOND TRUMPET SOUNDS

8 And the second angel sounded, and something like a great mountain burning with fire was thrown into the sea; and a third of the sea became blood (Rev. 8:8, NASB); 9 A third of the living creatures in the sea died, and a third of the ships were destroyed (Rev. 8:9, NIV).

SOMETHING CAST INTO THE SEA

The second angel sounded a warning concerning the far-reaching destruction of the seas during the naval side of the nuclear war. The timing of this event and the assessment of damages are clear. The calamity will take place directly following the opening salvos of the atomic war. Damages will include the death of a third of the creatures living in the sea and destruction of a third of all sea-going ships.

John's description of the cause of the disaster: "and as it were a great mountain burning with fire was cast into the sea" (Rev. 8:8), is not as easy to identify. At first glance a very large fiery meteor might be considered a good candidate for what will be cast into the sea. However, the Sixth Seal Atomic War imagery of "the stars in the sky falling to the earth" (Rev. 6:13, NIV), quickly rules out this possibility, since John did not identify the fiery object's trajectory as coming from the direction of the heavens, but likened it to an entire mountain, lifted suddenly by some tremendous force and cast into the sea.

Normally, when a writer uses either the word as or like to make a comparison between two things that are different in most respects, yet alike in some identifiable way, each entity is named. Not so here. According to the definition of a simile the unnamed "something" will have observable features that will produce negative effects on the high seas equivalent to a great mountain burning with fire being blown sky-high into the sea. Clearly then, "negative effects" provide the link between the imagery of the mountain-like burning mass and the unnamed something. Recognizing the "negative effects" linkage brings into focus the starting point that will lead to a positive identification of the mysterious unnamed "something." That is, it will be both logical and proper in this case to begin the analysis of the text with a review of past examples of destructive forces unleashed when volcanic mountains exploded in maritime regions of the world.

A REVIEW OF TWO PAST MARITIME DISASTERS

An event similar to the second trumpet imagery took place in August of 1883, when the Netherlands East Indies island of Krakatoa exploded. Krakatoa burst with a roar heard more than 2,000 miles from the island. The shock wave cracked walls 100 miles away and traveled three times around the world. As the volcanic eruption continued, vast quantities of pumice hurtled through the air, defoliating trees, and clogging harbors for months to come. Debris suspended in the air turned day into night over a radius of 130 miles. Floating pumice, up to 13 feet, blanketed the sea.

Krakatoa's blowout generated tidal waves more than 100 feet high. With a velocity in excess of 50 miles an hour, they swept away almost 300 towns and villages along the nearby coasts of Java and Sumatra. More than 36,000 people lost their lives.

In the early 1970's archaeologists and scientists pieced together the archaeological evidence of another ancient blowout on the Greek island of Thera or Santorini. Four thousand years ago, Santorini was a single mountainous mass, almost completely round. Some time about the year 1500 B. C., the island's inhabitants suddenly left. Shortly thereafter, a tremendous volcanic explosion blew the whole center of the island sky-high. Afterward, the sea rushed in to fill the red-hot wound of the crater.

Santorini's caldera, or crater, is five times the size of Krakatoa's. Quarry operations have disclosed that the ash blanket at Santorini reached a depth of 160 feet compared to a few inches at Krakatoa. For these reasons and others, geologists assume that the Santorini explosion must have had three or four times the force of Krakatoa's. The energy released by the blowout is estimated to have been equivalent to the blast of a 400-megaton nuclear bomb.

The molten hail produced by Santorini's eruption must have rendered all lands within a 100-mile radius (including central Crete) uninhabitable. The incursion of the sea into the gaping lava boil and subsequent rebound of the immense volume of water as it rushed outward again in a giant wave, wrecked harbors and flooded coastal lands around the Mediterranean basin. Some scholars estimate the returning waters' speed at more than 200 miles an hour and assign to them a height of 300 feet as they piled up on the northern coast of Crete.

These two past examples of volcanic blowouts provide a ready list of the negative effects inflicted on surrounding maritime regions by such large-scale disasters. Since the sixth seal prophecy introduced AWWI as the main destructive event of the opened Book of Revelation and since no other major subject has been introduced thus far, it follows that the "negative effects" inflicted on the seas by the unnamed "something" will be damages resulting from the naval action of planet earth's First Atomic War.

The world's atomic-armed nations are already well-prepared for tomorrow's naval nuclear war. Their arsenals include surface warships, combat aircraft, submarines and a vast array of the most savage conventional and nuclear weapons ever devised by the human race.

Once the Russian confederated forces begin arriving on the outskirts of Israel the superpowers' navies will be placed on the highest Def Con (Defense Condition) alert there is, just as a precaution against a preemptive nuclear first strike by the other side. The forces of smaller nations possessing a nuclear fighting capability will also be nervously priming their atomic weapons systems as the military action in the Middle East unfolds. Nerves will be taut, especially those of surface fleet commanders who will be all too aware of the vulnerability of surface ships in the face of nuclear weapons. (Admiral Hyman G. Rickover, the "father" of the U.S. nuclear navy, told a congressional committee in 1982 that a modern aircraft carrier would last "about two days" in a major war.)

Land-based troops will be even more tense, since either side could eliminate thousands in seconds simply by switching from a conventional to a nuclear artillery shell during the course of the battle.

In the midst of this supercharged environment, Ezekiel's predicted earthquake will suddenly rock the hills of Palestine. With the ground heaving under their feet, the chance of some jumpy soldier touching off a round from a battlefield nuke is highly probable. Exactly who will fire the first atomic shot is not given in Scripture and may well never be determined. Notwithstanding, according to Bible prophecy nuclear chaos will immediately erupt around the globe.

All out nuclear escalation should not surprise anyone. After all, the world's nuclear forces are not postured to respond in any other way. The existence of nuclear weapons simply precludes any response less than all-out nuclear war, once one side fires the first atomic shot. The whole idea of trying to fight a limited nuclear war can perhaps best be expressed by the analogy of a person attempting to warm cold hands by lighting just one end of a large puddle of gasoline.

Within minutes after the earthquake, the nuclear flames from the slugfest between the superpowers' navies will already be burning with fervent heat. Due to the effectiveness of satellite and aerial reconnaissance, most surface warships will already be in somebody's cross hairs when the earthquake hits. Consequently, the surface ship war should not last long.

UNDERSEA NAVAL COMBAT

The undersea naval combat is where the atomic war will be pushed to its logical conclusion, in a very methodical, cold-blooded, brutal fashion. The subsea weapon of choice will be the big nuclear missile-carrying, atomic-powered submarines that run deep and so silently that they are virtually undetectable. Operating at depths in excess of 400 feet, they are essentially invulnerable to a preemptive attack and seem certain to remain so for the foreseeable future. Both United States and Russian killer subs—called boomers by virtue of their range and mobility (which includes hiding beneath the polar ice of the Arctic Ocean)—are capable of launching a prompt retaliatory strike on any adversary nation from many directions, thereby complicating any attempt to thwart a counterattack by means of an anti-ballistic-missile (ABM) system. A 4-deck, 42 foot diameter by 560 foot long U.S. Trident boomer can launch 24 Trident I eight-warhead missiles, each in much less than a minute. Russia's Typhoon boomers have roughly the same firepower. From their sniper's nest at the top of the world, boomer subs can crunch up through thin spots in the polar ice and melt a city more than 5,000 miles away. One Trident sub, armed with Trident I missiles carrying 100-kiloton warheads, can destroy most of Russia's major cities.

The Trident I missile system is presently in the process of being replaced by the far superior Trident II, which can carry as many as 10 warheads, each with an explosive yield of 475 kilotons. The new 1989 Trident boomers, factory equipped with 24 Trident II missiles, will be America's most destructive weapons system. Compared to the total World War II air bombardment by all participants (equal to about 3 million tons of TNT), the Trident II's potential destructive force is overwhelming. One new Trident sub can fire 114 megatons of devastating power, equal to 38 World War II's, at some 200 targets in less than 20 minutes. This means one U.S. Trident, or Russian Typhoon boomer, could kill 100 million people or more in less than 60 minutes.

These sobering facts reveal the ease with which today's nuclear nations can fulfill the second trumpet prophecy. Obviously, once one side crosses the nuclear threshold following the great earthquake, the nuclear nations will order their naval forces to destroy the other side's sea-based fighting capability. Naval and air bases located on the rims of the continents and on islands in the sea will be fired on at will. "Mountains and islands will be moved out of their places" (Rev. 6:14). Atomic blasts will also blow coastal military bases and seaports miles into the sky. Much of their burning contents will then fall into the sea.

COMPOSITION OF THE UNNAMED SOMETHING

According to supercomputer calculations, a global nuclear war will inject hundreds of millions of tons of smoke, dust and other debris into the planet's atmosphere. If all of this fiery material fell into the sea in one great heap, it would easily add up to a "great mountain burning with fire cast into the sea."

In retrospect, John did not name the "something" he was comparing to a mountain-like burning mass simply because the fiery atomic material will actually originate from a wide variety of sources. That is, the unnamed "something" falling into the sea will be the sum of the burning, vaporized remains of fighting ships, islands and mountains, seaports, cities, etc., which the global atomic war will systematically reduce to a great mountain of burning ashes.

A THIRD OF THE SEA TURNS
THE COLOR OF BLOOD

According to the text, the net effect of this mountain of poisonous radioactive substances falling into the sea will turn a third part of the world's oceans a dark, blood-red color. The metaphorical statement: "and the third part of the sea became blood" (IGENT), is used here to point out the severe pollution of the sea by emphasizing the likeness of the dirty water's unnatural redish hue to blood. (It is important to recall here that John wrote Revelation in Greek and also that the origin of the word "metaphor" comes from the Greek words meta (beyond) + pherein (to carry). Hence a metaphor is a figure of speech in which one object is carried beyond, or likened to another as if it were that other, as "The soldier was a lion in battle.") Thus, the expression "the third part of the sea became blood" likens the unlivable condition of the polluted third of the oceans to blood, a matrix within which living creatures in the sea would not be able to survive.

A THIRD OF THE SEA DIES

The text goes on to detail the most destructive side-effect from the sea's polution—"and the third part of the creatures which were in the sea, and had life, died." Modern science also predicts early loss of phytoplankton from massive quantities of caustic atomic debris falling into the sea, which, in turn, will subsequently eliminate the support base for many marine species.

As for the third of the ships destroyed in the naval nuclear war, those riding at anchor in harbors will be demolished by the same nuclear bombs that knock out the seaports. Undoubtedly, whole battle groups of naval ships will also be destroyed by over-the-horizon nuclear-tipped cruise missiles, sub launched rocket-propelled nuclear depth bombs (SUBROC) and various other conventional and nuclear ship-attack torpedos and missiles.

The effects of what a nuclear antiship warhead will do to a fleet of ships are suggested by the Baker test explosion conducted by the United States at Bikini Atoll in 1946. Some 70 unmanned ships of various types were anchored around the site of the shallow underwater burst, which had an explosive yield of about 20 kilotons. The ships were damaged from underwater and atmospheric shock waves as well as surface water waves. For example, the aircraft carrier U.S.S. Saratoga, which was moored in the lagoon about 400 yards from "surface zero," had the central part of its island structure folded down onto the deck by a 90-foot wave generated by the explosion.

The much larger warheads available in today's nuclear arsenals would inflict far greater damage on a fleet. Clearly, the superpowers presently have more than enough firepower to destroy one-third of all sea-going ships.

THE THIRD TRUMPET SOUNDS

10 And the third angel sounded, and there fell a great star from heaven, burning as it were a lamp, and it fell upon the third part of the rivers, and upon the fountains of waters: 11 And the name of the star is called Wormwood: and the third part of the waters became wormwood; and many men died of the waters, because they were made bitter (Rev. 8:10–11).

ANALOGY OF STARS REUSED

The third trumpet angel reused the Sixth Seal Atomic War prophecy's visual analogy of stars falling from the sky to describe the awesome nuclear weapons of mass destruction that will be used to fight the world's First Atomic War. Here again, a great star falling from the heavens, burning as it were a lamp, could not be a literal star since even a star as small as the Earth's sun would incinerate the planet in a collision. As mentioned in the previous chapter, John categorically eliminated the possibility that the great star might represent a large meteor. Hence, reuse of the prophetic symbol for a nuclear bomb—i.e., stars— dictates that fulfillment of the third trumpet event will not only occur over the course of the First Trumpet Atomic War, but will also be an integral part of that war.

ANALYSIS OF THE TERM "GREAT STAR"

The analysis of the third trumpet text begins with a corollary to the prophetic symbol for a nuclear bomb: great symbolic stars equal great atomic bombs. The properties, therefore, which would make some starlike atomic bombs "great" over run-of-the-mill nuclear warheads must be identified before the correct meaning of the third trumpet event can be determined.

Explosive yield is one attribute that helps to determine whether or not a nuclear bomb is great or small. In general the 12.5 kiloton atom bomb that destroyed Hiroshima, Japan on August 6, 1945, is considered a minor nuclear weapon next to the 1-megaton warheads stockpiled in today's nuclear arsenals. (One megaton or one million tons of TNT would fill a freight train 300 miles long). Yet, the awesome destructive power of 1-megaton bombs are dwarfed by the superpowers' 10- to 20-megaton warheads. At first glance it might appear impossible to determine what specific throw-weight yields should be assigned to the group of starlike nuclear bombs warranting the rating of "great." However, when the aim points of the great starlike bombs are factored into the equation, the properties of a "great" atomic starlike bomb become readily apparent.

The text defines the aim points in terms of the "great star" (bombs) "fell upon the third part of the rivers, and upon the fountains of waters"—that is, the interiors of the continents where the majority of the world's rivers and lakes are found.

Therefore, any nuclear bomb capable of destroying critical targets such as military bases, hardened intercontinental ballistic missile launch sites, strategic command and control centers hidden under mountains, and industrial centers, located deep in the interiors of the continents, would meet the first requirement for being classified as a "great" starlike nuclear weapon.

The qualifying word "potential" has to be added here since according to the text the second mandatory feature of a "great" atomic bomb is that it must fall from heaven. This means that the starlike atomic bomb must have a powerful enough ICBM delivery vehicle to carry it through the heavens to the designated target, located deep in the interior of a continent. On planet earth that generally requires an ICBM launcher capable of traveling 5,000 or more miles through the heavens.

Putting these facts into perspective with respect to the third trumpet prophecy reveals that the great star falling from heaven, "burning as it were a lamp," or torch, symbolically represents nuclear warheads delivered to the interiors of the continents during the second stage of the First Trumpet Atomic War. The first stage of an atomic attack would probably be carried out by submarine-launched missiles and intermediate shorter ranged land-based launchers that could hit border and coastal targets, generally located on the rims of the continents. This initial stage of the war would be over in a matter of a few minutes. It would be an additional fifteen minutes or more before the big long range intercontinental ballistic weapons began falling from the heavens on targets deep in the interior of the continents.

Clearly then, the third trumpet imagery represents a second stage escalation of the initial atomic exchanges. The long range ICMB's used in the second stage would be aimed at hardened missile bases, command and control centers, industrial cities, and other military targets deep in the continental "heart lands." It is also possible that the great star falling from heaven represents warheads launched from space. Again it would take quite some time to get satellite-based warheads to target.

BIBLICAL STAR IMAGERY
VS. TODAY'S ANALOGIES

In the final analysis it doesn't matter how a warhead is delivered. The physical process of an atomic explosion remains the same: an intense flash of brilliant white light followed by an even brighter flash a moment later. For a one-megaton surface blast, a fireball would rise 8 miles into the air. People 30 miles away could be partially blinded from a single glance at the fireball. At the same time a surface blast would dig a crater 200 feet deep and 1000 feet wide, with temperatures at ground zero approaching those on the sun. Since the Earth's sun is actually a small star that gives off light from ongoing atomic explosions, the picture of a great star falling from heaven describes a twentieth century nuclear explosion perfectly.

During the course of an interview with Discover magazine reporters in 1985, nuclear weapons tester, Elbert W. Bennett, also compared the detonation of a nuclear bomb to a star. Bennett, who spent nearly three decades at Los Alamos testing nuclear weapons and analyzing the results, explained, "Conditions in a thermonuclear explosion are very much like the interior of a star, which is really nature's fusion reactor. There's no other way to get access to that sort of environment." Thus, both the Apostle John and Elbert Bennett agree that an atomic blast is, indeed, a great burning lamp!

RADIATION CONTAMINATED WATER

Today's scientists know for certain that an atomic war large enough to burn up one-third of the earth will leave the waters in the vicinity of the bombed areas highly radioactive. Radioactive isotopes—such as iodine 131, which can cause thyroid cancer—would settle into exposed water systems. With electric generating plants disabled in targeted areas, modern man's electric pumps for lifting well-water to the surface of the earth will be rendered useless. Accordingly, many survivors will be faced with the dilemma of drinking irradiated surface waters or dying of thirst. These twentieth century facts agree with the Bible's description of the coming atomic disaster: "and many men died of the waters, because they were made bitter."

John stated further that the name of the star is called Wormwood. Wormwood was a well-known bitter herb which has come to mean "grievous bitterness." His allegorical use of the word here does not imply that the starlike atomic bomb would be actually so called, but that this would be properly descriptive of its qualities. "And the third part of the waters became Wormwood," therefore, properly means they became bitter as Wormwood from the radioactive fallout released by great starlike nuclear bombs "falling upon the third part of the rivers, and fountains of waters," located deep in the heart lands of the continents.

Water polluted from AWWI's radioactive fallout will be bitter indeed. Today's scientists know that anyone drinking irradiated surface waters after an atomic attack will suffer a slow, painful death from radiation sickness. Starting with nausea, vomiting and diarrhea, victims would experience internal bleeding, ulcerations of the lips, and loss of hair within two weeks. Eventually their immune systems would break down, rendering them helpless against disease. Those exposed to smaller amounts of radiation could still die as a result of that exposure forty years later.

Thus ends John's firsthand report on how the world's First Atomic War will be fought. It's a grisly scene filled with the dead and the dying, and dazed, dehydrated survivors drinking radiation-laced surface water in the midst of a scorched wasteland.

Obviously absent in John's report is any mention of a victor. In fact, according to the next chapter's continuing prophetic report, without the intervening hand of God, the First Trumpet Atomic War would end all human life.

7 One Lone Eagle

The sounding of the Fourth Trumpet heralds the Bible's account of conditions on the Earth in the post-atomic war period. The Fourth Trumpet angel opens this subject with a description of the most damaging climatic wound inflicted on the planet by AWWI. The following analysis of the Fourth Trumpet prophecy reveals the striking parallels between the angel's review of this unprecedented climatic disruption and computer simulation predictions of the expected environmental consequences of nuclear war. This particular negative effect is especially interesting since according to the text it will be used by one lone eagle to lead many to Christ in the post-AWWI period.

THE FOURTH TRUMPET SOUNDS

12 And the fourth angel sounded, and the third part of the sun was smitten, and the third part of the moon, and the third part of the stars; so as the third part of them was darkened, and the day shone not for a third part of it, and the night likewise (Rev. 8:12).

AWWI IS OVER

The first thing to see here is that the atomic war is over. There is no further reference to the immediate destructive effects of starlike nuclear weapons. The monstrous weapons of mass destruction will have found their targets. The doctrine of nuclear deterrence—the absurd idea that major wars would become obsolete simply because no one would dare use atomic weapons for fear of the consequences of overwhelming retaliation—will be revealed as the vain hope that it is.

ONE-THIRD LESS LIGHT

According to the Fourth Trumpet angel's report, one of the early worldwide consequences of AWWI will be the inability of a third of the light from the sun, moon and stars to penetrate the planet's atmosphere.

ATOMIC SMOKE BLOCKS SUNLIGHT

Note how the text lists the negative effect, but not what will bring about the condition. This does not turn out to be an obstacle to the process of correctly identifying the cause, thanks to the First Trumpet angel's plainly stated announcement of "a third" of the earth, trees, and grass being burnt up (Rev. 8:7, RSV). Obviously a fire that will burn up all the grass on a third of the Earth's land mass along with one-third of the trees, (not to mention countless cities and towns) will loft unprecedented quantities of smoke into the planet's atmosphere. Hence, the fourth global disaster will be a direct consequence of the smoke, dust, and pyrotoxins spewed into the atmosphere by the first three trumpet events.

A review of the observable effects of the atomic bombs detonated over Japan at the close of World War II provides insight into how the smoke from AWWI will block out one-third of the sun's rays. The Nagasaki atomic explosion sent a cloud of gas and debris 50,000 feet into the air. At the time the isolated nuclear explosion over Nagasaki was not viewed as apocalyptic since it did not block out the sun's rays for any appreciable length of time. Nevertheless, it demonstrated that even a small atomic explosion can lift smoke to a high altitude where it has the potential to cause serious damage to the planet's atmosphere.

A future nuclear war involving the incineration of one-third of the Earth will not be brought about by the detonation of a few isolated nuclear bombs. Although computer calculations indicate as few as several hundred nuclear explosions could raise enough smoke and dust to dramatically reduce light levels at the Earth's surface, the atomic arsenals and war fighting strategies of the nuclear powers favor estimates ranging between 10 and 20 thousand nuclear explosions in an all-out atomic war (By the mid-1970s, the United States already had more than seven nuclear warheads for every large city, industrial complex, and military base in the world). When these staggering numbers are factored with the yields of today's nuclear warheads (40 to 1,000 or more times the destructive force of the atomic bombs dropped on Japan) the distinct possibility (indeed liklihood) of there being enough smoke entrained into the planet's atmosphere by AWWI to block out a third of the light from the sun, moon, and stars becomes chillingly apparent.

NUCLEAR WAR SMOKE STUDIES

The Scientific American article "The Climatic Effects of Nuclear War" (August 1984) supported the view that the immense clouds of smoke and dust raised by even a medium-scale nuclear war could bring about a global "nuclear winter." The authors (the TTAPS scientists) based their conclusions on computer simulations of the general circulation of the earth's atmosphere. Their study parallels the Fourth Trumpet biblical account of a third part of the light from the sun, moon, and stars being blocked as a result of a global nuclear war.

The TTAPS scientists calculated that the total smoke emission from a full-scale nuclear exchange could easily exceed 100-million metric tons. In many respects this is a conservative estimate.

Scientists working at the Max Planck Institute for Chemistry at Mainz, West Germany estimated that the total emission from a full-scale nuclear war would be closer to 300- million tons.

Later studies conducted by the U.S. National Academy of Sciences paralleled earlier findings, predicting global cooling from lingering atomic smoke clouds and severe hardship for any survivors.

Once it was determined that nuclear war would introduce massive quantities of smoke and dust into the earth's atmosphere scientists then had to investigate where it would go and how long it would remain aloft. Observation of naturally occur-

SHORTER POST-AWWI DAYS

In addition to keeping one-third of the sun's rays from reaching the surface of the Earth, the thick clouds of smoke will literally shorten the length of daylight normally available from dawn to dusk by a third, and the nightlight likewise. Nuclear war studies do not address this particular negative consequence of atomic warfare. Fortunately, the main features of the mechanism that will shorten the planet's post-AWWI days, are relatively easy to explain.

The first thing to note is that once high altitude atomic smoke clouds encircle the Earth they will effectively become a miles thick, overhead dark curtain. Under normal conditions the atmosphere is quite transparent to solar radiation at visible wavelengths; accordingly a large fraction of the incident sunlight passes through the atmosphere to the planet's surface. On the other hand a smoke-filled atmosphere becomes opaque and absorbs a significant portion of incoming sunlight. A large fraction of the absorbed light would be reradiated directly back into space at infrared wavelengths without ever reaching the surface. The total amount of sunlight prevented from reaching the Earth's surface (as a result of absorption and reradiation) is a function of the depth and optical density (opacity) of the smoke cloud. (Optical depth is a measure of opacity equal to the negative natural logarithm of the attenuation of an incident light beam by absorption and scattering.) For the purpose of understanding this prophecy just be aware that smoke clouds with greater optical depths have greater sunlight blocking capacities.

In the days following AWWI the sun's rays will traverse the least amount of smoke when the rays are perpendicular to the Earth's surface. As the day progresses through the afternoon and into the evening hours, the path of the sun's light to the surface gradually lengthens as the angle of penetration decreases to a horizontal position at sundown.

Therefore, less sunlight will penetrate the smoke cloud's steadily lengthening effective optical depth as the day moves toward the evening hours. Eventually, instead of one-third of all inbound solar radiation smitten, two-thirds will be smitten, and finally, as the sunlight's angle of penetration rotates toward the horizon, all visible light will be blocked out by the heavy pall of smoke. Predictably, sundown will occur well ahead of schedule. For example, instead of 12 hours of daylight at the equator, the smoke's "curtain effect" will literally shorten the length of an equatorial day by one-third to 8 hours. This same light blocking mechanism will likewise delay daybreak's arrival and decrease by one-third the length of time that light from the moon and stars will be visible.

To conclude this passage by saying that the smoke-induced side effects of AWWI are prophetic signs of Christ's Second Coming would be correct. However it would fail to reveal a very important redeeming aspect of AWWI's immense clouds of smoke. The full significance of the smoke's positive influence was revealed by Christ to His disciples during the course of His response to their question: "What shall be the sign of thy coming?" (Matt. 24:3). Christ's lengthy answer to this question included a number of signs and events that would come to pass before He returned to establish His earthly kingdom of peace. In the midst of His reply Jesus identified the most important unnatural phenomenon that will occur during the great tribulation and its awesome significance.

THE GREAT TRIBULATION KEY

21 For then shall be great tribulation, such as was not since the beginning of the world to this time, no, nor ever shall be. **22** And except those days should be shortened, there should no flesh be saved: but for the elect's sake those days shall be shortened (Matt. 24:21–22).

The presence of the keynote phrase, "great tribulation," raises a fair question: Is this the same Great Tribulation, which, according to the Sixth Seal prophecy, will begin the day a great earthquake touches off AWWI? The search for the answer begins with a review of the historical interpretation of the text.

THE HISTORICAL VIEW OF SHORTENED DAYS

For centuries there was general agreement among Christian theologians that this prophecy was fulfilled when a Roman army, led by Titus, began the systematic destruction of Jerusalem in 70 A.D. The fall of Jerusalem was incredibly violent. Five months after Titus began the siege, the walls fell, and over coast of North America, half a world away from the accident. Fortunately, the amount of radiation deposited on North America was not sufficient to pose a significant health threat.

A large-scale nuclear war involving the incineration of one-third of the Earth will dwarf Chernobyl's radiation-bearing cloud thousands of times over. Again, Christ's statement "no one would survive" teaches that AWWI will generate enough radioactive smoke to kill every person on the planet, if it were not for the thick, high altitude smoke's moderating influences that will stop the winds and shorten the days.

It is worthwhile comparing Christ's authoritative statement on just how close mankind will come to self-inflicted extinction with 40 biologists' findings on the long-term biological consequences of nuclear war. Their sweeping, controversial conclusion, published in the December 23, 1983 issue of Science, states: "extinction of the human species itself cannot be excluded."

So the "shortened days" from AWWI's globe-girdling, high altitude atomic smoke turns out to be part of a life-saving safety feature, put there by God; not, as has been commonly supposed, the death blow to the human race. The "shortened days" blessing in disguise also provides a good example of how God continually applies His love to the task of salvaging a dying race from its own commitment to destruction.

When the size of AWWI's foretold climatic catastrophe is coupled with Christ's statement that the Great Tribulation will be harsh enough to bring the human race to the edge of extinction, the sobering impact of His prophecy about a "great tribulation, such as was not since the beginning of the world to this time, no, nor ever shall be," comes into full focus. After all, an atomic war which, but for the intervening grace of God, would terminate the human species, unarguably fulfills the first requirement of the Great Tribulation: "such as was not since the beginning of the world."

The Bible's wealth of information about the world's First Atomic War and its aftermath could be put to practical use by today's nuclear war researchers since it answers the most incredibily complex and hotly debated scientific question of the nuclear age: How will a nuclear war disrupt the circulation of the Earth's atmosphere? The scientific nuclear-war studies end with typical disclaimers such as "These projections, of course, can be neither proved nor disproved, since there is no way to conduct an experiment." The Bible speaks with authority about the cause—"A third of the earth was burned up" (Rev. 8:7, NIV)—and about the effect—"A third of the sun was struck, and a third of the moon, and a third of the stars, so that a third of their light was darkened" (Rev. 8:12, RSV). With these sweeping biblical insights, today's scientists need not wonder whether or not the human race will survive a nuclear war. In fact, the Bible speaks with such force about the world's First Atomic War and its aftermath that even Christians who must overcome the handicap of being well-versed in the inherited misinterpretations of the past, find themselves awakened to the truth.

WHY THE DAYS WILL BE SHORTENED

Jesus ended His Great Tribulation prophecy with the statement: "but for the elect's sake those days shall be shortened." The elect here means Christians. The word *elect* in the Greek means "chosen," and "God chose them from the beginning to be saved, through sanctification of the Spirit and belief of the truth" (2 Thess. 2:13, RSV). Sanctification is the spiritual act of God freeing a man from his sins. God chose from the beginning to save all men who would believe in the truth that Jesus Christ is the Savior of the world: "But as many as received him, to them gave he power to become the sons of God, even to them that believe on his name" (John 1:12).

These "shortened days" will make it possible for Christians living during the Great Tribulation to bear witness. Jesus emphasized the Christians' presence directly following His explicit definition of these "shortened days."

> **23** "At that time if anyone says to you, 'Look, here is the Christ!' or, 'There he is!' do not believe it. **24** For false Christs and false prophets will appear and perform great signs and miracles to deceive even the elect—if that were possible. **25** See, I have told you ahead of time. **26** So if anyone tells you, 'There he is, out in the desert,' do not go out; or, 'Here he is, in the inner rooms,' do not believe it" (Matt. 24:23–26, NIV).

Christians often wonder aloud why God is so intent on keeping them alive through such a horrible time as the "great tribulation?" The answer is found in the fact that "for the elect's sake" includes people who will be living after AWWI who have not yet accepted Christ as their personal Savior. Thus, for the sake of the unbelieving who will yet trust in Christ, the days will be purposely shortened to keep Christians alive so that they will be able to spread the gospel during the dark days of the Great Tribulation. (This means God designed the physical structure of the planet in such a way that atomic war-produced smoke would automatically stop the winds and shorten the days.)

FLYING EAGLE BROADCASTS

Following the Fourth Trumpet angel's parallel "shortened day" message is a full explanation of who will take the lead in spreading the gospel of Christ after AWWI and how modern technology will be used to carry this evangelistic outreach to the far corners of the Earth.

> 13 And I saw, and I heard one eagle flying in mid-heaven saying with a great (loud) voice, woe, woe, woe to the ones dwelling on the earth from the remaining voices of the trumpet of the three angels being about to trumpet (Rev. 8:13, IGENT).

The Apostle John recorded that he saw one lone eagle flying in mid-heaven. He also noted that he heard this eagle warning the inhabitants of the earth, with a great loud voice, concerning the last three trumpets, "about to sound." This eagle is the same symbol used to represent the United States in Daniel's vision of the four beasts. The flying eagle's position in mid-heaven, coupled with its ability to voice a verbal warning "to the ones dwelling on the earth," symbolically depicts a U.S.-built communications satellite. The flying, speaking eagle imagery is a picture of the United States using its global communications satellites to broadcast the Bible's prophetic forewarnings of what the last three catastrophic trumpet events will bring upon the Earth in the post-AWWI period.

John described the location of the American satellite to be in mid-heaven. Communications satellites are in fact placed in the heavens, 22,300 miles beyond the surface of the earth. Thus, the U.S. eagle will deliver God's final warning messages to the nations from its satellite pulpits in space, precisely where John said they would be.

Commercial communications satellites routinely broadcast TV programs outside the United States. In addition they handle thousands of phone conversations and computer-to-computer communications. Just one of these satellites, Intelsat IV, carried 6,000 telephone calls, or could beam 12 color TV broadcasts, or combinations of the two among 25 countries, simultaneously, in the early 1970s. Millions of people can hear a U.S. satellite broadcast at any given time. Now that's speaking with a loud voice. Nineteen hundred years ago, when the Apostle John wrote about this eagle with the great loud voice, it would have been impossible for any man to speak loud enough to be heard by millions of people, in several countries, simultaneously.

Due to the awesome dimensions of the destruction wrought by the first four trumpet events, no one will doubt that the final three prophetic trumpet events will shortly come to pass. Consequently, U.S. Christians will have the opportunity not only to warn the world about the final events of man's reign on the Earth but also to explain God's plan for their escape—that escape being the gospel of salvation through Jesus Christ.

Notice that the U.S. eagle says "woe" three times. Each woe represents a period of grievous distress and great trouble on the earth. Each individual period of woe will begin with the consecutive sounding of the last three trumpets.

THE WATCHMAN NATION

The eagle's presence in mid-heaven indicates further that the United States will survive the world's first, all-out, continent-smashing nuclear war. Though surely not unscathed, the United States will definitely be capable of functioning after AWWI. Even more important, the United States will be a viable witness for God to the whole world during the closing days of man's reign and will thus fulfill the role of the "watchman" among the nations in the end times.

In the days of walled cities it was a custom to set a watchman on the city wall in times of danger to look for the approach of the enemy. Ezekiel explained the importance of the watchman's duties.

1 And the word of the Lord came to me saying, 2 "Son of man, speak to the sons of your people, and say to them, 'If I bring a sword upon a land, and the people of the land take one man

from among them and make him their watchman; 3 and he
sees the sword coming upon the land, and he blows on the
trumpet and warns the people, 4 then he who hears the sound
of the trumpet and does not take warning, and a sword comes
and takes him away, his blood will be on his own head. 5 He
heard the sound of the trumpet, but did not take warning; his
blood will be on himself. But had he taken warning, he would
have delivered his life. 6 But if the watchman sees the sword
coming and does not blow the trumpet, and the people are
not warned, and a sword comes and takes a person from
them, he is taken away in his iniquity; but his blood I will
require from the watchman's hand" (Ezek. 33:1–6, NASB).

Even as the watchman of old blew the trumpet and warned
the people when he saw the sword coming upon the land; so
also will the people of the United States see the final three
trumpet events coming and likewise sound the alarm to all the
people of the Earth. Notice that the watchman has a responsibility to sound the alarm and the people who hear have a duty
to respond. The people of the United States need to realize the
importance of the task required of them in the years just ahead.
They also need to ask God for direction and power to accomplish this mighty task. By the same token, when other nations
hear the U.S. broadcasts, it is imperative for them to turn from
their evil and heed God's message. In both cases, the responsibility of the United States as the watchman nation and the
responsibility of the listening nations comes down to personal
decisions on the part of individuals.

The next three verses clarify the importance of the watchman further.

7 "Now as for you, son of man, I have appointed you a
watchman for the house of Israel; so you will hear a message
from My mouth, and give them warning from Me. 8 When I
say to the wicked, 'O wicked man, you shall surely die,' and
you do not speak to warn the wicked from his way, that
wicked man shall die in his iniquity, but his blood I will
require from your hand. 9 But if you on your part warn a
wicked man to turn from his way, and he does not turn from
his way, he will die in his iniquity; but you have delivered
your life" (Ezek. 33:7–9, NASB).

To understand the meaning of this text, first realize that the unlocking of God's prophecies will originate in the United States and will become commonly known there, thanks to a free press and America's unequaled communications systems. U.S. Christians will organize and use their considerable resources and wealth to get God's message out to all the nations in the closing years of the age. However, some U.S. citizens will not respond to God's message of the hour, even though they will hear the truth of God's prophecies concerning the last days. Consequently, God will require the blood of those who die in other nations, at the hand of any U.S. citizen who hears God's prophetic message of the hour but refuses to help sound the warning.

Billions of people will die during the days of the last three trumpet events. Again, according to Christ's forewarning about a "great tribulation, such as was not since the beginning of the world to this time, no, nor ever shall be" (Matt. 24:21), this time of trouble will be more catastrophic than anything human history has ever witnessed.

Therefore, Christians should be "redeeming the time, because the days are evil" (Eph. 5:16), for "the night cometh, when no man can work" (John 9:4). U.S. Christians especially need to realize that when Jesus said that "this gospel of the kingdom shall be preached in all the world for a witness unto all nations; and then shall the end come" (Matt. 24:14), that U.S. Christians are the people who will carry out the bulk of this major task by utilizing their abundant wealth and freedom to spread God's final warning messages "as good stewards of the manifold grace of God" (1 Peter 4:10).

8 The Fifth Trumpet "Nuclear Winter"

The Fifth Trumpet angel begins his message with a visual presentation of an intercontinental ballistic missile weapons system and its workings, including the sophisticated procedure used to detonate the nuclear warhead carried inside its chambers. At the conclusion of his presentation, the Fifth Trumpet angel personally demonstrates the technique used to explode the warhead. As the rising smoke from the ensuing nuclear blast darkens the air and blocks out the sun, the Fifth Trumpet angel describes the incredible chaos and social upheaval that will follow in the wake of the world's First Atomic War.

THE FIFTH TRUMPET SOUNDS

1 And the fifth angel trumpeted; and I saw a star out of heaven having fallen onto the earth, and was given to it the key of the shaft of the abyss. 2 And he opened the shaft of the abyss; and went up a smoke out of the shaft as smoke of a great furnace, and the sun and the air was darkened by the smoke of the shaft (Rev. 9:1–2, IGENT).

John begins his account of the Fifth Trumpet event by referring back to the star he described in the Third Trumpet event: "and there fell a great star from heaven, burning as it were a lamp" (Rev. 8:10). "Having fallen" indicates the star was not in the act of falling, but had already fallen in this portion of the vision recorded by John. This past tense reference to his initial starlike nuclear bomb imagery positions the events about to be described as taking place following the First Trumpet Atomic War.

THE KEY OF THE SHAFT

"And was given to it the key of the shaft of the abyss." Before continuing his report on the aftermath events of the nuclear war John paused to describe in the language of his times both the procedure for detonating a nuclear warhead and the delivery system that carries the weapon to its target. Here, "it" refers to the nuclear warhead which upon being given a top-secret coded electronic "key" exploded with such a brilliant flash of light that it reminded John of "a great star falling from heaven, burning as it were a lamp" (Rev. 8:10).

Electronic keys must in fact be given to a nuclear warhead before it can be exploded. To foil anyone who might try an unauthorized detonation of a nuclear bomb, U.S. weapons designers use a sophisticated electronic system called PAL-Permissive Action Link. A tiny microchip-filled box inside the weapon prevents it from firing unless the authorized coded keys are punched in on control equipment from outside.

THE ARROW OF CHAOS

John described the intercontinental ballistic missile (ICBM) carrying the warhead through the heavens to its target as "the shaft of the abyss." By definition a shaft at that time was the long, slender rod forming the body of a spear, or of an arrow. Again by definition abyss was a word that meant unmeasurable chaos, involving utter confusion and disorder. Therefore, John was describing the missile and exploding atomic weapons he saw in his vision in terms of an arrow, which is a weapon that has similarities in appearance to a modern nuclear missile.

Therefore, verse one states that once the warhead carried by the warhead delivery vehicle (the "shaft of the abyss") was given the correct detonation "key," the bomb went off. The subsequent nuclear explosion, which came out of the missile's shaft, quickly escalated what had been a conventional war into the First Trumpet Atomic War. Thus, out of the missile's shaft came unprecedented chaos and disorder on the Earth.

Remember that John was describing a vision, or in other words, a "seeing." Just as modern moviemakers flash backward and forward in time to describe a series of events, so also does John go back to the Third Trumpet star falling from heaven, which pictorializes a nuclear explosion. Then he described the atomic weaponry. How apt it is to call a nuclear missile "an arrow of chaos." It is an arrow that can be fired from one side of the globe to the other and melt the very elements in incredible heat.

THE ANGEL OPENED THE SHAFT

"And he (the angel) opened the shaft of the abyss." In Greek the word *angel* means "messenger." Each of the seven trumpet angels delivered a very specific prophetic message to the Apostle John. The first four trumpet angels presented John with a panoramic vision of the message they were assigned to deliver. The Fifth Trumpet angel also delivered his message in visual form, but added another dimension to his presentation by personally demonstrating how a modern nuclear missile works. "He" does this by opening the "shaft of the abyss" from the outside. The angel's purpose for doing so is to illustrate how the warhead being carried inside the missile could only be set off when

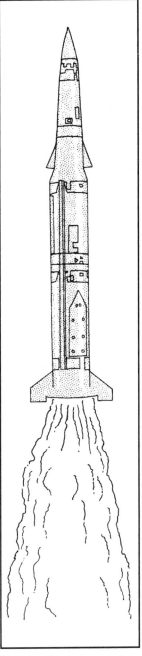

Pershing 2 missile soars in test flight.

someone from the outside gave "it" the top-secret detonation "key."

In addition to presenting visual and personal demonstrations to help John understand parts of specific prophecies, some of the angels add verbal instructions for further clarification of a subject. The reason they do so is because some technical concepts could not be conveyed to the technological age without accompanying verbal explanations.

Incidentally, the Fifth Trumpet angel's visual presentation of a missile weapons system, coupled with his demonstration of the procedure used to detonate its nuclear warhead, eliminates the possibility of using a meteor to explain the destruction caused by the "great star falling from heaven" (Rev. 8:10). A meteor does not need the sleek shaft of a missile to carry it through the heavens to the Earth; nor does it need someone from the outside to give it a top-secret coded key to prompt it to do its damage.

THE SMOKE-FILLED HEAVENS

John continued to describe the physical aspects of the atomic blast by pointing out that smoke went up out of the shaft "as smoke of a great furnace, and the sun and the air was darkened by the smoke of the shaft." The rising smoke of an atomic blast collects at the top of a columnar shaft where it forms a gigantic cloud that darkens the skies, (even on a clear day). Scientists estimate that the initial smoke clouds and accompanying urban firestorms would block the sun within the target zones to the extent that it would be too dark to see, even at noon. (A twenty-megaton atomic bomb detonated over a large city would generate a mushroom smoke cloud seventy miles in diameter, covering an area of 3,850 square miles.) A city engulfed in a massive firestorm sending smoke 10 to 12 miles into the stratosphere, is a "great" smoking "furnace" indeed!

John's account of smoke from atomic explosions filling the heavens and darkening the sun, completes the full explanation of the Sixth Seal's prophetic introduction to AWWI: "I watched as he opened the sixth seal. There was a great earthquake. The sun turned black like sackcloth made of goat hair, the whole moon turned blood red" (Rev. 6:12, NIV). (Sackcloth was a coarse black cloth, commonly, though not always, made of goat hair.) Thus, the idea conveyed here is that immediately after the great earthquake unleashes AWWI, "the sun will turn black" to the extent that it will be as dark over the target areas as it would be if the sun were covered with a huge garment made of black sackcloth. Likewise, "the whole moon turned blood red" pictures how the dispersion of the moon's light through the pall of dust and smoke will make it appear blood red in color. Twentieth century observations of the smoke produced by atomic explosions confirm the Sixth Seal Atomic War prophecy's original documentation of the matter.

Since the sun turning "black" is the first negative effect mentioned after the opening announcement of the Sixth Seal Atomic War: "There was a great earthquake"; it follows that the blocking of the sun's rays will be an indirect side effect of the "great earthquake" that will unleash the world's First Atomic War. Inasmuch as Ezekiel stated that the epicenter of the great earthquake will be "in the land of Israel" (Ezek. 38:19, NASB), and "on all My mountains, . . . Every [Russian] man's sword will be against his brother" (Ezek. 38:21, NASB), the smoking "atomic pistol" that will touch off AWWI seems to point to a Russian-built battlefield nuke!

THE SMOKING RUINS ON THE GROUND

At this point in the prophecy John turned his attention from the smoke-filled heavens to what will be happening amidst the smoking ruins on the ground.

THE LOCUST IMAGERY

3 And out of the smoke came forth locusts to the earth, and authority was given to them as the scorpions of the earth have authority (Rev. 9:3, IGENT). **4** And they were told that they should not hurt the grass of the earth, nor any green thing, nor any tree, but only the men who do not have the seal of God on their foreheads (v. 4, NASB). **5** And to them it was given that they should not kill them, but that they should be tormented five months: and their torment was as the torment of a scorpion, when he striketh a man (v. 5). **6** And in those days men will seek death and will not find it; and they will long to die and death flees from them (v. 6, NASB).

In Bible days clouds of locusts would appear from time to time in great numbers, darkening the sky when they passed overhead. These insects would devour all vegetation in their path. Consequently, vast destructive armies were often referred to as locusts by the prophets. One such example is found in the book of Judges.

> 3 For it was when Israel had sown, that the Midianites would come up with the Amalekites and the sons of the east and go against them. 4 So they would camp against them and destroy the produce of the earth as far as Gaza, and leave no sustenance in Israel as well as no sheep, ox, or donkey. 5 For they would come up with their livestock and their tents, they would come in like locusts for number, both they and their camels were innumerable; and they came into the land to devastate it (Judges 6:3–5, NASB).

The locust imagery, therefore, based on previous biblical imagery, is used here to represent a military force. "Out of the smoke . . . to the earth" establishes how the soldiers in this army will be transported to their destination points. They will "come forth" out of the post-AWWI smoke-filled skies as the aircraft carrying them come in for a landing "to the earth."

A PEACE-KEEPING ARMY

The verbal command—"and they were told that they should not hurt the grass of the earth, nor any green thing, nor any tree"—underscores the fact that the locust imagery represents an army of men, since insects would normally eat grass and other green vegetation. The command also reveals that the army will not be sent forth to destroy but rather to protect property such as grass, green crops, trees and other things of value. This verbal command coupled with the defined policy—"that they should not kill them"—shows that the soldiers will be an emergency peace-keeping force, not a conquering army. Thus, the army's main mission will be to establish law and order in various fractured communities struggling to survive the chaotic aftermath of AWWI.

THE NEED FOR MARTIAL LAW

It is easy to understand why hordes of dazed and injured survivors, demanding that something be done to help them, will recklessly riot against any authority, including armed soldiers. Equally understandable is the immediate implementation of martial law to quell anarchy. The typical survivor's first reaction will be panic, then anger. That anger will be directed at their respective governments that failed to protect them. Politicians won't be able to quiet angry hordes of desperate victims with a few soothing words of political rhetoric.

People living in the nuclear era are simply too well informed about the consequences of nuclear war. The survivors will know that the systematic weakening of their immune systems by the lethal effects of radiation will inevitably leave many of them to fall victim to fatal diseases. They will also know that any medical help will only be a token gesture. Young people in the prime of life, fully aware that they may well die in a matter of a few weeks or months, will want to strike back at the authorities who failed to protect them. These facts provide some insight into why the nuclear combatant nations will use harsh measures to control the raging mobs of victims after AWWI.

As a result of all this misery and chaos men will welcome death as a release from their suffering. Certainly the survivors in nuclear war zones will have reason to envy the dead.

Note however, that the fifth trumpet prophecy was not addressed only to survivors living in bombed areas, but to everyone living on the planet in the post-AWWI period. This can be determined from the prophecy's opening statement: "And out of the smoke came forth locusts to the earth," which means even as the Fourth Trumpet angel reported that the smoke from AWWI will shroud the entire planet, so likewise will combat troops appear out of that same atomic smoke to quell civil insurrections around the globe after the war.

The support for this position is underscored by the indefiniteness of the text as to where the troops will come from and who will dispatch them: "And out of the smoke came forth." "They were told that they should not hurt . . . And to them it was given that they should not kill them . . ." In short, the language is so general that it eliminates any attempt to precisely identify where the troops will come from and who will send them. Logically then, it follows that they will be dispatched from more than one location and by more than one authority. Thus, the prophecy will be fulfilled by individual nations (including those far removed from atomic battlegrounds) issuing general calls for martial law after the First Trumpet Atomic War.

Martial law would be an obvious measure in the post-AWWI period. The loss of a third of the world's food supplies to fire and toxic contamination will immediately create a global food shortage. Yet, the initial loss of food in the bombed areas will be minor compared to the sub-freezing temperatures and subsequent global crop damage expected from "nuclear winter." Also, loss of a third of the world's ships will make it difficult to distribute remaining food supplies.

In addition to famine, the destruction of thousands of cities will immediately translate into missing supplies of raw materials, spare parts and manufacturing components needed to run factories. Missing markets and capital will also contribute to the inability of societies to function normally. There will be mass unemployment and frantic hoarding of food and goods. Predictably, people will panic, demonstrations will turn violent, and according to this passage, martial law will be declared in nation after nation in a desperate attempt to restore order.

After AWWI, shortages of food and other goods will force governments everywhere to implement rationing and price controls. Basic animal feed stocks such as hay and chopped alfalfa, corn and sorghum fodder, will be in great demand due to the loss of a third of the world's grass and crops to AWWI's nuclear firestorms. Trees also will become highly prized for heating, cooking, and constructing shelter. Large numbers of people will go into the countryside searching for food and other commodities for their own use or to sell on the black market. Quite appropriately military units will be deployed outside cities to protect these vital resources from roving bands seeking a quick profit.

Thus, the general order—"And they were told that they should not hurt the grass of the earth, nor any green thing, nor any tree"—means that troops will be dispatched to protect dwindling supplies of basic food and fuel sources (such as trees), located on farmlands throughout the countryside. This will be a natural first step taken by all governments to insure their nation's survival in the face of gripping global famine.

THE SEAL OF PROTECTION IMAGERY

The army's other marching order to "hurt only the men who do not have the seal of God on their foreheads" shows that the occupation troops will only apply physical force to unbelievers. According to the text's seal imagery this clearly means that the people with seals will not be troubled by national guard units. The seal imagery provides some insight into who these people will be. For instance, according to the Sixth Seal the 144,000 sealed Jews will be a highly motivated group of evangelists committed to spreading the gospel of Jesus Christ during the days of the Great Tribulation. They will begin making their commitment to Christ when a powerful influence out of the East arrives on the world scene, sometime after AWWI ends. Hence, since the Eastern influence has not yet been introduced at the time of the Fifth Trumpet prophecy, the sealed Christians spoken of here will not be this group of 144,000 Jewish evangelists. Based on the consistency of biblical imagery, it is both logical and appropriate to conclude that the sealed people in the Fifth Trumpet prophecy will have the same basic Christian objectives as the 144,000 Jews who will make their appearance sometime after the Fifth Trumpet event comes to a close.

It is equally clear that John did not directly explain why these sealed Christians will not be troubled by post-AWWI martial law enforcement troops. However, in view of the fact that soldiers will be instructed not only to protect basic food and fuel supplies but also to "harm" the men who do not have the seal of God on their foreheads, it is reasonable to assume that national militias will be harming people caught stealing scarce commodities for resale on the black market. Despite the confusion of the times and the blurred line between hungry people taking what they need to survive and outright lawlessness for gain, it seems unlikely that dedicated Christians will allow themselves to become involved in situations that could be interpreted by soldiers as wholesale robbery. The logical conclusion of this premise strongly suggests that Christians will not be subjected to bodily harm by soldiers after AWWI simply because they will not be in harm's way.

Along with the order to harm anyone violating martial law, soldiers will be told "that they should not kill them." This is a typical order given to combat troops sent to restore order during national emergencies. The fair interpretation of this order would be that it will be generally followed by the various national militias restoring order after AWWI. It should be noted that the text does not say no one will be killed during the turbulent days of the Fifth Trumpet nuclear winter, but rather, the general policy will be "not to kill anyone."

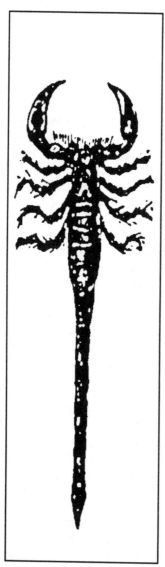

A scorpion.

THE SCORPION IMAGERY

John's initial statement regarding the soldiers—"and authority was given to them as the scorpions of the earth have authority"—begins a description of the typical national guard unit's mission assignment and how the soldiers will be instructed to conduct themselves while establishing order after the war. Unlike other insects, the scorpion is frequently thought of as an animal due to its large size (often twelve inches long in tropical climates), ugly appearance, and mean disposition. In fact, scorpions are so bad-tempered that they will lash out and strike at anyone or anything daring to cross their path. Not surprisingly, when people and scorpions meet, the people invariably recognize the scorpion's authority and back off accordingly. John's comparison of martial law enforcement troops to scorpions is a good one since combat soldiers are often thought of as mean-tempered brutes who will likely as not attack anyone daring to cross their path. Predictably, when civilians disobeying restrictions imposed under martial law (such as curfews) meet combat soldiers on patrol, the civilians will invariably recognize the soldiers' authority and either back off, or suffer the immediate unpleasant consequences of their folly.

John goes on to describe the painful injuries suffered by those who run afoul of martial law troops: "and their torment was as the torment of a scorpion, when he striketh a man." Verse 10 supplies the additional fact that the weapons of "authority" which will be used "to harm men" will resemble "tails like to scorpions." This is an apt description of the taillike rifles and machine guns carried by today's combat soldiers. The barrels of these weapons are similar to a scorpion's long tail, not only in appearance but also in function. Exactly what type of ammunition will be used in the soldiers' weapons cannot be specifically determined from the text; however, since a scorpion's sting and a bullet wound produce almost identical symptoms of pain, the ammunition used may well be ordinary bullets. For example, the scorpion's unusually painful sting, though seldom fatal, is one of the most malignant among insects. According to *Barnes' Notes*, "the place where a person is stung becomes inflamed and hardened; it reddens by tension, and is painful by intervals, being now chilly, now burning. The pain soon rises high, and rages, sometimes more, sometimes less. A sweating succeeds, attended by a shivering and trembling; the extremities of the body become cold and the members become pale." In many respects the suffering caused by a scorpion's sting and the symptoms of shock brought on by excessive bleeding from a "stinging" bullet wound are much the same. Clearly then, the presence of John's description of the scorpion-like stinging pain felt by a person hit by a modern bullet supports the interpretation that combat soldiers will shoot to stop, not to kill smugglers and rioting crowds of civilians after AWWI. After all, with the automatic firing capabilities of modern weapons, a well-armed military force could quickly kill a group of looters or a large unarmed mob of unruly civilians if that were the intent.

FIVE DREADFUL MONTHS

John stated that this period of extreme distress will last five months. The conditions of this five-month period correspond to the TTAPS group's analysis of variation in temperature at ground level in the Northern Hemisphere after a nuclear war. Their study predicts the average temperature decrease for various sized nuclear wars over the interior regions of the continents. Their simulations show a period of three months before temperatures climb above the freezing point of water, for a 5,000-megaton base-line nuclear war case. For a 10,000–megaton yield exchange (enough firepower to burn up a third of the earth), subfreezing temperatures could last almost six months. Although John does not explicitly use the word *famine* to describe the scientifically predicted "nuclear winter," he does forecast five months of famine-driven social and political upheaval in terms of its highly visible disruptive effects—the widespread mobilization of troops to protect basic food stocks remaining in the countryside. As we will see in the next chapter of this book, several biblical texts foretell extensive environmental damages resulting from AWWI. Therefore, it is reasonable to assume that the global famine induced by nuclear winter will be a major cause of the five-month period of intense human suffering reported in the Fifth Trumpet event.

THE LOCUST-SHAPED AIRCRAFT

John switched from a general briefing on how the typical mobilized national guard unit will go about restoring order after AWWI to a detailed description of the locust-shaped aircraft that will be used to support the transportation requirements of these military operations.

> 7 And the shapes of the locusts were like unto horses prepared unto battle; and on their heads were as it were crowns like gold, and their faces were as the faces of men. 8 And they had hair as the hair of women, and their teeth were as the teeth of lions. 9 And they had breastplates, as it were breastplates of iron; and the sound of their wings was as the sound of chariots of many horses running to battle (Rev. 9:7–9).

Here begins John's meticulous review of the functional capabilities and physical construction of the locust-shaped, troop-carrying aircraft. The statement "the shape of the locusts were like unto horses prepared unto battle" reveals that the locust-shaped vehicles will actually perform horselike services. That is, according to the text they will be outfitted in the same way the battle horses of old were "prepared unto battle," with seating gear for carrying men. Thus, though the overall outer appearance of the contraptions will be locust-shaped, they will be used like the horses of John's day to carry troops to war.

The large locust-shaped, horselike war vehicles are further described as having, "breastplates, as it were breastplates of iron." In other words, they will be covered with metal.

The phrase "and the noise of their wings was like the noise of many chariots with horses rushing into battle" (RSV), provides the additional fact that these metal war machines will also have locustlike wings that will make a tremendous noise.

The assembly of these three components of the locust-shaped, horselike contraption suggests the recognizable features of a modern helicopter. Helicopters are the only aircraft routinely designed and outfitted with mobile rotating wings capable of making a whirring noise similar to the sound of spinning chariot wheels. Further, the combination of the helicopter's running engine along with its whirling rotor-blades produces a definite thump, thump, thump sound as the chopper passes overhead. This unique, exceptionally loud noise resembles the hoofbeats of not one, but "many horses running to battle."

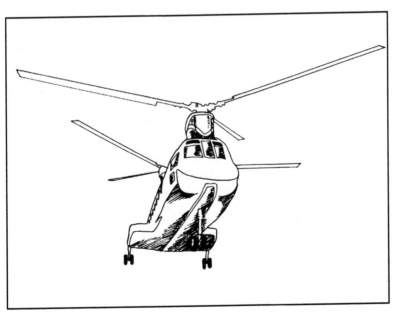

Note the helicopter's crownlike mast and the overall resemblance between the aircraft and a locust.

The circular mast supporting the helicopter's rotary wings, which is mounted above the cockpit, is similar in appearance to a circular crown worn on the heads of kings: "and on their heads, as it were, crowns like gold." "Like gold" does not, in any way, imply that the mast will be a golden color or made of gold, but rather that the crownlike mast will have the same round shape as a king's golden crown.

Now since John said the crownlike mast was "on their heads," the head has to be a reference to the helicopter's cockpit, upon which the crownlike mast is mounted. Logically then, the face of the headlike cockpit has to be the exterior, front end of the cockpit where the pilot's windows reside. Thus, the shapes of the locusts' faces appeared to John to resemble "the faces of men." That is, the metal vehicles' faces displayed rugged masculine features; they definitely did not have the gentle delicate curves found in a woman's face. Said in more specific terms, the front of the approaching gunships displayed the deadly grim, fierce determination found in the faces of warriors charging into battle, which is in keeping with the overall deportment of the locust-shaped war machines that "looked like horses prepared for battle" NIV.

Yet, these same heads with combat-ready faces had "hairs as hairs of women" (IGENT). A quick inspection of a modern helicopter's equipment fails to turn up anything akin to "hairs as hairs of women," (unless the whirling blades appeared to John to resemble a woman's long hair blowing in the wind). It may well be that the feature described here has not yet been invented and installed. Whether this be the case or not does not present a problem since the exact meaning of the hairs is not necessary to determine that John's description of the locust-shaped contraption properly identifies a helicopter.

The teeth like lion's teeth are a reference to the deadly bombs, rockets, and missiles that modern helicopter gunships carry as part of their offensive weapons package. Thus, the ferocious, lionlike teeth also emphasizes the battle-readiness of the locust-shaped war machines that "looked like horses prepared for battle" (NIV).

Helicopter gunships, like the battle horses of old, can also be used to break up unruly mobs rioting against the authorities. In the early 1980s, Afghanistan civilians rioted in the streets of Kabul against the Russian-established Afghan government. The Russians moved in quickly with their helicopter gunships and dispersed the mobs, by machine-gunning the crowds from the air. The Russian choppers swooped over buildings, without warning, and fired on the people below before they could escape. Dozens of civilians were killed or wounded by this action.

This surprise attack on Afghan civilians can be compared to a lion pouncing on an unsuspecting person before he can escape. Perhaps this is why the Apostle John compared the lethal firepower of modern-day helicopters, coupled with their swift maneuverability, to the deadliness of lions teeth, when the lion suddenly springs and attacks its prey.

> 10 And they have tails like to scorpions and stings, and the authority of them is to harm men with the tails of them five months (Rev. 9:10, IGENT).

The taillike weapons of authority identify the helicopter gunships' machine guns and the rifles of the soldiers riding inside. The long round barrels of the guns are similar in appearance to a scorpion's tail. The stinging pain inflicted on men by a scorpion's tail likewise closely resembles the pain caused by a "stinging" bullet. These weapons will be used to harm men for five months.

In summary, the opening statement—"out of the smoke came forth locusts to the earth . . . , And they were told that they should not hurt the grass of the earth, nor any green thing, nor any tree"—foretells the use of helicopter gunships to police the open countryside after the smoke begins to settle following the First Trumpet Atomic War. All things considered, radio–dispatched, troop-carrying helicopters will be the most effective way to protect vital commodities still remaining in rural storage bins from roving bands of robbers.

FIVE DREADFUL MONTHS RE-EMPHASIZED

John mentioned the five-month period of extreme misery for the second time in this passage, which indicates an emphatic warning. Christians should pay close attention to its significance with respect to God's warnings in the past to those who would listen before major calamities arrived. For example, Joseph stored grain for seven years in Egypt before a seven-year famine arrived (Gen. 41). Prior to Joseph's time, God warned

tant nations will have atomic craters where the capital cities housing their respective governments once stood, the commanders administering martial law will be the only semblance of government operating in many of these nations after the war. Obviously this opportunist will have to gain the backing of the world's military establishment as a first step in his bid for world power.

Other Scriptures covering the aftermath of AWWI show this man steadily acquiring a larger international following until he secures control of an all encompassing world government. All nations will then be subjected to the whims of this tyrant who will make his initial bid for power during the dark days of the global nuclear winter.

There is a saying that history repeats itself. At the end of World War I, (the war to end war), the League of Nations was established. The League's main objective was to preserve world peace. Less than twenty years after its founding, World War II broke out. At the end of World War II a new world body called the United Nations rose from the ashes of that conflict. According to Bible prophecy, out of the radioactive ashes of AWWI the nations will erect man's final international governing "beast" organization. History will repeat itself again.

THE FALSE HOPE OF WORLD UNITY

The threat of nuclear war is already acting as a catalyst to promote the idea of establishing a world government that would be chartered with the responsibility of ensuring peace and safety through disarmament. One recent book, *The Fate of the Earth*, by Jonathan Schell, proposed this solution. Schell discussed the doctrine of deterrence and concluded that there is no safety without complete world disarmament and the withering away of sovereign nations in favor of world government.

Scripture foretells the attempt by nations to establish peace and safety through the formation of a world government after the Initial Atomic War. However, the Bible discloses that disarmament efforts will fail completely; a second, even more devastating atomic war will break out in the closing days of the nuclear age.

The authority exercised by the world's final governing beast will completely dwarf the scope and power of previous international peace-keeping bodies. Man's last government will be given the authority to set up a new international financial system, new laws, and the power to enforce its policies on the Earth via sophisticated high-tech methods which will be discussed later.

THE FIRST WOE ENDS

12 The first woe is past; behold, two woes are still coming after these things (Rev. 9:12, NASB).

The five-month period of chaos following the First Trumpet Atomic War is referred to as the first woe. According to the Fifth Trumpet prophecy and Revelation 17:8 this woe marks the period when a future "world government beast" and its leader will begin "to come up out of the abyss," or unfathomable chaos following AWWI. This is the first of three woes about which the U.S. eagle will warn the world, directly after AWWI.

THE FIRST FIVE TRUMPETS REVIEWED

The five trumpet events mark a time unlike the world has ever seen.

(1) Trumpet 1 introduced the subject of the world's first nuclear war and its most immediate major impact—the destruction of one-third of the Earth by radioactive hail and fire.

(2) Trumpet 2 used the analogy of "something" like a "great mountain burning with fire cast into the sea" to describe the massive mountain of fiery atomic debris that will be cast into the sea over the course of AWWI. One-third of the world's oceans will promptly be contaminated by this mountain of poisonous substances to the extent that the affected seas will turn a blood red color and the creatures living in these waters will subsequently die. Also one-third of all ocean-going ships will be destroyed in the naval theater of the nuclear war.

(3) Trumpet 3 used the analogy of a "great star falling from the heavens, burning as it were a lamp," to describe the awesome weapons of destruction used in the First Trumpet Atomic War. The radioactive fallout from the starlike atomic

blasts will contaminate one-third of the world's rivers and lakes. Many survivors in the bombed areas will subsequently die from drinking poisonous waters.

(4) Trumpet 4 warned that a third of the light from the sun, moon, and stars will not be able to penetrate the planet's atmosphere as a direct consequence of the atomic war.

(*) A special announcement is inserted between the fourth and fifth trumpet events. It speaks of one "U.S." eagle flying in mid-heaven warning those dwelling on the Earth concerning the remaining three trumpet events yet to come.

(5) Trumpet 5 identified the immense clouds of smoke generated from starlike nuclear bomb-initiated firestorms as the primary reason a third of the sun's light will not be able to reach the Earth's surface. The Fifth Trumpet angel also warned that a future world leader will cunningly use a pro- phesied post-war five-month period of famine-driven hard- ship and social upheavel to launch his ruthless international political career.

The insertion between the fourth and fifth trumpets of one "U.S." eagle flying in mid-heaven to warn those dwelling on the Earth about the remaining three trumpet events is signifi- cant. Since the latest scientific studies predict a global nuclear winter within two or three days after a nuclear war takes place, it follows from the text that the U.S. eagle will come through this war in surprisingly good shape. Obviously, many U.S. cities and their communication facilities will be functioning during the two- or three-day interval between the Fourth and Fifth Trumpet events; otherwise U.S. Christians would not be on the job preaching the gospel and warning the world about the remaining trumpets yet to sound.

The meaning of the first five trumpets has not been under- stood since the Apostle John wrote Revelation, and, in fact, could not be understood until advanced studies of the smoke from nuclear warfare started being released in June of 1982. These recent studies by some of the world's foremost scientists awakened the general public to the realization that smoke from atomic warfare has the capacity to block out a large fraction of the sun's rays and lower land temperatures below freezing for months. Once these facts on the aftereffects of smoke from nuclear war were understood, God's warning messages to the nuclear generation also came into focus.

Consider the contrast between the Bible's account of the aftereffects of nuclear war with modern man's decades-long awakening to the facts of the matter. While today's experts overlooked the humblest of the side effects of nuclear war—the smoke of burning cities—for nearly forty years after the detonation of the first atomic bomb, the Bible emphasizes smoke as the most significant side effect.

9 A Biblical View of "The Day After"

What will the world be like when survivors emerge the day after a nuclear war? Some of the best scientific minds are attempting to find answers to this question. Much of their current research has centered around trying to determine if the probable outcome of a nuclear war will be a nuclear winter, and if so, what the impact would be on the global environment. Although the original TTAPS study predicting global nuclear winter in the wake of nuclear war has consistently held up, at least as a "first order" estimate, the complex variables used in the formula for nuclear winter are so rife with uncertainties that an authoritative scientific report on the concept is not available.

In direct contrast, the biblical account of what awaits the planet's survivors after a global nuclear exchange speaks with force and certainty. In fact, Jeremiah boldly introduced his prophecy with "thus saith the LORD God of Israel unto me" (Jer. 25:15). He detailed the nuclear destruction of the nations, unequivocally naming God as the source of his information. Yet the biblical account of the damaging effects from the world's First Atomic War precisely matches the observable destructive power of today's nuclear weapons.

From this indisputable portrait of the world's First Atomic War, the Bible proceeds to detail the extent of the aftermath damages that modern man has come to call "nuclear winter." These informative prophecies are followed, in turn, by a description of the world's second nuclear war. At its conclusion,

smoke-filled skies. This will cause the sudden destruction of crops around the world.

The volcanic blowout of Mount Tambora supports the predictions of nuclear war studies that suggest a bone-chilling "nuclear winter" brought on by the smoke pumped into the Earth's atmosphere from multiple atomic explosions. According to a study by the Smithsonian Institution, Mount Tambora erupted in April of 1815, on the island of Sumbawa, in the Indonesian archipelago. Scientists estimate that a single tremendous explosion from the volcano blew some twenty-five cubic miles of earth and rock into the atmosphere. The air was so filled with dust, smoke, and ash that it left an area 400 miles across in total darkness for three days. A substantial quantity of the volcano's smoke was carried into the stratosphere. This high-altitude smoke subsequently lowered temperatures in the Northern Hemisphere to the extent that crops were severely damaged in North America and many areas of Europe suffered outright famine.

If the smoke and dust spewed into the Earth's atmosphere from one volcanic explosion wrought this much damage on Northern Hemisphere crops, a global atomic war capable of lofting at least a hundred times the volumes of dust and smoke produced by Tambora will undoubtedly plunge the world into the dark, crop-freezing days so clearly detailed here by Isaiah.

THE CAUSE OF ATOMIC WAR IDENTIFIED

5 The earth also is defiled under the inhabitants thereof; because they have transgressed the laws, changed the ordinance, broken the everlasting covenant. 6 Therefore hath the curse devoured the earth, and they that dwell therein are desolate: therefore the inhabitants of the earth are burned, and few men left (Isa. 24:5–6).

After documenting the fact that all classes of people will be subjected to the death blow of an atomic bomb, Isaiah identified the cause of nuclear war as the collective result of men turning their backs on God's instruction and laws. He then described the consequences of this rebellion in terms of man's reckless use of nuclear bombs to defend his defiant way of life. Isaiah aptly summarized the violence of atomic warfare as "the curse" that devours the earth and burns the majority of its inhabitants.

GLOBAL CROP DAMAGES REPORTED

7 The new wine mourns, The vine decays, All the merry-hearted sigh. 8 The gaiety of tambourines ceases, The noise of revelers stops, The gaiety of the harp ceases. 9 They do not drink wine with song; Strong drink is bitter to those who drink it (Isa. 24:7—9, NASB).

At this point the prophecy begins to detail the agricultural damages that will occur in the post-AWWI period. The vine becoming sickly and decaying parallels the latest scientific findings that predict that extreme cold will bring about the death and decay of crops around the globe.

RADIOACTIVE HOUSES SHUT UP

10 The city of confusion is broken down: every house is shut up, that no man might come in (Isa. 24:10).

An air-burst atomic bomb can reduce a great city to charred rubble in a matter of minutes. The bomb's shock wave generates overpressures above buildings several times normal atmospheric pressure and winds of many hundreds of miles per hour. The overpressure will crush reinforced concrete structures and flatten or severly damage all but the strongest buildings within a radius of a mile to several miles of ground zero. If the bomb is large enough even the world's largest cities will be left completely "broken down" after a nuclear attack.

According to *Barnes' Notes*, the word rendered "confusion" does not denote disorder or anarchy, but is a word that expresses destitution of form. It occurs in Genesis 1:2: "And the earth was without form." The Greek Septuagint provides a crisp translation of this: "all the city has become desolate."

Isaiah described some houses still standing the day after the Atomic War. They will undoubtedly be buildings of brick and concrete located far enough away from ground zero to be left intact. However they will be "shut up" or off limits to men due to dangerous levels of atomic fallout. Truly, "no man may come in," because of the risk from radiation poisoning.

The Soviet Union's nuclear powerplant accident gave the world a preview of what the sudden release of large amounts of radiation into the air will do to nearby population centers left standing after a nuclear attack. Even though the Chernobyl reactor suffered only a partial meltdown, deadly radiation escaping into the surrounding environment made it necessary to evacuate 135,000 people living within an 18-mile radius of the stricken reactor. Their houses had to be "shut up so that no man may come in." Large sections of the contaminated zone are expected to remain closed to the population for four years or more until decontamination cleanup operations are completed.

Yet the contamination from the Chernobyl reactor explosion would be insignificant next to the far greater amount of radiation that would be released into the environment in a nuclear war. For example, a 1-megaton hydrogen bomb would produce 1,000 times more radioactivity within an hour of its detonation than the worst conceivable reactor accident.

In summary, today's documentation of the radiation effects from nuclear explosions over cities agrees with Isaiah's account that makes it clear that the day after AWWI ends there will be so much radioactive fallout on the ground that "every house is shut up so that none can enter" (RSV), for miles and miles in every direction!

GOOD TIMES CANCELLED

11 There is an outcry in the streets concerning the wine; All joy turns to gloom. The gaiety of the earth is banished. **12** Desolation is left in the city, And the gate is battered to ruins (Isa. 24:11–12, NASB).

The day after AWWI survival will be the primary concern of survivors fleeing the Earth's smashed cities. Isaiah noted that gaiety will not be a part of the scene. "All joy turns to gloom" on the Earth.

GLOBAL POST-AWWI FAMINE

13 For thus it will be in the midst of the earth among the peoples, As the shaking of an olive tree, As the gleanings when the grape harvest is over (Isa. 24:13, NASB).

"For thus it will be in the midst of the earth among the peoples" is a summary statement that applies all the previously described calamities to everyone left alive on the Earth after AWWI. That is, the survivors shall find themselves in a world where the "heavens together with the earth" are in the process of losing their former strength and vigor. This will cause the "vine" to "decay" as the agricultural crisis deepens during the dark days of the ensuing nuclear winter. Survivors fleeing bombed, "broken down" cities will also realize that the good times have become a thing of the past when they gaze back at the heaps of desolate rubble, "left in the city," they once called home.

According to Isaiah's prophecy, people will be frantically scavaging for food and shelter the day after the Atomic War ends. Those surviving in former lush agricultural areas will find themselves in a burned out wasteland. Where there had been abundant food and water, suddenly there will be nothing fit for human consumption. It will be akin to being lost in a desert. Survivors are compared to the destitute and poorest classes of old, who would go into the olive groves and vineyards after the harvest, to glean what few olives and grapes were left. There will be a frantic effort to collect every morsel of food.

As noted before, today's scientists believe a "nuclear winter" will set in on the Earth after an atomic war. Recent studies by scientists in Europe, the United States, and the U.S.S.R., suggest that the long-term climatic effects of a major nuclear war will introduce abnormally low temperatures (independent of season) over much of the Earth. This prolonged cold snap along with atomic smoke clouds blocking sunlight would prevent growth of most foods. With crop production essentially shut down and supplies of food in targeted areas either destroyed or contaminated, the spread of global famine would be unavoidable. In light of these grim findings, how apt it is to describe the condition of the Earth in the aftermath of a nuclear war "as the gleanings when the grape harvest is over."

GOOD NEWS FROM THE WEST

> 14 They raise their voices, they shout for joy. They cry out
> from the west concerning the majesty of the LORD. 15 There-
> fore glorify the LORD in the east, The name of the LORD, the
> God of Israel In the coastlands of the sea (Isa. 24:14–15, NASB).

It is hard to imagine people from the West "shouting for joy"
in the aftermath of atomic war. Yet Isaiah's narrative parallels
the same positive response prophesied in Revelation 8 concerning the Western nation of the United States launching a worldwide evangelistic outreach following the First Trumpet Atomic
War.

The joy of the people from the West recalls the words of
Christ when He warned of the violence of the last days.

> 31 So likewise ye, when ye see these things come to pass,
> know ye that the kingdom of God is nigh at hand (Luke
> 21:31).

AWWI is the first trumpet event prophesied to come to pass
at the time of the end. The last trumpet event is Christ's return
to establish His earthly kingdom of peace. The joyful news
proclaimed by the "people of the West" the day after AWWI,
therefore, will clearly be "Christ is coming." Western Christians
will use the prophetic fulfillment of the outbreak of AWWI to
convince the "people of the East" that Jesus Christ is the King
who will soon return.

GOOD NEWS SILENCED BY A BETRAYAL

> 16 From the ends of the earth we hear songs, "Glory to the
> Righteous One," But I say, "Woe to me! Woe to me! Alas for
> me! The treacherous deal treacherously, And the treacherous
> deal very treacherously" (Isa. 24:16, NASB).

The first part of this verse indicates that many people will
hear the facts about God's mighty deliverance of Israel from the
invading Russian forces. Many will promptly turn to God and
praise Him for His righteousness. Isaiah's documentation of
their positive response coincides with Ezekiel's prophecy that

states that all nations will know who God is after Russia's defeat.

Isaiah then shifts back to the physical condition of AWWI's survivors. "Woe to me" indicates they will be in grievous distress with a terrible affliction. The New International Version renders this as "I waste away, I waste away!" Waste away means to become physically wasted, losing flesh and strength. People will be simultaneously hit by inadequate food supplies and radiation sickness.

The Isaiah prophecy then moves to an extended period of time after AWWI. Isaiah indicated that the nations will establish disarmament treaties and other agreements following the war, such as pledges banning the use of atomic weapons. This is discernable from the phrase "the treacherous deal very treacherously," which means a deceptive double-cross and a betrayal of an agreement. The use of treachery and deceit in the pursuit of selfish national objectives will eventually usher in more atomic fighting. According to Scripture, once this second conflict begins it will quickly escalate into the world's Second Nuclear War (AWWII).

AWWII ERUPTS

The rest of Isaiah chapter 24 completes the description of the world's second all-out atomic war and the end of the matter.

> 17 Fear, and the pit, and the snare, are upon thee, O inhabitant of the earth. 18 And it shall come to pass, that he who fleeth from the noise of the fear shall fall into the pit; and he that cometh up out of the midst of the pit shall be taken in the snare: for the windows from on high are open, and the foundations of the earth do shake (Isa. 24:17–18).

THREE CAUSES OF DEATH

Isaiah listed the three main causes of death from the atomic holocaust here. Some will die of fear when they hear the incredible noise from the blasts rolling across the continents. Others will head for a "pit" or some type of bomb shelter when they hear the blast noise only to find people who were already in the bomb shelters running to get out. Due to the shaking of the Earth the bomb shelters will break up and collapse. However, head goes off. For instance, a one-megaton surface blast can excavate a crater 200 feet deep and 1000 feet in diameter. Between 100,000 and 600,000 tons of the soil displaced from the crater is actually vaporized and renucleated while the blast is lifting it to a high altitude.

At the same time the crater is being formed by the explosion, "the earth is reeling to and fro like a drunkard" as the initial concussion and high winds from the blast sweep several million tons of surface debris away. When AWWII is over the Earth will be left "utterly broken down."

AWWII WILL RUIN THE NATIONS

The prophet Jeremiah also foretold the atomic holocaust coming on the Earth in the latter days. One of his prophecies carefully spells out the fact that all the nations will be systematically ruined by AWWII. Jeremiah introduced this prophecy directly after he announced the imminent downfall of the kingdom of Judah.

> **15** For thus saith the LORD God of Israel unto me; Take the wine cup of this fury at my hand, and cause all the nations, to whom I send thee, to drink it. **16** And they shall drink, and be moved, and be mad, because of the sword that I will send among them (Jer. 25:15–16).

"The wine cup of this fury" symbolizes the production and stockpiling of nuclear weapons. The nations "drinking" from the "wine cup of this fury" is a picture of the nations using their stockpiled weapons in all-out nuclear war. God predicts that the nations will "be moved, and be mad," because of the nuclear weapons, or "nuclear sword," that will be among them.

In earlier times, U.S. nuclear strategy was predicated on the so-called MAD (mutually assured destruction) idea. Its basic "message" to be conveyed to missile launchers was the single command "retaliate." Nothing more needed to be said. Although the United States does not presently use this acronym to describe its nuclear strategy, man's use of nuclear weapons can only be labeled a mad act.

Once an atomic war breaks out, it will not matter what nuclear fighting strategy a nation has officially established since the choices available to many commanders will remain the same. They will have to use their warheads or face losing them to the enemy. Often the decision to "use them or lose them" will need to be made in the space of a few minutes. Other factors likely to contribute to rapid escalation of global nuclear war include widespread disruption of communications and the probable elimination of many national leaders and command structures in the opening atomic salvos. The early loss of communication links to appropriate command structures would quickly heighten the uncertainity and confusion of the moment. In the midst of these chaotic circumstances it is hard to imagine nuclear forces commanders calmly contemplating their next move. Furthermore, once an enemy's leadership and command structures are gone, who would be able to cooperate in terminating the war? The sum of these independent forces leave little hope for anything less than unchecked escalation to total nuclear war. Thus, when the atomic wars break forth it will be even as God has said; the nations will "be moved and be mad, because of the sword that . . . [He] will send among them."

17 Then took I the cup at the LORD's hand, and made all the nations to drink, unto whom the LORD had sent me: 18 To wit, Jerusalem, and the cities of Judah, and the kings thereof, and the princes thereof, to make them a desolation, an astonishment, an hissing, and a curse; as it is this day; 19 Pharaoh king of Egypt, and his servants, and his princes, and all his people; 20 And all the mingled people, and all the kings of the land of Uz, and all the kings of the land of the Philistines, and Ashkelon, and Azzah, and Ekron, and the remnant of Ashdod, 21 Edom, and Moab, and the children of Ammon, 22 And all the kings of Tyrus, and all the kings of Zidon, and the kings of the isles which are beyond the sea, 23 Dedan, and Tema, and Buz, and all that are in the utmost corners, 24 And all the kings of Arabia, and all the kings of the mingled people that dwell in the desert. 25 And all the kings of Zimri, and all the kings of Elam, and all the kings of the Medes, 26 And all the kings of the north, far and near, one with another, and all the kingdoms of the world, which are upon the face of the earth: and the king of Sheshach shall drink after them. 27 Therefore thou shalt say unto them, Thus saith the LORD of hosts, the God of Israel; Drink ye, and be drunken, and spue, and fall, and rise no more, because of the sword which I will send among you. 28 And it shall be, if they refuse to take the

spread from nation to nation in the form of words, threats, and military actions for centuries. Today's proliferation of nuclear know-how, manufacture of related atomic materials, and ultimately, nuclear weapons development and deployment, has become the final spreading of evil among the nations.

THE DEAD WILL NOT BE BURIED

Jeremiah's closing pronouncement "and the slain of the LORD shall be at that day from one end of the earth even unto the other end of the earth" is in keeping with today's estimates that hundreds of millions will die during and after a global nuclear war. His observation that the dead will be left on the surface of the earth like "dung upon the ground" and "they shall not be lamented, neither gathered, nor buried" (for lack of a safe way to enter the contaminated zones and bury them) is also correct. Even after it becomes safe enough to enter the contaminated zones, it would not be feasible to gather and bury a large fraction of the victims. The reason for this was accidentally found in the ashes of Nagasaki at the end of World War II.

The discovery was made by the first small detachment of Americans to enter Nagasaki in 1945, following the destruction of the city by the second American atomic bomb dropped on Japan at the close of World War II. When the team reached point zero, the designation for the exact center of the blast, one scientist noticed that the army officer next to him was standing in a circle of fine white ash (not thick enough to feel through a man's boot soles)—the remains of a person instantly incinerated by the heat from the explosion. Years later the army officer, Morton Sontheimer, recalled in an article published in the June 29, 1981 issue of Newsweek, that all of the spots of human ashes in the area "looked alike." There was "nothing left to bury." Although Mr. Sontheimer was not aware of it at the time, he had stumbled across the grim future fulfillment of Jeremiah's prophecy.

Jeremiah's panoramic preview of millions of spots of human ashes left on the ground after man's final global nuclear war, reminded him of a pasture with dung left lying upon the ground. His account of nuclear war—"they shall not be gathered, nor buried; they shall be dung upon the ground"—certainly matches what took place at Nagasaki.

Malachi recorded a complement prophecy about man's last nuclear war that details how people will be reduced to ashes from the heat generated by the atomic weapons used in that war.

> 1 For, behold, the day cometh, that shall burn as an oven; and all the proud, yea and all that do wickedly, shall be stubble: and the day that cometh shall burn them up, saith the LORD of hosts, that it shall leave them neither root nor branch. 3 And ye shall tread down the wicked; for they shall be ashes under the soles of your feet in the day that I shall do this, saith the LORD of hosts (Mal. 4:1, 3).

The use of the abrupt introduction "behold, the day cometh, that shall burn as an oven" or furnace, serves to impart the terrible and sudden burning nuclear destruction that will burst forth upon the heads of the wicked during man's last nuclear war. According to Malachi's account, the intense heat from the nuclear firestorms will "burn up the proud, yea and all that do wickedly." When it is over, the remains of the wicked will end up as "ashes under the soles of the feet" of the survivors.

THE SIGNIFICANCE OF ATOMIC PROPHECIES

The coming nuclear destruction of the nations is a common idea of this age. Today almost anyone could predict incredible devastation on the Earth to be an immediate consequence of a nuclear war. Ban-the-bomb demonstrators prove the point. What is news to most people today is the fact that the men who wrote the Bible began recording descriptions of atomic weapons and the calamities they would bring upon the human race over 3,000 years ago.

The important lesson to be learned from the biblical pictures of nuclear destruction is that, collectively, they validate the rest of the Bible's prophecies concerning the nuclear age. For example, if atomic weapons have come to be built according to the awesome scale of destruction spelled out in the Bible so long ago, then so also will Isaiah's prophecy foretelling two future global nuclear wars come to pass. The presence of this same impressive evidence makes it illogical to doubt Isaiah's closing statements describing Christ's return at the end of AWWII.

CHRIST'S TRIUMPHANT RETURN

> **21** And it shall come to pass in that day, that the LORD shall punish the host of the high ones that are on high, and the kings of the earth upon the earth. **22** And they shall be gathered together, as prisoners are gathered in the pit, and shall be shut up in the prison, and after many days shall they be visited (Isa. 24:21–22).

"And it shall come to pass in that day" refers to the day the nations will be systematically leveling the continents in the course of fighting AWWII. This is the day the prophet speaks of when the Lord shall step in and arrest those responsible for starting the world's Second Nuclear War. The kings of the Earth and various other people holding important positions of authority shall be shut up in prison "on that day" for their part in starting AWWII.

"Visited" in the phrase "and after many days shall they be visited" may also be translated as *found wanting or punished*. As used here it means the people in high places around the globe who will help start AWWII will be tried for their crimes, subsequently found guilty of mass murder and rebellion against God and sentenced accordingly.

> **23** Then the moon shall be confounded, and the sun ashamed, when the LORD of hosts shall reign in mount Zion, and in Jerusalem, and before his ancients gloriously (Isa. 24:23).

"The moon shall be confounded, and the sun ashamed" is a reference to the sun and moon's light being blocked by the immense clouds of smoke generated from numerous atomic explosions used in the fighting. The adjectives "confounded" and "ashamed" are used here in the sense that the light from these heavenly bodies will be considerably dimmed as a direct consequence of the planet's atomic-smoke filled atmosphere.

The pronouncement "when the LORD of hosts shall reign in mount Zion, and in Jerusalem" immediately follows the portrait of the sun and moon's light being darkened after AWWII. This places Christ's Second Coming and the establishment of His earthly kingdom immediately after that war. Isaiah's closing statement declares that Christ will descend through the smoke of AWWII and proceed to set up His earthly reign in Jerusalem.

"Before his ancients gloriously" specifically identifies the elders of His people to be His ancient people, the nation of Israel. After the overthrow of the world's kingdoms, those entrusted with authority under Christ's rule will subsequently witness His glorious reign of peace on Earth administered from Jerusalem.

JOEL'S PORTRAIT OF CHRIST'S RETURN

The following passages in Joel also fix the end of AWWII as the time when Christ shall establish His earthly kingdom.

> **30** And I will shew wonders in the heavens and in the earth, blood, and fire, and pillars of smoke. **31** The sun shall be turned into darkness, and the moon into blood, before the great and terrible day of the LORD come (Joel 2:30–31).

The "wonders in the heavens and in the earth" is a description of nuclear explosions on the Earth that shall send the "blood" of vaporized people, along with giant fireballs and "pillars of smoke," miles high into the heavens. Joel then identified the most immediate consequence of numerous "pillars of smoke" lofting vast quantities of black smoke into the Earth's atmosphere as "the sun shall be turned into darkness and the moon into blood." The sun being darkened from atomic smoke clouds by day is a known negative effect of nuclear explosions over cities. The description of the moon turned into blood simply means that the light difracting through the smoke and dust shrouding the planet will make the moon appear blood red in color at night.

Joel then lists the return of the Jews to their original homeland in the latter days and the subsequent establishment of the modern nation of Israel as the first events to look for in the prophecy's fulfillment.

> **1** "For behold, in those days and at that time, when I restore the fortunes of Judah and Jerusalem, **2** I will gather all the nations and bring them down to the valley of Jehoshaphat, and I will enter into judgment with them there, on account of my people and my heritage Israel, because they have scat-

tered them among the nations, and have divided up my land"
(Joel 3:1–2, RSV).

The restoration of "the fortunes of Judah and Jerusalem"
did not come to pass until the modern state of Israel was
established in 1948. This is the correct interpretation since, even
though a remnant returned to Jerusalem after the Babylonian
Captivity, a self-governing Jewish nation did not surface again
until 1948. Hence, Joel is alerting the people who will be living
"in those days," after the "fortunes" of the Jewish state have
been "restored," to look for a gathering of all the nations for a
world war.

Jehoshaphat means "the judgment of Jehovah." The valley
of Jehoshaphat as used here refers to an ancient judgment on
Judah's foes in which the confederated forces of the Ammo-
nites, Moabites, and the inhabitants of mount Seir fought
among themselves en route to attack King Jehoshaphat's forces
at Jerusalem. Before this confederated army was overthrown,
Jahaziel the prophet prophesied before King Jehoshaphat concerning the outcome of the invasion:

> 15 And he said, Hearken ye, all Judah, and ye inhabitants of
> Jerusalem, and thou king Jehoshaphat, Thus saith the LORD
> unto you, Be not afraid nor dismayed by reason of this great
> multitude; for the battle is not yours, but God's. 16 Tomorrow
> go ye down against them: Behold, they come up by the cliff
> of Ziz; and ye shall find them at the end of the brook, before
> the wilderness of Jeruel. 17 Ye shall not need to fight in this
> battle: set yourselves, stand ye still, and see the salvation of
> the LORD with you, O Judah and Jerusalem: fear not, nor be
> dismayed; tomorrow go out against them: for the LORD will
> be with you (2 Chron. 20:15–17).

Hence, the reference to the overthrow of Judah's foes in this
ancient battle serves to supply the manner in which all the
nations will be judged in the Second Nuclear War. In the final
battle of the age Israel will not have to overpower her enemies
since they will fight among themselves and destroy each other,
even as Judah's confederated enemies did in King Jehoshaphat's day.

The conclusion of Joel's prophecy repeats the description of
the destruction of the nations in a second all-out atomic war

"before the great and terrible day of the LORD comes" (Joel 2:31). Joel's use of repetition pronounces the certainty of the establishment of Christ's earthly kingdom of peace, immediately after AWWII.

> **14** Multitudes, multitudes in the valley of decision: for the day of the LORD is near in the valley of decision. **15** The sun and the moon shall be darkened, and the stars shall withdraw their shining (Joel 3:14–15).

The phrase "multitudes, multitudes," is a Hebraism for immense multitudes. "In the valley of decision" is a reference back to "the valley of Jehoshaphat," i.e., "the valley of judgment," where the nations shall meet their determined doom.

The statement that "the day of the LORD is near in the valley of decision" indicates that the return of the Lord to set up His earthly kingdom will be even at the doors when all the nations assemble their armies for one final, all-out, world war.

The repeated portrait of the sun and moon being darkened and the stars withdrawing their shining reaffirms the fact that this phenomenon will be a direct consequence of the smoke generated by AWWII.

> **16** The LORD also shall roar out of Zion, and utter his voice from Jerusalem; and the heavens and the earth shall shake: but the LORD will be the hope of his people, and the strength of the children of Israel. **17** So shall ye know that I am the LORD your God dwelling in Zion, my holy mountain: then shall Jerusalem be holy, and there shall no strangers pass through her any more (Joel 3:16–17).

"The heavens and the earth shall shake" describes the tremendous blast forces from the exploding nuclear bombs used in the fighting.

The sentence "So shall ye know that I am the LORD your God dwelling in Zion, my holy mountain" implies that the Jewish people will finally recognize Jesus Christ as the Lord God of Israel. They will believe He is their God and Savior because His return and presence in Jerusalem shall fulfill the prophecies recorded by their prophets. When Christ arrives in Jerusalem, "no strangers shall pass through Jerusalem any more" to attack the city, or disrupt His earthly reign of peace.

The Bible's report on the aftermath of nuclear war is of profound importance to those living during the closing days of the nuclear age. First, the Bible confirms today's scientific findings predicting global famine in the wake of large-scale nuclear war. Knowing the size of the First Nuclear War—"the third part of the earth was burnt up" (Rev. 8:7)—enables today's God-fearing people to prepare for the post-AWWI famine in advance. Yet, the famine resulting from the First Atomic War's nuclear winter aftereffects will be a minor inconvenience when compared to the prophesied Second Nuclear War that will leave the nations in ruins. In light of the fact that modern man's technically advanced civilization is about to be destroyed by the nuclear weapons of his own making, the first priority of God's people should be to use the time remaining before Christ returns to give His message of salvation to a dying world.

10 Leviathan— The Sea Monster

In view of the Bible's forecast of massive loss of life from global nuclear war, Christians may well feel that their chances of surviving AWWI are preposterously remote. Even worse, Christians often think there is nothing they can do to avoid the coming atomic catastrophe anyway, so what is God's point in instructing them about this war in advance? These instructions are as important as the ones given to Noah's generation. In the days of Noah people could follow God's advice and put forth the effort to build a boat to ride out the prophesied flood, or they could perish when the catastrophe arrived. The nuclear generation can prepare for the First Trumpet Atomic War according to God's plan or suffer the consequences for not heeding His instructions.

The guidelines on how to prepare for AWWI are found in the book of Isaiah directly after a song of praise prophesied to be sung by the Jews living in the restored nation of Israel. In Isaiah's day it was a song of hope for the exiled Jews living in Babylon.

THE RETURNING JEWS' SONG OF PRAISE

1 In that day this song will be sung in the land of Judah: We have a strong city; God makes salvation its walls and ramparts (Isa. 26:1, NIV).

The phrase "in that day this song will be sung in the land of Judah" identifies the first thing to look for in the prophecies' fulfillment—the return of the Jews to their ancient dwelling place "in the land of Judah."

The statement "God makes salvation its walls and ramparts" means that God would direct the Jews' return and be the protector of His people in the place of walls and fortifications. The complete fulfillment of the prophecy, however, will not occur until Christ removes the need to defend the restored Jewish State, the day He establishes His promised reign of peace.

Isaiah's prophecy continues to list the praises which "will be sung in that day in the land of Judah" when the Jewish people are enjoying the peace and safety established by Christ's just rule.

> 12 LORD, you establish peace for us; all that we have accomplished you have done for us. 13 O LORD, our God, other lords besides you have ruled over us, but your name alone do we honor. 14 They are now dead, they live no more; those departed spirits do not rise. You punished them and brought them to ruin; you wiped out all memory of them (Isa. 26:12–14, NIV).

"In that day" of peace and safety the Jewish people will praise God for all that He has done for them. They will give special thanks to God for His judgment of all those who oppressed them in former times. They will not have to honor or even remember the evil rulers who enjoyed injuring them in the past.

THE RESTORED NATION'S EXTENDED BORDERS

> 15 You have enlarged the nation, O LORD; you have enlarged the nation. You have gained glory for yourself; you have extended all the borders of the land (Isa. 26:15, NIV).

The borders of the restored Jewish nation are foretold to be extended a considerable distance beyond the boundaries of the original kingdom. Modern Israel has expanded its borders on more than one occasion, which is in keeping with the repeated reference to the enlargement of the restored nation's borders beyond its original frontiers.

REFLECTIONS ON THE JEWS' DISPERSION

16 LORD, they came to you in their distress; when you disciplined them, they could barely whisper a prayer (Isa. 26:16, NIV). **17** Like as a woman with child, that draweth near the time of her delivery, is in pain, and crieth out in her pangs; so have we been in thy sight, O LORD. **18** We have been with child, we have been in pain, we have as it were brought forth wind; we have not wrought any deliverance in the earth; neither have the inhabitants of the world fallen (vv. 17–18).

Here the song of praise shifts to the desperate condition of the Jewish people during the days of the Babylonian captivity and the succeeding centuries before they were once again established as a nation in 1948. During those centuries of calamity the people could barely call to God for help. The depth of their suffering and pain is compared to that of a woman crying out in pain as the time of her delivery draws near. The Jews initial efforts, from time to time, to re-establish their nation is further compared to a woman who is too weak to deliver her child— "we have as it were brought forth wind." The Jews simply did not have the power to deliver their land from the various pagan nations that ruled Palestine after the Babylonians conquered Jerusalem. Thus, the foreign inhabitants of the world did not fall, but remained in control of the ancient land of Israel until 1948.

ISRAEL'S RESTORATION FORETOLD

19 Thy dead shall live, their bodies shall rise. O dwellers in the dust, awake and sing for joy! For thy dew is a dew of light, and on the land of the shades thou wilt let it fall (Isa. 26:19, RSV).

The statement, "thy dead shall live," continues the allegorical description of the prostrate Jewish nation under the imagery of dead men. The introduction of this new imagery conveys the final disposition of the vanquished Jews' efforts to give birth to a restored Jewish state—their efforts eventually died. As the Jewish people moved from nation to nation, and over time to the far corners of the world, active movements to re-establish the nation of Israel among the list of nations died out. The Jews did not have a king, a government, or even a homeland to return to for hundreds of years. For all practical purposes they were a nation of dead men.

The purpose of the prophetic statement in the words "thy dead shall live, their bodies shall rise" is to draw attention to the future restoration of the Jewish people to their original homeland. The twentieth century witnessed large numbers of Jews awakening from the dust and ashes of oppression in foreign nations to return to the land of their forefathers. Their subsequent successful bid to once again become a bonafide nation among the nations, is certainly a remarkable fulfillment of Isaiah's prophecy.

As the dew that falls from heaven revives withered plants in parched earth, so would the Spirit of God be instrumental in bringing light to the land of the shades, or shadows, the deceased nation of Israel. The prophecy, therefore, promises God's hand in restoring to life and health the destroyed and dead nation of Israel.

Isaiah's review of the miraculous restoration of the nation of Israel is followed by an urgent message. The message is addressed to the people who will be living during the days when the reinstated nation has "extended all the borders of the land" (Isa. 26:15, NIV).

GUIDELINES FOR SURVIVING AWWI

20 Come, my people, enter your chambers, and shut your doors behind you; hide yourselves for a little while until the wrath is past (Isa. 26:20, RSV).

The prophecy's abrupt opening "Come, my people, enter your chambers, and shut your doors behind you" awakens God's people to the alarming speed with which an overwhelming calamity is already approaching them. (Even though the prophecy was recorded over twenty-seven centuries ago, the day the nuclear generation awakens to its meaning the danger will already be closing fast upon them.) Note here that "enter *your* chambers" and "shut *your* doors behind *you*" names the listener as the responsible party for carrying out this directive. "Hide *yourselves*" also directs the listener to personally implement these orders. The sum of this personalized possessive language eliminates the possibility that this prophecy is a reference to the supernatural rapture of the Church. The tone of the initial compelling call to attention, therefore, clearly urges the audience to literally "hide yourselves for a little while." The closing comment, "until the wrath is past," advises the listener to stay hidden until the danger has passed completely from the vicinity.

Careful inspection of the overall design of the introduction reveals what the alarming approaching danger might be. For example, the imagery of the prophecy is taken from the need to quickly seek shelter from the face of a raging storm until its fury is spent. Some translations substitute *indignation*, which is a word that can mean fury, for *wrath* here. The word *past* in Hebrew means "passes over." Thus, the general message of the text advises God's people to quickly seek shelter in the face of a future violent storm and to stay put until the full fury of that storm "passes over" them. The next verse reveals the nature of the coming storm to be a worldwide atomic firestorm.

> **21** For behold, the LORD is coming forth out of his place to punish the inhabitants of the earth for their iniquity, and the earth will disclose the blood shed upon her, and will no more cover her slain (Isa. 26:21, RSV).

The phrase "the earth will disclose the blood shed upon her, and will no more cover her slain" is equivalent to Jeremiah's graphic description of the vast numbers of dead left on the ground after a global nuclear exchange: "And the slain of the LORD shall be at that day from one end of the earth even unto the other end of the earth: They shall not be lamented, neither gathered, nor buried; they shall be dung upon the ground" (Jer. 25:33). Thus, the future storm God's people are exhorted to seek shelter from will be a global nuclear firestorm.

The statement "the LORD is coming forth out of his place to punish the inhabitants of the earth for their iniquity" identifies the heavens (the dwelling-place of God) to be the direction from whence the atomic attack will come. It does not mean that God himself will rain atomic fire on the Earth's inhabitants. To make certain no one would get this incorrect impression Isaiah carefully closed this prophecy with a detailed description of the weapons system that will rain the bulk of the atomic fire on the Earth's inhabitants in the last days.

ATOMIC MISSILE-FIRING SUBS

1 In that day the LORD with his sore and great and strong sword shall punish leviathan the piercing serpent, even leviathan that crooked serpent; and he shall slay the dragon that is in the sea (Isa. 27:1).

Isaiah named the weapons system which will launch the bulk of the city smashing nuclear-tipped missiles at the end of the age, "leviathan the piercing serpent." In ancient Babylon and Canaan, Leviathan was a mythological sea monster known for its ability to devour on a large scale. Isaiah's employment of this ancient marine symbol to represent a modern nuclear missile carrying submarine is excellent. For example, the 560 foot long U.S. Trident and the 600 foot long Soviet Typhoon boomer subs are not only monsters in size, but they are also capable of destroying 200 or more cities and their inhabitants in less than one hour.

Isaiah noted further that these Leviathan-like sea monsters are capable of inflicting lethal wounds on unsuspecting people in a manner which is similar in some respects to the deadly strike of a "piercing serpent." A "piercing serpent" delivers its deadly wound by piercing the flesh of its victim with its sharp fangs. People caught by the deadly winds of an atomic blast are likewise killed suddenly when they are pierced by sharp flying debris moving at many hundreds of miles per hour.

"Even leviathan that crooked serpent" is rendered "Leviathan the twisting serpent" in the RSV. Both crooked and twisting describe the tactical maneuvers of modern monsterlike subs locked in mortal subsea combat. In a confrontation, high performance submarines on both sides would twist, turn and dive, while simultaneously firing torpedoes and dodging them. Swirling battles in the ocean depths among today's advanced subs would be more like aerial combat than the stealthy, slow-moving submarine maneuvers of the past. Hence, Isaiah selected a Hebrew word equivalent to twisting or crooked to describe the phenomenal speed and agility with which modern man's huge underwater boats move when they are engaged in a slugfest beneath the waves.

In closing, Isaiah noted that these man-made sea monsters will conduct themselves with the cunning of a "dragon who lives in the sea" (NASB). Mythical dragons were often viewed as dreadful creatures, hiding in dens where they would silently wait for the right moment to pounce on an unaware prey. The primary objective of today's strategic missile toting subs, in the true tradition of the legendary dragons of old, is to remain completely silent and hidden from view until the day they receive war orders to annihilate whole cities full of unsuspecting people. Submarines can maintain a minimum detection profile for weeks by simply "camping" in a shallow coastal canyon—whose contours hide the submarine from all surveillance.

More and more in recent times the superpowers are opting to hide their big subs under the Arctic Ocean's permanent polar icecap. When submarines glide beneath the polar ice floes, they enter a different undersea world which is in effect a vast, water-filled cave. The waters may be 3 miles deep and the ice overhead, 30 or 40 feet thick. Danger is everywhere with huge "keels" of ice, instead of icebergs, extending as deep as 900 feet. Yet, in the midst of this inhospitable eerie kingdom there are spots known by their Russian name, *polynya*, where melting has reduced the thickness of the ice by a considerable amount. These cavernlike havens provide a safe place for subs to quietly "ice pick"—submarine jargon for parking a sub against the underside of the Arctic ice cap—for weeks on end. Once inside they are virtually free from enemy detection at the present time.

From their secure vantage points under the polar ice, specially designed subs such as the Soviet Typhoon boomer can break through several feet of ice just prior to missile launch. This creates a small patch of relatively open water through which their missiles can be fired. Thus missile-firing subs can burst out of their icy caverns to attack hapless cities in much the same way mythical dragons were perceived as bursting through the vines and brush hiding the entranceways to their dens, before attacking unwary prey.

It should also be pointed out that modern man's dragonlike subs do "live" submerged "in the sea" for extended periods of time. Nuclear powered Trident's, for example, have a ten-year

ing, emphasizes the absolute necessity of hiding in a first-class bomb shelter during a nuclear attack. NAPB-90 also echoes Isaiah's initial advice that once "your doors" are "shut behind you," stay securely locked in "until the wrath is past." That is, stay inside until the radioactive fallout in the air has diminished to the point where it is completely safe to breathe outside air again.

Today's Christians need to begin preparing for AWWI in a practical way. The first step should be the development of an economical plan for building full function fallout shelters. The standard unit should provide adequate protection from outside radiation penetration, an effective gamma radiation air filtering system, a safe method for securing or storing water, sewage facilities and ample space to store food and clothing—not only for the first few aftermath months when the outside radiation levels will be high, but also for the foretold famine and years of continuing crop contamination that will follow in the war's wake.

Needless to say, the construction of a bomb shelter represents a very large commitment in terms of planning, money, time, and raw work—just like building a massive boat to ride out the flood was for Noah and his family in their day. Yet the alternative carries a much higher price tag when the bombs come. A person cannot hope to live if the air being breathed contains lethal levels of radioactive fallout.

So in the days ahead it will be "just as it was in the days of Noah" (Luke 17:26, NIV). Some will heed God's advice to prepare for the coming atomic holocaust and set about building substantial bomb shelters and some will not. Many of those who choose not to do so will meet their end according to the words of Isaiah's prophetic vision: "and the earth will disclose the blood shed upon her, and will no more cover her slain" (Isa. 26:21, RSV).

THERE WILL BE TIME TO ESCAPE

One thing to keep in mind is that according to Ezek. 38:13 "Sheba, Dedan and the merchants of Tarshish" will protest when Russia begins moving massive numbers of troops into Palestine prior to their invasion of Israel. Although Bible prophecy shows that diplomacy will fail to get the Russians out, the diplomatic effort will take some time. Within that period of diplomatic parrying, Christians will be able to get out of the cities to their bomb shelters in the country where they can enter their chambers and shut their doors behind them. (Bomb shelters should probably be built at least 50 miles beyond any city or military target since bomb blast overpressures, heat, and severe radiation would kill the occupants inside the typical homemade shelter if it were built within the zones where the bombs would go off.) Christians who heed God's advanced instructions and seal themselves in behind the closed doors of their bomb shelters will live through the nuclear battles of the First Trumpet Atomic War.

According to John's prophetic imagery of one "U.S." eagle flying in mid-heaven warning those dwelling on the Earth concerning the remaining three trumpet events yet to come, a large number of U.S. Christians will survive AWWI inside their bomb shelters. They will also be positioned to launch a global evangelistic outreach during the days of the Fifth Trumpet Nuclear Winter. It is also obvious that these same U.S. Christians will be part of the world's greater body of believers referred to as having "the seal of God on their foreheads" in the post-AWWI period.

PART
4

THE BIBLE'S DEFINITION OF "THE TIME OF THE END"

11 The Captain of the Lord's Host

Although the majority of today's Christians believe they are living in the "latter days," there are widely differing interpretations of the Scriptures pertaining to those days. This regrettable situation creates confusion, and it is a stumbling-block to the unbeliever. These conflicts need to be resolved.

Believers are instructed to "all speak the same thing . . . in the same mind and in the same judgment" (1 Cor. 1:10). If Christians are all "taught of God" (John 6:45), then they ought to arrive at the same basic conclusions.

THE DEFINITION OF BIBLE PROPHECY

By definition Bible prophecy is the prediction of things future according to a direct communication from God to a member of the human race. The definition requires that every Bible prophecy must have a specific fulfillment. This fact raises two questions. Can Bible prophecy be understood before it comes to pass? And, if the answer is yes, how can the correct interpretation of prophecies pertaining to the end times be determined prior to their occurrence?

A SHEEPHERDER'S PROPHETIC PERSPECTIVE

According to the words of one of the sheepherders from Tekoa who became known as Amos the prophet, prophecy is meant to be understood before it comes to pass.

7 Surely the LORD God does nothing Unless He reveals His secret counsel To His servants the prophets (Amos 3:7, NASB).

Amos promised here that God will not allow judgment to come upon people without advance warning. This truth at once pronounces the lengthy list of prophecies addressed to the modern world to be of utmost importance to today's Christian community. In practical terms Bible prophecy allows the people who are living close to the time of a prophecy's fulfillment the opportunity to prepare for the event before it takes place.

JOEL'S CHARGE TO POSTERITY

When a prophesied event is a major calamity, the prophetic forewarning can mean the difference between life and death for the listener. The Bible documents several past examples of how such a prophetic forewarning enabled God's people to escape certain destruction. Noah and his family's deliverance from the great flood is one well-known case in point. The Bible's vivid description of the violent atomic wars that will be fought in the last days of the nuclear age is a more contemporary example. The prophet Joel was well aware of how important it would be for the people of the nuclear age to be apprised of his prophetic description of these future nuclear wars. His charge to subsequent generations to make sure his prophecy was passed on to the present age speaks for itself:

3 Tell ye your children of it, and let your children tell their children, and their children another generation (Joel 1:3).

THE SEARCH FOR CORRECT INTERPRETATION

Once the fundamental definition of Bible prophecy and the importance of knowing what the future will bring are understood, a serious investigation of how to establish the correct interpretation of Bible prophecies addressed to the time of the end can begin in earnest.

The prophets themselves do not offer much help in the area of interpretation since they never claimed to be the source of the visions. Nor did they add their own interpretations to the revelations they received from the Lord. Instead, they simply introduced their prophetic subject with statements such as "For thus saith the Lord God of Israel" (Jer. 25:15). Without exception they continued to name the Lord throughout their texts as the one who was speaking with authority about the future.

Daniel the prophet's closing comment to his series of prophecies to the nations of the last days provides an example: "And I heard, but I understood not" (Dan. 12:8). Here, in addition to acknowledging God as the author of the visions he recorded for posterity, Daniel emphatically stated that he had no understanding whatsoever of the specific meaning of these prophecies.

The fact that prophets such as Daniel often did not understand the prophecies they recorded raises an obvious question: How would the future generation to whom the "latter day" prophecies were addressed know that they were indeed the generation spoken of, instead of one yet to come? The answer to this question was supplied to Daniel in his final vision concerning the events leading up to the second coming of Christ.

DANIEL DEFINES THE TIME OF THE END

4 But thou, O Daniel, shut up the words, and seal the book, even to the time of the end: many shall run to and fro, and knowledge shall be increased (Dan. 12:4).

This directive decrees that the prophecies Daniel addressed to the nations of the last days would not be opened to anyone, until "the time of the end." Without exception, all other prophetic scriptures addressed to the nations of the last days were also sealed by this decree, until "the time of the end".

The command to "seal the book, even to the time of the end," is followed by a precise definition of when "the time of the end" would arrive: "many shall run to and fro, and knowledge shall be increased." The twentieth century's mass manufacture and widespread use of motorized transportation vehicles literally enabled men to move rapidly "to and fro" on the land, over the seas, and through the air. Twentieth century man's love affair with affordable and efficient methods of travel marked the fulfillment of the first sign to look for in determining "the time of the end." The second sign—"and knowledge shall be increased"—followed directly on the heels of the unprecedented transportation revolution. Over the course of a few decades the knowledge explosion of the twentieth century quickly outdistanced the sum of knowledge accumulated by all previous generations and continues to do so at an ever increasing rate.

TECHNOLOGY EXPLOSION
BROKE PROPHETIC SEALS

According to Daniel's prophecy, once the conditions of the definition of "the time of the end" have been met, then the seals withholding the meaning of Bible prophecies directed to the time of the end would be broken. Today's knowledge explosion has in fact removed many of the mysteries of Bible prophecy, especially those detailing modern man's achievements in technology. For while today's knowledge explosion was rapidly producing a vast array of new technical achievements, the presence of these same technologies began the process of opening up a number of "sealed" prophecies that had remained "closed" to the sons of men since ancient times.

To see how quickly a new invention unlocked the meaning of several prophetic passages, consider what occurred when America detonated the first atomic bomb. The ensuing explosion caused "the heavens and the earth to shake" (Joel 3:16) as the "whirlwind" (Jer. 23:19) from the blast sent "pillars of smoke" (Joel 2:30) high into the heavens, where it "turned the sun and air into darkness" (Rev. 9:2; Joel 2:31). Egypt's successful construction of a modern superdam astride the Nile river in 1964 shattered another ancient prophetic seal.

This seal had kept Isaiah's three prophesied events to look for prior to the second coming of Christ "shut up" from the understanding of men for centuries. In like manner, high-tech inventions such as computers, communications satellites, and space shuttle orbiters have systematically unlocked several other biblical prophecies of profound importance to today's world.

Collectively, modern man's inventions provide the insight needed to determine the correct interpretation of many mysterious Bible prophecies. These same inventions also serve to announce the twentieth century to be "the time of the end" (Dan. 12:9).

THE PROCESS OF INTERPRETING "TIME OF THE END" PROPHECY

A conversation Daniel recorded at the end of his book sheds more light on the relationship between today's inventions and the process of correctly interpreting Scriptures addressed to the time of the end:

> **8** "My lord, what will be the outcome of these events?" (Dan. 12:8, NASB). **9** And he said, "Go thy way, Daniel: for the words are closed up and sealed till the time of the end . . . (v. 9). **10** None of the wicked will understand, but those who have insight will understand" (v. 10, NASB).

The answer Daniel received states that a day will arrive in the future when God's people will come to understand "the outcome of these events;" but that day will not arrive until "the time of the end." Since verse four previously defined the arrival of a transportation revolution followed by a knowledge explosion as "the time of the end," then in practical terms the inventions coming out of modern man's increasing knowledge base are the visible items supplying the "insight" needed to correctly interpret "the outcome of these events." Today's prudent student of the Bible can acquire this "insight" by comparing a biblical description of a modern invention with the invention itself.

CHRONOLOGICAL LISTS OF EVENTS

Prophetic insight into "the time of the end" visions also requires a chronological list of the events leading up to the Second Coming of Christ. This list of events helps answer the question of how long will "the time of the end" continue before Christ returns. Isaiah's Egyptian "hourglass" prophecy provides one list of events leading up to Christ's return. His directions on how to tell time with this gigantic prophetic clock include the following steps:

(1) Look for the construction of a prophetic clock upon the ancient sands of modern Egypt "at the time of the end."

(2) The clock's workings will be set in motion the day a modern superdam successfully blocks the flow of the mighty Nile river.

(3) The systematic environmental collapse of the Nile Valley as a direct result of the High Dam's side effects will serve as the visible source of energy needed to keep the clock's precision mechanism running properly.

(4) The subsequent shadows of despair and desolation cast across the dying land of Egypt will serve as hands on the clock's face, pointing to the amount of time left in the period of years prophetically defined as "the time of the end."

(5) The total collapse of Egypt's entire agricultural system will cause the workings of the prophetic clock to grind to a stop.

(6) The utter ruin of Egypt will mark the end of the prophetic clock's usefulness, which in turn will signal the end of the period of time referred to as "the time of the end."

(7) Christ will return and set up His earthly kingdom of peace directly following the fulfillment of these events.

Isaiah's instructions teach that "the time of the end" will not be played out over the course of several centuries. The massive accumulation of environmental damage inflicted upon Egypt in the first twenty years following the 1964 blocking of the Nile supports this conclusion.

A more comprehensive chronological list of milestones leading up to the Second Coming of Christ was given to the apostle John in the form of the book of Revelation at the close of the first century. John's account was written for the purpose of tying together all previously given "latter day" prophecies into a complete picture of the events leading up to Christ's return at the end of the age. The book of Revelation begins with an overview of how the book came into the possession of the human race.

OVERVIEW OF THE BOOK OF REVELATION

1 The revelation of Jesus Christ, which God gave him to show to his servants what must soon take place; and he made it known by sending his angel to his servant John (Rev. 1:1, RSV).

The word revelation means to uncover. It applies to the act of removing whatever is covering up an object hidden from the beholders view. Since previewing future events is beyond the reach of mortal men, Jesus Christ removed this barrier for those who believe in Him by personally laying out the important milestone events of the future in the Book of Revelation.

"To show," from a Greek word that commonly denotes "to point out" or "to cause to see," is an appropriate translation here since symbols are employed throughout the book of Revelation to reveal the things of the future. God in His infinite wisdom determined that symbolic pictures were the best means for conveying the outcome of future events and so gave them to Christ to present to His servants.

"To show his servants," defines the audience receiving Christ's message as the people who believe in Him; i.e., the world's Christian community. This same restriction was established for Daniel's prophecies: "None of the wicked will understand, but those who have insight will understand" (Dan. 12:10, NASB). This means that only those who are interested in the things of the Lord—Christ's "servants"—will be given "insight" into these prophecies at "the time of the end" (Dan. 12:9). Dan. 12:3 confirms this truth and also defines the Christian's responsibility to the unbelievers around him:

3 "And those who have insight will shine brightly like the brightness of the expanse of heaven, and those who lead the many to righteousness, like the stars forever and ever (Dan. 12:3, NASB).

Today's Christians will be the first people to gain insight into the mysteries of Bible prophecy addressed to the modern world. These same Christians will use their insight into the mysteries of the future to lead many unbelievers around the world to Christ.

"What must soon take place" does not mean the events described in this book will take place shortly, but that when they do begin to happen they will start suddenly and continue to occur with speed until the day Christ returns. The Greek word rendered here as *soon* literally means "with speed." Since the book of Revelation lists the First Trumpet Atomic War as the first major event to occur at the time of the end, it can be readily seen that that war will break out suddenly and proceed with speed to its conclusion. Compared to mankind's previous 6,000 years of recorded history, the succession of events foretold to occur following AWWI will also come to pass in rapid succession.

In summary, John's introduction states that the book of Revelation is a message from Jesus Christ, the faithful witness, who taught men all that He heard from the Father (John 15:15). Christ is unique in being "the first-born of the dead" (Rev. 1:5, RSV). He not only rose from the grave, but rose from death to immortality. Moreover, His death was accepted by God as payment in full for the sins of all mankind. "And to as many as received him, to them gave he power to become the sons of God, even to them that believe on his name" (John 1:12). This fact enables those who believe in Christ to become part of His everlasting kingdom and "priests to His God and Father" (Rev. 1:6, RSV). It is Christ's power that enables Christ's servants to understand the mysterious "time of the end" events foretold in the book of Revelation.

7 BEHOLD, HE IS COMING WITH THE CLOUDS, and every eye will see him, even those who pierced him: and all the tribes of the earth will mourn over him. Even so. Amen (Rev. 1:7, NASB).

Here, John introduced the Second Coming of Christ as the primary reason for presenting the book's prophecies to Christ's servants. His return will be a major event which will not be missed by anyone dwelling on the planet.

According to Zechariah's complement prophecy, "even those who pierced him" is a specific reference to the modern nation of Israel's reaction to Christ's return.

10 "And I will pour out on the house of David and the inhabitants of Jerusalem a spirit of compassion and supplication, so that, when they look on him whom they have pierced, they shall mourn for him, as one mourns for an only child,

and weep bitterly over him, as one weeps over a first-born" (Zech. 12:10, RSV).

Thus, when Israel's citizens realize that Christ is the same Jesus that died on the cross long ago, they will repent for their personal rejection of Him and be grieved in soul. So also will many people around the world repent with sadness over their rebellion against God through their personal rejection of Christ.

JESUS CHRIST IS GOD

8 "I am the Alpha and the Omega," says the Lord God, "who is, and who was, and who is to come, the Almighty" (Rev. 1:8, RSV).

Alpha and Omega are the first and last letters of the Greek alphabet. The phrase is equivalent to saying that He has always existed and always will exist. Isaiah used this same language to identify God:

6 Thus saith the LORD the King of Israel, and his redeemer the LORD of hosts; I am the first, and I am the last; and beside me there is no God (Isa. 44:6).

Thus, the language in Revelation identifies Christ as God. Further, the expression, "who is, and who was, and who is to come," is the same one used to identify God the Father in verse four. Hence, this expression also serves to identify Christ as the eternal God; i.e., Christ is present today; He was present in the past; and He will be present in the future when He comes to establish His earthly kingdom of peace.

John repeated this same language at the end of Revelation 1 for the purpose of firmly identifying Christ as God.

CHRIST'S POWER AND AUTHORITY

17 And when I saw him, I fell at his feet as dead. And he laid his right hand upon me, saying unto me, Fear not; I am the first and the last: 18 I am he that liveth, and was dead; and, behold, I am alive for evermore, Amen; and have the keys of hell and of death (Rev. 1:17–18).

The reference to Christ's resurrection after His death on the cross immediately identifies the One speaking here as Jesus Christ.

The keys Christ holds to hell and death describe the magnitude of His power and authority. Mention of these keys at the close of His opening statements serves as a solemn reminder of the importance of the prophetic message that follows.

People often fail to see that Jesus Christ is God. Yet, when the Jews asked Him: "If thou be the Christ, tell us plainly" (John 10:24); Jesus plainly answered: "I and my Father are one" (John 10:30). The Jews certainly understood Christ's answer to be an affirmation that He was God, since they "took up stones again to stone him" (John 10:31) for such blasphemy. The Jews' violent reaction to Christ's declaration that He was God prompted Him to make the following additional statement on the matter:

> **37** "If I am not doing the works of my Father, then do not believe me; **38** but if I do them, even though you do not believe me, believe the works, that you may know and understand that the Father is in me and I am in the Father" (John 10:37–38, RSV).

The Jews understood Christ's additional statements on this subject to be a second declaration that He was God in the flesh; and they again attempted to punish Him in the same manner (John 10:39).

Many Jews in Christ's day rejected His message because He plainly told them He was God in the flesh. It is important not to repeat this past mistake when seeking the correct interpretation of Bible prophecy addressed to the time of the end. For failure to believe Christ's plainly spoken statement that He and his Father were one (John 10:30) immediately calls into question the validity of every statement Christ ever made. Needless to say, those who persist in fashioning Christ into someone who is a little less than God, "the almighty" (Rev. 1:8), will find their attempts to understand the correct interpretation of Christ's prophecies instantly shattered on the rocks of further doubt and unbelief.

> **1** And I saw in the right hand of Him who sat on the throne a book written inside and on the back, sealed up with seven seals. **2** And I saw a strong angel proclaiming with a loud

voice, "Who is worthy to open the book and to break its seals?" 3 And no one in heaven, or on the earth, or under the earth, was able to open the book, or to look into it (Rev. 5:1–3, NASB).

At this point in the vision, John is shown the closed book of Revelation resting in the right hand of God. A strong angel then invites anyone who considers himself worthy and able, to step forward and break the seven seals and open the book. "And no one," neither human nor angelic beings, in all the universe of creation, "was able to open the book" and view what its contents had to say about the future.

4 And I began to weep greatly, because no one was found worthy to open the book, or to look into it; 5 and one of the elders said to me, "Stop weeping; behold, the Lion that is from the tribe of Judah, the Root of David, has overcome so as to open the book and its seven seals" (Rev. 5:4–5, NASB).

John is then told to "stop weeping" because Jesus Christ, who was born into the tribe of Judah in the line of David, "has overcome so as to open the book and its seven seals." How Christ acquired the power to open the book is explained in verse 9:

9 And they sang a new song, saying, "Worthy art Thou to take the book, and to break its seals; for Thou wast slain, and didst purchase for God with Thy blood men from every tribe and tongue and people and nation" (Rev. 5:9, NASB).

The new song sung by the heavenly host speaks of fallen man's redemption through Christ's blood and death, with which He purchased the souls of all those who would believe in Him. The price Christ paid also made Him worthy to reveal to His servants those things that would come to pass in the future.

After this John sees Christ open the seven seals of the book. The first six seals present a general introduction of what is contained in the book. When Christ breaks the seventh seal, the book is opened.

THE REVELATION COMPLETES
ALL END TIME VISIONS

It should be pointed out that the opened portion of the book of Revelation contains the central message of the document. The introductory material preceding the opening of the seven seals serves only to set the stage for the main prophetic communication of the book.

The opened book of Revelation begins with the sounding of seven trumpets. Each trumpet's warning message will take place over the course of a future period of time. The trumpet time-periods vary in duration. Some will last only a matter of days; others will span years. Each trumpet warning highlights the most important events taking place during the days of the prophecy's fulfillment. Collectively, the trumpet prophecies detail the most significant milestone events leading up to the establishment of Christ's earthly kingdom of peace. The first trumpet event describes the world's First Atomic War. The seventh trumpet time-period ends with the world's Second Atomic War. The overwhelming majority of biblical prophecy addressed to "the time of the end" fills in the details of what will come to pass between these two nuclear wars. In fact, most of the rest of the book of Revelation simply supplies further information on what will take place during the time the trumpet events are coming to pass.

This outline of the book of Revelation's overall design completes the list of items needed to determine the correct interpretation of Bible prophecies addressed to "the time of the end." That list includes:

(1) Daniel's definition of when "the time of the end" would arrive: "many shall run to and fro, and knowledge shall be increased."

(2) The knowledge explosion's introduction of modern achievements in technology and by-product supply of the "insight" needed to correctly interpret "the outcome" of "the time of the end" events.

(3) Prophetic insight into "the time of the end" visions also requires the book of Revelation's master chronological list of events leading up to the Second Coming of Christ.

(4) Prophetic insight is only given to those who have received Christ's "power to become the sons of God" (John

1:12), Christ's "servants." Christians know that Jesus Christ is God in the flesh, the author of the Bible's prophecies about "the time of the end" events.

(5) A basic understanding of the overall design of the book of Revelation gained from a comparison between the text's prophetic descriptions of today's modern inventions and the inventions themselves.

Ezekiel's account of the Russian-led invasion of Israel provides a practical example of how the process of determining the correct interpretation of a "time of the end" prophecy actually works. For instance, it would not be clear from Ezekiel's brief statement—"And I shall send fire upon Magog and those who inhabit the coastlands in safety" (Ezek. 39:6, NASB)—whether or not Ezekiel was referring to a global thermonuclear war. However, when a comparison is made between Ezekiel's text and the Revelation description of the First Trumpet Atomic War, the scriptural facts reveal that both prophecies are indeed addressing the same subject.

Confirmation of this position begins with a review of the principal points made in both prophecies. Ezekiel opened his prophecy with a lengthy description of the massive size of a Russian-led invasion force against the restored nation of Israel. He then interrupts his report on the course of the ensuing battle with an announcement that the war in the Middle East has suddenly escalated into an unprecedented global conflict involving the "sending" of "fire upon Magog and those who inhabit the coastlands in safety" (Ezek. 39:6, NASB). The first trumpet prophecy describes this same unprecedented global nuclear fire-fight in greater detail: "and there occurred hail and fire having been mixed in with blood and it was cast to the earth; and the third (part) of the earth was burnt (up)" (Rev. 8:7, IGENT). Ezekiel followed his announcement of the global atomic war with a description of a worldwide awakening to God's presence in the larger scheme of all things: "and they shall know that I am the LORD" (Ezek. 39:6). The Revelation account again echoes Ezekiel's report with a specific reference to how one "U.S." eagle flying in mid-heaven will use its global satellite broadcasting facilities to teach the world about the Creator God of all mankind.

Thus, the precisely corresponding Revelation trumpet prophecies about the First Atomic War provide the cross veri-

The Captain of the Lord's host simply asked Joshua to humble himself and take off his shoes. The Captain then briefed Joshua on the battle plan He had prepared against the city of Jericho.

> 2 And the Lord said unto Joshua, See, I have given into thine hand Jericho, and the king thereof, and the mighty men of valour (Joshua 6:2).

The Captain assured Joshua that indeed Jericho would be destroyed. The Captain of the Lord's host also informed Joshua that He was going to knock the formidable walls of Jericho down and give Joshua the plan of attack. Joshua and his fellow soldiers' part in the battle turned out to be a relatively minor role.

> 3 And ye shall compass the city, all ye men of war, and go round about the city once. Thus shalt thou do six days. 4 And seven priests shall bear before the ark seven trumpets of rams' horns: and the seventh day ye shall compass the city seven times, and the priests shall blow with the trumpets. 5 And it shall come to pass, that when they make a long blast with the ram's horn, and when ye hear the sound of the trumpet, all the people shall shout with a great shout; and the wall of the city shall fall down flat, and the people shall ascend up every man straight before him (Joshua 6:3–5).

Dr. John Garstang, then director of the British school of archaeology in Jerusalem and of the Department of Antiquities of the Palestine government, excavated the ruins of Jericho, 1929–1936. He found pottery and jewelry that provided evidence that the city had been destroyed about 1400 B.C., coinciding with the time of Joshua. Garstang's team unearthed a number of details that confirmed the biblical account in a most remarkable way.

"The wall fell down flat" (Joshua 6:20). Dr. Garstang found that the wall actually did "fall down flat." The wall was double, the two walls being about 15-feet apart. The outer wall was 6 foot thick while the inner wall was 12-foot thick; both being about 30-feet high. They were built on faulty uneven foundations, of bricks 4-inches thick and 1-to-2-feet long, which were held together with mud mortar. The two walls were linked together by houses built across the top. Dr. Garstang found that the outer wall fell outwards, and down the hillside, dragging the inner wall and houses with it, the streak of bricks gradually getting thinner down the slope. Also found, tilted outward, were four courses of the palace foundation walls. Dr. Garstang found indications that the wall was shaken down by an earthquake, a method which God could have used as easily as any other.

It is important for the nuclear generation to seize the spiritual truths in this historical battle. The Captain has surveyed Satan's awesome fortress—"Spaceship Earth"—with its vast armies, missile bases, and massive nuclear weapons arsenals— countless millennia before today's generation arrived on the scene. He has already been there, circled the walls, and drawn up the battle plan. The Captain has stood there, sword in hand, waiting for us to come through the mist to the dawn of the nuclear age. It is our turn to answer His only question: "Will you follow Me?"

As we head into the nuclear battles of the atomic age, we need to ask the Captain for direction and ever remember that the battle is the Lord's. The chapters ahead will show that God has promised to give into our hands "Fortress Earth" and victory over Satan and his forces, even as the Captain delivered Jericho into Joshua's hand in his day. In fact, God himself will break into Satan's stronghold and destroy the evil empire he controls on planet Earth at the end of the nuclear age.

Being assured of victory ahead of time, we should confidently follow the Captain's orders. The job at hand is much the same as Joshua and the Israelites' assignment in their day. The first assignment is to walk around "Fortress Earth" sounding the warning trumpets of the coming judgments upon the earth and the imminent return of the Captain of the Lord's host. The second is to invite all who will listen to turn from the path that leads to destruction and follow the Captain who has already provided escape from eternal damnation through Jesus Christ's death on the cross.

12 The Sixth Trumpet World War

The sounding of the sixth trumpet begins a period of appalling tribulation on the earth. The Bible refers to this time of trouble as the second woe. One would think that the nations would be ready for an immediate peace conference after an atomic war burns up a third of the Earth. Instead, at some point in time following a five-month period of post-AWWI turmoil, another world war will break out. This massive conflict will apparently cause greater loss of life than the First Atomic War.

THE SIXTH TRUMPET SOUNDS

13 And the sixth angel sounded, and I heard a voice from the four horns of the golden altar which is before God, 14 Saying to the sixth angel which had the trumpet, Loose the four angels which are bound in the great river Euphrates. 15 And the four angels were loosed, which were prepared for an hour, and a day, and a month, and a year, for to slay the third part of men. 16 And the number of the army of the horsemen were two hundred thousand thousand: and I heard the number of them (Rev. 9:13–16).

drinking water. Iraqi Information Minister Tariq Aziz said the Syrian action endangered about 3 million Iraqis living in the arid southern region and destroyed 60 million dollars worth of crops. At Al Ramla, about 10 miles outside of ancient Babylon, the river bed shrank from its normal 400 yards width to about 100 yards and only 7 feet deep. As a result, weeds grew in most irrigation ditches leading out from the river and the crops died. Further south of Al Ramla the plight of villagers was even more desperate.

THE FIRST BINDING AGREEMENT

As tension over the situation grew, both Syria and Iraq massed troops on their common border. Fortunately, they eventually resolved the crisis when Syria accepted a Saudi Arabian sponsored formula on August 14, 1975, which allowed more water to flow downstream into Iraq. The agreement was implemented when Syria literally "bound" the dam's water-flow regulating intake gate machinery at the diplomatically determined open position which would let more water flow downstream. Since the binding of Tabqa's physical intake gates kept the peace between Syria and Iraq, severance of this agreement could very possibly renew hostilities in the future. In short, the four-angel team may have bound themselves in the Euphrates for the express purpose of demonstrating how the water regulating intake gates of modern superdams could be abruptly "loosed" from an open "bound" position and lowered to a closed position over a dam's water intake tunnels. If the Syrians carried out this abrupt action at the Tabqa dam sometime after AWWI, the dramatic stopping of the river's flow could well ignite a conflict with the downstream state of Iraq, which, in turn, could escalate into the Sixth Trumpet World War.

This interpretation, of course, requires the presence of three more superdams astride the Euphrates to represent the three other members of the Sixth Trumpet's four-angel team. Each additional dam would also need to have the water flowing through them bound by some similar international agreement.

THREE OTHER "ANGELS" BOUND

A check of superdam construction along the Euphrates River, which rises in Turkey and flows across Syria and Iraq, reveals three other superdams in the river's path. All three are part of the ambitious Turkish dam construction and irrigation program, termed the South East Anatolian Project (SEAP). Two of the dams, the Keban and Karakaya, were completed in 1974 and 1987, respectively, while the biggest, the Ataturk, is expected to be finished by 1992. In all, the SEAP scheme will enable Turkey to proceed with plans to develop two million hectares of irrigated and partially irrigated land, of which nearly 1.5 million will be watered by the Euphrates. Ataturk alone will allow 700,000 hectares on the Urfa Plain to be irrigated and enable 2,400 megawatts of electricity to be generated.

Completion of the SEAP scheme promises an economic boon for Turkey, but for Syria and Iraq projected drastic reductions in the volume of water flowing downstream bodes future agricultural and economic hardships. For example, before Turkey began building dams on the Euphrates, the river's average annual flow at the Turkish-Syrian border was about 30 billion cubic meters. The SEAP scheme could involve the removal of up to 14bn cubic meters of water from the river annually. If evaporation losses are added, the total reduction could be as high as 17bn cubic meters annually.

This would leave only about 13bn cubic meters of water per year crossing into Syria. The implications, particularly in the long term, are grave. For one thing, the water flowing into Syria has already declined dramatically as a result of impoundment behind Turkey's Keban and Karakaya dams. On several occasions in recent years, low water levels in the Lake Assad reservoir behind Syria's Tabqa dam has restricted output from the 800MW power station to only one third of capacity. In the longer term, further reductions of Euphrates water entering Syria could be a major constraint on Syria's ambitious plans to expand the amount of new land under irrigation from 61,000 to 640,000 hectares.

Predictably, the Euphrates has become a burning issue in Syrian-Turkish relations, despite a Syrian-Turkish water agreement which provides for a minimum annual flow to Syria of 19.7bn cubic meters. Yet it is readily recognized by both states that once the SEAP project is completed as planned, lower flows would appear inevitable.

However, there are signs of Turkish flexibility. In July of 1987 the two states signed a further Euphrates protocol. No details were released, but it was understood to have centered on an equitable formula for water-flow levels after the completion of the Ataturk Dam.

The presence of Turkey's three SEAP superdams and Syria's Tabqa dam, "in the great river Euphrates," fits the first specification to look for in the Sixth Trumpet prophecy's fulfillment. The present Syrian-Turkish and Syrian-Iraqi agreements governing the volume of water flowing through the four superdams on the Euphrates provide a recognizable literal reflection of the imagery of four angels bound in advance of the coming Sixth Trumpet World War.

THE TIMING OF THE SIXTH TRUMPET WAR

The original Greek refers to the timing of this event with the words: "and were loosed the four angels having been prepared for the hour and day and month and year" (Rev. 9:15, IGENT). This means there will be a specific hour, of a particular day, of a certain month, of a unique future year, when the four powerful objects will be loosed. Jamieson, Fausset and Brown's analysis of this phrase reinforces this opinion. "The Greek article (*teen*), put once only before all the periods, implies that the hour in the day, and the day in the month, and the month in the year, and the year itself, had been definitely fixed by God. The article would have been omitted had a sum-total of periods been specified." Thus, the fulfillment of the unbinding of these four powerful objects can be expected to occur quickly, within a period of one sixty-minute hour.

The intake gates of the four superdams astride today's Euphrates river are designed to be "loosed" on short notice from their present "treaty bound" open positions and quickly lowered over their respective intake tunnels. Therefore, the symbolical order to "loose," or unbind, the four superdams' water-regulating intake gate machinery could be carried out within the 60-minute time period specified in this prophecy.

Left unsaid here is what set of converging forces would prompt Turkey and Syria to do so. After all, this action would dry up the river and abrogate the long-standing Euphrates superdam water-flow agreements that had been essential to keeping the peace between Turkey, Syria, and Iraq. And in keeping with this prophecy, it would invite a fierce confrontation between two or more of the three Euphrates water-sharing states. Clearly, if Turkey and Syria ever decided to stop the river's flow they would have to be willing to accept the risk of a destructive war with their neighbors in the region.

A LARGER RISK

The reality of this ever-present risk of war defines another specification for the prophecy's fulfillment. That is, the gates of the four superdams are likely to be loosed only if a larger danger threatens, making it a far greater risk to Turkey and Syria not to stop the river's flow.

DROUGHT AND FAMINE

An obvious candidate for a larger post-AWWI danger to these nations would be famine in the face of an unrelenting drought. Revelation 11, which concludes the chronology of events foretold to occur over the course of the sixth trumpet time period, mentions just such a globe-gripping drought. Its insertion late in the sixth trumpet narrative indicates that the drought will be a delayed negative consequence of AWWI which will not reach its full force until sometime after the Sixth Trumpet World War is over. At its worst "it will not rain" (Rev. 11:6, NIV) for 1,260 consecutive days.

This prophetic information implies that rain showers will occur less and less frequently after AWWI. Then, sometime after the worst five months of the Fifth Trumpet Nuclear Winter have passed (thanks to enough smoke settling out of the planet's atmosphere to allow a warming trend to begin on the Earth's surface), it will suddenly become widely known (probably through scientific observations, weather studies, etc.), that the consistent lack of rain will not be a short-term negative effect of AWWI, but a long-lived global climatic disruption. Quite predictably, (and in keeping with the four bound angel's mission statement), once the persistent character of the post-AWWI drought is understood, the governments of Syria and Turkey will order the intake gates on their respective Euphrates superdams "loosed" from their "treaty-bound" open positions. The lowered gates will effectively stop the river's flow. Water still left impounded behind the dams could then be used to grow food for Turkey and Syria's hungry people during the continuing drought. Following the implementation of this action, Iraq, of course, would be left to contend with the water conservation efforts of both the upstream states.

Total impoundment of the waters behind the upstream states' four superdams would reduce the volume of water reaching Iraq to a mere trickle. Clearly, Iraqi crops along the Euphrates would be promptly ruined and the Iraqi nation's ability to weather the long-term drought-driven famine would be greatly diminished. In the face of such desperate circumstances it is hard to imagine that Iraq would not go to war.

MODERN WEAPONS OF WAR

At this point in the prophecy John turns his attention from the sequence of events leading up to the Sixth Trumpet War to a detailed description of the vehicles and weapons that will be used in the fighting on the ground.

> **17** The horses and riders I saw in my vision looked like this: Their breastplates were fiery red, dark blue, and yellow as sulfur. The heads of the horses resembled the heads of lions, and out of their mouths came fire, smoke and sulfur. **18** A third of mankind was killed by the three plagues of fire, smoke and sulfur that came out of their mouths. **19** The power of the horses was in their mouths and in their tails; for their tails were like snakes, having heads with which they inflict injury (Rev. 9:17–19, NIV).

The *horses* the Apostle John saw in vision were modern weapons of war and the *riders* the crews that operate them. In fact, the sum of his descriptive language draws a surprisingly crisp picture of a modern battle tank. For example, the word rendered breastplate denotes a protective coat of mail covering the whole body. The breastplates, therefore, correspond to a modern tank's armor-plated steel body that protects its engine and crew.

"The heads of the horses resembled the heads of lions" describes the tank's turret. This large round object sets on top of the body of the tank and in some respects resembles the prominent head of a male lion.

The fire, smoke, and sulfur proceeding out of the horses' mouths corresponds precisely to what is discharged from a tank's main cannon when a shell is fired from it. Collectively, they are the exhaust emissions from burning gunpowder that come out of the cannon's barrel, along with the projectile, when the shell is detonated. Furthermore, the cannon is attached to the bottom of the turret, right where a mouth would be expected to reside in an analogy between a lion's head and a tank's turret.

The tails, likened to "snakes having heads with which they inflict injury," correspond to smaller automatic machine guns that are part of a modern battle tank's standard offensive weapons package. The "tails like snakes" is an apt description of the barrel of the weapon. The head of the snake-like tail is a reference to the flash suppressor on the muzzle of a machine gun's barrel. Its location on the discharging end of the weapon allows this slightly larger, round piece of metal to diminish the amount of visible fire, or flash, emitted in the aftermath of the bullet leaving the barrel. Flash suppressors make it harder for an enemy to detect the location of the weapon being fired. This feature and a snake's head are much the same in size and appearance.

By these three plagues, "the fire, smoke and sulfur," one third of mankind will be killed. These three items proceed out of the mouths, or barrels, of today's advanced weapons of war. For example, a modern tank's powerful turret-mounted cannon is used to bombard and knock out large targets, while its smaller onboard machine guns are used to destroy ground troop resistance. Hence, this mobile, well-equipped army can be expected to use battle tanks to spearhead its invasion into the Middle East and elsewhere over the course of the Sixth Trumpet World War. This was quite a sight for the Apostle John to see. In John's day armies killed people with swords, spears, arrows and sling stones.

The inspection of the horses John saw in vision is complete, except for an explanation for the coloring of their breastplates. Hindsight immediately reveals that the colors of the breastplates were not necessary to the task of positively identifying these horses as modern tanks. The presence of this fact suggests that there must be some subtle connection between the colors of the breastplates and what is hidden just beneath their surface, which is in some way relatively important to the larger mission of the whole tank.

John chose naturally occurring things from the environment around him to describe the colors of the breastplates— items which would remain the same in form and color from

This is probably the most chilling symbolic prophetic action in the Bible. To see why this is so, consider the two major catastrophic events John had just witnessed: the First Trumpet Atomic War which burned up one third of the earth and the Sixth Trumpet World War which brought death to one third of the human race. Then, before John can possibly absorb the magnitude of these events, this mighty angel comes down from heaven with a little book that is open for John to view. But, before the angel presents the book to John, he uses body language—the physical act of setting one foot on the sea and the other foot on the land—to symbolically illustrate that the little book's message pertains to the whole world, not just part of it.

THE NARRATIVE DIVIDED

The mighty angel's interruption effectively splits the narrative of the seven trumpet milestones into two distinct parts. The first part encompasses the Initial Atomic War and the subsequent trumpet events, up to and including the Sixth Trumpet World War. The second part is composed of the remaining sixth trumpet events and the events that will occur during the seventh trumpet time period. Together these two parts yield a damage assessment report of the entire seven trumpet tribulation epoch. The mighty angel's interruption effectively divides the damages inflicted on the earth during this time of trouble into two measurable components. The angel's reason for doing so is to make a dramatic comparison between the level of destruction up to the conclusion of the Sixth Trumpet War, and what will occur following the end of that war. One third of the earth will be burned up in the First Trumpet Atomic War but two thirds of the earth will be left unburned. In the same manner one third of humanity will die in the Sixth Trumpet World War, but two thirds will survive. Hence, the angel's dramatic interruption of the seven trumpet narrative, coupled with his prophetic body language, in effect says: whereas some people were relatively unaffected by the previous calamities, everyone will be subjected to the traumatic events described in the little book.

These facts reveal that despite the enormous disruptions caused by the first grouping of trumpet events, substantial numbers of people will be left relatively unscathed from it all.

However, the events prophesied to take place during the days when the seventh trumpet is about to sound will definitely touch everyone on the planet. Even as the earth is made up of land and water, so also will the foreboding events foretold in the little book engulf the entire world. Clearly, the fulfillment of the angel's symbolic action will literally include all the earth's waters, and all the earth's land, and all the earth's inhabitants, in the second half of the tribulation epoch.

NOT YET

5 And the angel which I saw stand upon the sea and upon the earth lifted up his hand to heaven, 6 And sware by him that liveth for ever and ever, who created heaven, and the things that therein are, and the earth, and the things that therein are, and the sea, and the things which are therein, that there should be time no longer. (Rev. 10:5–6).

There are two other noteworthy variations in the reading of the expression: "there should be time no longer." The NIV renders it, "There will be no more delay!" In Albert Barnes' time three other knowledgeable authorities on the subtleties of the Greek language—i.e., Mr. Elliott, Mr. Lord, Mr. Daubuz—translated the expression as, "the time shall not be yet." Verse seven provides a clue to the proper interpretation of the declarative expression.

7 But in the days when the seventh angel is about to sound his trumpet, the mystery of God will be accomplished, just as he announced to his servants the prophets (Rev. 10:7, NIV).

The days between the end of the Sixth Trumpet War and the sounding of the seventh trumpet are defined here as the period of time when the prophecies concerning the last days of man's reign on the earth will be completed. Now inasmuch as the greatest prophetic "mystery of God" through the centuries has been the question of when Christ will return, it follows that the culmination of the finished mystery of God cannot become reality until Christ returns and sets up His promised earthly kingdom of peace. Accordingly, the statement that "the mystery of God will be accomplished" defines the day the seventh are actually swallowing the book—living and dying during the day-to-day fulfillment of the final events of the age—they will find that the events described in the little book will be bitter indeed.

THE NARRATIVE CONTINUES

11 Then I was told, "You must prophesy again about many peoples, nations, languages, and kings" (Rev. 10:11, NIV).

The final directive to John emphasizes the main point of the mighty angel's message, "The time is not yet when the mystery of God shall be finished." Therefore, "you must prophecy again" about the events which will come to pass in the years following the Sixth Trumpet War, since they will concern "many peoples, nations, languages, and kings."

Contrary to a commonly held viewpoint, the Sixth Trumpet World War will not be the final battle of the age for an obvious reason—too many survivors. According to Isaiah the prophet, far fewer than two thirds of the human race will survive the final nuclear war of the age:

9 Behold, the day of the LORD comes, cruel, with wrath and fierce anger, to make the earth a desolation and to destroy its sinners from it. **10** For the stars of the heavens and their constellations will not give their light; the sun will be dark at its rising and the moon will not shed its light. **11** I will punish the world for its evil, and the wicked for their iniquity; I will put an end to the pride of the arrogant, and lay low the haughtiness of the ruthless. **12** I will make men more rare than fine gold, and mankind than the gold of Ophir (Isa. 13:9–12, RSV).

After filing his firsthand report on the mighty angel's unexpected interruption, John continued to transcribe the rest of the seven trumpet visions. His first entry upon resuming this task describes an assignment that he was instructed to carry out immediately.

A PROPHETIC ASSIGNMENT

1 And was given to me a reed like to a staff, saying: Rise and measure the shrine of God and the altar and the (ones) worshipping in it (Rev. 11:1, IGENT).

The Greek word for reed is *kanon*, which means a measuring line or rule. The ancient Hebrew word, *kaneh*, also means "a reed". The English word, canon, as derived from these ancient languages, refers to the canon of Scripture—the books of the Bible which are officially accepted by Christ's earthly Church as the inspired Word of God. Hence, even as the ancients used a hollow stalked, cut reed, as a measuring-stick for keeping the construction of a building true to the designer's plan, so also is John instructed here to use the Holy Scriptures (the measuring reed of the Church containing the rules of the Christian faith) to determine the true dimensions of every aspect of Christ's earthly Church. Specifically, the command instructs Christians living in the time to which the prophecy refers, to carefully consider the entire Church and all its workings, to see which features measure up to the specifications God set forth in His original plan for building His earthly Church.

The reference to the reed being "like to a staff" sums up the fact that God's written Word is strong, like "an iron staff" (Rev. 12:5, IGENT), which "cannot be broken" (John 10:35). The Hebrew shepherds were well acquainted with the worth of a staff which would not break; especially when severe thunderstorms blew in torrential rains from the Mediterranean, making steep mountain paths treacherously slick. Needless to say, if a shepherd's staff broke while he was traversing one of those perilous mountain trails, his chances of surviving the fall without serious injury were slim indeed. Hence, the symbolic portrait of a "reed like to a staff," (as employed here to represent the canon of Scripture), serves to emphasize the importance of the unbreakable character of God's written Word. Accordingly, the imagery discloses that at the time of the fulfillment of this prophecy Christians will be facing the worst storm of oppression in the history of Christ's earthly Church. During this period of great tribulation Christians will need to rely completely on God's unbreakable "iron staff" for support and guidance; for they will be engaged in a fight to the finish against the forces of the buyers and sellers and money-changers that Jesus cast out of the outer court of the temple. In fact, many of today's Christian church goers use the church as a means for furthering their business and social objectives, in much the same way the money-changers of Christ's day did.

Hence, the additional instruction to "cast" the outer court "out outside and measure it not," properly means that all counterfeit Christians are to be separated from the true body of Christian believers in the days following the end of the Sixth Trumpet World War. Indeed, the use of the forceful words, "cast out," implies that these imitation Christians are not merely to be passed by, or omitted, but rather that they are to be decisively separated from the true body of believers.

A SETBACK FOR THE CHURCH

The rest of this verse lists two major developments resulting from the Sixth Trumpet War. "Because it was given to the nations," reveals the most significant outcome of that war. The meaning is that the "outside court," the visible outward trappings of Christianity, will be given into the hands of the nations. This implies a transfer of control and ownership of the outer court. For instance, such items as church buildings, schools, colleges, theological seminaries, various denominational headquarters buildings and the people running the administrative infrastructure of the world's Christian community, will come under the control of a new religious order set up by the nations. (Later chapters of the mighty angel's little book reveal how the nations will establish a new international religion, directly following the Sixth Trumpet War). John disclosed here that the leaders of the world's various Christian denominations will willingly hand over the sum of their assets to the coming new international religious order. When this wholesale transfer of Christendom's tangible outer court assets takes place, all committed Christians will separate themselves from the new false religion being set up by the nations.

"And the holy city they will trample forty and two months." The holy city is a definite reference to Jerusalem, which, according to this verse, will also come under the control of the nations for a forty-two month period of time. This development will be the second significant outcome of the Sixth Trumpet War. The presence of the reference to the Israeli loss of full control over

Jerusalem indicates that the modern Jewish state will suffer severe damage at the hands of the 200-million man army, when it invades the Middle East. Once again, the rest of the mighty angel's little book will confirm this position.

Seeing the concentrated storm of oppression rolling in on His earthly Church after the Sixth Trumpet War in ancient times, the Captain of the Lord's Host instructed His servant John to write down His battlefield orders centuries before today's generation arrived at the dawn of the nuclear age. The orders say to rise—get up and prepare for the battle at hand; to measure the shrine of God—review the entire battle plan for successfully completing the building of Christ's earthly Church; to measure the altar—check the foundation of your faith, the plan of salvation for mankind through the death and resurrection of God's Son Jesus Christ; and measure the ones worshipping with you—make certain all impostors are physically removed from the Christians' ranks, for it will be a matter of life-and-death when the battle is joined.

The Captain then briefs His troops on the immediate course of the battle. For instance the enemy has overrun and confiscated the outer court— all of Christendom's physical facilities and assets are under the enemy's control. Further, they have seized the holy city of Jerusalem. The loss of Christendom's physical facilities will be a definite setback for the Church. The loss of Jerusalem, on the other hand, will not present any immediate problems for the Christian camp; however, the enemy will gain much moral encouragement from their control over it since it has long been recognized as the holy city called by God's name.

THE CAPTAIN'S COUNTEROFFENSIVE

The Captain then proceeds to spell out in great detail how He will conduct the war at hand. His immediate response to the seizure of His servants' property and the occupation of the holy city of Jerusalem will be a frontal assault against the combined might of the enemies' amassed forces. The counteroffensive will be the most unique operation ever undertaken in the history of the world. The task force God sends forth, to engage the enemy that sent the rampaging 200-million man army across the Euphrates into the Middle East, will consist of two soldiers. This may sound absurd, but it is precisely what the mighty angel's

God confirmed this promise of nationhood with Abraham's son Isaac and grandson Jacob. One of Jacob's twelve sons, Joseph, had a dream that gives the meaning of the twelve stars.

9 And he dreamed yet another dream, and told it his brethren, and said, Behold, I have dreamed a dream more; and, behold, the sun and the moon and the eleven stars made obeisance to me. 10 And he told it to his father, and to his brethren: and his father rebuked him, and said unto him, What is this dream that thou hast dreamed? Shall I and thy mother and thy brethren indeed come to bow down ourselves to thee to the earth? 11 And his brethren envied him; but his father observed the saying (Gen. 37:9–11).

The stars in this dream represent Jacob's sons who eventually formed the twelve tribes of Israel. Therefore, the woman's crown of twelve stars helps to clearly identify her as the nation of Israel.

2 And she being with child cried, travailing in birth, and pained to be delivered (Rev. 12:2).

The woman "with child, travailing in birth," directs attention to Israel's unique place in history as the nation God selected to bring His Son into the world. This additional information completes the evidence needed to establish the woman's true identity.

Many Old Testament Scriptures foretold the birth of God's anointed one. Jeremiah prophesied that this child was to come through the kingly line of David.

5 Behold, the days come, saith the Lord, that I will raise unto David a righteous Branch, and a King shall reign and prosper, and shall execute judgment and justice in the earth (Jer. 23:5).

Figuratively speaking the nation of Israel was in labor for hundreds of years while they waited for this King to be born. From the days of Abraham, when the nation was conceived, it was a long hard struggle for tiny Israel to survive against her more powerful neighbors.

A GREAT RED DRAGON APPEARS IN HEAVEN

3 And was seen another sign in heaven; and behold, a great red dragon, having seven heads and ten horns and on the heads of him seven diadems, **4a** and the tail of him draws the third (part) of the stars of heaven, and cast them to the earth (Rev. 12:3–4a, IGENT).

At this point God begins to reveal more detail concerning Daniel's vision of the Fourth Beast.

The red dragon represents Red China. For centuries the dragon appeared as China's national symbol and the Imperial Dragon was the badge of the royal family. This same symbolism appears in today's newspapers and magazines where China is often shown as a dragon in political cartoons.

In the picture of the dragon, the word "red" serves to positively identify the dragon as present day China. During the twentieth century, communist political radicals became known as "Reds." Hence, it was quite natural for the world to refer to the nation of China as "Red China," after Mao Tse-Tung's Communist Revolutionaries gained control of the country.

It is also important to note that the Devil, or Satan, has always been portrayed symbolically as a dragon, or serpent. These facts, coupled with the phrases stating that the woman and dragon appeared in heaven, document the origin point of a war between God and Satan, which began in heaven. This entire chapter details this battle: past, present, and future, and man's part in it.

THE DRAGON'S TAIL

The dragon's tail brings to mind the great wall of China which is the most massive monument ever built to Satan's dragon symbol. The initial span was built by Shih Huang Ti, "First Emperor," who established the Ch'in dynasty in 221 B.C. He erected the 20-foot high wall to keep out the Tatars to the north. The wall has some 25,000 connecting towers and a paved road on top wide enough for five horses to gallup abreast. The wall begins on a promontory overlooking the Pacific, called the Old Dragon Head. From the Dragon Head it snakes, loops and doubles back on itself, meandering across plains and valleys, scaling mountains, plunging into deep gorges and leaping raging rivers, for 3,700 miles to the Gobi desert. Why the wall takes such an odd course is not known. One ancient belief is that it was laid out to follow the contortions of a celestial dragon.

This ancient belief provides a glimpse of Satan's influence on the wall's builder. The "First Emperor" of China was a world class exponent of evil who is remembered for the death he brought to tens of thousands. Endless numbers of his own countrymen died from hunger, disease, and exhaustion building the wall. Their bodies, buried in the foundations together with those who were bricked up alive for failing to work hard enough, have earned the wall the grim appellation of "the longest cemetery on earth." The wall and the First Emperor's countless other construction projects led to the bankruptcy of the nation.

Nevertheless, the First Emperor's great wall served Satan's purposes very well. Through succeeding centuries, millions of Chinese manned the wall that wound across the hills like a great dragon. Though not always successful in keeping invaders out, it did preserve Satan's idea of the unity of all peoples "within the wall." It kept China intact during the long periods of national upheaval and foreign incursion and served to weld its population into the largest homogenous group of people on the face of the earth. The wall also generally served to keep change and God's truth out. This is the nation Satan will use to accomplish his purposes in the last days.

CHINA'S RELIANCE ON MAN

Revelation 12's opening imagery also reveals the key role the modern nations of Israel and Red China will play in the final battles of the age. God chose the nation of Israel to represent Him on the earth in ancient times. Satan, on the other hand, will select the nation of Red China to champion his cause during the closing days of the nuclear age.

The Book of Genesis records God's reason for choosing the nation of Israel.

17 And the Lord said, Shall I hide from Abraham that thing which I do; Seeing that Abraham shall surely become a great and mighty nation, and all the nations of the earth shall be blessed in him? 18 For I know him, that he will command his

children and his household after him, and they shall keep the way of the Lord, to do justice and judgment; that the Lord may bring upon Abraham that which he hath spoken of him (Gen. 18:17–18).

According to this text, God chose Israel because Abraham chose to rely on God, rather than man, to solve his problems and taught his children after him to keep the way of the Lord. In contrast, consider University of Chicago professor Ping-ti Ho's synopsis of China's past and present attitude toward God: "No other major culture in the world so consistently relied on man rather than God . . . a reliance on the human spirit and will, faith in his ability to solve his own difficulties—that is the Chinese attitude toward mankind."

SEVEN HEADS AND TEN HORNS

The ten horns in Daniel's vision of the four beasts are shown here attached to Red China along with seven heads. Revelation 17 mentions the additional fact that the seven heads are seven kings or countries. In the imagery of the dragon then, China is at the center of a united group of nations who are represented as seven heads and ten horns. The seven heads are shown to be more powerful than the organization represented by the ten horns since the heads are wearing diadems, or crowns. The crowns stand for authority. Therefore the seven crowned countries will establish policy and make decisions for this power structure.

CHINA'S EMERGING PROMINENT ROLE

In the early 1970s China launched a campaign of around-the-world rapprochement with Western European nations, the United States, and Japan. China's objectives then and now: an alliance that will counterbalance Russian military power and development of China into an industrial giant through an infusion of Western technology and know-how.

In 1979, China's Vice Premier, Teng Hsiao-p'ing, dramatically stated that Sino-American rapprochement should be turned into an anti-Soviet alliance. Stressing Sino-American ties, Teng argued that the two nations share a common destiny and should unite with other countries against the Soviet Union.

Teng went on to say, "if we really want to be able to place curbs on the polar bear, the only realistic thing for us is to unite. If we only depend on the strength of the United States, it is not enough. If we only depend on the strength of Europe, it is not enough."

China has already taken several other first steps toward obtaining her future position of prominence in the fourth power structure. While Eurovision carried the official signing of a Treaty of Accession to the European Common Market by Britain, Ireland and Denmark, in January of 1972, Red China began preparing the nation for its coming role as the body of the Great Red Dragon beast. Unobtrusively her newspapers began reporting events in the market and reprinting translations of papers produced by the Common Market's headquarters in Brussels on such topics as the value-added tax, Eurodollars, and tariffs.

China's interest in the Market's trade news points out her vast technological deficiencies, which contribute to her active interest in forming trade agreements with the industrial rich nations. Even now a multitude of missions move between Europe and China and as early as the summer of 1972 the Common Market took 40 percent of China's trade.

In the last days of the nuclear age, Satan will fire the imagination of people around the globe with the lofty idea of uniting all peoples under a new world order. Red China will be Satan's chief standard bearer of this ideology of international unity; which, according to Daniel's prophecy of the four beasts, is the fourth wind of revolutionary change to sweep the earth in the last days of the age. China will sell this appealing ideology under the premise that a powerful world government will be able to establish lasting peace on the planet.

As China's trade gains momentum with the industrial affluent nations, it will become more apparent as to who the seven heads and ten horns represent. Notwithstanding, today it can be said with certainty that the developed nations are presently supplying Red China with the sophisticated equipment and technological know-how needed to attain a powerful position. In time this technological bonanza will enable Red China to operate from a position of colossal strength. China will then be able to effectively champion Satan's cause to unite the nations into an all encompassing world government beast.

A DECISIVE MILITARY VICTORY

The closing statement, "And the tail of him draws the third (part) of the stars of heaven, and cast them to the earth," completes the introduction of the Great Red Dragon power structure. It shows a devastating Chinese invasion of Israel in which one-third of the tribes will be lost to the invading forces. Prophecies covered later reveal that this invasion of Israel will be part of a much larger Chinese military action that will decisively change the world's future balance of power.

12 STARS REPRESENT 12 TRIBES

The "stars" in this description again represent the tribes of Israel. Daniel's reference to the "stars of heaven" being "cast to the earth" in his ram-goat prophecy supports this interpretation.

8 Therefore the he goat waxed very great: and when he was strong, the great horn was broken; and for it came up four notable ones toward the four winds of heaven. 9 And out of one of them came forth a little horn, which waxed exceeding great, toward the south, and toward the east, and toward the pleasant land. 10 And it waxed great, even to the host of heaven; and it cast down some of the host and of the stars to the ground, and stamped upon them (Dan. 8:8–10).

After seeing this part of the vision Daniel is told the meaning of the prophecy by the angel Gabriel.

21 And the rough goat is the king of Grecia: and the great horn that is between his eyes is the first king. 22 Now that being broken, whereas four stood up for it, four kingdoms shall stand up out of the nation, but not in his power. 23 And in the latter time of their kingdom, when the transgressors are come to the full, a king of fierce countenance, and understanding dark sentences, shall stand up. 24 And his power shall be mighty, but not by his own power: and he shall destroy wonderfully, and shall prosper, and practise, and shall destroy the mighty and the holy people (Dan. 8:21–24).

virgin shall conceive, and bear a son, and shall call his name
Immanuel (Isa. 7:13–14).

6 For unto us a child is born, unto us a son is given: and the
government shall be upon his shoulder: and his name shall
be called Wonderful, Counsellor, The Mighty God, The Everlasting Father, The Prince of Peace. 7 Of the increase of his
government and peace there shall be no end, upon the throne
of David, and upon his kingdom, to order it, and to establish
it with judgment and with justice from henceforth even for
ever. The zeal of the Lord of hosts will perform this (Isa.
9:6–7).

Here again God foretold that His Son would come through
the kingly line of David. God explicitly promised that this child
would be born of a virgin and would be named Immanuel,
which means "God with us." The child would be God Himself,
in the flesh, and His reason for coming was to bring order and
life to mankind, who live in a world of chaos and death.

God emphatically states that His Son will "rule all nations
with a rod of iron . . . upon the throne of David." Today's world
does not contain even one Jew who can convincingly trace his
lineage directly to King David. This means that past records
contain the only verification of who God's Son is. That verification was recorded by the Jewish authors of the New Testament
which opens with the following account.

1 The book of the generation of Jesus Christ, the son of David,
the son of Abraham. 2 Abraham begat Issac; and Isaac begat
Jacob; and Jacob begat Judas and his brethren (Matt. 1:1–2).

The genealogy continues to King David, his son Solomon,
and finally ends with Joseph who was Christ's foster father.

16 And Jacob begat Joseph the husband of Mary, of whom
was born Jesus, who is called Christ. 17 So all the generations
from Abraham to David are fourteen generations; and from
David until the carrying away into Babylon are fourteen
generations; and from the carrying away into Babylon unto
Christ are fourteen generations (Matt. 1:16–17).

The third chapter of the book of Luke gives the genealogical record of Mary, the mother of Jesus, which also goes back to King David. These records are the only genealogical documents in existence that trace the lineage of any man directly to King David.

The last part of Revelation 12:5 ends with the statement "and her child was caught up unto God, and to his throne." This refers to the fact that although Christ died, He conquered death, when He arose from the grave and returned to God the Father in heaven. The last time Christ's disciples spoke with Him before He returned to heaven is recorded in the Acts of the Apostles.

> 6 When they therefore were come together, they asked of him, saying, Lord, wilt thou at this time restore again the kingdom to Israel? 7 And he said unto them, it is not for you to know the times or the seasons, which the Father hath put in his own power. 8 But ye shall receive power, after that the Holy Ghost is come upon you: and ye shall be witnesses unto me both in Jerusalem, and in all Judaea, and in Samaria, and unto the uttermost part of the earth. 9 And when he had spoken these things, while they beheld, he was taken up; and a cloud received him out of their sight (Acts 1:6–9).

When Christ ascended in open daylight in the presence of His apostles, they could not doubt that His work was approved, and that God would carry it onward. It was a confirmation of the truth of the Christian faith.

THE WOMAN FLEES

> 6 And the woman fled into the wilderness, where she hath a place prepared of God, that they should feed her there a thousand two hundred and threescore days (Rev. 12:6).

The narrative now returns to the events that will take place at the time of Red China's invasion of Israel. As the Chinese come sweeping into Israel many of the people will flee to the wilderness, probably the Sinai desert area to the south. The prophecy then states that "they" feed her there for "a thousand two hundred and threescore days," which is about three-and-one-half years by today's calendar.

SATAN CAST OUT OF HEAVEN

7 And there was war in heaven: Michael and his angels fought against the dragon; and the dragon fought and his angels, 8 And prevailed not; neither was their place found any more in heaven. 9 And the great dragon was cast out, that old serpent, called the Devil, and Satan, which deceiveth the whole world: he was cast out into the earth, and his angels were cast out with him. 10 And I heard a loud voice saying in heaven, Now is come salvation, and strength, and the kingdom of our God, and the power of his Christ: for the accuser of our brethren is cast down, which accused them before our God day and night. 11 And they overcame him by the blood of the Lamb, and by the word of their testimony; and they loved not their lives unto the death (Rev. 12:7–11).

This passage recaps a battle that took place in heaven in which Satan and his angels were defeated and confined to the Earth. Jesus Christ spoke of this impending battle just before His death.

27 Now is my soul troubled; and what shall I say? Father, save me from this hour: but for this cause came I unto this hour. 28 Father, glorify thy name. Then came there a voice from heaven, saying, I have both glorified it, and will glorify it again. 29 The people therefore, that stood by, and heard it, said that it thundered: others said, An angel spake to him. 30 Jesus answered and said, this voice came not because of me, but for your sakes. 31 Now is the judgment of this world: now shall the prince of this world be cast out. 32 And I, if I be lifted up from the earth, will draw all men unto me. 33 This he said, signifying what death he should die (John 12:27–33).

According to this passage, Satan, "the prince of this world," was "cast out" of heaven when Christ died on the cross and took the judgment of every man on Himself. Satan thought he had won the battle when Christ died on the cross. However, death could not hold Christ since God accepted His perfect life and death as payment for the sins of all mankind. Hence, when Christ arose from the grave He not only conquered death, but Satan who had the power of death.

Christ's victory at once made it impossible for Satan to accuse Christ's followers in heaven "before our God day and night" since they were henceforth vested with the power to overcome Satan "by the blood of the Lamb." Christ's death also marked the beginning of the kingdom of God which He spoke of when He started His ministry.

> **14** Now after that John was put in prison, Jesus came into Galilee, preaching the gospel of the kingdom of God, **15** And saying, The time is fulfilled, and the kingdom of God is at hand: repent ye, and believe the gospel (Mark 1:14–15).

In order for a man to become a living member of the kingdom of God he must realize that he has fallen short of what God intended him to be, repent, by asking God's forgiveness, and believe the gospel. The gospel is eternal life through faith in Jesus Christ. Christ explained the gospel many times in his ministry. A good example is found in the gospel of John.

> **16** For God so loved the world, that he gave his only begotten Son, that whosoever believeth in him should not perish, but have everlasting life. **17** For God sent not his Son into the world to condemn the world; but that the world through him might be saved. **18** He that believeth on him is not condemned: but he that believeth not is condemned already, because he hath not believed in the name of the only begotten Son of God (John 3:16–18).

It is every man's responsibility to either accept Christ as his personal Savior or reject Him. Each one must make this choice for himself.

SATAN PERSECUTES THE WOMAN

> **12** Therefore rejoice, ye heavens, and ye that dwell in them. Woe to the inhabiters of the earth and of the sea! for the Devil is come down unto you, having great wrath, because he knoweth that he hath but a short time. **13** And when the

dragon saw that he was cast unto the earth, he persecuted the
woman which brought forth the man child (Rev. 12:12–13).

About A.D. 70, just a few years after Israel's leaders rejected
Jesus, the Romans, led by Titus, besieged, conquered and destroyed Jerusalem. During the war Satan used Rome's legions
to kill a great number of the population and carry many of the
Jews into captivity. This was another of Satan's all-out attempts
to destroy the nation of Israel. These efforts continue to this day
and will continue until Christ returns to set up His earthly
kingdom.

TWO WINGS OF A GREAT EAGLE

14 And to the woman were given two wings of a great eagle,
that she might fly into the wilderness, into her place, where
she is nourished for a time, and times, and half a time, from
the face of the serpent (Rev. 12:14).

The narrative again returns to Red China's future invasion
of Israel. "Two wings of a great eagle" foretells the additional
fact that the United States will help the Israelis escape China's
overwhelming hordes by providing aircraft to fly Israel into a
desert area. The airborne wing of America's armed forces quite
appropriately uses two wings of a great eagle to simultaneously
represent the nation under whose flag they fly and their main
mission, which is to defend U.S. airspace. God employs this
same symbolism to show that the United States will use its
airpower to quickly evacuate Israeli civilians from the on-
slaught of Red China's massive invasion force.

Since this verse repeats the earlier account of the Israelis'
flight into the desert, "a thousand two hundred and three score
days" and "a time, and times, and half a time," represent
approximately the same period of time, which is about three-
and-one-half years. The cross-documentation of this escape
also shows that it will be the Americans who will feed the
Israelis in a desert area for three-and-one-half years, the same
period of time when one world government "beast" will be
systematically extending its control over the entire world.

THE DRAGON PURSUES THE WOMAN

> 15 And the serpent cast out of the mouth of him behind the woman water as a river, in order that he might make her carried off by the river. 16 And the earth helped the woman, and the earth opened the mouth of it and swallowed the river which the dragon cast out of the mouth of him (Rev. 12:15–16, IGENT).

The intermixing of Satan's serpent and dragon symbols and Red China's dragon symbol in this passage is necessary to the task of explaining Revelation 12's overview of a spiritual battle between God and Satan and man's interactions in this battle. The serpent in this text identifies Satan's ever present wrath toward the woman (Israel) as the source of inspiration for China's plans of conquest which will culminate in a massive attack against Israel. (Even in today's politics the Chinese have consistently taken a hostile position toward Israel. For example, in the early 1970s Red China was the chief supporter of Palestine's Arab commandos and in the fall of 1971 Peking refused to accept a congratulatory telegram from Israel, even though Israel voted for Red China's admission to the United Nations.) The text's imagery will find fulfillment in God's nation, Israel, being attacked by "water as a river" in the form of Satan's tool, Red China, sending a river of men against Israel.

Overflowing waters are often used in Scripture to represent attacking armies. Jeremiah used this terminology when he prophesied the defeat of Pharoah's army by King Nebuchadnezzar of Babylon.

> 7 Who is this that cometh up as a flood, whose waters are moved as the rivers? 8 Egypt riseth up like a flood, and his waters are moved like the rivers; and he saith, I will go up, and will cover the earth; I will destroy the city and the inhabitants thereof (Jer. 46:7–8).

The reference to "the serpent cast out of the mouth of him behind the woman water as a river" identifies Satan as the serpent and author of the decision to send a pursuing force after the fleeing Israelis. The river of men coming out of the serpent's "mouth" suggests that Red China will use Satan-inspired anti-American propaganda to encite neighboring Arab states to turn on the United States for helping the Israelis escape. Although the text does not go into any detail, it is highly probable that some of the Arab states will assist the Chinese in their pursuit of the fleeing Israeli refugees.

Note that this passage shows the direction of the attack to be "behind the woman." The passage also does not mention any decisive U.S. action in the battle, only the American evacuation of Israeli citizens. China's invasion force will be so massive that America will not be able to intervene effectively on Israel's behalf. The United States will simply use its available aircraft to remove civilians out of the invading army's path. Obviously, Red China will overrun Israel. But Satan will not be satisfied with land alone, since his real objective is the annihilation of the Jewish people. Hence, Satan will send his river of men after the fleeing Israelis.

It is precisely at this moment of Israel's helplessness that the earth, which God alone created, will open "the mouth of it," and swallow up in death the pursuing force. Exactly what will bring on the sudden death of this army is not entirely clear. It may be that an earthquake will cause the ground to cave in under the feet of the pursuing army. The exact cause of death is not especially important, however, since the main objective of this prophecy is to foretell the failure of Satan's determined attempt to annihilate the Israeli refugee remnant encamped in the desert.

Notice the use of pronouns in this last verse. "It," in the phrase, "and the earth opened the mouth of it," quite appropriately refers to the earth as "it". But in the phrase, "and swallowed the river which the dragon cast out of the mouth of him," the dragon is not referred to as "it." Therefore, "him" has to refer to Satan and not "it," the Red Chinese beast, or invading power structure. Yet, water as a river most definitely refers to the army of men that are swallowed. The conclusion is that Red China, who has beligerently used Satan's coat of arms for centuries, will become an extension and tool of Satan himself. When Satan speaks Red China will act accordingly.

THE REST OF THE WOMAN'S SEED

17 And the dragon was enraged over the woman, and went away to make war with the rest of the seed of her, the ones

keeping the commandments of God and having the witness
of Jesus; **18** and he stood on the sand of the sea (Rev. 12:17–18,
IGENT).

Red China will be furious at Israel after losing the pursuing
force. However, China's rage from this event onward will be
directed at "the rest of the seed of her, the ones keeping the
commandments of God and having the witness of Jesus." Examination of this passage in a broader context reveals that these
witnesses of Jesus will be U.S. Christians whose influence will
cause the United States to intervene on Israel's behalf. In a
spiritual sense, all who keep the witness of Jesus are the seed,
or descendents of Israel. They are the "rest of the seed," the wild
olive branches "grafted in among them" (Rom. 11:17).

> **28** There is neither Jew nor Greek, there is neither bond nor
> free, there is neither male nor female: for ye are all one in
> Christ Jesus. **29** And if ye be Christ's, then are ye Abraham's
> seed, and heirs according to the promise (Gal. 3:28–29).

At this point in the prophetic flow of events China will be
thwarted in her attempt to completely crush Israel, but at least
a defeated Israel will not be a focal point for conflict with her
Arab neighbors. This fact will help the nations work toward
their goal of unity and peace. China will let the refugees remain
in the desert and go about the task of establishing complete
control over the world's nations. To obtain this goal China will
make every effort to crush the opposition—mainly the world's
Christians and especially U.S. Christians. This is a process that
will occupy China throughout the remaining three-and-one-
half years of man's reign on the earth.

Beneath all these events lies the fact that this prophecy is
about a long-standing spiritual battle. Satan knows that Christ's
followers are the foe with real power. Jesus said, "All power is
given unto me in heaven and in earth" (Matt. 28:18). It is Christ
who will terminate Satan's control and destruction of the nations, at the end of the age.

The fact that the United States will feed a number of Israelis
in desert refugee camps right through the violence of the three-
and-one-half year reign of man's final one-world government
demonstrates that America will have some power and uni-
lateral decision-making ability, even during the desperately

oppressive last days of the age. However, as the domination of the world government "beast" grows, the power of the United States to act independently will be systematically and inexorably curtailed.

Prophecies covered previously have already shown that the United States will be God's nation for preaching the gospel during the closing days of the nuclear age. This passage proves that the American post-AWWI, world-wide evangelistic outreach will be effective. People around the globe will hear the gospel, accept Christ as Lord of their lives and also obey His command to spread the good news of salvation. Satan recognizes the spread of Christianity as a potent force on the earth that will threaten to disrupt his plan for controlling the nations through Red China. Hence, China will abruptly shift its war against Israelis specifically, to all Christians in general—"the ones keeping the commandments of God and having the witness of Jesus."

The chapter ends with Red China standing on the "sand of the sea." In other words, in the days following the Sixth Trumpet World War China will emerge from the sea of people on the earth to the position of the world's number one power.

PREVIOUS ATTACKS AGAINST THE WOMAN

A look back in time reveals other nations being used by Satan in his efforts to destroy Israel. In the days of Moses, Satan worked through Egypt in an attempt to destroy the young Hebrew nation and thus Christ, who was to be born out of Israel. In the days of Christ, Satan used Rome, and the Jews themselves, who plotted Christ's death on the cross. However, Christ conquered death and lived again, thus defeating Satan's attempt to destroy God's promises concerning Christ. Then there were the days of Hitler when Satan's nation of the hour was Germany. Again Satan tried to destroy the nation of Israel through the German war machine and death camps. Satan's persistent attempts to destroy Israel are transparent enough. If he could destroy Israel, then God's everlasting prophecies concerning Israel could not be fulfilled and God's word would fail. Thus, although Satan has never been successful in discrediting God, or in altering God's prophesied events, he has never given up his attempts to do so.

Red China, therefore, is just one of many nations that have been used by Satan in an all-out effort to destroy Israel. The prophecy in Revelation does not portray Red China as being more evil than other nations; it simply states that Red China will be Satan's premier nation in the final battles of the age. Also, it does not imply that China will be without Christians. Just as there were those in Germany during World War II who were truly God's people, so too will China continue to have witnesses for Jesus during the closing years of the age. Past examples of God's people dwelling in the midst of Satan's strongholds abound. The Apostle John made reference to this very situation in a message he wrote to the church in Pergamum.

> **12** "To the angel of the church in Pergamum write: these are the words of him who has the sharp, double-edged sword. **13** I know where you live—where Satan has his throne. Yet you remain true to my name. You did not renounce your faith in me, even in the days of Antipas, my faithful witness, who was put to death in your city—where Satan lives" (Rev. 2:12–13, NIV).

The chart on the next page shows the approximate dates of the four beasts described in Daniel's vision. The Red Chinese Dragon power is the first stage of the fourth and final beast. The next chapter will examine the development of the final stage of the Fourth Beast.

RED CHINA'S VISIONS OF CONQUEST

The destruction of the modern state of Israel will not be Red China's only reason for invading the Middle East. Red China would not need a 200-million man army to subdue tiny Israel who may well have only four or five million Jewish citizens when this war takes place. A review of the historical and prophetic facts leading up to China's future invasion provides additional support for this view.

A prime candidate for a more ominous threat to China before the Sixth Trumpet World War breaks forth would be their long-standing arch rival, Russia. Later Revelation references show the Russians not only surviving AWWI, but also continuing on to the end of the age as a vital world power. This infers that despite massive Soviet losses on the hills

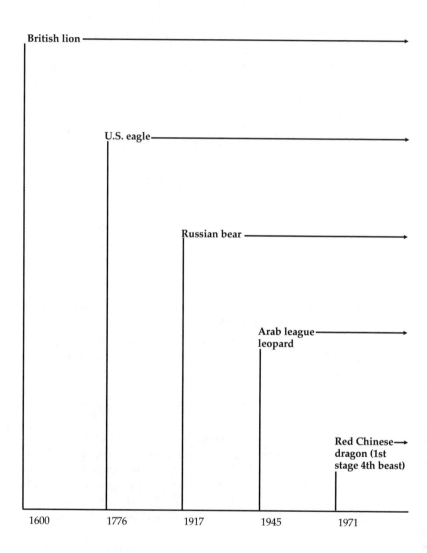

British lion ──▶

U.S. eagle──────────────────────────────────────▶

Russian bear ──────────────────────────▶

Arab league──────────▶
leopard

Red Chinese──▶
dragon (1st
stage 4th beast)

1600   1776   1917   1945   1971

*British lion empire established around 1600.
*Red Chinese dragon began forming about 1971 with expansion of trade.
However, the Red Chinese Dragon, which is the first stage of the fourth
beast, is by no means a complete power structure yet.

of Palestine, surviving Russian troops will still possess the potential to control many countries throughout the oil-rich Middle East in the post-AWWI period.

Therefore, since the four-angel team's symbolic message shows that the Euphrates dispute will unleash a violent war between the world's great powers, and since the Russians will still be present in the Middle East after AWWI, it is reasonable to assume that the Russians will become embroiled in the Euphrates river conflict. The invasion of Israel will apparently be accomplished during Red China's massive drive to push all remaining Russian confederated forces off the strategic land bridge between Africa and Asia.

China's future military move into the Euphrates conflict will be a continuation of her ongoing competition with Russia for influence throughout the Middle East and Africa. For example, both Syria and Iraq have a treaty of friendship with Russia. Yet in 1982 Iraq bought one-quarter of all its weaponry used in its war against Iran from China; that accounted for half of China's arms-export total in 1982.

Moreover, for years the Russians have been encircling Red China, starting with Russian dominance of Outer Mongolia and the transfer of the Japanese Kuriles to the Soviets after World War II. Then, in 1971, the Russians signed a "Treaty of Friendship" with India, which is basically a military pact that guarantees Moscow a privileged position in India. Indian military men train in Russia, and Russia is India's largest single export market. Next, following the American withdrawal from Vietnam, the Soviets began using Vietnamese naval facilities on China's southern flank. In return, Russia supported Vietnam's occupation of Laos and Cambodia. The most recent examples of Russian encirclement of China include their violent take-over of Afghanistan on China's western flank and use of North Korea's year-round port at Najin by Russian merchant ships and tankers. North Korea also allows the Russians to transport oil and other supplies from Najin by rail to Vladivostok when that city's harbor is closed by ice. This situation is particularly irksome to the Chinese since North Korea had promised its giant neighbors for decades that it would not allow the other to establish a base on North Korean territory.

Through the years Red China has only been able to make token responses against the Russian bear's moves. However, the Chinese are persistently working to build a military industrial complex that will be able to counter the Russian threat. This effort will continue. Finally, following AWWI, Red China will make her move against a dramatically weakened Russia.

The following quote appeared in a 1981 issue of the official Soviet newspaper Izvestia: "Peking has its own ax to grind: to cause a clash between the U.S.A. and the U.S.S.R. so as to dominate the world after the nuclear conflict." According to Bible prophecy, this assessment of Red China's long-range foreign policy objectives will come to pass following AWWI.

FAMINE WILL INTENSIFY THE WAR

Famine will be a second compelling reason for China to send a 200-million man army against the Russians. Clearly, the "nuclear winter" aftereffects of AWWI will halt world-wide production of most foods. Consequently, the Chinese will be confronted with millions of rioting, starving people in a matter of months, once the "nuclear winter" does its damage. Faced with this desperate situation, the Chinese leadership will march a 200-million man army out of the country with a twofold purpose in mind. One objective will be to break the Russian bear's back. Another will be to pillage and confiscate the food supplies of other nations. Great misery will befall those nations that have been allies of the Russians against China, when this well-equipped, hungry army marches out of China into their lands. The Bible declares that a third of the world's population will be killed as a result of this Chinese army fighting its way into the Middle East.

The reason the number of casualties will be so high is obvious. When food is scarce, people fight to the death to keep what food they have because the alternative is starvation.

An assessment of the coming Chinese threat, written by Alexander Solzhenitsyn, one of the most astute political analysts of our times, appeared in *Time* magazine in 1980. He warned against an alliance with Communist China, calling it a betrayal of both Taiwan and the oppressed people of China themselves. He labeled such an alliance a "mad, suicidal policy" and predicted that supplying China with American weapons would create a power "no force on earth" could stop. Bible prophecy supports this assessment. The unequaled manpower of China, well-armed, will burst its boundaries and descend like a flood upon the nations at the end of the age.

14 The Last Beast

Red China will emerge from the Sixth Trumpet War as the world's most powerful nation. The margin of her military triumph will place the Chinese in a position to dominate the decimated nations. According to Scripture, China will then promptly launch a movement that will set the stage for the entrance of the last beast. Red China itself will not be the last beast. Daniel's introduction of the Fourth Beast (7:7) eliminates this possiblity since China is one of many nations ruled by a communist form of government: "and it was diverse from all the beasts that were before it" (Dan. 7:7). Clearly the Fourth Beast's instrument of government will not be patterned after a political system used by one of the first three beasts.

Red China alone then, is not the "dreadful and terrible" (Dan. 7:7) Fourth Beast, but only the first stage of the last beast's development. Satan will use Red China's might after the Sixth Trumpet War to promote his plan for the construction of an all-encompassing international government "over every tribe and people and tongue and nation" (Rev. 13:7, IGENT).

THE FOURTH BEAST'S RISE TO POWER

1 And I saw a beast coming up out of the sea, having ten horns and seven heads, and on the horns of it ten diadems, and on the heads of it names of blasphemy (Rev. 13:1, IGENT).

315

raeli Yom Kippur War when the Arabs slowed the amount of oil they were exporting. Arab cuts in production quickly drove the price of oil through the roof and resulted in their emergence as a new kind of superpower. The Arabs' success centered on their control of 62 percent of the world's known oil reserves. Another contributing factor was the industrialized nations' woeful dependence on Arab oil to keep their industries running smoothly. At the time, Western Europe was importing 60 percent of its oil out of the Persian Gulf while Japan was importing 90 percent of its needs.

The oil glut since the Yom Kippur War has not lessened the long term economic importance of the Arab nations enormous oil reserves. These reserves will be the primary strength of the leopardlike body of the last beast. Even as the body of a beast contains its life-supporting blood, so will Arab oil be the life-blood of the industrialized nations in the closing days of the age.

John's picture of the last beast indicates that the world will eventually move from the oil surpluses of the mid 1980s back to the oil shortages of the 1970s. Lack of available oil supplies will be especially acute after the trumpet wars ruin much of the world's petrochemical industry. Following those devastating wars the vast quantities of easily accessible Arab oil will be central to the world's reconstruction efforts. Arab oil will provide the base needed to rebuild the international economy and it will also supply the Arab states with the leverage to make a successful bid for a central position in the formation of the final beast of the age.

THE BEAR'S CONTRIBUTION

Daniel's description of the Fourth Beast says, "It devoured and brake in pieces, and stamped the residue with the feet of it" (Dan 7:7). "And it shall devour the whole earth, and shall tread it down, and break it in pieces" (Dan. 7:23). Unfortunately for the people on this planet, "the feet" of the Fourth Beast will be "as" the feet of the Russian bear. This imagery shows that the Soviet's law enforcement system will be the main Russian contribution to the one-world government's three-and-one-half year reign of terror.

The Soviet law enforcement system was built around the Russian Red Army and the Soviet State Security Committee

(KGB). In the decades following the 1917 Bolshevik Revolution these feet of the modern Russian bear perfected communism's procedures for violating human rights and eliminating "undesirables." According to John's symbolic comparison, man's future world government will pattern its law enforcement system after the same violent methods used to control the Soviet people.

THE LION'S CONTRIBUTION

And the mouth of the last beast is "as the mouth of a lion," a mouth that will speak in English. Hence, English will be the official language of the world government. This isn't surprising. English is the language of diplomacy, business, and the international scientific community. It is also the dominant language of medicine, electronics, aviation and space technology, international advertising, radio, television, and film.

English is the world's most studied language. Eighty percent of Russian children study English starting in the fifth grade. By 1985, 250 million Chinese were actively learning the language—more than the number speaking it in the United States. Six years of English language are required in Japanese schools. In Burma, English-language classes are mandatory from kindergarten through college, and in France 83 percent of French students attending state secondary schools chose to study English as their foreign language in 1984. In Western Europe it is the second language of most bilingual people and its use is spreading rapidily in Eastern Europe with the enlarging of trade and tourism.

Modern India, with 179 different languages, relies on English to unify the country. At the start of the 1971 Indo-Pakistan war, the late Prime Minister Indira Gandhi informed the Indian nation about the war which had just begun, speaking first in English, then Hindi.

Although English is the native tongue of only a dozen countries it is widely spoken or studied in more than 90 others. Examples of its use as a universal medium of exchange go on and on around the planet.

When an Argentine pilot lands his airliner in Turkey, he and the ground controller converse in English.

When Japanese executives cut deals with Scandinavian entrepreneurs in Bangkok, they communicate in English.

In Mexico, English-speaking secretaries can double their wages; in Egypt their pay goes up ten times.

When the PLO's chief Yasir Arafat met with the Polish Pope, John Paul II, at the Vatican in 1982, the meeting was conducted in English—a language that both men could speak.

When pop singers from Hong Kong to Heidelberg ring out their songs, the lyrics often are in English.

Perhaps most significant of all, English is the medium for 80 percent of the information stored in computers around the world.

Considering its widespread use it is not a surprise to learn that English will be the language used by man's last government on the earth. What is surprising is that the Apostle John recorded this prophecy nineteen centuries ago during the time of the Roman Empire—a time when Britain was nothing more than an outpost on the fringe of the civilized world. In John's day the people living in the British Isles did not speak English. In fact, it was almost 400 years after John wrote Revelation that English finally arrived as a rude tongue spoken by obscure Germanic tribes who invaded the Isles in oared warships. Yet, 1,500 years later, the English language encompasses the globe. Obviously, only God could have known in John's time that an insignificant island on the edge of the European continent would one day field the universal language of the nations.

THE STROKE OF DEATH

> 3 And one of the heads of it as having been slain to death, and the stroke of the death of it was healed. And all the earth wondered after the beast, 4 and they worshipped the dragon, because he gave the authority to the beast, and they worshipped the beast saying: Who is like to the beast, and who can to make war with it? (Rev. 13:3–4, IGENT).

According to the imagery here, one of the heads, or countries, will be completely devastated in some way; yet will manage to recover afterwards. Revelation 13:14 explains the situation in more detail. Instead of referring to the beast as "it," which is the neuter gender form of the pronoun, the pronoun "who" is used, which here is the masculine gender. Verse fourteen provides the additional fact that the leader of this country (pronoun "who") will also receive a wound unto death, but his wound will be mysteriously healed. Predictably, people will wonder, or speculate curiously, about his mysterious recovery. The spectacular nature of this event will cause people to worship Red China for giving them this superhuman ruler. At the same time they will begin to worship the leader who will be given authority by China to preside over the new world government. In essence, when these people say, "who is like the beast," they will be saying the dictator is the beast or government. They will also be giving their allegiance to this person, declaring that no one else could possibly take his place.

People around the world will also say, "who can make war with it?" Because an attempt to remove this dictator would result in a war with "it"—the world government and the armies of the nations that will back that government.

It is important to differentiate between the "dictator beast" and the "world government beast." The Interlinear Greek-English translation of these Scriptures can be very helpful in this regard. (Incorrectly translated pronouns in several other English versions of the Bible often confuse the intended message of these texts.)

A 42 MONTH GOVERNMENT

5 And was given to it a mouth speaking great things and blasphemies, and was given to it authority to act forty-two months. 6 And it opened the mouth of it in blasphemies against God, to blaspheme the name of him and the tabernacle of him, the ones tabernacling in heaven (Rev. 13:5–6, IGENT).

According to John's report, the Fourth Beast government will last 42 months, or approximately three-and-one-half years. During this same period of time the United States will be feeding Israeli refugees in a desert place. John also notes that the "world government beast" will launch a massive propaganda campaign against God, God's name, and those that dwell in heaven with God.

WAR AGAINST CHRISTIANS DECLARED

7 And it was given to it to make war with the saints and to overcome them, and authority was given to it over every tribe and people and tongue and nation (Rev. 13:7, IGENT).

The last beast's propaganda war against God will be directed at God's people on the earth who are referred to as saints. As a result of this worldwide campaign to discredit God, the witnesses of Jesus will be subjected to unrelenting persecution.

John forewarns further that the "world government beast" will be given authority over every group of people and nation on the face of the earth. This will be the first time since the days following the great flood in Noah's time that one government will extend its rule over the entire planet.

The previous chapter reviewed Red China's role in initiating war against Christians directly following the Sixth Trumpet World War. Here, the imagery of the last beast supplies the additional fact that Red China will delegate "authority to the beast." This shows that the Chinese will be the chief exponents of the ideology of world unity and the driving force behind the international government's war against the saints. Thus, it will be Red China who will transform the beast into an instrument of war against the world's Christian community. Once that transformation is complete, the Fourth Beast will methodically carry this Chinese initiated war against Christianity to the far corners of the earth.

The Chinese-backed world government will use every conceivable means to crush the Christian opposition, until Christ returns and puts an end to the violence. This process will be akin to Hitler's domination of Europe and his war on the Jews—it happened in stages, not all at once. When Germany was no longer safe, Jews were still free in rural occupied Holland. Later they would flee to Vichy France, where, even though Nazi collaborators ruled, Jews were left alone. When the Germans occupied France completely, Jews were safe in Monaco for a time, and so it went throughout the war. Hitler kept advancing, but he was destroyed before he was able to crush the Jews completely. So it will be with the final beast and its war on the saints.

A DICTATOR PROCLAIMED A GOD

8 And all that dwell upon the earth shall worship him, whose names are not written in the book of life of the Lamb slain from the foundation of the world (Rev. 13:8).

PAUL'S INSTRUCTIONS

The Apostle Paul described this dictator who would establish himself as a god, in a letter to the church of the Thessalonians.

1 Now concerning the coming of our Lord Jesus Christ and our assembling to meet him, we beg you, brethern, 2 Not to be quickly shaken in mind or excited, either by spirit or by word, or by letter purporting to be from us, to the effect that the day of the Lord has come (2 Thess. 2:1–2, RSV).

Paul's main objective in this chapter is to correct an erroneous impression that had been made on the minds of the Thessalonians that Christ had returned, or was about to return. Paul then described two events which will take place prior to Christ's second coming.

3 Don't let anyone deceive you in any way, for that day will not come until the rebellion occurs and the man of lawlessness is revealed, the man doomed to destruction. 4 He will oppose and will exalt himself over everything that is called God or is worshiped, so that he sets himself up in God's temple, proclaiming himself to be God. 5 Don't you remember that when I was with you I used to tell you these things? (2 Thess. 2:3–5, NIV).

First, Christ would not come until there should be a great rebellion against God's truth. The days of this prophecy's fulfillment will find men abandoning their beliefs in God and the values they once had.

The second event to take place prior to Christ's return will be the appearance of the man of sin doomed to destruction. This man's character is such that it cannot be mistaken; he will be opposed to God, will exalt himself above all that is called God, and will sit in the temple showing himself as a god. Despite

God's warning in advance, people who are not Christians will worship this world "dictator beast" who will make the ridiculous claim that he is God.

THE LAMB'S BOOK OF LIFE

The reference to "the lamb having been slain from the foundation of the world" is employed here to remind people that when the world was first created, God prepared a lamb, Christ, who would and did come to die for man's sin. All those who repent of their sin and rebellion against God and accept Christ as God's Son, the Savior of the world, receive His gift of everlasting life. From that day of alignment with Jesus Christ onward, a Christian's name can never be blotted out of God's book of life.

Moses recorded this spiritual truth about God's book of life during a time of crisis when the Israelites had built an idol of gold to worship:

> 31 And Moses returned unto the LORD, and said, Oh, this people have sinned a great sin, and have made them gods of gold. 32 Yet now, if thou wilt forgive their sin—; and if not, blot me, I pray thee, out of thy book which thou hast written. 33 And the LORD said unto Moses, Whosoever hath sinned against me, him will I blot out of my book (Exodus 32:31–33).

Moses was clearly told here that God will blot the names of those who sin against Him out of His book of life.

The Book of Ezekiel records whose names were originally written in God's book of life:

> 4 Behold, all souls are mine; as the soul of the father, so also the soul of the son is mine: the soul that sinneth, it shall die (Ezek. 18:4).

God wrote every man's name in His book of life in the beginning. However, the person who sins against God will die and the sinning person's name will be blotted out of God's book of life.

The Book of Romans states which men are classified as sinners.

23 For all have sinned, and come short of the glory of God; (Rom. 3:23).

Everyone is a sinner. However, all sins shall be forgiven unto the sons of men except one.

28 Verily I say unto you, All sins shall be forgiven unto the sons of men, and blasphemies wherewith soever they shall blaspheme: **29** But he that shall blaspheme against the Holy Ghost hath never forgiveness, but is in danger of eternal damnation (Mark 3:28–29).

These verses teach that all sins are forgiven unto the sons of men, but a man will not be forgiven the sin of rejecting the message of the Holy Spirit. Furthermore, a man is in danger of eternal damnation, which is ultimately the blotting out of a person's name from the book of life, if the individual chooses to reject the message presented by the Holy Spirit.

Jesus Christ spoke of the Comforter, or Holy Spirit's work, before He died for the sins of mankind.

26 But when the Comforter is come, whom I will send unto you from the Father, even the Spirit of truth, which proceedeth from the Father, he shall testify of me (John 15:26). **8** And when he is come, he will reprove the world of sin, and of righteousness, and of judgment (John 16:8).

The message presented to humans by the Holy Spirit consists of the following truths:

(1) Everyone is a sinner and a member of a dying race.
(2) God is righteous and has provided a way of escape through personal repentance and acceptance of His Son, Jesus Christ, as Savior and Lord.
(3) Rejection of God's salvation through Jesus Christ and denial of the fact that Jesus is the Son of God will result in judgment and the blotting out of a person's name from the book of life. In essence, the Holy Spirit's whole mission is to testify of Jesus Christ.

There are two editions of the book of life. The first edition was written before man was created. It contained the names of every person who would be born into the human race. The second edition does not contain the names of the people who reject Jesus Christ as the Savior of the world, since God blots their names out of the book of life for committing this unforgivable sin. This final edition of the book of life is called the Lamb's book of life since only the names of those who receive Christ will be found written therein at the end of time.

Thus, John emphatically states that all the names of those who shall worship the coming self-proclaimed dictator-god "are not written in the book of life of the Lamb." John's unyielding statement on this subject immediately warns Christians that all those who will worship the "dictator beast" should be viewed for what they are—treacherous enemies of God's people.

It is important for Christians to understand in advance that the people who will worship the beast are not to be regarded as weak Christians who are simply trying to straddle the fence. For in the days of man's final global government, there will be no middle road—every person will have to choose between Jesus Christ and Satan's man-made god.

ETERNAL CONSIDERATIONS

9 If anyone has an ear let him hear. 10 If anyone is for captivity, to captivity he goes; if anyone by a sword will kill, it behoves him by a sword to be killed. Here is the endurance and the faith of the saints (Rev. 13:9–10, IGENT).

"If anyone has an ear let him hear," means: "Stop!" Don't just read words, but stop, and consider what is coming and what position you should take. The faceless day-to-day operating machinery of the coming one-world government will systematically enslave people in a ruthlessly dehumanizing and unprecedented manner. The "world government beast" will also persecute and kill Christians for not becoming a part of the new-world religion.

The magnitude of the violence that the "world government beast" will bring upon the earth will not only touch everyone, it will also require everyone to take a side. Unfortunately, all those who go along with the world government's program in either an active or passive way will become participants in the process of enslavement and murdering. Moreover, the government will require them to worship a man-concocted god.

Another obvious irony is brought to light here in the statement: "If anyone is for captivity, to captivity he goes; if anyone by a sword will kill, it behoves him by a sword to be killed." Initially the Fourth Beast's main thrust will be directed at the witnesses of Jesus Christ. But those who join the Fourth Beast will soon find that they also are being oppressed by the system. In the end they will not be successful in saving their lives.

Read again Isaiah's prophecy concerning the number of people left alive at the end of man's venture with the rule of all nations under one central governing body.

> 12 I will make mortal man scarcer than pure gold, And mankind than the gold of Ophir (Isa. 13:12, NASB).

The closing remark: "Here is the endurance and the faith of the Saints," is a reference to one of God's immutable laws.

> 7 Be not deceived; God is not mocked: for whatsoever a man soweth, that shall he also reap (Gal. 6:7).

Christians are very familiar with this law. They will not become a part of the system in order to save themselves because they have been taught that those who sow murder will reap murder and those who become a part of a devil-invented religion will reap the hell "prepared for the Devil and his angels" (Mt. 25:41). Therefore, they will endure the hardships and follow God's teaching even unto death. Christians know that in the end truth will prevail and they will reap a new life in the presence of Christ, forever free of the violence and hatred of this world.

THE LAMB BEAST

> 11 And I saw another beast coming up out of the earth, and it had two horns like to a lamb, and spoke as a dragon (Rev. 13:11, IGENT).

Here, "two horns like to a lamb" identifies this power structure as a religious organization. It will be established in concert with the one-world government "beast." The beast's "two horns like to a lamb" represent two prominent national powers that will assist in the initial design and on-going shared control of this religious power structure. The fact that it will speak like a dragon indicates that Satan's nation, Red China, will be instrumental in the initial design and promotion of the new "Religious Beast."

China will use the facilities of an international organization to push Satan's ideology of unity into the religious sector. "Come, let us all sit down and worship in peace and harmony." It will sound fine, but the new religion's foundation will be as weak as the mortal men who will design it. Consequently, this future ecumenical religious movement will end in disaster.

In the beginning of Daniel's vision four beasts came up out of the world's sea of people. Daniel's imagery foretold how each of these four political movements would emerge from the popular support of the sea of people under them. History proves that large numbers of people did become excited over a new idea of change in the case of the first three beasts.

In contrast, the lamb beast will not develop out of the sea of people, but rather, it will come up out of the earth. The implication seems to be that a few people in established governments will design this new religious order. In fact, the rest of Revelation 13 describes exactly how a group of international power brokers in high places will carefully orchestrate widespread enthusiasm for their new international religion.

The reference to the lamb beast "coming up out of the earth" also establishes its earthly, man-initiated origin. Neither its doctrine nor power will come from God in heaven. The idea of the one-church lamb beast movement and the people who will lend their support to its construction will all belong to the enemy, Satan, and the forces he controls.

In summary, the blueprints for the "world government beast" will begin forming in men's minds during the unsettled state of affairs following AWWI, but the finished product will not be established until the world passes through the convulsions generated by the Sixth Trumpet World War. Behind the scenes the international power brokers will also draw up a plan to set up a new international religious order. This new spiritual power will initially appear on the world scene as a non-threatening, benevolent organization.

WORLD CLASS DECEPTION

12 It exercises all the authority of the first beast in its presence, and it makes the earth and its inhabitants worship the first beast, whose mortal wound was healed. **13** It works great signs, even making fire come down from heaven to earth in the sight of men (Rev. 13:12–13, RSV).

Red China will set up the "Religious Beast" with the same "authority of the first beast," for the express purpose of opening up a second front against the Christians whom Satan is trying so diligently to crush. People will find out very quickly that the new spiritual order is an equal partner with the new international government, in authority, law enforcement, and violence. Thus, the "Religious Beast" will become inextricably intertwined with the "world government beast" in its war against Christians.

The new-world "Religious Beast" will stage a spectacular "magic show" which will even include fire coming down out of heaven. The world government and Red China will supply the "Religious Beast" with whatever resources it needs to awe the world with its "magic show." Part of their objective will be to bring people under the umbrella of the newly created religious organization.

The statement that "it makes the earth worship the first beast" implies that the "great signs" will be so spectacular that people will get the impression that the "earth" and its elements are responding to the "Religious Beast's" commands. These counterfeit miracles will lend a certain mystique to the new religion's propaganda campaign. The simulated miracles will help persuade people to go along with the new secular and spiritual order. That is, to respect, to revere and honor both the laws of the new world government and the precepts of the new religious order.

THE IMAGE MAN

14 And it deceives the (ones) dwelling on the earth because of the signs which it was given to it to do before the beast, who has the stroke of the sword and lived (again). **15** And it was given to it to give spirit to the image of the beast, in order

that the image of the beast might even speak, and might make
in order that as many as might not worship the image of the
beast should be killed (Rev. 13:14–15, IGENT).

The group manipulating the "Religious Beast" will erect an
image, or statue, in honor of the world leader who will receive
a mortal wound. Sometime after the statue is in place they will
bring the image of this world leader to life. The image will "even
speak." Everyone will then be ordered to worship the image
that will appear to be alive. The sensational effect of the speaking image will convince many that the image of their mortally
wounded leader has come to life as a god.

Of course this world leader, who will receive a fatal wound,
will not arise from the dead. The introduction of the "Image
Man" in verse 14— and "it," the Religious Beast, "deceives," or
tricks, "the (ones) dwelling on the earth"— verifies the point.

The statement that those who will refuse to worship "the
image" of the beast (i.e., not the person) "should be killed"
explains the deception further. Clearly, the "Image Man" coming to life will be nothing more than a well-orchestrated hoax.

What people will really be worshipping after the talking
image is unveiled cannot be precisely determined from the text.
The object of their worship may be a life-like animated character, or robot; or perhaps the medics and technicians of the day
will manage to patch up this individual's dead body and use it
like a robot to direct and awe the masses in public speeches.

On the other hand, the goal of those who will design this
plot is readily apparent from the text. The manipulators behind
the scenes will consider the simulation of this popular leader
coming back to life as a god paramount to the successful implementation and continuing advancement of their new international government. Their order to kill anyone who will
refuse to worship the image reveals their intense determination
to insure the success of the new religion.

The "Image Man" event reveals a cunning attempt by Satan
to mimic Jesus Christ's resurrection from the grave after being
dead for three days. Immediately following the simulation of
the "Image Man" coming to life, Satan's forces will claim that
this world leader has conquered death and become a god, equal
to Christ. Despite the realism of the performance, it will be
nothing more than a well-orchestrated lie concocted by those
who will be running the "Religious Beast" power structure.

CHRIST'S FOREWARNING

Jesus warned His people concerning such counterfeits when He talked to His disciples about the end times.

> 4 And Jesus answered and said unto them, Take heed that no man deceive you (Mt. 24:4). 24 For false Christs and false prophets will appear and perform great signs and miracles to deceive even the elect—if that were possible (Mt. 24:24, NIV). 25 Behold, I have told you in advance (Mt. 24:25, NASB).

Thanks to Christ's warnings in advance, Christians will not be deceived. Christians know from scripture exactly how Christ will return.

> 7 BEHOLD, HE IS COMING WITH THE CLOUDS, and every eye will see Him, even those who pierced Him; and all the tribes of the earth will mourn over Him. Even So. Amen (Rev. 1:7, NASB).

Christ's return will definitely not be a mysterious dark secret.

THE MARK OF THE BEAST

> 16 And it makes all men, the small and the great, both the rich and the poor, both the free men and the slaves, in order that they should give to them a mark on the right hand of them or on the forehead of them (Rev. 13:16, IGENT), 17 So that no one can buy or sell unless he has the mark, that is, the name of the beast or the number of its name (v. 17, RSV). 18 Here is wisdom. The one having reason let him count the number of the beast; for it is the number of a man. And the number of it (is) six hundreds (and) sixty-six (v. 18, IGENT).

The "Religious Beast" will use the Fourth Beast's global computer systems to enforce the decree demanding that everyone worship its life-like idol. Once the installation of the world government's institutions become fully operational, today's ongoing movement to eliminate paper business transactions and money will be complete. The world will literally have a cashless, checkless economic system in place. The facilities of a future global monetary system will make it relatively easy to force people to cooperate with the new religious order.

John's text warns of a coming day when every person on the planet will be required to have the "mark, the name of the beast or the number of the name of it" (Rev. 13:17, IGENT) placed permanently on the persons right hand, or forehead. The detail in God's word is always precise. Some people do not have a right hand; however, everyone has a head! At any rate, a person will be required to have one of the three acceptable computer access identifiers, or the person will not be allowed to buy, sell, or even receive pay for his work through the world's central computer system.

In addition to one of the three acceptable computer access identifiers, every person will need a unique identification number. Most likely a personal identification number will also be placed permanently on each individual. These unique numbers will allow the global computer system to correctly identify and credit or debit an individual's account through electronic point-of-sale computer terminal devices.

If a person's identification number is not in the global computer system, then the individual will have to exist completely outside of the established international financial system. In short, the person will not be able to "buy or sell." The master plan will be to let all those who will refuse to join the system slowly starve to death, unless the international security police find them first and execute them for being a threat to the security of the one-world government.

The international government will also have a coat of arms, or mark, a name, and a number. The number will be the number of the name of it and it will be the number of a man. "Here is wisdom," states that some peculiar knowledge, or skill, will be required to understand the relationship between the number 666 and the name of the man who will play the most prominent role in establishing and controlling the world government. Verse 18 further exhorts those who have "reason," or unique understanding based on specialized skills, to "count" the number of the beast, since the number 666 will be connected to the name of this specific man. The word count in the original Greek means compute. Today's generation, with its computerized banking and government social-security systems, can readily understand that a unique number can be entered into a computer that will compute, or find, a man's name that corresponds to his personal identification number. Thus, God has revealed in advance the specific computer access identification number of the future world leader who will be worshipped as a god, so that people will be able to positively identify him at the time of the end by connecting his number 666 with his name.

In summary, Red China will use the facilities of the beast's computerized monetary sword to overcome and kill Christians around the globe. The beast's financial computers will systematically separate the true Christians from the unbelievers who are simply going through the motions of Christianity as they mill around in the outer court of today's Christian churches. During the days of this economic persecution the true body of believers will not have to spend time trying to determine which people should be "cast out outside" the Church, since the beast's computers will be systematically separating Christ's servants from the unbelievers using the mark of the beast.

The next few chapters cover a number of Bible passages that provide today's generation with an incredibly clear picture of the operational control procedures that will be used by the last beast to carry out its future reign of terror. In order to understand the larger message of these Scriptures it is necessary to begin with a review of an ancient prophecy that was written at a time when a remnant of Jews returned from Babylon to Jerusalem to rebuild the temple.

PART
6

THE PROPHETIC
SIGNIFICANCE OF
MAN'S VENTURE
INTO SPACE

15 Wake Up!

John's description of the mark of the beast and how it will be used to establish a centrally controlled, computerized international financial system, provides only part of the larger prophetic statement on this subject. The other part was recorded by Zechariah the Prophet over 600 years before the Apostle John wrote the Revelation. Zechariah spelled out how modern space technology will be used to control and enforce the coming world government's global financial system. Collectively, his prophecies complete the Bible's comprehensive revelation about the destiny of modern man's construction of a computer-driven, satellite-linked, international financial system.

WHAT ARE THESE THINGS?

Zechariah's opening statements introduce the key subject needed to understand his prophecy—a future civilization's venture into the vastness of space. His introduction also identifies the generation living during the advent of the space-age as the one to whom the prophecy is addressed.

> 8 I saw by night, and behold a man riding upon a red horse, and he stood among the myrtle trees that were in the bottom; and behind him were there red horses, speckled, and white (Zech. 1:8). 9 And I said, What are these, my Lord? And the

angel that spoke with me said to me, I will shew thee what
these things are (v. 9, TSVGE).

Zechariah plainly stated that he saw a man "riding upon a
red horse . . . and behind him there were red horses, speckled,
and white"; but then he turns around in the next sentence and
asks the angel, "What are these things?" These seemingly contradictory statements show that the things Zechariah saw were
not living horses, but rather, a new invention that would appear
on the earth in the future.

The weird looking contraption in Zechariah's vision was a
startling sight for an ancient man to behold. Zechariah called
the thing a horse, not because it looked like one, but simply
because the man was riding upon it. In his day there were only
two basic modes of overland transportation available to a person—human foot or horseback. Hence, even as the prophet
Ezekiel used the language, "horses and horseman, all of them
splendidly attired" (Ezek. 38:4, NASB), to foretell the use of
modern motorized vehicles to transport Russian troops to the
invasion of Palestine in the latter days, so does Zechariah call
the spaceship that he saw a man riding upon in his vision, a
horse. It was clear to an ancient man that if a person was riding
instead of walking, then the "thing" being ridden had to be
something akin to a horse.

Zechariah's stated question, "What are these, my Lord?"
also declares that the "horse," which "stood among the myrtle
trees," was not standing among living myrtle trees, but rather,
some structure that was similar in appearance. The structure
Zechariah saw in vision was a gantry. Gantries are the steel
beamed towers that are built on the side of a rocket-ship's
launch pad. They serve as the spaceship's service tower while
the craft is being prepared for launch. Zechariah did not compare the gantry to a tower, however, since towers were enclosed
in his day. They were not rough framed structures with open
gaps between the beams. As Zechariah cast about for something
to compare the service tower to, he settled on the evergreen
called a myrtle tree, since it grew to a height of 30 feet and had
a lot of air-space between its branches, like the gantry he was
observing.

The next two verses bring the angel's explanation of "what
these things are" into sharper focus.

Space shuttle and gantry.

THEIR MISSION EXPLAINED

10 So the man who was standing among the myrtle trees answered, 'These are they whom the LORD has sent to patrol the earth' (Zech. 1:10, RSV).

It should be noted here that the Septuagint version renders the last part of this verse as "These are they whom the Lord has sent to go round the earth." Note that both translations reveal "what these things are" since today's manned military space-ships are often "sent forth to go round the earth" with explicit orders to "patrol the earth" below.

LAUNCH SITE DESCRIBED

At this point, the statement that "he stood among the myrtle trees that were in the bottom" can be brought into sharper focus. The word *bottom* denotes the lowest part of anything, as distinguished from the top. Zechariah used the word *bottom* here for lack of a better analogous word to describe the massive concrete and steel launch pad that supports a spaceship being prepared for flight. Zechariah may also have mentioned the fact that the horselike things stood at the bottom of the tall treelike structures because it did not make logical sense to him. From Zechariah's firsthand observation, it was visibly evident that the horselike thing needed the myrtle treelike thing to help it go forth into the heavens, from whence it could continue its journey round the earth. Although Zechariah does not say so, he apparently wondered why this flying horselike thing did not depart from the top of the treelike structure, in accordance with normal birds, who use a tree as a perch from which they launch themselves into flight.

Using some everyday language, Zechariah's original report could read: I saw by night, and behold a man was riding upon a red horselike contraption that was standing upright next to a tall framed structure that was similar in appearance to a myrtle tree. All of a sudden the horselike thing, that was standing at ground level next to the tall open-beamed scaffolding structure, shot straight up into the sky where it proceeded "to go round the earth."

A GOOD REPORT

When the spaceships returned from making their patrols round the earth, they submitted the following report to the angel of the Lord.

11 So they answered the angel of the LORD who was standing among the myrtle trees, and said, "We have patrolled the earth, and behold, all the earth is peaceful and quiet" (Zech. 1:11, NASB).

Here again the Septuagint renders "We have patrolled the earth" as "We have gone round all the earth."

When the Soviet Union launched the world's first artificial satellite, Sputnik 1, on October 4, 1957, the world's major powers were not engaged in any serious armed conflicts. That period of relative peace was still holding on April 12, 1961, when the first manned space flight was completed by Soviet cosmonaut, Yury A. Gagarin, who successfully circled the globe in the spaceship, Vostok 1, in 1 hour and 48 minutes. Thus, the historical record confirms that "all the earth was peaceful and quiet" when the space-age arrived.

THE FIRST REPOSSESSION OF JERUSALEM

Zechariah abruptly dropped his introductory space-age prophecy here and turned to an entirely different subject. This subject addresses the main concern of the Jews of his day who were living as captives in Babylon.

12 Then the angel of the LORD said, 'O LORD of hosts, how long wilt thou have no mercy on Jerusalem and the cities of Judah, against which thou hast had indignation these seventy years?' (Zech. 1:12, RSV).

The angel asked the Lord how long it would be before Jerusalem and the cities of Judah would be rebuilt. The angel also noted that the Jewish nation had been subjected to severe punishment during the seventy years since Nebuchadnezzar, king of Babylon, began the final siege of Jerusalem which led to the destruction of the kingdom of Judah.

13 And the LORD answered gracious and comforting words to the angel who talked with me. 14 So the angel who talked with me said to me, 'Cry out, Thus says the LORD of hosts: I am exceedingly jealous for Jerusalem and for Zion. 15 And I am very angry with the nations that are at ease; for while I was angry but a little they furthered the disaster. 16 Therefore, thus says the LORD, I have returned to Jerusalem with compassion; my house shall be built in it, says the LORD of hosts, and the measuring line shall be stretched out over Jerusalem.'" (Zech. 1:13–16, RSV).

The Lord replied that He was jealous for Jerusalem and Zion and declared that He had already returned to Jerusalem for the purpose of rebuilding the temple and the city.

Both of these prophecies were fulfilled long ago. The temple was completed during the sixth year of Darius (Ezra 6:15), (which already had its foundation laid at the time Zechariah was recording this prophecy [Hag. 2:18]), while the rebuilding of Jerusalem's walls was completed eighty years after Zechariah recorded his prophecy.

THE SECOND REPOSSESSION OF JERUSALEM

This prophecy is followed immediately by a second prophecy foretelling a second return of the Jewish nation to the cities of Judah and Jerusalem.

> **17** "Cry again, 'Thus says the LORD of hosts: My cities shall again overflow with prosperity, and the LORD will again comfort Zion and again choose Jerusalem.'" (Zech. 1:17, RSV).

The command, "Cry again," was issued here to announce a second prophecy about the cities of Judah and Jerusalem concerning a second return of the Jewish nation to their original homeland that would take place in the future. This is the correct interpretation since "I have returned to Jerusalem," in verse 16, is in the past tense while "the Lord will again choose Jerusalem," in verse 17, is in the future tense.

Insertion of a reference to the second return here announces the first important event to look for following the Soviet's first successful manned space flight "round the earth"—Israel's repossession of the ancient holy city of Jerusalem. This prophecy was fulfilled in June of 1967 during the Arab-Israeli Six-Day War, six years after the Soviet's first manned space flight "round the earth." Hence, the word *again* was used four times here to positively identify the text in verse 17 as a reference to the Jews second return to Jerusalem at the time of the end.

WAKE UP!

Immediately before continuing his prophetic portrait of the destiny of today's space technology, Zechariah was awakened by the angel who spoke with him.

1 And the angel that talked with me came again, and waked
me, as a man that is wakened out of his sleep (Zech. 4:1).

Zechariah was amazed to be awakened by the angel to
whom he had been talking right along. The angel had been
showing and telling him a number of things. Zechariah was
watching, asking questions, and was very interested in the
angel's presentation. But suddenly, he found himself being
awakened, just as if he had been "wakened out of his sleep."
He was amazed because he was so certain that he had been
awake and paying attention to God's message. Zechariah's
awakening in the middle of his vision prophetically represents
the awakening of Christians living during the time of the end
to the meaning of his space-age prophecies. Here again the
historical record bears witness that everyone on planet Earth
continued sleeping for several years after the arrival of manned
space flight, and after the Jews repossesed Jerusalem in 1967,
before Zechariah's space-age "wake up" report explaining the
significance of these events was finally understood.

A CANDLESTICK WITH SEVEN LAMPS

2 And said unto me, What seest thou? And I said, I have
looked, and behold a candlestick all of gold, with a bowl upon
the top of it, and his seven lamps thereon, and seven pipes to
the seven lamps, which are upon the top thereof: 3 And two
olive trees by it, one upon the right side of the bowl, and the
other upon the left side thereof (Zech. 4:2–3).

The angel showed Zechariah a golden candlestick with
seven lamps on it. Revelation 1:20 states that the "seven candlesticks are the seven churches." Therefore, this prophecy is directed to these seven churches which represent Christ's work
on the earth. Zechariah's narrative eventually reveals that this
prophecy is addressed to Christ's Church during the time when
man's last government will be ruling the entire world.

The candlestick was in the Jewish tabernacle in the days of
Moses, and later in the temple at Jerusalem. It was a symbolic
representation of God's house and its light-bearing qualities.

Through the ages gold has been viewed as man's most precious metal. The "candlestick all of gold" represents the priceless worth of Christ's earthly Church to God.

The olive oil represents the Holy Spirit who feeds the oil of truth to the seven lamps, or churches. Burning oil gives light. Light is a symbol of God's truth which He gives to Christ's earthly Church. The Church in turn gives the light of truth to a dark world.

The two olive trees, on either side of the bowl located upon the top of the candlestick, puzzled Zechariah and prompted him to ask the following question:

ZECHARIAH'S QUESTION IGNORED

4 So I answered and spake to the angel that talked with me, saying, What are these, my lord? 5 Then the angel that talked with me answered and said unto me, Knowest thou not what these be? And I said, No, my lord. 6 Then he answered and spake unto me, saying, This is the word of the Lord unto Zerubbabel, saying, Not by might, nor by power, but by my spirit, saith the LORD of hosts. 7 Who art thou, O great mountain? Before Zerubbabel thou shalt become a plain: and he shall bring forth the headstone thereof with shoutings, crying, Grace, grace unto it (Zech. 4:4–7).

Zerubbabel was the grandson of King Jehoiachin, who had been carried to Babylon. Zerubbabel was appointed governor of a remnant of Jews by King Cyrus, who had just conquered Babylon. Zerubbabel returned to Jerusalem with the remnant to rebuild the temple of God. The people dwelling in the area, to whom the Jews' land had been given, opposed the reconstruction of the temple and Jerusalem's wall, and they successfully held up the work.

ASSURANCES OF SUCCESS

Zechariah's prophecy assured Zerubbabel that God himself would remove the mountain of opposition opposing the work. Zerubbabel was also told that there would be a celebration when he put the last finishing stone in place at the completion of construction.

8 Moreover the word of the LORD came unto me, saying, **9** The hands of Zerubbabel have laid the foundation of this house; his hands shall also finish it; and thou shalt know that the LORD of hosts hath sent me unto you (Zech. 4:8–9).

Again the angel stated that Zerubbabel himself would finish the temple. This was good news, since the opposing inhabitants of the land had succeeded in halting construction for fifteen years. The angel went on to say that Zechariah would know that his prophecy was from God when the temple was completed because he was prophesying about its completion at a time when everyone was convinced this temple would never be built.

10 For who hath despised the day of small things? for they [the seven eyes of the Lord] shall rejoice, and shall see the plummet in the hand of Zerubbabel with those seven; they are the eyes of the LORD, which run to and fro through the whole earth (Zech. 4:10).

Previously a celebration had taken place upon completion of laying the temple's foundation. This event took place the second year after the remnant had returned from Babylon. Most people shouted for joy, but the older men, who had seen the first temple, wept, because this temple did not begin to compare with the splendor of the original. The angel warned against despising a "small" beginning of God's work on the earth, because this tiny temple would one day grow into a mighty body of believers. The eyes of the Lord were not only watching, but rejoicing, because God's eyes search the earth for men who will do God's work and Zerubbabel was such a man. The rest of Zechariah's prophecy is addressed to God's people who will be building Christ's Church in the face of relentless opposition, during the final days of the nuclear age.

ZECHARIAH'S SECOND INQUIRY IGNORED

11 Then answered I, and said unto him, What are these two olive trees upon the right side of the candlestick and upon the left side thereof? (Zech. 4:11).

ZECHARIAH'S THIRD INQUIRY

> **12** And I answered again, and said unto him, What be these
> two olive branches which through the two golden pipes
> empty the golden oil out of themselves? (Zech. 4:12).

Zechariah inquired about the meaning of the two olive trees
for the second and third time, respectively here, since their
significance was not clear to him. The angel deliberately remained silent and simply did not answer Zechariah's second
inquiry. This puzzled Zechariah, so he restated his question in
more detail the third time. He focused on the two branches that
were attached to the olive trees that empty the golden oil of
truth from God out of themselves to Christ's earthly Church.

Here, the branches—literally "ears" in Hebrew—are a specific reference to the clusters of olives on the olive trees'
branches. That is, even as ears of corn are full of grain, so the
olive branches are full of olives. Thus, since the angel did not
answer Zechariah's first two inquiries as to what the two symbolic olive trees represented, he directed his question to the
olive clusters that were the source of the oil for the candlestick's
seven lamps.

God's people have been asking about the significance of
these two olive trees, their attached branches and the prophecies adjoining them for the last 2,500 years. These prophecies have not been clear to men and God has remained silent
to all questions asked about them during the intervening centuries.

The fact that Zechariah asked the same question twice in a
row, at the end of the vision, prophetically signals that the full
meaning of the message would not be revealed until the time
of the end. The angel finally answered Zechariah when he
restated his question the third time.

THE OLIVE TREE IMAGERY EXPLAINED

> **13** And he answered me and said, Knowest thou not what
> these be? And I said, No, my lord. **14** Then said he, These are
> the two anointed ones, that stand by the Lord of the whole
> earth (Zech. 4:13–14).

The angel replied that "these are the two anointed ones," or literally, "the sons of fresh oil," that stand by the Lord of the whole earth. A later chapter of this book will reveal that these two olive trees are two witnesses who will continue to build Christ's Church during the final days of the nuclear age. They will continue the building job that Zerubbabel started, in even more incredibly troublesome times than Zerubbabel faced in his day.

They will be standing against the forces of hell with the Lord Himself and they will be armed for the fight—with the fresh oil of truth from God the Holy Ghost. These two will preach the gospel of Jesus Christ with the unlocked mighty technological prophecies of truth, which have been written down in advance by God's prophets of old.

The olive clusters represent the technological prophecies of truth which immediately follow Zechariah's "wake up" message. Hence, the two witnesses' main mission will be to deliver the prophetic oil of truth to Christ's earthly Church at the close of the age. Figuratively speaking, they will accomplish this task by squeezing oil from the olive clusters in their hands. That is, they will explain the Bible's technological prophecies to God's people who will be building Christ's Church during the time of the end.

This completes Zechariah's introduction to his larger prophetic message concerning the building of Christ's Church during the closing days of the technological age.

16 The Eye in the Sky

Modern technology has eliminated hard physical labor for millions of people living in the twentieth-century. The invention of electricity and numerous innovative machines has freed men from former back-breaking tedious tasks. These labor saving advances should give men more time to attend to spiritual matters. Yet, for many, the reverse is true. Instead of developing a closer relationship with God, they have lost all contact with spiritual things.

Knowing the mind of today's unbelievers, God directed His servant Zechariah to record a startling technological prophecy twenty-five centuries ago, which would help awaken people from their spiritual slumber. Contained within this prophecy is a description of how some of the twentieth century's most sophisticated technical equipment will be deployed as a weapon against Christians at the end of the age. This high-tech inquisition against the Church will take place during the time when one world government will rule over the entire earth.

THE FLYING ROLL

1 Then I turned, and lifted up mine eyes, and looked, and behold a flying roll (Zech. 5:1).

A roll was an ancient book in the form of a rolled manuscript, usually made of parchment. Ancient parchments were commonly called scrolls. When rolled up they were called rolls or volumes. A rolled up scroll was cylindrical in shape and looked like a modern roll of paper towels. Rolls were communication devices that allowed men to send and receive information.

Although Zechariah had no idea what he was viewing at first glance, twentieth century people can make the connection between a flying roll and a modern communications satellite without difficulty. Commercial communications satellites were first deployed in the heavens in the mid 1960s. At roughly 22,300 miles beyond the surface of the earth they send and receive, simultaneously, thousands of phone calls, TV broadcasts, and computer-to-computer data transmissions, from continent to continent, in mere fractions of a second.

THE ROLL'S DIMENSIONS

2 And he said unto me, What seest thou? And I answered, I see a flying roll; the length thereof is twenty cubits, and the breadth thereof ten cubits (Zech. 5:2).

A cubit was not a precise measurement in ancient times but for centuries it has been considered to be roughly 18 inches in length. Therefore, the satellite Zechariah saw was about 30 feet long and 15 feet in diameter.

Compared to America's first widely used 17-by-8 foot cylindrical commercial communications satellites, Zechariah's satellite was almost twice as large. By the 1980s, however, the overall dimensions of the more sophisticated Intelsat VI models had increased to approximately 12 feet in diameter and a length of 38 feet upon being fully extended like a telescope after positioning in orbit. By April of 1994 Christian TV host, Paul Crouch, announced that Trinity Broadcasting Network would begin broadcasting to Africa and South America with the latest Hughs Galaxy 5 satellite, which is almost exactly 30-by-15 feet. An examination of the historical development of the space program and the rest of Zechariah's space-age prophecy will shed more light on the significance of this prophetic satellite's 30-by-15 foot dimensions.

In the early days of man's venture into space the U.S. Congress recognized the need for international coordination and standardization of global satellite communications. As a consequence of their foresight the Communications Satellite Act was enacted in August, 1962, which declared that it would be the policy of the United States "to establish in conjunction and cooperation with other nations as expeditiously as practicable a commercial communications satellite system." In Europe, a conference on satellites concluded that international satellite communications should be organized in such a way as to permit all nations to participate in the ownership, management, construction, and design of the system. Discussions between the United States and European nations resulted in an agreement to form Intelsat. Intelsat stands for International Telecommunications Satellite Consortium. Nineteen nations signed the original pact on August 20, 1964. Other nations followed, raising the number of members to 109 by 1983. Intelsat's main objective is to create a global commercial communications system using satellites as the relay vehicles. One of its fundamental tasks is to establish a set of standards for the basic components of that system, which, in turn, has a direct influence on the measurements of items such as the overall dimensions of the communications satellites.

The United States is one of the world's leaders in space. In fact, the United States was the first nation to develop a sophisticated operational space shuttle system. The space shuttle orbiter is a cargo ship that plies the oceans of space, making regular runs into earth's orbit and back. It is destined to be the workhorse of the '80s and '90s, carrying tons of equipment and people into space over a period of fifteen to twenty years.

One of the shuttle's primary functions is to launch communications satellites into higher orbit from its cargo bay. Later, if a satellite needs to be brought back to earth for repairs, the shuttle's remote-controlled arm stuffs it back into the shuttle's cargo bay for the return trip. Interestingly, the shuttle's cylindrical cargo bay happens to be 60 feet long and 15 feet in diameter. It is designed to carry more than one satellite at a time. In fact, it is able to carry two large disabled communications satellites back to earth for repair that have a length of approximately 30 feet and a breadth roughly equal to 15 feet.

Zechariah's continuing space-age prophecy spells out how a future world government will use 30-by-15 foot communications satellites to control a global monetary system. God provided the exact dimensions of tomorrow's satellites in ancient times so that people could not shrug off Zechariah's accurate description of modern man's satellites. Although the satellites prophesied to be used by a future world government are not yet available for inspection, the similarity in size between today's satellites and the one shown to Zechariah has to be classified as nothing less than remarkable. After all, how could Zechariah possibly have surmised what size a satellite should be twenty-five centuries before man invented one? For even if Zechariah ingeniously conceived the idea of a global communications system in his day, there would have been no way for him to estimate the correct size of the container required to house the components needed to perform the actual communications transmissions.

THE ROLL'S MISSION EXPLAINED

3 Then said he unto me, This is the curse that goeth forth over the face of the whole earth: for every one that stealeth shall be cut off as on this side according to it; and every one that sweareth shall be cut off as on that side according to it. 4 I will bring it forth, saith the Lord of hosts, and it shall enter into the house of the thief, and into the house of him that sweareth falsely by my name: and it shall remain in the midst of his house, and shall consume it with the timber thereof and the stones thereof (Zech. 5:3–4).

As stated previously the "world government beast" will use its computerized, cashless-checkless, monetary system to gain control "over every tribe and people and tongue and nation" (Rev. 13:7, IGENT). Computers and the communications satellites described in this prophecy will be the high-tech instruments used to keep track of everyone's daily business transactions, "buying and selling." According to the text, one of the benefits of this future international financial system will be its ability to eliminate thievery and cheating in business transactions such as writing bad checks.

Zechariah specifically stated that everyone who tries to steal will be "cut off," or banished, "as on this side according to it." Likewise, everyone who swears falsely in God's name in the

Note the resemblance between a modern communications satellite and a flying roll.

course of doing business "shall be cut off on that side according to it." The "beast's" central computers will make these decisions according to what its data banks have to say about the individual's account. If a person is trying to beat the system, or is wanted for another crime, he will be caught when he attempts to use the global computer network. Punishment will consist of being "cut off," or denied access into the world's computerized economic system.

National computer systems, already in use, are designed to catch criminals and cheaters, such as doctors and pharmacists that misuse the federal medicaid program. Another example is the Treasury Enforcement Communications System, or TECS, which is run by the U.S. Customs Service. TECS contains data from several bureaus, including the Drug Enforcement Administration, and the names of thousands of known or suspected smugglers. At a number of airports, agents type into computer terminals the name of every person who passes through customs. Those who are not given the okay by the computer may be taken aside for further questioning. Smugglers fear TECS, or "the beast" as they call it, and try to avoid airports where it is used.

The fact that computers with connecting satellite links are going to be used to catch criminals doesn't sound too ominous. However, God labeled this equipment and its use as a "curse that goeth forth over the face of the whole earth." His forceful indictment warns of a coming day when computers and their associated connecting satellites will be used as a weapon of oppression against innocent people. Revelation 13's full explanation of how this electronic equipment will be turned against Christians confirms this prophetic indictment.

ZECHARIAH'S LEVITICAL ANALOGY

"And it shall remain in the midst of his house, and shall consume it with the timber thereof and the stones thereof." Zechariah employed the language used by Moses to describe the early Hebrew's procedure for removing the plague of leprosy to show how Christians will be treated at the end of the age.

> **44** Then the priest shall come and look, and, behold, if the plague be spread in the house, it is a fretting leprosy in the house: it is unclean. **45** And he shall break down the house, the stones of it, and the timber thereof, and all the morter of the house; and he shall carry them forth out of the city into an unclean place (Lev. 14:44–45).

> **45** And the leper in whom the plague is, his clothes shall be rent, and his head bare, and he shall put a covering upon his upper lip, and shall cry, Unclean, unclean. **46** All the days wherein the plague shall be in him he shall be defiled; he is unclean: he shall dwell alone; without the camp shall his habitation be (Lev. 13:45–46).

The Jews were very familiar with the dreaded disease of leprosy and the procedure for utterly destroying a house that had the plague within its structure. In Zechariah's day they dug the foundation stones of a leprous house right out of the ground. Timbers, stones, and mortar were carried outside the city. When the demolition was completed there was absolutely nothing left.

According to Zechariah's prophetic analogy, satellites shall enter a person's house, shall remain in the midst of his house, and shall consume it with the timber thereof and the stones thereof. The prophetic message is clear. Electronic satellites will enter the Christian's house and dwell there day and night when the central computer system identifies and classifies a Christian as a "leper" for not receiving the "beast's" mark. The "high priest satellite" will quarantine the Christian's house by denying him access to the world's computerized economic system. The Christian will have the option to lift the quarantine by taking the mark of the beast and its accompanying oath of allegience. But if he continues to align himself with the true God of heaven, then the satellite will shut him out of his bank account and eventually his house, when he is unable to pay his taxes. In the end the Christian will lose all of his assets, and many their lives by starvation. Like the leper of old who lived "alone," outside the camp, Christians will be forced to live outside of the world's computerized economic system. Therefore, in the last days, the satellite that will come into a Christian's house and remain in the midst of his house, will be "the curse that goeth forth over the face of the whole earth."

THIS IS THEIR EYE

> 5 Then the angel that talked with me went forth, and said unto me, Lift up now thine eyes, and see what is this that goeth forth. 6 And I said, What is it? And he said, This is an ephah that goeth forth. He said moreover, This is their resemblance through all the earth (Zech. 5:5–6).

An ephah was a large basket, equal to about a bushel. It was used by the Hebrews to measure a unit of grain. In short, it was a measuring device.

The Douay version of the Bible renders the sentence "this is a vessel going forth" as "This is their eye in all the earth." The Douay translation agrees with the plain meaning of the Hebrew, which reads "this is their eye. . . ."

Despite the differences between the King James and Douay, both versions accurately describe a modern space reconnaissance, photo-intelligence-gathering satellite. Photo-recon surveillance satellites are essentially measuring devices. Instead of measuring amounts of grain, they use a variety of techniques to measure such items as amounts of radiation that objects on the earth give off, temperatures at varying altitudes over the entire globe, or different wavelengths of light reflected by various plants on the earth's surface. With infrared cameras, satellites are able to sense variances in heat given off by objects such as heating and air conditioning units inside underground missile silos. All collected data is in turn dumped out of the ephah, or beamed via radio signals, back to earth, where computer systems and the men that run them analyze its contents.

Some satellite-gathered information is used for peaceful enterprises but most is used for military purposes. Peaceful uses include improvements in communications, weather forecasting, crop-disease control, drug control, mineral exploration, etc. Using various sophisticated instruments such as infrared photography, surveillance satellites can identify diseased crops from healthy ones, hard wood forests from soft ones, differentiate between field corn, popcorn, and sweet corn, as well as other conventional crops, and can locate marijuana and heroin poppy fields from 575 miles above the earth. Satellites are even sensitive enough to track crop-killing frosts. By one estimate, Florida citrus growers save $35 million a year because satellite data tell them precisely when to turn on the burners in their orange groves.

The United States launched a peaceful Earth Resources Technology Satellite (ERTS) in 1972 for the purpose of seeking information about improving agriculture, forestry, and land use. Interestingly, this satellite was referred to as the "Orbiting Eye" at the time.

Zechariah, while looking up, was told by the angel that "this is their eye through all the earth." The angel's additional verbal description makes it possible to positively identify the flying ephah as a photo-recon surveillance satellite. For example, many of America's intelligence satellites are in north-south polar orbit, a route that permits them to circle the globe every 90 minutes as the earth turns under them. Thus, their cameras are able to "eye," or view, each part of the globe every few hours "through all the earth."

Nearly half the spy satellites deployed are in geosynchronous orbit at an altitude of 23,500 miles where each remains above a point on the equator, moving at the same speed as the earth. These are called "staring" satellites because they keep a single area under constant surveillance rather than circling the earth. Most of them are used for early warning of the launch of ballistic missiles and for communications.

Today's top secret military satellites are referred to as our "eyes in the sky." Zechariah's reference to them as "their eye through all the earth" is perfect.

Some 40 percent of military satellites do photographic reconnaissance. Their cameras can pick out a golf ball on a green or read an automobile license plate from hundreds of miles above the earth. U.S. photo-recon satellites report on every square mile of the Soviet Union. They routinely take thousands of black and white photos of the entire Russian land mass. Their complex cameras can zoom in on anything suspicious and take close-up color photos or infrared pictures if needed.

In 1611, King James's translators correctly rendered the last phrase of verse six as "this is their resemblance through all the earth." Satellite photographs are in fact exact two dimensional resemblances of three dimensional objects.

Due to the need to monitor arms-control agreements, eye-in-the-sky satellites are also equipped to identify military objects that are camouflaged, obscured by clouds, or buried underground. U.S. satellites locate some camouflaged Russian equipment with multispectral cameras that photograph the

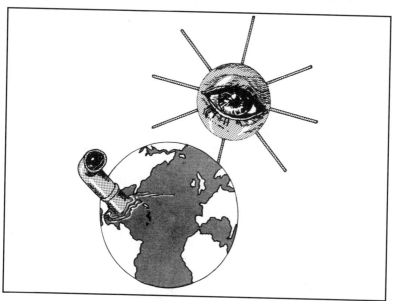

Eye in the sky satellite cartoon.

same scene in different colors. This technique uses a number of different filters, in order to penetrate the artificial camouflage. The latest breed of radar-imaging satellites are used to "see" objects on Earth's surface through clouds and in darkness.

In addition to photographing the earth's surface, military recon-satellites also monitor the radio traffic and radar transmissions of foreign military units and private communications of foreign leaders. For years, the U.S. National Security Agency used a "ferret" satellite to eavesdrop on the conversations of Premier Nikita Khrushchev and other Soviet leaders as they chatted with each other and with Kremlin offices over the radiotelephones in their cars.

In summary, the "ephah" satellite that Zechariah was shown going forth through all the earth is a very good eye indeed. It not only sees and photographs everything on the face of the earth below, but records the conversations of people as well.

A PROPHETIC SPACE WOMAN

7 And, behold, there was lifted up a talent of lead: and this is a woman that sitteth in the midst of the ephah (Zech. 5:7).

At this point in the vision the angel directed Zechariah's attention to the contents of the ephah-like spaceship. A "talent"—lit., "a round piece," i.e., lid or cover—"of lead was lifted up." This is a good description of the prophetic spaceship's heavy circular hatch door. When the hatch door was "lifted up" Zechariah was able to see inside and record the fact that it was occupied by a woman.

The location of the woman sitting (at the spacecraft's master control console), "in the midst of the ephah" shows that the woman will be in command of the reconnaissance spaceship. Her seated position symbolically demonstrates that the "woman that sitteth in the midst of the ephah" will oversee the international government's spaceborne espionage operations during the last days of man's reign on the earth.

According to Jamieson, Fausset, and Brown's *Commentary on the Whole Bible*, a talent of lead fashioned into an ephah lid would weigh 125 pounds troy. Even though a lead cover of this weight would provide far superior protection for the ephah's contents (since it would not be easily bumped off by man or beast or blown away by strong winds), it is highly unlikely that ephah lids were made of lead in Zechariah's day. It is also important to note that spaceship hatch doors are not made of lead—the metal is too soft to be used in such a role, and it is also too heavy. In view of these observations it appears that this prophetic hatch door was made of lead to symbolically reveal the fact that extra efforts would be taken to secure the contents of this future "eye-in-the-sky," spy spaceship mission. The elaborate security surrounding today's super-secret recon-satellite operations supports this interpretation. The fact that the formidably heavy lead cover was prophetically "lifted up" also supports this hypothesis. This action infers that without God's prophetic intervention, no one would be aware of the commanding role that the "woman that sitteth in the midst of the ephah" would play in the future world government's space-borne espionage operations.

WICKEDNESS FROM SPACE

8 And he said, This is wickedness. And he cast it into the midst of the ephah; and he cast the weight of lead upon the mouth thereof (Zech. 5:8).

A few years ago the standard U.S. spy satellite was the big 50-by-10 foot cylindrical, 11 ton photo-recon satellite called Big Bird. It was crammed full of highly sophisticated photographic and communications equipment. Big Bird sent most of its photos to earth electronically, but when maximum resolution was called for, an actual film cassette was dropped in a special re-entry packet or canister. The canister was caught in midair, as it floated by parachute through the latter part of its descent, by specially equipped aircraft based in Hawaii.

Also, in the 1970s, the manned Skylab craft had cameras that could be aimed like guns, using bore sights, to concentrate on specific targets. These high resolution Skylab films were carried back to earth manually by each returning Skylab crew.

Drawing on this background the actions of the angel can be seen to demonstrate the procedure used to retreive film packs that are attached to the outside hull of some of today's spacecraft. The angel then proceeded to cast "it" into the midst of the

10 And I said to the angel that spoke with me, Whither do these carry away the measure? 11 And he said to me, To build it a house in the land of Babylon, and to prepare a place for it; and they shall set it there on its own base (Zech. 5:10–11, TSGVE).

Substitution of the word "measure" for "ephah" here emphasizes the ability of reconnaissance spaceships to "see" the entire planet, including the atmosphere, with data collected by onboard sensors that measure minute differences in temperature, radiation emissions, and surface-reflected wavelengths.

THE MYSTERIOUS SPACE WOMAN IDENTIFIED

One thing unaddressed in Zechariah's prophecy is a precise definition of who or what the symbolic "woman that sitteth in the midst of the ephah" represents. In fact, the only conclusion that can be drawn from Zechariah's text is that the exact identity of the symbolic space woman is a mystery. It turns out that this does not slow down the process of determining who or what the mysterious space woman represents since her most striking

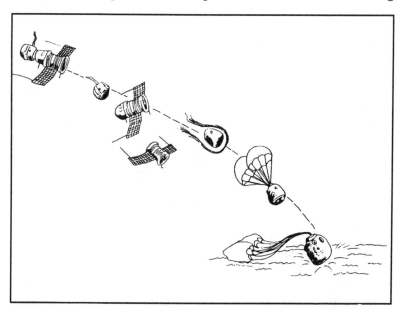

Russia's 1971 manned Soyus 11 ferry spacecraft looked much like the manned ephah revealed in vision to Zechariah twenty-five centuries ago.

trait—mysteriousness—immediately provides a unique characteristic that can be used to pinpoint her true identity. The future location of the mysterious space woman's "own" space-age "base, in the land of Babylon," provides one other essential clue to the symbolic woman's true identity.

Determining who or what the mysterious space woman prophetically represents requires a search of other Scriptures that speak of a mystery woman in connection with the ancient land of Babylon. Such a reference to a mystery woman, named Mystery Babylon, is found in Revelation 17. According to this passage Mystery Babylon will be a great city that will have "a kingdom over the kings of the earth" (Rev. 17:18, IGENT).

The answer to Zechariah's question "Whither do these bear the ephah?" plainly states, "To build it a house in the land of Babylon." It follows therefore that the mystery "woman that sitteth in the midst of the ephah" is the same mystery woman spoken of in Revelation 17 as the world's future capital city—Mystery Babylon.

Unlikely as it may seem at the beginning of the decade of the '90s, Zechariah stated that the mystery woman in charge of the ephah, or the spaceborne spying operation, will establish "her own base in the land of Babylon," which is the land within the borders of the modern day nation of Iraq. Despite the present unattractiveness of the lower Tigris-Euphrates basin for the building site of an international capital city, Zechariah's text shows that Mystery Babylon will be established on the same plain that originally supported the ancient kingdom of Babylon.

Tomorrow's international capital city of Babylon will also have a house, or temple built, which will be the command and control center for the "Religious Beast's" anti-Christian operation. This false temple will house the world's massive central computers, which will control the photo-intelligence-gathering "ephah" operation and the cashless and checkless international financial system. The whole operation will be administered by Mystery Babylon, depicted here as a "woman that sitteth in the midst of the ephah."

With the mystery woman's true identity established, her initial introduction can be brought into sharper focus. For instance, since Zechariah had no trouble seeing a man riding upon a red horselike spaceship in Zech. 1:8, it seems inconsistent that a circular hatch door had to be "lifted up" in Zech. 5:7 for him to see a woman inside. The explanation seems to be that the lead cover was opened to dramatize God's prophetic act of exposing Mystery Babylon's future evil objective—the use of a sophisticated international financial system and global space-borne enforcement patrols to destroy the Christian opposition to the "Religious Beast's" man-made god. The imagery suggests further that the world capital's "hidden agenda" (the annihilation of Christianity), carefully crafted in secret behind elaborate security measures (symbolically represented here by a massive lead cover), will not only be exposed by God, but ultimately defeated by God in the fullness of time.

ANALYSIS OF TWO FLYING WOMEN IMAGERY

A review of the imagery of the lamb beast which "had two horns like to a lamb, and spoke as a dragon," provides a clue to the identity of the two flying women in Zechariah's prophecy. (The lamb beast is the one arbitrarily designated as the "Religious Beast" in this book.) The lamb beast was the organization that pretended to represent Jesus Christ, but spoke like a Red Chinese Communist Party official. Also, according to the standard prophetic definition for a horn attached to a beast—that is, one horn equals one country—the two horns on the false lamb beast represent two nations that will play a key role in setting up the "Religious Beast." Since one symbolic horn is used to represent one nation and one symbolic woman is used to represent tomorrow's capital city, Mystery Babylon, it follows that the two women bearing the ephah represent two cities.

Since Scripture plainly teaches that the lamb beast will masquerade as an exponent of Christianity, it follows that the two cities who will support the initial establishment of a new global religious order would already house some major Christian religious organizations. Such cities would be more likely to take an active interest in setting up a one-world church movement. Furthermore, support from cities housing historically recognized Christian religious sects would lend credence to tomorrow's anti-Christian Religious Beast's claim that it represents God's true religion on the Earth.

It is highly probable that these two influential religious centers are already headquartered in two present-day cities somewhere on the planet. During the days when the seventh trumpet is about to sound, it will become clear as to which two cities will lead the movement to establish a new international religion centered in "the land of Babylon."

God had Zechariah record these space-age facts during the time when Zerubbabel was building a temple for God in the face of tremendous opposition. In like manner, God will add souls daily to His Church during the closing days before Christ returns, despite the coming sophisticated space-age opposition.

17 Top Secret

After the cargo planes load up the "ephah" spaceship and take off for the land of Shinar, Zechariah "turns" and finds himself inspecting the top secret command and control center of the most evil empire that will ever rule planet Earth. Zechariah's report on what he heard and saw during the angel's presentation provides a closer look at Mystery Babylon's fully operational space-age base, including the rockets and spaceships which will launch the satellites into orbit. These heretofore closed prophecies turn the light on a subject that has rested in darkness for centuries.

TWO MOUNTAINS OF BRASS

1 And I turned, and lifted up mine eyes, and looked, and, behold, there came four chariots out from between two mountains; and the mountains were mountains of brass (Zech. 6:1).

Imagine how startled Zechariah must have been, as he watched the flames from thousands of horsepower rocket engines blast space-age chariots into the heavens. It certainly had to be a sight to behold for a man living in ancient times.

Any spectator who watched the space-shuttle Columbia's maiden launch at Cape Canaveral would agree. As the

Shuttlecraft's 6.4 million pounds of flaming thrust roared to life, about 300,000 gallons of water poured down around the ship's base to dampen the mighty vibrations. Despite all the water, 6,000 degree fahrenheit exhaust flames roared across the launch pad, charring cables, tearing handrails from their moorings, melting water-spray nozzles and scorching grass up to a mile from the pad. Columbia's rapid ascent created such a great shock wave that light fixtures, fire-alarm boxes, and the electrical panel doors were damaged or completely torn away. Although the main structural beams of the 347-foot service tower survived intact, the elevator doors were buckled out of their frames.

Unlike ordinary mountains of rock and dirt, the two mountains Zechariah saw were man-made. They will be composed of tons of brass and brazen silicon parts, miles of fine brass and copper wires, copper pipes for water-cooled computer systems, an assortment of TV screens, radar-tracking scanners, various communications devices and all the other high-tech apparatus needed to run a space-age launch and mission control center.

One of the brass mountains represents Babylon's launch control center. The electronic gadgetry, computers, and other instruments at this site will be used strictly for launch control. This brass mountain will be an updated version of the launch control space center at Cape Canaveral in the United States.

The other brass mountain, located on the other side of the base, will be the mission control center. It will be a beefed-up version of America's Houston mission control center. All daily communications with the astronauts, flight and re-entry procedures, scientific experiments, mission planning, etc., will be handled from this center. This half of the base will also be in charge of daily operations for the coming world-wide, cashless and checkless monetary system, associated communications satellites, photo-recon enforcement patrols, and related monitoring equipment. At this point Zechariah recorded his impressions of the chariots he saw lift off from the base.

HORSES "IN" THE CHARIOTS

2 In the first chariot were red horses; and in the second chariot black horses; 3 And in the third chariot white horses; and in the fourth chariot grisled and bay horses (Zech. 6:2–3).

In Zechariah's day a chariot was usually pulled by a team of four horses. Yet Zechariah states that the "horses" were "in" the chariots, instead of outside, pulling the chariots. For centuries Zechariah's prophecy seemed inaccurate and puzzled Bible scholars. Today it is clear that Zechariah's account is flawless. Spacecraft rocket engine "horses" are "in" the "chariots." In fact, the three main rocket engine "horses" of the latest U.S. space shuttle orbiters do not pull their "space chariot," but rather, ride in the rear section of the "chariot" as they push the spacecraft into orbit.

The four space chariots are distinguished by the colors of the horses riding in them. According to Zechariah's introductory statements in chapter 1:8—"I saw by night, and behold a man was riding upon a red horse"—the world's first manned horselike spaceship would be red in color. As previously noted, that rocket-powered spaceship was launched by the Russian Red Army. Zechariah went on to report that there were red, speckled, and white horses behind the first red horse. Here again the historical record shows that the Soviets not only launched the world's first two artifical satellites and the first manned space flight around the earth, but also the second manned space flight round the earth on May 5, 1961. The Americans and other nations eventually followed the Russians into space with both unmanned and manned spacecraft, but they were forever behind those first two Red Army, communist-built, red horselike spaceships.

The Apostle John's vision of the four horsemen (Rev. 6) provides support for the position that the unique colors of the horses in each chariot represent specific nations. In John's vision each rider goes forth on a different colored horse; one to dramatically alter the world's economic order, the other three to conquer and make war. In all four cases, the colors of each rider's horse represented the nation, or coalition of powers, originating and supporting each rider's action in the vision. Here again the Bible employs colors to identify nations in prophetic text. Thus, Zechariah's space-age vision is consistent with John's four horsemen vision inasmuch as both use different colored horses to help identify the nations, or coalitions of powers, supporting the action portrayed in these visions.

The speckled horse, then, by virtue of its position in the Zechariah 1:8 text, stands for the United States and its manned space program, which followed closely on the heels of the

Soviets' first two successful manned space flights around the Earth.

The rationale for assigning the United States to the speckled horse symbol appears reasonable. It must be viewed with caution, however, since the meaning of the Hebrew word translated "speckled" in Zechariah 1:8, and "grisled and bay" in Zechariah 6:3, is uncertain. For example, the word has also been translated as "dappled gray," "dappled and many colored," "piebald and ash-colored," "ashen gray," "brown," "sorrel," and "strong dappled." The uncertainty surrounding the translation of this word makes it difficult to establish the significance of the speckled horse's color. For that matter, (at the time of this writing) the nations represented by the black and the white horses and the significance of the colors black and white also remain a mystery. Fortunately, the major points of Zechariah's space-age prophecy are easily understood, despite the unresolved questions about color. It is also important to note God's promise that "my word . . . shall not return unto me void" (Isa. 55:11). Needless to say, the correct color of the horses in the last chariot cannot be lost; therefore, there will come a day when the significance of the colors will cease to be a mystery.

WHAT ARE THESE, MY LORD?

4 Then I answered and said unto the angel that talked with me, What are these, my lord? (Zech. 6:4).

After watching the four space chariots leap into the sky on pillars of impossibly bright flame, Zechariah asked, "what are these, my lord?" Here again Zechariah's question makes it clear that the things shown to him were not ordinary chariots.

MULTIDIRECTIONAL CHARIOTS

5 And the angel answered and said unto me: These chariots go forth to the four winds of heaven, after presenting themselves before the Lord of all the earth (Zech. 6:5, THS).

The angel explained that the spacecraft "go forth," or are launched, "to the four winds of heaven." Like the winds, spaceships and the satellites they launch travel over the face of the whole earth.

PERMISSION PROCEDURES

The reference to the spaceships going forth "after presenting themselves before the Lord of all the earth" is similar to the language Zechariah used earlier to describe the two sons of fresh oil who "stand by the Lord of the whole earth." According to that imagery, the two sons of fresh oil will "stand by the Lord," spiritually to receive God's permission to carry out their mission and to receive fresh prophetic instructions from the Lord to sustain them in their work, which is to preach the gospel of Jesus Christ to the world through the seven churches.

A question naturally surfaces here: Does this mean these spacecraft will also be required to request permission from God to carry out their space missions? The answer to this question is found in the Bible's story of the man called Job. The story begins on a day when Satan came to present himself before the Lord. At this meeting Satan told the Lord that the only reason Job served God was because God had blessed him. Satan went on to say that Job would curse God to His face if he lost all that he had. Upon hearing Satan's request to injure Job, God gave Satan permission to move against Job within the boundaries of the following instructions.

> **12** And the Lord said unto Satan, Behold, all that he hath is in thy power; only upon himself put not forth thine hand. So Satan went forth from the presence of the Lord (Job 1:12).

God's reply to Satan teaches that Satan and his followers are powerless to harm God's people outside the knowledge of God and without first obtaining God's permission. Accordingly, the reference to "these chariots go forth to the four winds of heaven, after presenting themselves before the Lord of all the earth" teaches that just as Satan had to "present himself before the Lord" (Job 1:6) and receive permission to persecute Job, so will Satan and his space-age forces be unable to persecute Christians at the close of the age without God's permission. Thus, this passage warns Christians in advance of a coming day when Satan's forces will use space-age technology to wreak havoc against God's people on the earth.

INDEPENDENT FLIGHT PATHS

6 The chariot with the black horses goes toward the north country, the white ones go toward the west country, and the dappled ones go toward the south country (Zech. 6:6, RSV).

The angel that talked with Zechariah continued his explanation of what these things are by pointing out that in addition to "going forth to the four winds of heaven," the chariots have the power to travel through the heavens, in different directions, independent of air currents—north, west and south, according to the RSV. (Some translations render the individual flight paths of the chariots as north, south, east, and west.) Modern spacecraft, in keeping with the angel's description, circle the entire planet, in every direction, independent of which way the winds are blowing.

THE CHARIOTS DEPART

7 "When the strong ones went out, they were eager to go to patrol the earth." And He said, "Go, patrol the earth." So they patrolled the earth (Zech. 6:7, NASB).

POWERFUL HORSES

The sentence "When the strong ones went out, they were eager to go to patrol the earth," accurately describes a modern, rocket-powered spaceship launch. When launch control computers give them the final command to depart, the tremendous pent-up, bomblike forces unleashed at the moment of liftoff blast them into the heavens, out of sight, in a matter of minutes.

The New International Version of the Bible captures the intensity of the pre-liftoff moment: "When the powerful horses went out, they were straining to go throughout the earth." The Revised Standard Version provides an equally crisp picture of the moment of departure: "When the steeds came out, they were impatient to get off and patrol the earth." The shuttlecraft's three main rocket engines strain against lock arms for six seconds as the engines build up thrust. These complex engines, which burn fuel at the rate of half a ton per second, deliver a thrust of more than one million pounds (roughly equal to the power output of twenty-three Hoover Dams). The whole shuttlecraft rocks nineteen inches forward during the initial six-second warm-up, then it rocks back, and in that moment the solid rocket engines ignite, providing five million pounds in additional thrust. Almost instantly, the craft is streaking toward space. In two minutes and twelve seconds, it is thirty miles high and traveling at 2,891 miles an hour. "When the steeds came out, they were impatient to get off and patrol the earth" indeed!

THE CHARIOTS' MISSION

The angel's command to "Go, patrol the earth" serves to define the military nature of the "space" chariots' mission. Even as horses and chariots were used to patrol the borders of kingdoms in ancient times, so do today's nations deploy sophisticated, reconnaissance surveillance spacecraft to guard against a surprise attack from an enemy.

TRANSLATION COMPARISONS

The Septuagint's translation of this verse stated that the angel told the space chariots to go and "compass" the earth. This is precisely what today's space vehicles do when they are in their respective orbits, circling the globe every 90 minutes at 17,000 miles per hour.

The King James Bible rendered the first part of this text as "and the bay went forth, and sought to go that they might walk to and fro through the earth." This translation also captures an accurate picture of today's shuttle orbiters since they are the first spacecraft engineered to make more than one trip "to and fro through the earth" on a regular basis. Prior to orbiters, only expensive, one-way rockets could put astronauts and man-made satellites into earth orbit. The U.S. space shuttle fleet of the '80s and beyond removed this handicap by introducing the world's first reusable space transportation system. Manned shuttles ride into earth orbit atop "rocket horses" and glide back to earth after completing their mission. While other rocket ships are used once and discarded, the shuttles are expected to fly round-trips, to-and-fro between earth and orbit, repeatedly, for 100 missions or more.

A strikingly equivalent description of the space shuttle orbiter to that of the Bible's appeared in the January 12, 1981 issue of *Time* magazine. "The shuttle is envisioned as a hot-shot, to-and-fro pickup truck of a vehicle . . . the shuttle will honor round-trip reservations, going up and coming down intact, not once, but time and time again."

Americans have unknowingly borrowed one other word from Zechariah's original spaceship report by nicknaming the U.S. fleet of orbiters the "workhorses" of the '80s. Twentieth-century man still calls his transportation vehicles horses.

All things considered, Zechariah's description of shuttle orbiters is perfect: "walking to and fro through the earth," going into and out of earth orbit, using space shuttles not once, but time and time again, "compassing" the earth.

THE NORTHERN MILITARY OPERATION

8 Then cried he upon me, and spake unto me, saying, Behold, these that go toward the north country have quieted my spirit in the north country (Zech. 6:8).

The forceful introduction, "Then cried he upon me," under-scores the importance of the angel's summary proclamation concerning these various satellites and space vehicles. The lan-

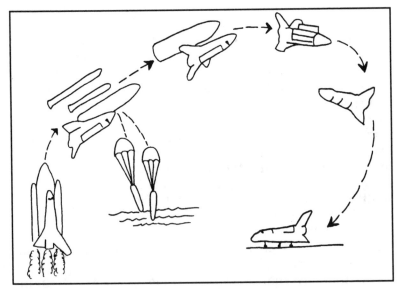

The space shuttle at work from launch to re-entry and landing.

guage used parallels the language God used to describe His anger at Russia for invading Israel in the latter days.

> **18** And it shall come to pass at the same time when Gog shall come against the land of Israel, saith the Lord GOD, that my fury shall come up in my face (Ezekiel 38:18).

The peculiar Hebraic phrase "my fury shall come up in my face," metaphorically expresses God's anger. Zechariah's transcription of the angel's proclamation communicates the same emotion, since "quieted" means "caused to rest" in Hebrew, while the Hebrew word Zechariah used for spirit means "anger." Therefore, the angel's pronouncement states that modern man's rocket ships will carry God's anger "north" and cause His judgment to rest on that (Russian) northern land. Insertion of the word "Russian" here appears to be going beyond the text without a shred of justification; however, closer inspection will reveal that this is the correct interpretation of the angel's summary proclamation.

Support for this position begins with the premise that the Bible employs a definite prophetic language to define the events of the last days. The language is composed of keynote phrases, words, numbers, and unique, well-defined symbols. These four features of the language clarify our understanding of prophetic events. They connect two or more prophecies at appropriate meaningful points. A comparison between Ezekiel's prophecy about the Russian invasion of Israel and Zechariah's spaceship vision demonstrates the effectiveness of prophetic language.

As noted previously, the first connector between Ezekiel's and Zechariah's prophecies is found in Ezekiel's declaration: "when Gog shall come against the land of Israel, says the Lord GOD, my wrath will be roused" (Ezek. 38:17, RSV). (Ezekiel's prophecy defines Gog as the ruling body over the land of Magog—Russia.) Zechariah's spaceship prophecy uses Ezekiel's same language to explain how God's wrath toward Russia will be appeased: "those who are going to the land of the north have appeased My wrath in the land of the north" (Zech. 6:8, NASB).

The second shared feature between these two prophecies is found in Ezekiel's thrice repeated statement that Israel's invader will come from the "uttermost parts of the north." The keyword "north" serves to positively identify Russia as the future invader since Russia is more north of Israel than any other nation on the planet. Zechariah's spaceship prophecy again echoes Ezekiel's report with the insertion of the keyword, north, in his summary declaration that these rocket ships will cause God's judgment to rest "on the land of the north." Thus, this precise correspondence of facts between Ezekiel's and Zechariah's prophecies makes it possible to determine that "the land of the north" in Zechariah's prophecy is the same land of Russia identified in Ezekiel's prophecy.

Left unsaid here is how the rocket-powered space chariots "that go toward the north country" will cause God's judgment to rest on that northern Russian land. That task was left for others, such as Ezekiel and John, to prophetically describe. Their prophecies explain how Russia's judgment will arrive in the form of man-made atomic fire during the days of the world's First Nuclear War.

Zechariah's spaceship prophecy teaches that God will not personally rain fire on the northern nation of Russia; instead, the sophisticated rocket ship technology of other nations will deliver God's devastating atomic judgment on Russia during the closing days of the nuclear age.

Zechariah completed his report on Babylon's space-age base with an explanation of how the temple Zerubbabel started building so long ago relates to the general design of this space-age prophecy.

TWO CROWNS

> **9** And the word of the LORD came unto me, saying, **10** Take of them of the captivity, even of Heldai, of Tobijah, and of Jedaiah, which are come from Babylon, and come thou the same day, and go into the house of Josiah the son of Zephaniah; **11** Then take silver and gold, and make crowns, and set them upon the head of Joshua the son of Josedech, the high priest; **12** And speak unto him, saying, Thus speaketh the LORD of hosts, saying, Behold the man whose name is The BRANCH; and he shall grow up out of his place, and he shall build the temple of the LORD (Zech. 6:9–12).

God instructed Zechariah to take some of the silver and gold, which the visitors had brought as an offering from the exiles in Babylon, and make crowns. Zechariah then placed these crowns on the head of Joshua. Joshua was a priest and for this ceremony a symbol of Christ who would come in the future. The "branch" ("sprout" in Hebrew) represents Christ who would come in the future and build the temple. Within the distinctive narrative strategy of this prophecy, the temple symbolically represents Christ's earthly body of believers.

> 13 Even he shall build the temple of the LORD; and he shall bear the glory, and shall sit and rule upon his throne; and he shall be a priest upon his throne; and the counsel of peace shall be between them both (Zech. 6:13).

Hence, at the end of the age, Christ will finish building the temple of the Lord, which is the body of believers in Christ. At that time He will rule in person as King of the earth, and He will also rule as priest of all the earth. Thus, the two crowns signified the combining in Christ of the two great mediatorial offices of priest and king. Under Christ's just rule the world will dwell in peace.

> 14 And the crowns shall be to Helem, and to Tobijah, and to Jedaiah, and to Hen the son of Zephaniah, for a memorial in the temple of the LORD. 15 And they that are far off shall come and build in the temple of the LORD, and ye shall know that the LORD of hosts hath sent me unto you. And this shall come to pass, if ye will diligently obey the voice of the LORD your God (Zech. 6:14–15).

The crowns were placed in the temple that Zerubbabel completed, as a memorial to the fact that God pledged Christ would one day come and complete the building of the body of believers. The passage goes on to say that people in far away places would help build the Church of Christ in the years ahead.

Zechariah's prophecy declared the arrival of the space age to be one of the signs of Christ's Second Coming. According to Zechariah's text, the establishment of global satellite communications systems, followed by the widespread deployment of "eye in the sky" photo-recon surveillance satellites, will be the first things to look for in the prophecy's fulfillment. Now inasmuch as global communications systems and photo-intelligence gathering spacecraft have already been deployed by the nations in the order spelled out by Zechariah, it is reasonable to assume that the rest of his prophesied events will also come to pass. This means that the nations will apparently begin planning an international city (referred to in Scripture as "Mystery Babylon") for the purpose of setting up a grand international financial system, before the rocket powered space chariots "that go toward the north country" are launched. Zechariah's visions suggest further that "Mystery Babylon" may actually be built before the nations unleash AWWI.

18 The Sebat Generation

Jerome, (340–420 A.D.), referred to Zechariah's work as "...that most obscure book of the prophet Zechariah." Down through the succeeding centuries Zechariah's book remained locked, waiting for future technology to forge the keys that would open its message. Without exception, those who attempted to unlock Zechariah's book before the appointed time came into view, failed to frame so much as a vague outline of its profound significance to modern man.

THE DISCIPLES QUESTION

To say Zechariah's description of man's breathtaking flight into space is one of the signs of Christ's Second Coming is correct, yet it tells only part of the story. For there is another dimension associated with the dawn of the space age that cannot be discovered in Zechariah's prophecy alone. In fact, if Jesus Christ had not mentioned the subject when His disciples asked, "What shall be the sign of thy coming?" (Mt. 24:3), no one on Earth would have been aware of the full import of man's venture into space.

In response to His disciples question, Jesus listed a number of signs and events that would come to pass before He returned to establish His earthly kingdom of peace. Jesus ended His list of events with a brief description of the world's Second Atomic War.

> **29** Immediately after the tribulation of those days shall the
> sun be darkened, and the moon shall not give her light, and
> the stars shall fall from heaven, and the powers of the heavens
> shall be shaken: **30** And then shall appear the sign of the Son
> of man in heaven: and then shall all the tribes of the earth
> mourn, and they shall see the Son of man coming in the
> clouds of heaven with power and great glory (Mt. 24:29–30).

"Immediately after the tribulation of those days" is a direct
reference to the great tribulation brought on by AWWI, which
Christ had commented on at length before making this statement. Christ then used the same language found in Joel's
portrait of AWWII to describe the immense quantities of smoke
that will be lofted into the earth's atmosphere over the course
of the nations fighting that second, all-out atomic war.

> **14** Multitudes, multitudes in the valley of decision: for the
> day of the LORD is near in the valley of decision. **15** The sun
> and the moon shall be darkened, and the stars shall withdraw
> their shining (Joel 3:14–15).

Christ also used the Apostle John's analogy of "the stars of
heaven fell unto the earth" (Rev. 6:13) to describe air-burst
atomic weapons, which will be used by the nations to wage
man's last nuclear war. Christ's use of this same language
establishes the timing of His return to be directly following a
global nuclear war; which, according to later chapters of the
book of Revelation, will be the world's Second Atomic War.

THE PARABLE OF THE FIG TREE

Christ followed His documentation of the timing of His
return with a definition of which future generation will be
present during the decades immediately preceding His promised Second Coming. Christ presented His definition in parable
form.

> **32** Now learn a parable of the fig tree; When his branch is yet
> tender, and putteth forth leaves, ye know that summer is
> nigh: **33** So likewise ye, when ye shall see all these things,
> know that it is near, even at the doors (Mt. 24:32–33).

Some Bible scholars have viewed the fig tree as a symbol of the restored nation of Israel. However, there is no other biblical or historical evidence to support this position. Moreover, the Apostle Luke's more detailed account of Christ's parable of the fig tree points to a different meaning.

LUKE'S PARABLE OF THE FIG TREE

29 And he spake to them a parable; Behold the fig tree, and all the trees; **30** When they now shoot forth, ye see and know of your own selves that summer is now nigh at hand (Luke 21:29–30).

Christ named not only the fig tree but also *all* the trees in this parable. "The fig tree and all the trees," therefore, represent *all* the prophesied signs and events leading up to Christ's Second Coming, which is in keeping with what He had been talking about immediately preceding His interjection of this parable. Thus, the equivalent statements, "when the trees now shoot forth," or "when the branches are yet tender, and putteth forth leaves," symbolically announce the rapid fulfillment of "all" the Bible's "time of the end" prophecies during the days preceding Christ's return.

In practical terms of application, "when ye shall see all these things," i.e., the establishment of the modern Jewish nation of Israel on the ancient hills of Palestine; men running to and fro and knowledge being dramatically increased; the collapse of Egypt's entire agricultural system in the days following the construction of a mighty dam astride the Nile river; the invention, production and deployment of atomic weapons and the nuclear missile systems capable of delivering them to targets half a world away; the arrival of space travel, and the widespread use of global satellite communications and "eye in the sky" photo-recon spy satellites, then "know that it is near, even at the doors," when Christ will return and establish His earthly kingdom.

According to Luke's account, "know that it is near" is a specific reference to Christ's establishment of His kingdom on earth.

31 So likewise ye, when ye see these things come to pass, know ye that the kingdom of God is nigh at hand (Luke 21:31).

Jesus concluded His parable of the fig tree with the following profound pronouncement.

THE "SHALL NOT PASS" GENERATION

34 Verily I say unto you, This generation shall not pass, till all these things be fulfilled. 35 Heaven and earth shall pass away, but my words shall not pass away (Mt. 24:34–35).

Jesus stated here that "all" the prophesied milestone events leading up to His Second Coming will occur within the life span of one generation. Christ's plainly spoken statement immediately demands that "this generation" must in some unique way be positively identified. If this generation could not be unmistakeably identified at the time of the end, then how could they be convinced that Christ was talking to them and of what earthly value would Christ's parable of the fig tree be to anyone?

A LOGICAL SEARCH FOR "THIS GENERATION"

Christ's instruction—"Now from the fig-tree learn the parable" (Mark 13:28, IGENT)— commands His servants, at the time of the end, to diligently study the Scriptures to discover the complete meaning of the parable of the fig tree, including the exact identification of the generation to whom the parable is addressed. In view of the parable of the fig tree and all the trees' central symbolism (trees putting forth leaves), it is reasonable to assume that the text defining "this generation" might also contain a reference to trees putting forth leaves when their branches are yet tender in the spring of the year. Those who proceed to investigate the matter on this premise will come to the night of "the four and twentieth day of the eleventh month, which is the month Sebat" (Zech. 1:7), when Zechariah the prophet was shown a series of visions detailing man's future venture into the silent void of space.

7 Upon the four and twentieth day of the eleventh month, which is the month Sebat, in the second year of Darius, came the word of the LORD unto Zechariah, the son of Berechiah, the son of Iddo the prophet, saying, 8 I saw by night, and behold a man riding upon a red horse, and he stood among the myrtle trees that were in the bottom; and behind him were there red horses, speckled, and white (Zech. 1:7–8).

Zechariah took great care to record the year, month, day, and even the time of the day when he received this vision. At first glance, the information appears to be redundant. After all, the prophecies that follow are addressed to people who would be living hundreds and hundreds of years in the future; what possible difference could it make to them as to what the time and date was when Zechariah received his vision?

THE SEBAT CONNECTION

The ancient Babylonian month of Sebat coincides with the eleventh month of the Jewish sacred lunar calendar, which runs from the new moon in February to the new moon in March. The word *sebat* means a "shoot," in Chaldee, for the month when trees begin to shoot or bud. God chose to reveal man's initial step into space to Zechariah during the month of Sebat for the distinct purpose of using the meaning of the month to connect the parable of "the fig tree, and all the trees" to Zechariah's manned space flight vision. Even as the rapid fulfillment of "end time" Bible prophecy was compared to budding trees (which allow men to judge that spring and summer are near) to alert people living during the closing days of the age to the nearness of Christ's Second Coming, so was the month of Sebat selected to announce man's initial step into space for the express purpose of tying the fulfillment of that event to the timing of Christ's return. Specifically, the Sebat connection turns out to be the key which unlocks the Bible's mysterious definition of the generation which "shall not pass, till all these things be fulfilled."

A GENERATION'S MOST BASIC FEATURE

Before this key can be explained, the most essential element of the definition of a generation must be established. Since the people living within a given generation pass away at different points over time, it follows that the most fundamental feature common to all the members of a specific generation is the date around which they enter into the world.

This basic property of a generation requires the presence of a unique entry date for the "end time" generation spoken of in the parable of "the fig tree and all the trees." The date, Sebat 24, 519 B.C., found in Zechariah's introduction to his first-manned-space-flight-around-the-earth prophecy, along with the "Sebat connection," budding tree imagery, provides the information needed to discover the unique entry date for this "end time" generation.

Neither Zechariah's first manned space flight prophecy, nor the date he received the vision, Sebat 24, 519 B.C., meant anything to the human race prior to the prophecy's fulfillment. Within the Sebat connection's budding tree imagery, however, the valueless state of Zechariah's vision changed abruptly the day the Russian's successfully launched the first manned space flight around the earth, on April 12, 1961.

The Soviet's successful flight marked the fulfillment of one of the "budding tree" signpost event prophecies (foretold to come to pass within the life span of the "end time" generation). Moreover, closer examination of Sebat 24, 519 B.C., reveals that it was not recorded for the purpose of drawing attention to the date Zechariah received his manned space flight vision, but rather to point to the date of the fulfillment of that event as the unique arrival date around which the "end time" generation would be born into the world.

The Sebat connection, therefore, provides the key that identifies the generation spoken of in the parable of "the fig tree and all the trees" as the one that witnessed the dawn of manned space flight, according to Zechariah's prophetic vision of that event.

With the definition of the Sebat generation understood, Christ's parable of "the fig tree and all the trees" announces man's first journey into space, "round the earth," as the date to begin the final countdown to the day of His promised return. According to this same parable, the generation that witnessed Soviet cosmonaut Yury A. Gagarin's first manned space flight "round the earth," on April 12, 1961, "shall not pass away, till all these things be fulfilled."

THE DEFINITION OF A GENERATION

"This generation" must necessarily be defined further since many people who were eighty, or older, in 1961, did not live to see Christ return. The fourteenth chapter of the book of Numbers documents an ancient historical event that spells out God's definition of a generation.

After Moses led the children of Israel out of the land of Egypt, they refused to cross into the Promised Land because of their fear of the inhabitants. God subsequently sentenced them for their unbelief and rebellion to forty years of wandering in the wilderness. During that forty year period, everyone who was twenty years old and upward died. The generation of children which witnessed their parents and grandparents rebellion were nineteen years old and under at the time. Forty years later this generation of children also witnessed, and were a part of, the Israelites' triumphant entry into the Promised Land.

Therefore, according to biblical historical precedent, anyone who was nineteen years old, or under, at the first space flight around the earth on April 12, 1961, is part of the generation identified in the parable of the fig tree, which "shall not pass, till all these things be fulfilled." This means the people who were nineteen or under on April 12, 1961, will witness Christ's return at the close of the age.

A word of caution needs to be interjected here concerning the forty years the congregation of Israel was sentenced to wander in the wilderness for their faithlessness. First, that forty year period had nothing to do with the longevity of a generation. It was a sentence for a crime, nothing more, nothing less. Further, the Bible does not refer to the Israelites who died in the wilderness during that forty years as a generation, but as a congregation. This is logical since several generations died in the wilderness; namely, parents, grandparents and great-grandparents.

The Sebat connection between Christ's parable of "the fig tree, and all the trees" and Zechariah's manned space flight vision identifies the generation Christ referred to as the one that witnessed the dawn of manned space flight. This identification does not hinge on the longevity of that generation nor does it establish the exact number of years to the day of Christ's return.

The linkage between Christ's parable of the fig tree and Zechariah's space-age prophecy, does however, serve notice to everyone that Christ will return before the generation of children who were nineteen, or under, on April 12, 1961, pass from this earth. In real terms, the expected life span of this generation provides a good approximation of the number of years remaining, within which Christ will return. Scripture sets some very definite limits on just how long any generation can expect to live.

THE LIFE SPAN OF A GENERATION

3 And the LORD said, My spirit shall not always strive with man, for that he also is flesh: yet his days shall be an hundred and twenty years (Gen. 6:3).

Therefore, in light of the limits God set on man's longevity over 4,000 years ago, (which are still prevailing despite the best research efforts of today's medical scientists), coupled with the readily available observation that most people do not even live ninety years today, it is reasonable to assume that the majority of the Sebat generation will not live more than eighty years after 1961 (The length of our days is seventy years—or eighty, if we have the strength; yet their span is but trouble and sorrow, for they quickly pass, and we fly away (Ps. 90:10, NIV). This means that Christ will return and establish His earthly kingdom sometime before, or shortly after the start of the fourth decade of the twenty-first century. Although this does not establish a precise date for Christ's return; it does eliminate the possibility that His return is yet scores of generations into the future.

God defintely designed Zechariah's prophetic description of the dawn of manned flight into space and the parable of the fig tree in such a way that Christ's servants could pinpoint the generation that will be living through the unprecedented period of violence and destruction leading up to Christ's return. God singled out space technology to identify man's last free–wheeling generation simply because it will yield the most deadly weapon ever devised by the human race. (Its lethal effectiveness relegates the destructive power of atomic weapons to mere crude stone clubs.) For while a nuclear bomb can reduce a huge city and its millions of inhabitants to ashes in a matter of seconds, infinitely more sophisticated high-tech space technology can silently reach into that same city and selectively murder only those millions labeled undesirable by a handful of future international power brokers. With this sinister technology no one will be able to "buy or sell unless he has the mark, that is, the name of the beast or the number of its name" (Rev. 13:17, RSV). This high-tech system of selective persecution and death, already under construction by the forces of darkness, has the potential to remove Christ's servants and the Christian faith from the face of the earth. Seeing this plot against His servants in ancient times, the Captain instructed Zechariah to precisely identify the generation that will bear the brunt of this coming attack against His Church. In light of the Captain's advance warning, today's Sebat generation of Christians, who will shortly face the methodical stalking death from outer space, should wake up to the urgency of the hour and make the time they have left count for Christ's work.

THE PARABLE OF THE TEN VIRGINS

Jesus followed the parable of the fig tree with a second parable, the parable of the ten virgins. In this parable Christ compared His return in the latter days to that of a bridegroom coming to his marriage ceremony.

> 1 Then shall the kingdom of heaven be likened unto ten virgins, which took their lamps, and went forth to meet the bridegroom. 2 And five of them were wise, and five were foolish. 3 They that were foolish took their lamps, and took no oil with them: 4 But the wise took oil in their vessels with their lamps. 5 While the bridegroom tarried, they all slumbered and slept. 6 And at midnight there was a cry made, Behold, the bridegroom cometh; go ye out to meet him. 7 Then all those virgins arose, and trimmed their lamps. 8 And the foolish said unto the wise, Give us of your oil; for our lamps are gone out. 9 But the wise answered, saying, Not so; lest there be not enough for us and you: but go ye rather to them that sell, and buy for yourselves. 10 And while they went to buy, the bridegroom came; and they that were ready went in with him to the marriage: and the door was shut. 11 Afterward came also the other virgins, saying, Lord, Lord, open to us. 12 But he answered and said, Verily I say unto you, I know you not (Mt. 25:1–12). 13 Watch ye therefore, because ye know not the day nor the hour (Mt. 25:13, IGENT).

The parable's use of the words wise and foolish refers only to the conduct of the ten virgins in regard to the oil. The oil represents God's abundant truth concerning the gospel of Jesus Christ that is readily available to men before Christ returns. Five of the virgins were wise and accepted the gospel of Christ and secured His oil of truth for themselves. The other five were foolish and did not bother to secure Christ's oil of truth, or make Him a part of their lives.

All ten virgins knew the bridegroom was coming, but no one knew when he would actually arrive. This has been the case since Christ left His disciples and returned to heaven over 1,900 years ago. Christians know Christ said He would return, but they do not know when He will return. Moreover, "while the bridegroom tarried" longer than expected, Christians grew weary of trying to sort out the contradicting opinions concerning the timing of Christ's return, quit watching, and fell fast asleep. The parable's main message, therefore, is that people need to wake up and "watch" the prophesied events of the end times unfold so that they will be ready for Christ's imminent return.

The cry, "the bridegroom cometh," raises the question: Why did everyone wake up to this? After all, the ten symbolic virgins knew the bridegroom was coming before they went to sleep. So why would people suddenly wake up to one more oft repeated cry, "Christ is coming," to the extent that they will rise up with one accord and hastily set about making last minute preparations for His arrival?

The command "go ye out to meet him" provides some clues to the answer of the question. The virgins immediately arose, set about trimming their lamps, and checked their supply of oil. This shows that no one challenged the authority backing the command. Notice also that the authority driving the action is definitely not vested in whomever delivered the cry, since not so much as one word is said about the person, or persons, who carried out this task. This implies the authority driving the action must be vested in the greater message of the cry. That greater message turns out to be the complete body of prophetic evidence defining when Christ will return. Moreover, according to the greater context of the parable, the biblical evidence contained within this late hour cry will speak with such force that no one will seriously doubt the prophetic truth of the message.

Once it is understood that, "Behold, the bridegroom cometh," serves only as a symbolic announcement of the cry's much larger message, the task of locating the full text of the cry can proceed without difficulty. Since the parable's imagery centers around the theme of people abruptly awakened to new prophetic truth concerning when Christ will return, it follows that the cry's full definition of the timing of Christ's Second Coming will be found in some other prophecy containing "wake up" imagery. This same imagery, of course, was also employed in Zechariah's "wake up" introduction to his space-age prophecies foretelling the building of Christ's Church during the closing days of the technological age. The visible evidence of Zechariah's unfolding prophecies bears testimony to the truth of the prophetic cry: "Behold, the bridegroom cometh." Hence, Zechariah's unabridged definition of the timing of Christ's return documents the full text of the cry: "Behold, the bridegroom cometh."

Keep in mind that Christ used both the parable of the fig tree and the parable of the ten virgins to help answer His disciples' question: "Tell us, when will these things be, and what will be the sign of Your coming, and of the end of the age?" (Mt. 24:3, NASB). Christ designed each of these parables to specifically pinpoint the timing of His return through the selection of definite symbols to connect each parable to Zechariah's full, space-age explanation of the matter. The parable of the fig tree uses the imagery of trees beginning to bud to precisely define the "Sebat generation" that will see Christ return within their lifetime. The parable of the ten virgins employs the imagery of sleeping people, suddenly awakened, to define the approximate time when the "Sebat generation" will "wake up" to Zechariah's prophetic definition of who they are and when Christ can be expected to return. Together, the two symbols spell out when Christ will return and when the Sebat generation will wake up to these prophetic facts.

With the basic design of these two parables in hand, the significance of the parable of the ten virgins' greater prophetic cry comes into full focus. For example, the "wake up" connection between the parable of the ten virgins and Zechariah's full text of the cry "Behold, the bridegroom cometh," declares that "at midnight," a very late hour just prior to Christ's return, the "wake up" message of Zechariah's space-age prophecies will be delivered to the world. Everyone will be awakened to God's message of the hour—not only the King is coming, but *when* Christ will return! Zechariah's space-age prophecies will finally cease to be a mystery. For the first time, people will know that Christ will physically return before the Sebat generation passes from the scene.

A review of Zechariah's text sharpens the prophetic objectives of these two parables. According to Zechariah 1, the first manned space flight "round the Earth" is the first event to look for in the prophetic fulfillment of these two parables. Soviet cosmonaut, Yury A. Gagarin, fulfilled this prophecy on April 12, 1961, when he successfully circled the globe in the spaceship, Vostok 1. The next event to look for, Israel's repossession of Jerusalem, also came to pass according to Zechariah's prophetic time table.

> **17** "Again, proclaim, saying, 'Thus says the LORD of hosts, "My cities will again overflow with prosperity, and the LORD will again comfort Zion and again choose Jerusalem'" (Zech. 1:17, NASB).

The word "again" is used four times here to positively identify this text as a reference to the Jews' second return to Jerusalem at the time of the end. "Again," also separates this foretold second return to Jerusalem from the prophesied first return (following the Babylonian Captivity), which is mentioned in the preceding verse. Thus, Zechariah followed his prophecy foretelling the first manned space flight "round the Earth" with a proclamation stating that the Jews would "again" repossess Jerusalem following the completion of that flight. Six years after the Soviet's first manned space flight, the Jews captured Jerusalem during the 1967 Arab-Israeli Six-Day War.

Abruptly, Zechariah dropped the subject of space technology at the end of chapter 1. Chapters 2 and 3 cover other prophetic subjects. Then, as abruptly as the subject of space technology was dropped at the end of chapter 1, Zechariah is suddenly awakened: "And the angel that talked with me came again, and waked me, as a man that is wakened out of his sleep" Zech. 4:1). The abrupt awakening of Zechariah signals the resumption of the angel's space-age "wake up" narrative. Note further that Zechariah was in a sense mentally asleep during the angel's presentation of chapters 2 and 3. Zechariah's slumbering, unknowing state, parallels the years the Sebat generation was unaware of the prophetic significance of the first manned space flight "round the earth." Even as the angel wakened Zechariah to the rest of the prophetic explanation of the prophesied first- manned space flight "round the earth," so will the Sebat generation be suddenly awakened to the prophetic significance of Zechariah's space-age "wake up" message. At a very late hour the Sebat generation will "wake up" to who they are and the prophesied fact that Christ will return to rule the world in their time.

THE SEBAT GENERATION'S RESPONSIBILITIES

The parable of the ten virgins warns that once Christ removes the Church, the door will be shut. There will be no time for preparation afterwards. No one else will be admitted into the marriage feast in heaven. Therefore, it is imperative that Christians wake up and respond to the urgency of the hour. Even as the virgins should have been awake and watching events unfold as the bridegroom approached, so should today's Christians be alert to the signs of the times. Those who are not Christians should also wake up and lose no time in asking Christ into their lives. For He is "not willing that any should perish, but that all should come to repentance" (2 Pet. 3:9).

Consider for a moment the significance of God's message to today's high-tech space-age world. The Sebat generation is steeped in science and engineering. The constant cross–polination of new ideas emerging from these structured disciplines produces a steady stream of innovation, which, in turn, intensifies the pace of modern-day life. People are becoming increasingly busy just trying to keep up. But what will be the end of all this busy, busy effort? In other words, what is this generation really trying to accomplish and where is it headed? Because of the Sebat generation's lack of understanding and direction, nobody knows! The Captain issued Zechariah's high-tech space-age prophecies in ancient times. The Captain knew what today's advanced civilizations would be doing 2,500 years ago; He also knew that it would take the Bible's indisputable prophetic oil of truth foretelling the end of the space age to wake the Sebat generation up and bring them to a saving knowledge of Jesus Christ.

6 "Thus says the LORD, . . . 'there is no God besides Me. 7 'And who is like Me? Let him proclaim and declare it; Yes, let him recount it to Me in order, From the time that I established the ancient nation. And let them declare to them the things that are coming And the events that are going to take place'" (Isa. 44:6–7, NASB).

9 Behold, the former things are come to pass, and new things do I declare: before they spring forth I tell you of them (Isa. 42:9).

9 "Remember the former things long past, For I am God, and there is no other; I am God, and there is no one like Me, (Isa. 46:9, NASB). 10 I make known the end from the beginning, from ancient times, what is still to come. I say: My purpose will stand, and I will do all that I please" (v. 10, NIV).

6 "From now on I will tell you of new things, of hidden things unknown to you. 7 They are created now, and not long ago; you have not heard of them before today. So you cannot say, 'Yes, I knew of them'" (Isa. 48:6–7, NIV).

Only God can describe space-age chariots, satellites, and all the high-tech hardware needed to support a modern space program hundreds and hundreds of years before man builds this equipment. In view of the authority of God's word, everyone should examine the Bible's plan for saving man's eternal soul.

18 Come now, and let us reason together, saith the LORD: though your sins be as scarlet, they shall be as white as snow; though they be red like crimson, they shall be as wool (Isa. 1:18).

20 Behold, I stand at the door, and knock: if any man hear my voice, and open the door, I will come in to him, and will sup with him, and he with me (Rev. 3:20).

23 For the wages of sin is death; but the gift of God is eternal life through Jesus Christ our Lord (Romans 6:23).

11 For the scripture saith, Whosoever believeth on him shall not be ashamed. **13** For whosoever shall call upon the name of the Lord shall be saved (Romans 10:11, 13).

8 For by grace are ye saved through faith; and that not of yourselves: it is the gift of God: **9** Not of works, lest any man should boast (Eph. 2:8–9).

11 And this is the record, that God has given us eternal life, and this life is in his Son. **12** He that hath the Son hath life; and he that hath not the Son of God hath not life (1 John 5:11–12).

12 Neither is there salvation in any other: for there is none other name under heaven given among men, whereby we must be saved (Acts 4:12).

6 I am the way, the truth, and the life: no man cometh unto the Father, but by me (John 14:6).

16 For God so loved the world, that he gave his only begotten Son, that whosoever believeth in him should not perish, but have everlasting life. **17** For God sent not his Son into the world to condemn the world; but that the world through him might be saved (John 3:16–17).

2*b* Behold, now is the accepted time; behold, now is the day of salvation (2 Cor. 6:2*b*).

PART
7

"Mystery Babylon's"
All-out Effort
To Destroy
Christianity

19 Mystery Babylon

Mystery Babylon, tomorrow's world capital, will oversee the most evil empire that will ever rule the Earth. According to Scripture, the city will be built on the land where the ancient kingdom of Babylon once stood.

Revelation 17 describes the decline of the last beast's powerful seven heads, the ten horns' rise to prominence, and the beast's relationship with the ruling capital city, Mystery Babylon. The chapter also exposes the world capital's main objective as nothing less than the elimination of the Christian religion from the face of the Earth.

> 1 And one of the seven angels who had the seven bowls came and spoke with me, saying, "Come here, I shall show you the judgment of the great harlot who sits on many waters, 2 with whom the kings of the earth committed acts of immorality, and those who dwell on the earth were made drunk with the wine of her immorality." 3 And he carried me away in the Spirit into a wilderness; and I saw a woman sitting on a scarlet beast, full of blasphemous names, having seven heads and ten horns. 4 And the woman was clothed in purple and scarlet, and adorned with gold and precious stones and pearls, having in her hand a gold cup full of abominations and of the unclean things of her immorality (Rev. 17:1–4, NASB).

THE GREAT HARLOT

The Apostle John was shown "the judgment of the great harlot who sits on many waters." The harlot represents the international government's capital city. The imagery of "many waters" stands for the world's people that Mystery Babylon will control through the new religious order and the computerized international financial system. The city's relationship with the world government is depicted here as a woman sitting on a seven headed, ten horned, "scarlet"- colored beast. In other words, the nations that will set up tomorrow's international government will support the cost of running the capital city.

THE SCARLET-COLORED BEAST

The color scarlet or red reveals Red China's hand in molding the international government's bureaucratic machinery into a murderous tool of oppression. Once in place, the Chinese will use the ruthless institutions of the world government to dominate and control the nations. This interpretation is based on the authority of John's initial introduction of the Fourth Beast: "And the dragon gave to it the power of it and the throne of it and great authority" (Rev. 13:2, IGENT).

In recent years Red China has acknowledged the failure of its communist economic policies and rushed to embrace free-market practices. During the same period of economic change, however, the Communist Party's firm central political control over the people has remained absolute. Authorities still watch, program, and keep a detailed dossier on each Chinese citizen. All dissent is simply liquidated. Such was the case in 1989 when the Red Army brutally crushed the democracy movement in Tiananmen Square. According to the imagery of the last beast's scarlet color, hard-line communists will ultimately prevail over any future Chinese democracy movements. The beast's scarlet color also serves to forewarn everyone that Red China's hard-line communist policies will eventually come to dominate the governing character of the Fourth Beast.

A CUP OF ABOMINATIONS

The reference to the harlot having in her hand a gold cup full of abominations and unclean things of her immorality shows that this religious capital city will enrich itself through the instruments of treachery, oppression, murder and other acts of abomination. For example, Christians who will not be able to buy or sell will lose all their property and other assets to the international government. Thus, the Fourth Beast will finance its murderous operation, in part, through the sale of confiscated goods and assets of undesireables such as Christians.

Yet despite the methodical murder of vast numbers of innocent people, the religious leaders running the world capital will claim that they are doing God's will by saving mankind from another nuclear war. They will apparently justify the murder of Christians who refuse to worship the life-like image of their charismatic leader on the grounds that Christian dissent could stir up unrest that would lead to another devastating conflict.

THE MOTHER OF HARLOTS

5 And upon her forehead a name was written, a mystery, "BABYLON THE GREAT, THE MOTHER OF HARLOTS AND OF THE ABOMINATIONS OF THE EARTH." 6 And I saw the woman drunk with the blood of the saints, and with the blood of the witnesses of Jesus. And when I saw her, I wondered greatly (Rev. 17:5–6, NASB).

The Apostle John wondered why the mysterious name, "Babylon the great, the mother of harlots and of the abominations of the earth," was written on the harlot's forehead. A history of ancient Babylon's origin, found in the writings of the Jewish historian, Josephus, provides some insight into this mystery.

Josephus noted that after the great flood the sons of Noah settled in the plain of Shinar. Although God had instructed them to spread abroad, they chose to remain in one place. Their leader, Nimrod, described by Josephus as "a bold man, and of great strength of hand," persuaded the people to credit their own efforts rather than God's for their prosperity and to consider it cowardice to obey God.

According to Josephus, Nimrod's goal was to bring everyone under his control for the purpose of enhancing his own personal power and importance. To accomplish his objective Nimrod convinced people that God was unjust and led a rebellion against God's instruction by building a tower and the city called Babylon. Although Nimrod's plan got off to a good start, Genesis 11 reports that the rebellious kindgom was destroyed when God stepped in and confounded the peoples' language and so scattered its inhabitants abroad.

According to the book of Daniel, another great kingdom of Babylon was built by Nebuchadnezzar about 1600 years later. Nebuchadnezzar, like Nimrod, attempted to conquer and control all the people on the earth. Nebuchadnezzar also led a rebellion against God by demanding that all people bow down and worship a golden idol that was 90 feet high and 9 feet wide. Despite Nubuchadnezzar's well organized effort, he also failed to conquer and control all the earth's people. Both his kingdom of Babylon and its false religion came to an end.

The city of Babylon that will rule the world at the end of the nuclear age will be patterned after these first two kindgoms. The last Babylon will have as its central objective the control of all the earth's people, will lead a rebellion against God, and will set up a false religion complete with a life-like image for people to worship. Yet despite its late arrival on the world scene, the last Babylon is called "the mother of harlots." At first glance, this reference seems inconsistent with its latter position in the flow of human history. After all, since the last Babylon is the third Babylon to come to world prominence, one would expect it to be referred to as the daughter of the second Babylon or the grandaughter of the first. However, examination of the prophetic facts show that whereas the first two Babylons eventually failed in their bid to rule over all the people on the earth, the last Babylon will successfully accomplish this feat for three-and-one-half years. Note further that the Babylon of Nebuchadnezzar's day had to rely on informers to enforce the commandment to bow down and worship the golden image, while the last Babylon will have a world-wide, satellite-linked, computer-based banking system to enforce the worship of its lifelike image. Obviously, the procedures used by the first two Babylons to persuade the masses to turn from God were elementary next to the prophesied use of space-technology by the last Babylon to enforce its God-opposing policies. Clearly, the first two Babylons were mere children compared to the last, "Babylon the Great," when it comes to creating a false religion and forcing all the people on the earth to go along with an all-out rebellion against God.

THE MYSTERIOUS IMAGERY EXPLAINED

> 7 And the angel said to me, "Why do you wonder? I shall tell
> you the mystery of the woman and of the beast that carries
> her, which has the seven heads and the ten horns" (Rev. 17:7,
> NASB).

The angel then proceeded to complete his explanation of the
rise of the last beast and its relationships between the woman,
the seven heads, and the ten horns.

> 8 The beast that thou sawest was, and is not; and shall ascend
> out of the bottomless pit, and go into perdition: and they that
> dwell on the earth shall wonder, whose names were not
> written in the book of life from the foundation of the world,
> when they behold the beast that was, and is not, and yet is
> (Rev. 17:8).

John is told here that this coalition of powers will exist
before the First Trumpet Atomic War takes place. He is also told
that it will cease to exist ("and is not") immediately following
the destruction of one-third of the earth by that atomic war.
Naturally, after numerous cities and possibly whole countries
are left in ruins from atomic warfare, there will be a period of
time when there will not be any viable world power structures
in place, or international summit meetings. Then, "out of the
bottomless pit" ("abyss" in the Greek), or period of chaos
following AWWI, a new set of binding agreements between
nations will be formed, or revived, which will be similar to the
international alliances that existed before the atomic war occurred. Yet, even though the nations will succeed in consolidat-
ing into a powerful world government, the last beast will fail
completely and "go to destruction" (IGENT).

This passage also teaches that while the world's unbelievers
will wonder after the "beast" and blindly follow it "to destruction," the world's Christian community, whose names are written in the Lamb's book of life, will not render homage to it.

The statement that the beast "was, and is not, and is about
to come up out of the abyss" (IGENT) provides the key to a full
understanding of the rest of this prophecy. For example, since
the text states that the final form of the Fourth Beast will develop
out of the atomic ashes and chaos of the post-Atomic War

period, it follows that the seven heads and ten horns represent nations that will be allied in some meaningful way before the war erupts. The imagery reveals further that these coalitions of nations will establish a cohesive power-sharing arrangement with each other and the "woman" after the war. Thus, the seven heads and ten horns represent bonafide nations that will exist, directly before, and immediately after, AWWI.

SEVEN HEADS ARE SEVEN KINGS

9 Here is the mind having wisdom. The seven heads are seven mountains, where the woman sits on them, and are seven kings (Rev. 17:9, IGENT).

The seven heads are identified here as "seven mountains," which "are seven kings," or countries. In Scripture, "mountains" are sometimes used to symbolically represent prominent powers—especially ones that are opposed to God's work. For example, Jeremiah refers to Babylon as a "destroying mountain" (Jer. 51:25), even though the city was located on a plain in his day. The symbolic statement that "The seven heads are seven mountains, where the woman sits on them," shows that these seven countries will underwrite Babylon's initial construction costs and the development of a computerized international financial system.

FIVE FELL

10 The five fell, the one is, the other not yet come, and whenever he comes it behoves him to remain a little while (Rev. 17:10, IGENT).

"The five fell" indicates that AWWI will devastate five of these seven heads/nations. A sixth will be relatively unscathed and in a position of strength. The seventh head/country will rise to a position of prominence when a charismatic leader gains control of that country at some point following the First Trumpet Atomic War. This leader will only last a short time. Again, the language implies that this leader will not survive his deadly wound.

The plan to establish a world financial center and the actual construction of the city will apparently take place before the outbreak of the Initial Atomic War. This conclusion may be derived from careful examination of the following facts: 1) Seven influential heads/nations shoulder the financial cost of building this city. 2) "Five fell," which shows that five of these nations are left prostrate as a direct result of the massive destruction wrought on them by AWWI. Obviously, these devastated five heads/nations would not be in a financial position to fund the building of Babylon following the war. Therefore, it is reasonable to look for this world financial center and a preliminary version of its supporting international monetary system to be established prior to the outbreak of AWWI.

THE BEAST IS AN EIGHTH

11 And the beast which was and is not, even he is an eighth, and is of the seven, and to destruction goes (Rev. 17:11, IGENT).

The fact that the seven-headed, ten-horned beast will cease to function, or exist, following the devastation wrought by AWWI, is stated again here for emphasis. The added informative statement that "even he is an eighth, and is of the seven" shows that the individual who will gain control of the world government will eventually rise out of the group of seven, to an eighth position of higher authority. At this point, the eighth head will be the dictator of the world.

The following prophecies list the major posts the coming world dictator will fill over the course of his rise to great heights of power.

(1) Daniel 7:8 states that this dictator will begin his career as the leader of a little country. This little country will then rise up among the ten horns and succeed in pulling three of the ten up by the roots. Thus, the little country will uproot three of the ten horns, and at the same time it will force a realignment of the ten-horned group of countries.

(2) Revelation 17:10 states that during the chaos following the First Trumpet Atomic War this dictator will manage to get control of one of the "Big Seven" heads, a major step up the power ladder.

(3) Revelation 17:11 shows the dictator rising above the "Big Seven" to an eigth powerful position, from which he will be promoted to the office of king of the world, or president of presidents.

(4) Revelation 13:14 records the fact that the dictator will receive a deadly wound after attaining his position. Revelation 17:11 closes with a complementary message concerning this ruler's deadly wound—"and to destruction goes." In other words, he will not fall like the first five heads, but will physically be destroyed.

Unfortunately, the dictator's violent policies and vicious government machinery will continue to grind up the world after he receives his deadly wound.

THE TEN HORNS ARE TEN KINGS

12 And the ten horns which you saw are ten kings, who have not yet received a kingdom, but they receive authority as kings with the beast for one hour (Rev. 17:12, NASB). **13** These have one mind, and shall give their power and strength unto the beast (v. 13).

John is told here that the powers represented by the ten horns do not exist in his day but that they will rise up on the earth in the future and be given ruling authority with the final configuration of the "Fourth Beast" world government. This special ruling authority will be granted for "one hour," i.e., the relatively short period of time that the final form of the Fourth Beast will be running the world. This organization will be the single most powerful component of the last beast, since the ten-crowned horns are the first item mentioned in the initial description of the Fourth Beast in Revelation 13:1.

The statement "These have one mind, and shall give their power and strength unto the beast" indicates that the ten countries will, in some respects, be wholly independent of each other; but, on the issue of promoting the world government and the new computerized international monetary system, they will be completely united. They will willingly give their power and strength to the establishment of the new "world government beast" and the dictator who will initially run it.

There has been much misunderstanding since John wrote the book of Revelation concerning whom the seven heads and ten horns represent. Often, authors have assigned ancient nations such as Chaldea, Egypt, the Babylon of Daniel's day, Persia and Greece, to represent the five heads that fell. Yet, Daniel explicitly stated in the vision of the four beasts that "these four beasts are four kingdoms that shall rise up on the earth" (Dan. 7:17, TSVGE). Since Daniel had the vision of the four beasts during the reign of Belshazzar, who was the last king to rule Babylon, obviously the Babylon of Daniel's day was not one of the four beasts. Furthermore, one can easily understand that the various nations that will come together to form the fourth power structure would also have to arise in the future to Daniel's time, otherwise they could not be integral components of the final governing beast of the age. Since the seven-headed, ten-horned beast in John's Revelation account is an expanded description of the Fourth Beast in Daniel's vision, it is clear that these seven heads and ten horns represent bonafide nations that will exist directly before and immediately after AWWI.

The prophetic events of the end times are rapidly coming to pass. The atomic weaponry and space-age equipment necessary to fulfill the major prophecies of the last days are already in place, and the Sebat generation continues to grow older with each passing day. Therefore, it appears that the time of the First Trumpet Atomic War is even at the door, within the next decade or two.

TODAY'S INTERNATIONAL ALLIANCES

With this premise in mind, today's international alliances and organizations should be examined with respect to the Bible's description of the formation of the last beast. According to the Revelation text, the seven heads and ten horns will be the most powerful components of the Fourth Beast and they will share that power between them. Furthermore, their power will be based on their consolidated economic leverage since John's text clearly shows that the beast's main source of strength will rest on its ability to control the international financial system. All things considered, it is reasonable to expect the coalitions of nations depicted as heads and horns to be bound together in an economic alliance, rather than a military confederation.

In terms of raw international financial power Russia and her Satellites are not good candidates for the positions of heads or horns. Although the Russians have succeeded in building an intimidating military machine, it has cost her dearly in terms of non-military production, wealth, and basic economic power. Yokohama City University Professor, Tsuneaki Sato, calculates that as much as 50 or 60 percent of all Soviet industrial capacity may be devoted to arms production. The results of over emphasis on arms production raised Soviet-block debts held by Western banks and governments to 80 billion dollars in 1982. This huge debt coupled with the virtual bankruptcy of Poland in the early 1980s prompted Western banks to deny all but a trickle of Western credit to the Soviet-block. In spite of a Soviet sell-off of large quantities of oil, diamonds, and gold to raise hard cash, Soviet deposits with Western banks dropped from $8.5 billion to $3.6 billion in 1982. "That's the level of a Sri Lanka or a Malaysia," said one U.S. banker, "and you just don't let that happen. Cash is the last thing you use if you have anything else." In view of the current economic realities of the closing years of the twentieth century, it is reasonable to expect the seven heads and ten horns to develop out of Western initiated economic alliances and organizations. (From the Bible's description of the Great Red Dragon Beast, these two Western dominated economic organizations can be expected to actively assist Red China in her efforts to become a modern industrial power during the closing years of the age.)

THE "BIG SEVEN"

Within the framework of today's international financial facts, a search of Western-sponsored economic bodies best fitted to the Bible's description of the seven heads leads to an alliance of seven nations commonly referred to as the "Big Seven." This alliance is made up of the non-communist world's seven strongest industrial powers. They are Britain, Canada, France, Italy, Japan, Germany, and the United States. The "Big Seven" have had an economic summit meeting once a year since 1975 for the purpose of discussing international financial affairs such as economic ties with China. Since they are the most powerful Western nations trading with Red China, they are the best candidates for the seven crowned heads of the Great Red Dragon Beast at the present time. The seven heads of the Western Alliance are not only a very powerful force in today's world, they are led by seven very real heads of states (as the 1983 political cartoon below so graphically shows).

THE COMMON MARKET RULED OUT

According to the imagery of the Great Red Dragon Beast, the ten horns will initially be less powerful than the seven crowned heads. For a number of years the European Economic Community (EEC), often referred to as the "Common Market," was considered a good candidate to fulfill the prophecies concerning the ten horns. However, when Spain and Portugal joined the EEC on Jan. 1, 1986, the Common Market ceased to be a possibility, since its active membership went from ten to twelve.

THE GROUP OF TEN

A second less known ten nation group are the finance ministers of the Group of Ten (G-10)—the insiders' club of the 177-nation International Monetary Fund (IMF). The G-10 nations are Belgium, the Netherlands, France, Germany,

The unfinished symphony of nations.

Italy, Great Britain, Canada, Japan, Sweden, and the United States. The Group of Ten's finance ministers are the inner circle from the major industrial powers who make almost all of the world's important monetary decisions.

The G-10 member nations are trading with Red China today and seven of them are also members of the "Big Seven" group. The possibility that some of the heads and horns will be the same countries is highly probable since nations invariably become members of several international organizations. The G-10 members and the bankers who attend International Monetary Fund meetings, represent their parochial national interests, but, compared to the "Big Seven's" summits that often address a variety of topics, G-10 meetings tend to stick to the technical business and banking issues of the global economy.

In recent years the IMF's "Group of Ten" wealthiest industrialized nations have systematically consolidated and extended their influence on the world economic scene, despite a dislike of the Fund's policies by Russia and many third world governments. Says Paul Singer, an Economist at the University of Sao Paulo, Brazil, "the power of the IMF is absolute. No foreign country can get a single cent now without an extended agreement with it."

Directly following the First Trumpet Atomic War there will be a tremendous need for a new economic system to help bring order out of chaos. Obviously the Fourth Beast's main source of power will be its new economic system, complete with electronic money. Considering the IMF's broad base of power, which enables the G-10 members to force democracies and dictatorships alike into adopting IMF imposed economic measures, the G-10 nations certainly fit the biblical description of ten economic horns rising to an absolute position of economic power "for one hour" with the beast at the end of the age.

Closer examination of the International Monetary Fund's structure reveals several features that make this organization a likely candidate for the crowned ten horns of the last beast. The IMF was created at the Bretton Woods conference in 1944 for the purpose of keeping order in the international monetary system. Under the IMF charter, the member governments have agreed on broad lines of international policy—for the first time in history.

The Fund's role was limited to helping member states—45 at the beginning, 148 by 1985—ride out balance of payments difficultie‹. A country in deficit could apply to the IMF for low-interest loans. In return, the IMF required the debtor government to put its economic house in order. When the deficits were "structural," reflecting permanent changes in a country's terms of trade, such adjustments could be painful: currency devaluation, tax increases, reduced government spending, tight controls on monetary growth. But if the immediate impact was harsh, the long-term goals were healthy, sustainable growth and high employment.

The ten most economically powerful nations in the Fund are awarded their position of importance and voting power on the basis of their contribution to the Fund's pool of resources. In time some less developed nations may grow in economic stature and eventually displace several nations that are currently among the ten most powerful in economic importance. (Dan. 7:8 foretells a "little horn" one day forcing the restructuring of the "ten horned" economic organization. This restructuring will result in the uprooting of three of the ten members and their subsequent replacement by three more economically powerful members.)

The IMF's growing influence on the world scene makes it a good candidate for the prophesied ten-horned economic organization slated to "receive authority with the beast for one hour," directly following the Sixth Trumpet World War. The Fund's current subordinate role to the governments in charge of the world's "Big Seven" sovereign industrial powers also fits the imagery of the ten horns' position during the time when these two organizations will assist Red China in her rise to world prominence.

In light of the Bible's forecast of the eventual withering away of many of the traditional vested powers of sovereign nations in favor of world government, the reversal of the dominant role between a group of nations like the "Big Seven," and the ten most powerful members of the IMF, falls within the realm of a reasonable possibility.

According to Bible prophecy a new international monetary organization will be established directly following the Sixth Trumpet World War, which will include all nations.

This new organization will be massively funded and on the order of a global central bank, capable of creating its own computerized money. At that time the organization represented by the ten crowned horns will overshadow the previously crowned seven heads in power and influence on the world scene.

One other observation should be mentioned concerning the "Big Seven" summit meetings and the statement "And the beast which was and is not, even he is an eighth, and is of the seven" (Rev. 17:11, IGENT). The European Commission President also attends the annual "Big Seven's" summit meetings, and he, the "eighth" head, invariably appears in news photographs along with the seven official heads of state representing the "Big Seven" powers. Thus, even though the "Big Seven" wield the official power at these summits, the EEC has its "eighth" head present to represent the Common Market's growing global economic clout. In other words, in recent times, "even he"—the position of EEC Commission President—"is an eight, and is of the seven," inasmuch as the EEC Commissioner is definitely present at the "Big Seven" summits as an official observer of the proceedings.

Whether or not the European Common Market succeeds in establishing the EEC as an eighth powerful head, from which a future leader eventually gains control of a comprehensive world government, remains to be seen. The wise will certainly remain open to other possibilities.

At the same time, the striking parallels between the "little horn, speaking great things" (prophesied to rise up among the ten horns [Dan. 7:8]), and the EEC's growing economic influence, should not be overlooked.

Since the Common Market's founding in 1957, its proponents have promised the Europeans "great things" through the removal of all barriers to the free movement of goods, services, and capital among EEC member states and through the eventual establishment of political unity through the creation of a United States of Europe.

According to present schedules, the 12 EEC countries will become a single marketplace of 320 million consumers, nearly equal to the combined populations of the U.S. and Japan, by the end of 1992. If events unfold according to the European Community's plan, they are expected to become the most lucrative trading bloc in the world. These developing events should not be viewed as positive identification of the eighth head, but rather, as a subject that should be kept under continuing observation.

WAR WITH THE LAMB

14 These shall make war with the Lamb, and the Lamb shall overcome them: for he is Lord of lords, and King of kings: and they that are with him are called, and chosen, and faithful (Rev. 17:14).

The ten nations, along with the beast, will use their powerful economic leverage to make war against the faithful followers of Jesus Christ, the Lamb. At the end of the age, Christ will return with His faithful and defeat the beast and destroy the international financial system represented here by ten crowned horns.

15 And he saith unto me, The waters which thou sawest, where the whore sitteth, are peoples, and multitudes, and nations, and tongues (Rev. 17:15).'

The world capital city of Babylon will rule over all the Earth's nations, peoples, and multitudes with their numerous diverse languages.

MYSTERY BABYLON UNDER ATTACK

16 And the ten horns which thou sawest upon the beast, these shall hate the whore, and shall make her desolate and naked, and shall eat her flesh, and burn her with fire (Rev. 17:16).

The ten horns will be enthusiastic about setting up an international capital city and will "give their power and strength unto the beast." However, with the passing of time this relationship will sour. They will soon learn to hate the capital city and the oppressive bureaucrats running it. Eventually the Ten will devise a plan to strip the city of its power and "shall eat her flesh;" which implies the confiscation of the goods and wealth the capital will amass during its three-and-one-half year reign of terror.

The reason the nations' relationship with the capital city will change from love to hate is obvious. At first, only Christians and other undesireables will be killed. But once the international government gets its secret police firmly in place, suddenly no one will be immune from being labeled undesireable. Everyone will be subjected to living in absolute fear. Eventually the ten most influential nations will come to the point where they have had enough. As a final solution they will wipe the international capital city off the face of the earth with atomic fire.

The statement "the ten horns . . . shall eat her flesh, and burn her with fire" points out that the future international government and its powerful economic institution will not entirely displace the governments of individual nations, nor will it gain real control over the military forces of the world's nations. However, the Ten most economically affluent nations will agree to let the international capital city regulate the world economy without hinderance. At the same time, apparently in the interest of world peace and economic recovery, the Ten will go along with the world capital's sinister and violent liquidation of anyone opposing their grand plan, including the wholesale removal of the individual rights of the common man.

THE FULFILLMENT OF GOD'S WORDS

17 For God hath put in their hearts to fulfil his will, and to agree, and give their kingdom unto the beast, until the words of God shall be fulfilled (Rev. 17:17).

This verse does not mean that God will force these ten nations to help establish a Satan-inspired one-world government. To do so would introduce a gross contradiction since the last beast's primary objective is the destruction of Christ's earthly Church. Obviously God would not ally Himself with these ten nations by giving them a plan of action against His people. Quite the contrary is the case. The book of Revelation is a written warning to all nations, hundreds of years in advance, not to join a one-world government movement. That warning is still being sounded by God's people today and will be intensified in the years ahead. Instead, the ten nations will agree to give their power to the beast, in spite of the Bible's forewarnings against this folly.

13 "These have one purpose and they give their power and authority to the beast. **14** "These will wage war against the

Lamb, and the Lamb will overcome them (Rev. 17:13–14*a*, NASB).

The ten nations will consciously agree to "give their power and authority to the beast." They will also agree with one accord to suppress Christians opposed to the establishment of the anti-Christian world government. The Ten's combined effort to annihilate God's people will be, in effect, a declaration of war against God Himself.

A comparison between John's statement, "For God hath put in their hearts to fulfil his will, . . . and give their kingdom to the beast, until the words of God shall be fulfilled," and Isaiah's forceful introduction of AWWI, "Behold, the LORD maketh the earth empty and maketh it waste, and turneth it upside down, . . . and the land shall be utterly emptied and utterly spoiled: for the LORD hath spoken this word" (Isa. 24:1, 3), removes any lingering uncertainty concerning the correct meaning of this passage. For instance, even as "Behold, the LORD maketh the earth empty" does not mean God will literally bring AWWI upon the Earth, but rather, AWWI will come to pass according to the infallible Word of God; so does John's equivalent statement, "For God hath put in their hearts to fulfil his will" not mean that God will literally force the leaders of the ten-horned group to give their kingdoms unto the beast. Instead, John's prophetic statement means the rulers of the ten nations will give their kingdoms unto the beast according to the infallible, pre-recorded, foreknowledge of God.

The prophets of Israel made startling unbending statements such as "For God hath put in their hearts to fulfil his will" to emphasize the certainty of an unparalleled future event coming to pass. In this case, the unprecedented act of not one, but ten future powerful rulers handing their kingdoms over to a newly formed city of administrators was so implausible (and still is) that the natural reaction would be to dismiss the statement as far-fetched, or simply write it off as an error on John's part. Hence, in an effort to counteract this natural reaction, John employed the typical bold language of the Hebrew prophets for the sake of underlining the certainty of the actual fulfillment of this event.

Note further that the qualifying statement "Until the words of God shall be fulfilled" is equivalent to Isaiah's clarifying comment, "for the LORD has spoken this word" (Isa. 24:3). That is, God will not force the ten kings to relinquish their power to the beast, but rather, the ten will agree among themselves to do this unprecedented act according to the "words of God." Moreover, the word "until" also declares that the Ten will eventually decide among themselves to strip the world capital of its power, in keeping with the previous verse, "And the ten horns which thou sawest upon the beast, these shall hate the whore, and shall make her desolate and naked, and shall eat her flesh, and burn her with fire" (Rev. 17:16).

THE LAWLESS ONE

The Apostle Paul wrote a letter to the church of the Thessalonians that explains how these people will be tricked into handing their kingdoms over to the beast.

> **9** The coming of the lawless one will be in accordance with the work of Satan displayed in all kinds of counterfeit miracles, signs and wonders, **10** and in every sort of evil that deceives those who are perishing. They perish because they refused to love the truth and so be saved. **11** For this reason God sends them a powerful delusion so that they will believe the lie **12** and so that all will be condemned who have not believed the truth but have delighted in wickedness (2 Thess. 2:9–12, NIV).

Paul's prophecy parallels Revelation 13's description of the "Religious Beast's" use of great signs and wonders to convince people that they should worship the image of the beast. Paul goes on to explain that because they will refuse to believe the truth and be saved, God will send them a powerful delusion so that they will believe the lie. "The lie" will be the "Religious Beast's" counterfeit miracle that will be realistic enough to make people believe that the world leader has come to life through a man-made image. Once these Christ-rejecting people actually believe the image has come to life as a god, the ten nations will willingly give their kingdoms to the beast and support the establishment of the anti-Christian world government. For rejecting God's plan of salvation through Christ's death and resurrection and for delighting in their man-made false God, they will be condemned.

Thus it will come to pass in the last days of the nuclear age that politicians, bureaucrats, and other evildoers will flock to the international capital city for the purpose of attaining positions of authority in the emerging world government. They will eagerly vie with one another for these positions, despite the warnings being preached by God's people concerning the prophesied judgment of Babylon. In the end God's words of judgment against the place will be fulfilled—the city and its inhabitants will be utterly destroyed by fire.

> **18** And the woman whom thou sawest is the great city having a kingdom over the kings of the earth (Rev. 17:18, IGENT).

John ends this prophecy by identifying the woman as the symbolic representation of the capital city that will reign over the nations of the earth. Thank God for limiting her days to a period of 42 months.

20 Firstfruit

Despite Mystery Babylon's employment of a computerized international financial system to silence those naming the name of Christ, the gospel will go forth with vigor during the days of the great tribulation. Revelation 14 highlights the dedicated effort the 144,000 "sealed" Jews, "from all the tribes of Israel" (Rev. 7:4, NIV), will put forth to help reach the lost for Christ during the closing days of the tribulation era. The chapter also describes the main technology Christians will use to accomplish this task.

THE 144,000

1 And I looked, and behold, the Lamb was standing on Mount Zion, and with Him one hundred and forty-four thousand, having His name and the name of His Father written on their foreheads (Rev. 14:1, NASB).

The 144,000 identified here are the same persons first introduced in the Sixth Seal Atomic War prophecy. According to that initial overview, "another angel ascending from the rising of the sun, having the seal of the living God" (Rev. 7:2, NASB), commanded four angels "standing at the four corners of the earth, holding back the four winds of the earth, so that no wind should blow on the earth or on the sea or on any tree" (Rev. 7:1, NASB), "saying, 'Do not harm the earth or the sea or the trees, until we have sealed the bond-servants of our God on their foreheads'" (Rev. 7:3, NASB). By way of review, the four-angel team assumed bodily positions at the four points of the compass to project the idea of the four winds of the Earth being held back by a future nuclear war-induced temperature inversion. Independently, their team leader deliberately ascended "from the rising of the sun" to call attention to some special influence in "sealing" the servants of God going out from the East, in the post-AWWI period.

The reference here to the 144,000 "having His name and the name of His Father written on their foreheads" reveals that the task of "sealing" the 144,000 with Christ's everlasting seal of salvation will be completed at this point in the prophetic flow of Revelation events. This means that the special contribution from the East to the process of influencing the 144,000 to accept Christ's "seal" of salvation must already be explained in the passages leading up to this text. A recheck of the main message of the two preceding chapters—Red China's victorious emergence from the Sixth Trumpet World War as the planet's number one power and her subsequent establishment of a Chinese-backed governing body over the nations—confirms this assumption.

The day after AWWI burns up a third of the Earth, U.S. Christians will launch a successful satellite-based evangelistic outreach to every corner of the planet. These "Flying Eagle" broadcasts will explain that AWWI and the post-AWWI global hot-air inversion are the fulfillment of Bible prophecy. They will also report Red China's sudden dispatch of a 200-million army into the Middle East and subsequent Sixth Trumpet World War victory as continuing examples of the fulfillment of prophesied end time events.

The "144,000" will be among the multitudes around the globe who will hear the U.S. satellite broadcasts. With the dramatic fulfillment of the trumpet prophecies unfolding before them, the 144,000 will finally embrace the U.S. Christian broadcasters' claims that Jesus Christ is the Savior of the world. Thus, it will take the fulfillment of the "stopped winds" and the rise of Red China to world power to convince the 144,000 to make a personal commitment to Christ.

THE WINDS BEGIN TO BLOW AGAIN

Once the 144,000 Jews have been "sealed"—according to the four-angel team leader's command to "not harm the earth or the sea or the trees, until we have sealed the bond-servants of our God on their foreheads" (Rev. 7:3, NASB)—the planet's winds will begin to blow again. Although Revelation does not spell out the duration of the global temperature inversion it will last somewhat longer than five months since the text describes the worst five months of the Fifth Trumpet Nuclear Winter before introducing the subject of the Sixth Trumpet World War. This means the global temperature inversion will last five months, plus whatever length of time it will take to fight the Sixth Trumpet War. Moreover, since John announced the completion of the task of "sealing" the 144,000 directly following his report on the establishment of the Fourth Beast and the workings of its computerized international financial system, it follows that the global hot-air inversion will also continue through the length of time it will take to set up a world government in the post-Sixth Trumpet World War period.

(Whether it will take a few months, or several years, to fight the Sixth Trumpet War and set up a world government afterwards, remains to be seen. In view of the magnitude of these two events, it is hard to imagine that both could be completed within the span of a few months.)

THE LAMB ON MOUNT ZION

In the statement "And I looked, and behold, the Lamb was standing on Mount Zion," "the Lamb" symbolically represents Christ, who is "the Lamb of God, which taketh away the sin of the world" (John 1:29). John used "Mount Zion" and a number of other emblematic objects to portray several concepts. In this manner the vision panoramically sketches the 144,000's conversion to Christianity and their unique spiritual relationship with Christ during the closing years of the great tribulation epoch.

Mount Zion, the southwestern hill in the city of Jerusalem, was a name also used for the whole city. Since it was the center of worship, it became an emblem of heaven—the dwelling-place of God.

2 I am jealous for you with a godly jealously. I promised you to one husband, to Christ, so that I might present you as a pure virgin to him. 3 But I am afraid that just as Eve was deceived by the serpent's cunning, your minds may somehow be led astray from your sincere and pure devotion to Christ (2 Cor. 11:2–3, NIV).

Thus, "these are they which were not defiled with women," is a symbolic way of saying that the 144,000 will not defile their spiritual relationship with Christ through the process of incorporating convoluted doctrines and philosophies spawned by the presumptuous thoughts of men. This means the 144,000 will not become a part of "MYSTERY, BABYLON THE GREAT, THE MOTHER OF HARLOTS" (Rev. 17:5) ecumenical "One Church" movement, nor will they be defiled by any of her sensational religious teachings. Instead, they will follow the Lamb withersoever he goeth, "in doctrine, for reproof, for correction, and for instruction in righteousness" (2 Tim. 3:16).

The phrase "These were redeemed from among men, being the firstfruits unto God and to the Lamb" (Rev. 14:4), specifically shows that the 144,000 Jews, "from all the tribes of Israel," will not only hear the American "Flying Eagle" broadcasts explaining the unfolding trumpet prophecies, but also that they will be the first "from among men" around the globe to accept the broadcasters' claims that Jesus Christ is the Son of God, the Savior of the world. Thus, even as the first ripe strawberries, apples, or oranges are referred to as the firstfruits of the greater harvest that will soon follow, so also will the 144,000 Jews be the first of the larger harvest "from among men" (both Jews and Gentiles) to come to Christ during the post-AWWI period.

5 and in the mouth of them was not found a lie; they are unblemished (Rev. 14:5, IGENT).

According to the statement "and in the mouth of them was not found a lie," the 144,000 will actively tell others about their new found faith in Jesus Christ. "They are unblemished," means that incorrect teachings and sensational doctrines constructed by the Fourth Beast's false religious movement will not weaken or compromise them.

THREE ANGELS IN MID-HEAVEN

Directly following his symbolic vision of the 144,000 Jews' relationship with Christ, John records a panoramic sketch of the high-tech equipment Christians will use to deliver the gospel to the far corners of the Earth during the closing years of the nuclear age.

THE FIRST ANGEL

6 And I saw another angel flying in mid-heaven, having an eternal gospel to preach over the ones sitting on the earth and over every nation and tribe and tongue and people (Rev. 14:6, IGENT), 7 Saying with a loud voice, Fear God, and give glory to him; for the hour of his judgment is come: and worship him that made heaven, and earth, and the sea, and the fountains of waters (v. 7).

John took special care to point out the in-flight location of this strange (to him) angelic presentation, by recording that while the angel was speaking in a "loud voice," preaching the everlasting gospel "over" the ones sitting on the earth, he was also engaged in the physical act of "flying in mid-heaven." The angel chose this unique location so that he could personally demonstrate how a modern communications satellite will be used to preach the "eternal gospel" of salvation throughout the entire world.

The angel personally demonstrated how a modern communications satellite works; so this prophecy reveals that Christian broadcasters will use communications satellites, more and more, in the days leading up to Christ's return. They will eventually succeed in delivering the gospel "over" everyone on the earth. Christian programs will also warn that the hour of God's judgment will shortly come to pass. Christian broadcasters will reason with people to turn to God who "made the heaven, and earth, and the sea, and the fountains of waters."

THE SECOND ANGEL

8 And there followed another angel, saying, Babylon is fallen,
is fallen, that great city, because she made all nations drink of
the wine of the wrath of her fornication (Rev. 14:8).

"And there followed another angel" with a second proclamation, who personally demonstrated the important role
that a second strategically placed communications satellite will
play in delivering God's Word to the world. The message that
will be broadcast by this satellite foretells the complete overthrow of the anti-Christian world capital, Mystery Babylon.

THE THIRD ANGEL

9 And another angel, a third, followed them, saying with a
loud voice, "If any one worships the beast and its image, and
receives a mark on his forehead or on his hand, **10** he also
shall drink the wine of God's wrath, poured unmixed into the
cup of his anger, and he shall be tormented with fire and
sulphur in the presence of the holy angels and in the presence
of the Lamb. **11** And the smoke of their torment goes up for
ever and ever; and they have no rest, day or night, these
worshipers of the beast and its image, and whoever receives
the mark of its name" (Rev. 14:9–11, RSV).

A third angel personally demonstrated the importance of a
third precisely positioned communications satellite that will
broadcast a third important message to those on the earth. His
proclamation declares that everyone who will worship the
beast's lifelike image and join the world government's economic system, by taking the mark of its name, will certainly be
judged by God.

Today's communications satellites are placed 22,300 miles
above the Earth's surface where they travel at the same relative
speed as a corresponding point on the earth below. To an
earthbound onlooker, the satellite appears to be stationary. In
fact, geostationary, or geosynchronous, is the term used to
describe this orbit. In principle, it takes three properly positioned satellites to provide continuous global broadcast coverage to those "sitting on the earth." The satellite technology that

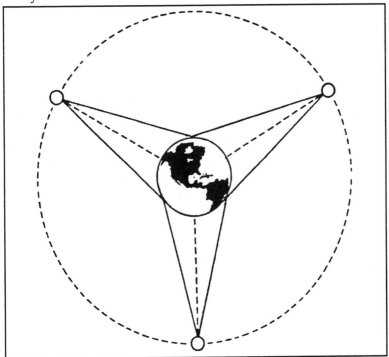

In principle, three satellites placed in geostationary orbit—fixed above a single point 22,300 miles above the equator—can provide continuous global communications coverage.

could be used to fulfill the evangelistic effort described in this passage is already available. This prophecy also foretells the three most important messages that Sebat Christians will be broadcasting via satellite during the closing days of the nuclear age.

In summary, a three-angel team was sent on this prophetic mission simply because a task force of three provided a logical way to demonstrate the technical necessity of employing three properly positioned satellites in "mid-heaven" before continuous global broadcasts could be delivered "over the ones sitting on the earth."

PERSEVERANCE OF THE SAINTS

12 Here is the perseverance of the saints who keep the commandments of God and their faith in Jesus. **13** And I heard a

voice from heaven, saying, "Write, 'Blessed are the dead who
die in the Lord from now on!'" "Yes," says the Spirit, "that
they may rest from their labors, for their deeds follow with
them" (Rev. 14:12–13, NASB).

"From now on," indicates that Christians using satellites to
preach the gospel will come under increasing persecution as the
domination of the world government grows. Many Christians
will be killed for their evangelistic efforts and for speaking
against the evil excesses of the international government. Nevertheless, God encourages Christians to continue preaching
despite the cost, reminding them that death releases a Christian
from the labor of this world and brings him into the Lord's rest.
Even after the Christian is gone, the results of his work follows—those who have turned to Christ.

The emblematic description of the 144,000 Jews' impeccable
Christian testimony, immediately before the symbolic vision of
Christendom's use of global communications satellites to
preach the gospel "over the ones sitting on the earth," shows
the 144,000 converted Jews will join forces with those Christians
already engaged in the task of leading the world's multitudes
to Christ.

At the close of Christ's ministry His disciples asked, "what
shall be the sign of thy coming, and of the end of the world?"
(Mt. 24:3*b*). Christ responded with the following message to
Christians concerning the persecution they will be confronted
with during the closing days of the nuclear age. Christ's message complements the Revelation 14 account about these coming times of trial.

CHRIST'S WARNING

9 Then shall they deliver you up to be afflicted, and shall kill
you: and ye shall be hated of all nations for my name's sake.
10 And then shall many be offended, and shall betray one
another, and shall hate one another (Mt. 24:9–10).

Jesus warns Christians that they will be hated of all nations
and killed for His name's sake, just prior to His coming. Jesus
also identified a large number of people within the framework
of the Christian Community who will be offended when they

find the tribulation days upon them and, fearful for their own lives, will quickly disassociate themselves from uncompromising believers who will be the immediate objects of the world government's wrath. Predictably, these false Christians will hate Christ's true followers and will turn them over to the international authorities who will be seeking their lives.

CHRIST'S DEFINITION OF THE END

Jesus answered His disciples' question as to when to expect the end of the age with the following statement.

14 And this gospel of the kingdom will be preached throughout the whole world, as a testimony to all nations; and then the end will come (Mt. 24:14, RSV).

Christians will use modern satellite broadcasting technology to preach the gospel of the kingdom "throughout the whole world, as a testimony to all nations; and then the end will come." Christians will preach the gospel until the world government silences their message. At that time (according to the last half of Revelation 14, covered in the final chapter of this book), Christ will remove all Christians from the Earth. He will then proceed to judge the anti-Christian world government and those supporting its actions.

21 The Captain's Last Two Soldiers

Zechariah's space-age prophecy introduced two sons of fresh oil "standing by the Lord of the whole Earth," but the rest of his book makes no further reference to them. As a matter of fact they are not mentioned again until the eleventh chapter of the book of Revelation.

> 1 And was given to me a reed like to a staff, saying: Rise and measure the shrine of God and the altar and the (ones) worshipping in it. 2 And the outside court of the shrine cast out outside and thou mayest measure it not, because it was given to the nations, and the holy city they will trample forty and two months (Rev. 11:1–2, IGENT). 3 And I will give power unto my two witnesses, and they shall prophecy a thousand two hundred and threescore days, clothed in sackcloth (v. 3).

This passage reviews the major outcomes of the Sixth Trumpet World War. First, all of Christendom's financial assets will come under the control of the new international religious order that will be set up by the nations after the war. This action will mark the beginning of a globally organized war against Christians. Further, the holy city of Jerusalem will come under the control of the nations for forty-two months.

42 MONTHS AND 1,260 DAYS

In response to these gains made by Satan's forces, the Captain of the Lord's host "will give power unto His two witnesses, and they shall prophecy a thousand two hundred and threescore days." The use of forty-two months and 1,260 days here indicates that 42 months, 1,260 days and a time and times and half a time, all refer to the same three-and-one-half year period of time—the time when the Fourth Beast will rule the world.

TWO OLIVE TREES AND TWO CANDLESTICKS

4 These are the two olive trees, and the two candlesticks standing before the God of the earth (Rev. 11:4).

In Zechariah's prophecy, the "two olive trees," one on each side of a candlestick with seven lamps thereon, represent the two "anointed ones" (literally, "the sons of fresh oil") teaching God's space-age prophecies to Christ's earthly church during the days leading up to the outbreak of AWWI. Here, the definite statement "these are the two olive trees, and the two candlesticks standing before the God of the earth" declares that the same two "anointed ones" will not only fulfill the mission symbolically defined in Zechariah's two olive trees prophecy, but also the mission defined by the two candlesticks' imagery. The two candlesticks symbolize the decidedly different mission of the two witnesses during the Fourth Beast's three-and-one-half-year reign of terror.

The book of Revelation's introductory prophetic picture of Christ walking among seven candlesticks reveals the mission of the two witnesses. The seven candlesticks represent Christ's entire earthly church. John introduced the two witnesses' second mission after the reference to Jerusalem being placed under the control of the nations for 42 months (the same 42 month time period assigned for the duration of the Fourth Beast in Rev. 13:5). It follows that once the Fourth Beast succeeds in snuffing out the light going forth from Christ's long-established churches, the two witnesses will assume the leadership role after the church has been driven underground. During those violent days, the only visible light remaining intact from the "seven churches" will be going out through the Captain's two witnessing candlesticks. These two soldiers of the cross will be Christ's visible earthly church.

The unique narrative connection between Zechariah and John's prophecies teaches that once the space-age has advanced to the level described in Zechariah's prophecy, the two witnesses will begin to shed much light on events pertaining to the approaching end of man's reign on the Earth. Initially, the "sons of fresh oil" will explain future events in terms of the Bible's abundant supply of technological prophecies, especially those describing the world's First Atomic War and the construction of an oppressive international government in the post-AWWI period. Upon the establishment of that world government, the two witnesses will spend their remaining three-and-one-half years leading the Christian movement to evangelize the world, despite the Fourth Beast's determined effort to keep them from doing so. Note further that since the two "anointed ones" will be preaching during the Fourth Beast's reign of terror, the space-age will close within the life-span of these two witnesses.

CLOTHED IN SACKCLOTH

One might wonder why the two witnesses will wear sackcloth. Sackcloth was a coarse cloth used for making sacks and rough garments in Bible days, commonly made from camel or goat hair. Garments made from this type of cloth were a symbol of mourning and were worn during times of grief and calamity. The witnesses may wear these traditional mourning clothes as an expression of grief over the atomic disaster brought on the Earth by man's rebellion against God. On the other hand, they may wear some type of sturdy garments for more practical reasons such as keeping radioactive fallout off their skin and for protection against the dramatic increase in ultraviolet radiation expected in the wake of a global atomic war.

THE WITNESS OF TWO IS TRUE

The assignment of two witnesses to this prophetic end time mission is in keeping with the Mosaic judicial procedure—the witness of two is true. God, being just, does not condemn any man to death on the word of one witness.

6 At the mouth of two witnesses, or three witnesses, shall he
that is worthy of death be put to death; but at the mouth of
one witness he shall not be put to death (Deut. 17:6).

During extraordinary times in Israel's past, God sent men
in pairs to warn people of impending judgments. Examples
include: Moses and Aaron, Caleb and Joshua, Ezekiel and Daniel, Zerubbabel and Joshua. The two witnesses will carry out
their final mission during the most extraordinary times ever
witnessed by man.

The two witnesses will exhort all men to repent and turn to
Christ. They will use God's space-age prophecies to prove
God's existence and good intentions toward all men.

FIRE DEVOURETH THEIR ENEMIES

5 And if any man will hurt them, fire proceedeth out of their
mouth, and devoureth their enemies: and if any man will hurt
them, he must in this manner be killed (Rev. 11:5).

The day the world government takes power will mark the
beginning of ever increasing opposition to the witnesses' space-
age prophetic message of truth and hope. Predictably, those
supporting the international government will find the witnesses' message inflamatory and disruptive, especially their
general call for men to turn to Christ and separate themselves
from the international government's religious movement.

According to this text and the Fourth Beast's declaration of
"war with the saints" (Rev. 13:7), there will be a determined
effort, not only to silence the two witnesses' testimony, but also
to "hurt them." John described the witnesses' response to this
offensive against them in the words "fire proceedeth out of their
mouth, and devoureth their enemies."

Should the language of Revelation 11:5 be interpreted in a
figurative or literal sense? Similar language used in Jeremiah's
prophecy of Jerusalem's fall at the hands of the Babylonians
provides one possible parallel text.

14 Wherefore thus saith the LORD God of hosts, Because ye
speak this word, behold, I will make my words in thy mouth
fire, and this people wood, and it shall devour them (Jer. 5:14).

The prophetic words from Jeremiah's mouth came to pass when the Babylonians burned Jerusalem and carried those remaining alive back to Babylon as slaves. If a symbolical meaning of "fire" is intended in Revelation 11:5, it would find fulfillment when the witnesses' enemies eventually meet their death at the hands of the post-AWWI plagues and Second Atomic War, both of which are prophetically spelled out in the rest of the Revelation.

On the other hand, if the immediate death of the witnesses' enemies by literal fire is the intended meaning of the text, parallel passages exist for this also. In a confrontation between King Ahaziah of Samaria and Elijah the prophet, literal fire settled the matter.

> **9** Then the king sent unto him a captain of fifty with his fifty. And he went up to him: and, behold, he sat on the top of an hill. And he spake unto him, Thou man of God, the king hath said, Come down. **10** And Elijah answered and said to the captain of fifty, If I be a man of God, let fire come down from heaven, and consume thee and thy fifty. And there came down fire from heaven, and consumed him and his fifty (2 Kings 1:9–10).

Thus, when the captain threatened Elijah in his day, God killed Elijah's enemies with actual fire. God's intervention not only kept Elijah's enemies from harming him, but more importantly, it removed all doubt concerning his commission as a prophet of God.

The two witnesses will be up against the same all-out opposition that Elijah faced in his day. In fact, according to Revelation 11:7, the Fourth Beast will finally succeed in killing them after waging war against the two witnesses for 1,260 days.

Since "the two candlesticks" represent the two witnesses openly assuming the leadership role left after the church has been driven underground, destruction of the two witnesses' enemies provides the only plausible explanation. Otherwise how could the two openly preach for 1,260 days against the evils of a powerful international government determined to silence them? The second half of this verse confirms the manner in which their enemies will be killed. The phrase "and if any man will hurt them, he must in this manner be killed" repeats what was previously said and redirects the cause of death back to the initial description—by "fire."

NO RAIN FOR 1,260 DAYS

> **6** These have the authority to shut heaven, in order that rain may not rain(fall) the days of the prophecy of them, and authority they have over the waters to turn them into blood and to strike the earth with every (kind of) plague as often as they may wish (Rev. 11:6, IGENT).

It will not rain on Earth during the entire 1,260 days of the two witnesses' final prophetic mission. Since the text places the timing of their prophecy directly after the text covering the Sixth Trumpet World War, it is reasonable to assume that the globe-gripping drought will be a delayed negative consequence of AWWI. A United Nation's study released in May of 1988 titled "Study on the Climatic and Other Global Effects of Nuclear War," reported that lowered temperatures and various other disruptive climatic effects of nuclear war might be compounded by a decrease in rainfall of as much as 80 percent over land in temperate and tropical latitudes.

(As today's scientists continue to gather data on the expected global environmental disruptions caused by nuclear war, their calculated conclusions are becoming more and more in harmony with the Bible's account of what will actually come to pass.)

The two witnesses' authority "to shut up the sky so that it will not rain during the time they are prophesying" does not necessarily demand that they will invoke supernatural power to stop the rains. Instead, the intended meaning seems to be that they will declare that it will not rain for 1,260 days on the authority of this very prophecy in God's Word. This position is in keeping with the first reference to their power in verse 3: "And I will grant authority to my two witnesses, and they will prophesy for twelve hundred and sixty days." (Rev. 11:3, NASB). This verse identifies God's remarkable prophecies about the last days of the nuclear age as the source of the witnesses' God-given "authority."

WATERS TURN BLOOD RED

In the same vein, the sense of the metaphorical statement "and authority they have over the waters to turn them into blood" (IGENT) seems to be that the two witnesses will prophesy according to the authority of God's Word—e.g., "The third angel poured out his bowl on the rivers and springs of water, and they became blood" (Rev. 16:4, NIV). This prophecy (covered in the next chapter) does not mean that the Earth's waters will actually turn into blood but rather that they will become contaminated from AWWI's long-term atomic fallout to the extent that they will eventually take on the unnatural redish hue of blood.

AUTHORITY OVER PLAGUES

The witnesses' authority "to strike the earth with every kind of plague as often as they want" would find fulfillment in the two witnesses pointing out the parallels between the Bible's descriptions of the post-AWWI plagues and the observable environmental consequences of that war—e.g., no rain, waters turning bloodred, and soil contamination from long term atomic fallout.

The closing comment, "as often as they may wish," in turn, seems to indicate that as often as they preach on the post-AWWI plagues, people will be able to look at the accumulating evidence and see for themselves the fulfillment of Bible prophecy in their time. Thus, God will commission the two witnesses to testify of these mighty prophecies coming to pass after AWWI in front of the rulers, bureaucrats, and general population so that they will know that God's word is true.

THE WITNESSES KILLED

7 And whenever they finish the witness of them, the beast coming up out of the abyss will make war with them and will overcome them and will kill them (Rev. 11:7, IGENT).

At the end of the number of days God has alloted the witnesses to preach to the world, the beast will be allowed to "overcome them and kill them." God will decide their prophetic mission is finished at the end of 1,260 days, not the murderous bureaucrats running the international government.

The statement about "the beast coming up out of the abyss" and making "war with them," refers to the fact that the Fourth Beast will form out of the atomic ashes of the First Trumpet Atomic War.

> 8 And their dead bodies shall lie in the street of the great city, which spiritually is called Sodom and Egypt, where also our Lord was crucified (Rev. 11:8).

John reported here that the two witnesses will give their final message of warning and hope in the city of Jerusalem. God will then allow the "beast" to end their lives.

> 9 And some of the peoples and tribes and tongues and nations see the corpse of them three and a half days, and they do not allow the corpses of them to be placed in a tomb (Rev. 11:9, IGENT). 10 And they that dwell upon the earth shall rejoice over them, and make merry, and shall send gifts one to another; because these two prophets tormented them that dwelt on the earth (v. 10).

The two witnesses' strong stand against the evil excesses of the Fourth Beast and its man-made god will be a constant source of aggravation to the bureaucrats running the world government. No one likes to be told that they are following a false way. When the televised news of their death is flashed around the world, there will be widespread rejoicing. But the rejoicing will be premature.

THE WITNESSES RAISED FROM THE DEAD

> 11 And after three days and an half the Spirit of life from God entered into them, and they stood upon their feet; and great fear fell upon them which saw them. 12 And they heard a great voice from heaven saying unto them, Come up hither. And they ascended up to heaven in a cloud; and their enemies beheld them. 13 And the same hour was there a great earthquake, and the tenth part of the city fell, and in the earthquake were slain of men seven thousand: and the remnant were

affrighted, and gave glory to the God of heaven (Rev. 11:11–13).

Three-and-one-half days after the two witnesses are murdered, God will raise them from the dead before the eyes of those dwelling on the Earth. People will be terrified when the two witnesses stand up on their feet and step off the Earth and into the clouds. A great earthquake within the same hour, which will topple a tenth part of the city and kill seven thousand, will intensify the survivors' fears. God will raise the witnesses from the dead in a spectacular manner, in a final effort to convince people to repent and believe the two witnesses' testimony concerning Jesus Christ.

Once again God will demonstrate His abundant love—even for these arrogant, Devil-worshipping people who will be celebrating the murder of His last two visible soldiers of the cross. Truly, God is not willing that any should perish. One result of God's mercy and His miracle of raising the witnesses from the dead, will be that many will finally believe the two witnesses' message and give glory to God.

END OF THE SECOND WOE

14 The second woe is past; and, behold, the third woe cometh quickly (Rev. 11:14).

The two witnesses' departure to heaven will mark the end of the period of time referred to as the second woe. The second woe time period spans the entire Sixth Trumpet World War, plus the Fourth Beast's three-and-one-half year reign of terror.

Consider the plight of surviving Christians at this point in the history of the church. They lived through the Initial Atomic War, the incredible cold, famine, and chaos of the post-Atomic War nuclear winter, and the Sixth Trumpet World War, which brought death to one out of every three people on the Earth, only to be confronted by a world government that sought their lives for the next three-and-one-half years. They endured misery and suffering and witnessed death on every side. Christ himself said, "for then shall be great tribulation, such as was not since the beginning of the world to this time, no, nor ever shall be (Matt. 24:21). Yet, they were encouraged through it all by the testimony of the two witnesses. These two visible soldiers of the cross were a constant reminder to everyone that God was in control and had not forgotten them.

After the beast succeeds in killing the two witnesses, surviving Christians will lose the comfort of their leadership. Christ's earthly church will be at its most vulnerable point since the day after Christ died on the cross. The world government will be in full control. If Christians speak the name of Christ to anyone, they will be killed. Christians will not be able to do anything but look to God, and He will not disappoint them.

THE SEVENTH TRUMPET SOUNDS

> **15** And the seventh angel sounded; and there were great voices in heaven, saying, The kingdoms of this world are become the kingdoms of our Lord, and of his Christ; and he shall reign for ever and ever (Rev. 11:15).

When the seventh trumpet sounds, the hope that will sustain the Sebat Christians through the great tribulation will become a reality. They will be caught up to meet the Lord in the air. Christians commonly refer to this coming event as the Rapture. The Apostle Paul described the Rapture in letters to the Corinthians and the Thessalonians.

> **51** Behold, I tell you a mystery; we shall not all sleep, but we shall all be changed, **52** in a moment, in the twinkling of an eye, at the last trumpet; for the trumpet will sound, and the dead will be raised imperishable, and we shall be changed. For this perishable must put on the imperishable, and this mortal must put on immortality. **54** But when this perishable will have put on the imperishable, and this mortal will have put on immortality, then will come about the saying that is written, "DEATH IS SWALLOWED UP IN VICTORY. **55** "O DEATH, WHERE IS YOUR VICTORY? O DEATH, WHERE IS YOUR STING?" **56** The sting of death is sin, and the power of sin is the law; **57** but thanks be to God, who gives us the victory through our Lord Jesus Christ (I Cor. 15:51–57 NASB).

> **13** But we do not want you to be uninformed, brethern, about those who are asleep, that you may not grieve, as do the rest

who have no hope. **14** For if we believe that Jesus died and rose again, even so God will bring with Him those who have fallen asleep in Jesus. **15** For this we say to you by the word of the Lord, that we who are alive, and remain until the coming of the Lord, shall not precede those who have fallen asleep. **16** For the Lord Himself will descend from heaven with a shout, with the voice of the archangel, and with the trumpet of God; and the dead in Christ shall rise first. **17** Then we who are alive and remain shall be caught up together with them in the clouds to meet the Lord in the air, and thus we shall always be with the Lord. **18** Therefore comfort one another with these words (1 Thess. 4:13–18, NASB).

Paul's reference to the Rapture of the church at the time of the sounding of "the last trumpet" is identical to the seventh trumpet Revelation account of this same event. Directly following Christ's timely rescue of His people from the international government's relentless persecution, the judgment of those who oppressed them will begin.

16 And the twenty-four elders who sit on their thrones before God, fell on their faces and worshipped God, **17** saying, "We give Thee thanks, O Lord God, the Almighty, who art and who wast, because Thou hast taken Thy great power and hast begun to reign. **18** "And the nations were enraged, and Thy wrath came, and the time came for the dead to be judged, and the time to give their reward to Thy bond-servants the prophets and to the saints and to those who fear Thy name, the small and the great, and to destroy those who destroy the earth" (Rev. 11:16–18, NASB).

Those in heaven will rejoice when God steps in and rescues the Christians and judges the destroyers of the Earth. Although the people running the world at the end of the age will be turning the planet into a wasteland with their atomic wars and insane policies, seemingly unchecked, God will not allow them to continue their evil indefinitely.

19 And the temple of God which is in heaven was opened; and the ark of His covenant appeared in His temple, and there were flashes of lightning and sounds and peals of thunder and an earthquake and a great hailstorm (Rev. 11:19, NASB).

God's ark of the covenant is shown to John to remind Christians of God's pledge of faithfulness to His covenant in saving His people and punishing their and His enemies. Part of God's judgment will be administered in the form of an earthquake and a great hailstorm. These judgments will only come upon those left behind after Christ receives the Christians unto Himself.

The days when God's wrath will be delivered upon "those who destroy the earth" should remind everyone of the fact that the human race is living on planet Earth as rent-free tenants. Certainly no one would expect a rich man, who let someone live in one of his valuable homes rent-free, to overlook the systematic ruin of the place in his absence. So likewise God will not excuse man's abuse of the Earth and nuclear destruction of the planet when He returns at the end of the age.

The review below shows the major events that will occur before Christ returns to reign over the Earth.

SUMMARY OF FIGURE 2

1. The first four trumpets will probably take place within a couple of weeks time.

2. The fifth trumpet signals the beginning of an unprecedented "nuclear winter". During those dark days the final form of the Fourth Beast will begin forming.

1260 days:

3. In the midst of the Red Chinese Dragon invasion of Israel, U.S. aircraft will evacuate large numbers of Israelis to a desert area.

4. Following Red China's invasion of Israel, God will commission the two witnesses to testify against the newly installed international government for 1,260 days.

5. The 1260 day time-period will end when the two witnesses are raised from the dead and called up to heaven.

6. The seventh trumpet Rapture of the church will occur after the two witnesses departure.

42 months:

7. Jerusalem will be trodden down by Red China's forces.

8. The Fourth Beast will be given authority over all the Earth's nations. The Seventh Plague Nuclear War will end the forty-two month time-period. Further, Mystery Babylon will be utterly destroyed by this nuclear war.

Time and times and half a time:

A less specific period of time is given to the three-and-one-half years when the Fourth Beast will be in power and part of the Israeli nation will be camped in the desert.

Once the Christians are taken out, the Israelis will be on their own. Also, once Babylon is nuked the Fourth Beast won't have its computerized capital city control center to run the world. However, the Fourth Beast will still be nominally in control through the international army massed in the Middle East.

The third woe will end when the assembled international army is destroyed at the Battle of Armageddon. Christ will then establish His earthly kingdom.

ORDER OF EVENTS BEFORE CHRIST RETURNS

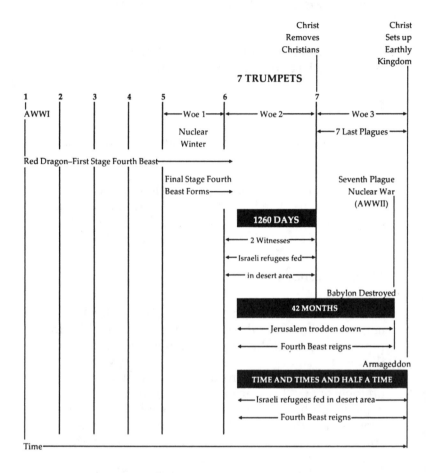

Figure 2: This chart shows the order of events that will take place through time before Christ returns to establish His earthly kingdom. It should help one understand the next two chapters, which cover the final judgments on those who will take the mark of the beast. (Note that 1,260 days, 42 months and a time and times and half a time are not drawn proportionally—all three refer to the same three-and-one-half year time period.)

PART
8

THE FALL OF MAN'S ANTI-CHRISTIAN WORLD GOVERNMENT

22 The Seven Last Plagues

Directly following the sounding of the seventh trumpet, the raptured Christians will celebrate with Christ in heaven their deliverance from the anti-Christian world government. God's promise that the formidable anti-Christian "beast" would be destroyed will then proceed without delay. John's prophecy of the seven last plagues provides a summary description of the pouring out of God's wrath on "those who destroy the earth."

> 1 And I saw another sign in heaven, great and marvelous, seven angels who had seven plagues, which are the last, because in them the wrath of God is finished (Rev. 15:1, NASB).

After Christ rescues His faithful followers, seven last plagues will be unleashed on those who took the mark of the beast. These plagues will complete the wrath of God, which will be poured out on those who persecuted His people. Collectively the plagues describe the final fall of rebellious man and the overthrow of the planet's future anti-Christian world government.

THE REDEEMED CHRISTIANS IN HEAVEN

> 2 And I saw what appeared to be a sea of glass mingled with fire, and those who had conquered the beast and its image

445

and the number of its name, standing beside the sea of glass
with harps of God in their hands (Rev. 15:2, RSV).

Those who walked with God through the relentless persecution imposed by the world government will rejoice and
praise God for delivering them from the beast.

3 And they sang the song of Moses the bond-servant of God
and the song of the Lamb, saying, "Great and marvelous are
Thy works, O Lord God, The Almighty; Righteous and true
are Thy ways, Thou King of the nations. 4"Who will not fear,
O Lord, and glorify Thy name? For Thou alone art holy; For
ALL THE NATIONS WILL COME AND WORSHIP BEFORE THEE, For
Thy righteous acts have been revealed" (Rev. 15:3–4, NASB).

The song of Moses was a song of thanksgiving and praise.
Moses taught the Israelites to sing this song after God delivered
them from Egyptian bondage (cf. Exodus 15).
The raptured Christians will also sing the song of the Lamb,
Jesus Christ, their great liberator. Their deliverance from the
anti-Christian world government will parallel the Israelites'
rescue from Egyptian bondage.

SEVEN FINAL JUDGMENTS PREPARED

5 And after that I looked, and, behold, the temple of the
tabernacle of the testimony in heaven was opened (Rev. 15:5).

After John sees in vision the redeemed Christians celebrating in heaven, he then sees the preparation made for the execu-
tion of the seven final judgments upon those left behind on the
Earth.
"And, behold, the temple of the tabernacle of the testimony" is not the whole temple, but a very specific part of the
temple. The first tent or tabernacle was erected by Moses in the
wilderness for the service of God. Later, the Israelites applied
the same word to the temple that was built in Jerusalem. It was
called the "tabernacle of testimony," because it was a testimony,
or witness, of the presence of God among the people. The word
temple here does not refer to the whole of the building called the
"temple," but only to the holy of holies, the residence of God.

This was the sacred dwelling-place of God, usually closed from all access, that was now opened, implying that God himself orders the command to execute the judgment of the beast.

> 6 And out of the temple came the seven angels with the seven plagues, robed in pure bright linen, and their breasts girded with golden girdles. 7 And one of the four living creatures gave the seven angels seven golden bowls full of the wrath of God who lives for ever and ever (Rev. 15:6–7, RSV).

The seven angels come from the presence of God and each one is to execute a single plague. "Clothed in pure white linen" represents their holiness. Having their breasts girded with golden girdles symbolizes their high rank and God-given authority to carry out their assigned judgments.

The golden bowls full of the wrath of God alludes to an ancient form of punishment in which a person drank a goblet full of poison. These bowls therefore are emblems of God's divine wrath.

> 8 And the temple was filled with smoke from the glory of God and from his power, and no one could enter the temple until the seven plagues of the seven angels were ended (Rev. 15:8, RSV).

Smoke is the usual symbol of God's presence in the temple. The meaning is that the smoke, or singular purpose of God's presence to judge the beast, so filled the temple that no one could enter it until the bowls of wrath were poured out. That is, no one could possibly enter to make intercession, or turn away God's wrath. The angels have been sent forth and will not be recalled.

THE SEVEN BOWLS OF WRATH

> 1 Then I heard a loud voice from the temple telling the seven angels, "Go and pour out on the earth the seven bowls of the wrath of God" (Rev. 16:1, RSV).

The rest of this vision describes the seven last plagues under which the world government will fall. Examination of the first five of the seven reveals that they are a description of the destruction of the Earth's environment from the long-term global aftereffects of AWWI.

Today's scientists have left many of the questions pertaining to the extent of the Earth's long-term biological damage from nuclear war open for further study. Confident predictions are simply overwhelmed by the infinite number of unknown environmental interactions introduced by the long-term effects of global nuclear war. Yet the Bible foretells the final consequences of AWWI without hesitation, including the exact order of the death of the Earth in the first five of the seven last plagues.

THE FIRST BOWL POURED OUT

2 So the first angel went and poured his bowl on the earth, and foul and evil sores came upon the men who bore the mark of the beast and worshipped its image (Rev. 16:2, RSV).

Though the plague was poured upon the Earth, yet its effects were seen upon men. This terrible skin plague will be a direct consequence of the cummulative effects of AWWI's radioactive and pyrotoxin fallout entering the soil.

An example of the relentless long-term effects of soil contamination from toxic chemicals came to light in the late 1960's when twenty-seven cows mysteriously died on Arthur Godfrey's Virginia farm. Subsequent investigation revealed that they were poisoned by high levels of arsenic in the grass. It turned out that the arsenic in the soil was left from the spraying of an orchard that had existed on the land fifty years prior to this incident.

According to the first plague prophecy, as hundreds of millions of tons of radioactive smoke, dust, and pyrotoxins continue to fall back on the Earth during the post-AWWI years, the problems of soil contamination will unavoidably increase. Crops grown on the befouled soil will become less and less fit for human consumption. Eating the tainted crops will introduce a number of health problems. Those left behind after the Rapture of the church will eventually break out with "loathsome and malignant" (NASB) sores from the cumulative build up of fallout poisons in their systems. (Note here that Christ's timely rescue will save Christians from the full force of the long-term aftereffects of AWWI.)

THE SECOND BOWL POURED OUT

3 The second angel poured his bowl into the sea, and it became like the blood of a dead man, and every living thing died that was in the sea (Rev. 16:3, RSV).

At the time John wrote this prophecy 1900 years ago, it must have been hard to imagine that every living thing in the oceans could die. But today the possibility of the oceans dying is readily understood.

Back in 1971, Swiss marine explorer Jacques Piccard, testifying before a United Nations symposium on the environment in Geneva, warned that if nothing is done, all the oceans will be dead before the end of the century. At the same symposium, French undersea explorer Jacques Cousteau estimated that the vitality of the seas, in terms of fish and plant life, had declined some 30 percent to 50 percent in the previous twenty-year period.

Prediction of the ocean's death in modern times is based on the fact that they serve as the Earth's largest dump. The main danger to marine life comes from wastes that are exceptionally long-lasting, or highly toxic. These include pesticides, a range of radioactive materials, aerosols such as those used in dry cleaning, and some resilient compounds like the "degreasers" used widely by industry to remove grease from manufactured parts. The main threat from these chemicals is that once they are there, they stay there. The chemical effects of each gallon of oil spilled in the ocean, for example, depletes the oxygen in 400,000 gallons of sea water, thus decimating all fish life in the area.

Unprecedented quantities of toxic substances will eventually end up in the oceans after AWWI. Their ominous effects will inexorably increase until they reach the deadly levels described in the second plague prophecy. At the same time light reductions brought on by the post-AWWI smoke-clogged skies will essentially terminate phytoplankton productivity. Loss of surface phytoplankton, the primitive plant life that generates most of the Earth's oxygen and provides the support base for many marine and fresh water animal species, will fatally disrupt the entire marine life cycle. The combination of these two destructive forces will eventually leave the world's oceans not only void of life, but a color similar to the dark almost black blood of a dead man.

Note here that the full effects of the worldwide atomic fallout will completely devastate the planet's land before the oceans die. This is logical since fallout poisons need only penetrate a few inches of topsoil to cause severe contamination of the Earth's surface. The oceans' depths, on the other hand, are measured in miles. This factor enables the seas to absorb larger quantities of poisonous substances before reaching a lethal saturation point. Therefore it will require a longer period of time for the oceans to become sufficiently toxic to eliminate all sea life.

THE THIRD BOWL POURED OUT

4 The third angel poured his bowl into the rivers and the fountains of water, and they became blood (Rev. 16:4, RSV).

After "the third angel poured his bowl into the rivers and the fountains of water," John wrote down his metaphorical observation: "and they became blood." Although God could turn the waters into blood if He so desired, the meaning parallels John's previous description of the pollution of the seas: "and it became like the blood of a dead man" (Rev. 16:3, RSV). Thus, plague three foretells the death of man's two primary sources of water: rivers, which are dammed for the purpose of storing water in giant reservoirs, and fountains of waters, or wells and lakes, which supply water to cities and communities that do not have access to other water sources.

Unsettling reports of rivers choked with municipal sewage, lakes polluted by acid rain, and contamination of subsurface water supplies from the dumping of chemical wastes have become commonplace in modern times. Efforts to reduce these trends have often been disappointing. The construction of the largest toxic dump in the United States ended this way. The clay-lined pit built on a 2,400 acre lot near Emelle, Alabama, was called the Cadillac of landfills. The engineers who designed the pit expected it to keep dangerous chemicals safely interned for thousands of years. No such luck. Seven years after its completion in 1977, officials of the Environmental Protection Agency (EPA) reported that the Emelle landfill was leaking. Unfortunately the EPA also revealed that dangerous chemicals are percolating down through layers of soil into underground water reservoirs at as many as 16,000 other landfills throughout the United States.

The destructive effects of AWWI will pollute the world's fresh water supplies on an unprecedented scale. Atomic blasts will pervert the face of the Earth and add massive amounts of radioactive fallout to the Earth's surface. The ensuing death of most vegetation will leave the land exposed to the unchecked forces of soil erosion. Once normal weather patterns return some years after the atomic war, subsequent run-off from rain storms in the bombed third of the Earth will foul the rivers and fountains of water on a scale previously unknown. However, this prophecy foretells the effects of long-term continuing fallout eventually fouling rivers and subsurface water supplies around the globe. (The Bible's description of the inexorable extension of the war's adverse effects to the far corners of the Earth confirms the best educated suspicions of today's scientists.)

The order of succession in the death of the third big component of the Earth's ecosystem is again correct. Rivers, reservoir, and lake water will undoubtedly become contaminated as quickly as the oceans; however, subsurface fountains of water, or well water, will take much longer to become dangerously contaminated—thanks to the cleansing capabilities of the soil that surface waters pass through. Yet, despite the soil's effective filtering mechanism, the water table's first line of defense against pollutants will eventually succumb to the overwhelming volume of toxic atomic fallout seeping through the ground. Hence, even though this process will take longer than the pollution of the oceans, in due time AWWI's massive volume of radioactive pyrotoxin fallout will succeed in penetrating water tables everywhere, including underground water reservoirs of nations far removed from the atomic war zones.

5 And I heard the angel of the waters say, Thou art righteous, O Lord, which art, and wast, and shalt be, because thou hast judged thus. 6 For they have shed the blood of saints and prophets, and thou hast given them blood to drink; for they

are worthy. 7 And I heard another out of the altar say, Even
so, Lord God Almighty, true and righteous are thy judgments
(Rev. 16:5–7).

Christians are reminded here that a righteous God will
surely judge those who murder His people. The employees
working for the world government during the tribulation will
systematically shed the blood of God's innocent people without
a second thought. Yet their enforcement of the policy that will
not allow Christians to buy or sell for not taking the mark of the
beast will subject many Christians to slow painful death from
lack of adequate food, water, and shelter. In the end those who
take the mark of the beast will find themselves reaping in kind,
water as unfit to drink as blood.

THE FOURTH BOWL POURED OUT

8 The fourth angel poured his bowl on the sun, and it was
allowed to scorch men with fire; 9 men were scorched by the
fierce heat, and they cursed the name of God who had power
over these plagues, and they did not repent and give him
glory (Rev. 16:8–9, RSV).

In today's scientific terms what John called fire from the sun
is now called ultraviolet (UV) radiation. UV radiation, a form
of light invisible to the human eye, causes sunburn and skin
cancer. Overexposure to these rays has also been linked to
cataracts and weakening of the immune system.

The immediate question raised here is what will prompt the
dramatic increase in UV light reaching the Earth's surface during the days of the fourth plague. The key to establishing the
correct answer to this question is provided in the two words
"was allowed." For instance, the statement that the sun "was
allowed" to scorch men with fire infers that the Earth's normal
UV radiation blocking mechanism will be altered to the extent
that there will be a substantial increase in the amount of UV
light striking the planet. Since the main theme of the seven last
plagues prophecy is the long-term repercussions of AWWI, it is
reasonable to assume that the plague of intense heat from the
sun will be another delayed negative consequence of AWWI.

Inspection of the planet's ozone layer and its workings reveals why this will be the case. Ozone gas, a highly reactive form of oxygen found about 15 miles up in the stratosphere, serves as a shield for humans and other organisms against an overdose of solar UV radiation by absorbing most of these harmful rays. But the paper-thin (three-millimeter deep) layer is fragile, susceptible to a number of chemicals that convert ozone back into ordinary oxygen. For example, it is suspected that the accelerating use of nitrogen fertilizers, which are converted by bacteria into nitrogen oxides that eventually rise into the stratosphere, could result in the destruction of as much as 15 percent of the ozone layer. Even worse are man-made chlorofluorocarbons (CFCs) used in air conditioners and fast-food plastic foam containers. Atmospheric studies conducted by the University of California, Irvine, in 1974, revealed that when CFCs escape from abandoned refrigerator coils, or evaporate from plastic foam, they float toward the heavens where they can act like high-altitude Pac-Men, devouring ozone in the stratosphere at a voracious rate. Atmospheric studies conducted in the late 1980s also found substantial evidence that a number of man-made air-borne chemicals are methodically destroying the planet's ozone layer.

Today's scientific findings provide documented examples of the far greater ozone-shredding conditions that will be generated by massive volumes of ozone-attacking pyrotoxins blasted into the stratosphere over the course of AWWI. The United Nations 1977 annual State of the Environment Report estimated that a large-scale nuclear war would blast enough nitrogen oxides into the atmosphere to reduce the ozone layer by as much as 70 percent for a period of from five to ten years. The United Nation's findings can be viewed as a fairly accurate prediction of what will happen to the ozone layer after AWWI since they echo John's fourth plague description of people receiving severe sunburns from the dramatically increased burning power of the post-AWWI sun.

The original Greek names the sun's "great heat" as a second feature of the fourth plague's stressful effects upon men. Climatic findings in the late 1980s revealed that some of the gases routinely spewed into the air by today's industrial society—by burning fossil fuels and cooling buildings—are trapping heat in the Earth's atmosphere and warming the planet. Carbon dioxide, the biggest offender, accounts for about half the warming. Since 1958 concentrations of carbon dioxide in the atmosphere have increased 11 percent. To make matters worse, man is systematically destroying rain forests that naturally absorb carbon dioxide. With fewer trees on the planet, more carbon dioxide remains in the air. In general, the fourth plague's grim forewarning—"And men were burnt [with] great heat"—confirms the 1980's preliminary climatic studies of the "greenhouse effect." An atomic war that will leave "a third of the earth burnt up" (Rev. 8:7) will dramatically increase the volume of carbon dioxide and other heat-absorbing gases in the atmosphere. Note too that the 1,260 post-AWWI rainless days will eliminate a large fraction of the planet's oxygen-producing/carbon dioxide-devouring trees and plants. Then, at the time of the fourth plague, when the stratospheric smoke clears enough to allow the sun's light to reach the surface of the Earth, the world will be caught in the grip of a blistering heat wave.

For a few years after AWWI people will not be subjected to the full wrath of the sun's intense heat because massive amounts of atomic smoke left in the stratosphere will absorb most of the sun's light and/or reradiate it directly back into space before it can ever reach the Earth's surface. Scripture shows that this smoke-filtering effect will exist for at least four years after AWWI. However, once there is a substantial clearing of the smoke, at the time of the fourth of the seven last plagues, the intense burning effect of the sun will hit the inhabitants of the Earth with its full force. (Again the Bible places the fourth plague consequence of AWWI in its correct position of occurrence.)

According to John's report, the sun's fierce heat will be so hot that people will be severely burnt if they stay outside for even a short period of time. Yet instead of asking God's forgiveness for their hate, which is what will ultimately touch off AWWI in the first place, the typical person will blame God for the heat and curse His name.

THE FIFTH BOWL POURED OUT

10 The fifth angel poured his bowl on the throne of the beast, and its kingdom was in darkness; men gnawed their tongues in anguish **11** and cursed the God of heaven for their pain and sores, and did not repent of their deeds (Rev. 16:10–11, RSV).

The long-lived air pollution generated by AWWI will apparently promote ideal conditions for a persistent temperature inversion, which will plunge the "beast's" capital city into darkness. (A temperature inversion is a layer of cool air held in place by a layer of warm air above it—which prevents polluted cool air from blowing away.) Similar situations caused by smog and stagnant air masses—sometimes called "hot-air inversions"—have plagued many modern cities.

It is clear from the description of people biting their tongues that Mystery Babylon's plague of darkness will be especially frustrating for the city's inhabitants. Mention of their "pain and sores" here indicates preceding plagues will continue. There will be an accumulation, not a mere succession, of plagues. Thus, the plague of darkness will be the final stress for a population already unable to cope with the calamities engulfing them.

At this point in the history of man, the earth will be slowly dying. The human race will also be dying. Humans will be sitting in the middle of total ruin that they alone created. People will be eating food laced with poisons, smelling an ocean full of rotting plant and animal life, drinking water unfit for human consumption, and either suffering from a third-degree sunburn or taking extraordinary measures to avoid one. In addition to all this misery, the inhabitants of the world capital will be breathing toxic air while they grope in the dark with bodies racked with painful sores. One would think that people would repent for turning the paradise God provided for them into a dying ash heap. Instead, they will blame God for what they have done and curse Him all the more.

THE SIXTH BOWL POURED OUT

12 And the sixth angel poured out his bowl upon the great river, the Euphrates; and its water was dried up, that the way might be prepared for the kings from the east (Rev. 16:12, NASB).

The place to begin an analysis of the plague represented by the contents of the sixth bowl is with an examination of the bowl imagery itself. According to the initial command of "go and pour out on the earth the seven bowls of the wrath of God" (Rev.

16:1 RSV), the symbolic bowls of wrath will be filled in the heavens before they are poured onto the Earth. Clearly, the plagues represented by the contents of the first five bowls will come from the heavens. That is, the contamination of the Earth's soil, oceans and rivers and fountains of waters will be the cumulative long-term consequence of hundreds of millions of tons of radioactive smoke, dust, and pyrotoxins settling out of the planet's post-AWWI atmosphere. AWWI's ozone–destroying negative effects and the capital city's plague of darkness will likewise originate in the heavens.

The source of the plague represented by the contents of the sixth bowl, therefore, will also come from AWWI's unprecedented pollution of the heavens, in keeping with the original command: "go and pour out on the earth the seven bowls of the wrath of God." Specifically, this means the waters of "the great river, the Euphrates," will dry up in the face of the unrelenting post-AWWI drought, which, according to the prophecies preceding the seven last plagues narrative, will be a direct consequence of the meteorological disturbances generated by AWWI's globe-girdling pall of smoke.

Keep in mind, at the same time, that Turkey and Syria may well accelerate the Euphrates drying process by shutting the intake tunnel gates of their respective superdams astride the river. The greater significance of the Euphrates river drying up *to prepare a way* for the kings from the east supports this premise. The sixth plague language is similar to the language used to describe the post-AWWI Euphrates river dispute—"Loose the four angels which are bound in the great river Euphrates . . . which were prepared . . . to slay the third part of men" (Rev. 9:14–15)—that will pave "the way" for the world's great powers to become embroiled in the Sixth Trumpet World War. Hence, reuse of the word *prepared* here implies that AWWI's long-lived drought will eventually spawn another fierce dispute over Euphrates water at the time of the sixth plague. The ensuing regional conflict would then rupture the peace Red China established in the area after the Sixth Trumpet World War, which, in turn, would "prepare the way," or prompt, Red China and her eastern allies—literally, "the kings from (the) rising of (the) sun"—to "prepare" for another great war in the Middle East.

It appears that Turkey and Syria will stop the Euphrates river flow at the time of the sixth plague in a desperate attempt to hoard dwindling water supplies. This sequence of events provides one logical reason for the prophesied outbreak of a conflict in the region.

The absence of Christians during the days of the seven last plagues is an important point. After all, the international government will base its promise of establishing lasting world peace on its success at eliminating the uncompromising Christian opposition. Yet, the world government will fail completely to enforce the peace, once the Christians are gone. Obviously it will not be possible to blame Christians for the final war of the nuclear age.

PREPARATIONS FOR WAR

13 And I saw coming out of the mouth of the dragon and out of the mouth of the beast and out of the mouth of the false prophet, three unclean spirits like frogs; 14 for they are spirits of demons, performing signs, which go out to the kings of the whole world, to gather them together for the war of the great day of God, the Almighty (Rev. 16:13–14, NASB).

In the midst of the utter environmental collapse of the Earth, the world's three principal ruling groups will mount a massive propaganda campaign to encite the nations to prepare "for the war of the great day of God, the Almighty." The principal power brokers listed in the order of their importance are the Red Chinese Dragon, the "world government beast," and the false prophet. (The false prophet will head up the "Religious Beast" organization. He will be the master magician who will use great signs and wonders to convince people to worship the man-made image.)

The reference to the messages coming out of their mouths being "unclean spirits like frogs," shows that all three organizations will feed lies to the masses. They will use modern television advertising methods to systematically hammer their devil-inspired agenda into people's minds—the same propaganda will be rerun over and over on the world's TV networks. John compares their use of repetition to the repetitive endless croaking of frogs in the night. Their propaganda campaign will be successful and all nations will begin gathering troops "for the war of the great day of God, the Almighty." ("The war of the great day of God, the Almighty" is so named because God will return on that day and put the affairs of this world in order.)

Note here that the text does not mention the world leader who received a death wound. The absence of a reference to him indicates that the world leader will not be an important ruler during the final days of the age, which, in turn, supports the position that he will not survive his death wound.

> **15** ("Lo, I am coming like a thief! Blessed is he who is awake, keeping his garments that he may not go naked and be seen exposed!") **16** And they assembled them at the place which is called in Hebrew Armageddon (Rev. 16:15–16, RSV).

THE PLACE CALLED ARMAGEDDON

The three powers will gather the nations' armies "at the place that is called in Hebrew Armageddon," or "mountain of Meggido." Meggido was distinguished for being the place of the decisive conflict between Deborah and Sisera, the captain of Canaan's army. In this battle Israel destroyed Jabin, king of Caanan (Judges 4). Had Israel lost this battle, her ability to continue as a nation would have been in doubt. Hence, the name Megiddo became emblematic of any decisive battlefield. The word "mountain" in the term Armageddon seems to have been used in part because the ancient town of Megiddo was in a mountainous region, though the battles Israel fought there were fought in a valley adjacent. The final outcome of the battle between Satan's forces, embodied in the armies of the nations, and the armies coming with Christ upon His return to set up His earthly kingdom, will be determined here. The actual battleground, where Satan's mountain of opposition will be defeated, will probably range over an area of a couple of hundred square miles. At this battle, Christ will decisively defeat Satan and his forces.

I AM COMING AS A THIEF

The insertion "lo, I am coming as a thief" is a warning to everyone. Christ's return will be sudden, "like a thief." Futhermore, Christ will be coming to break into Satan's world government for the purpose of utterly destroying it.

The interjected statement "Blessed is he who is awake, keeping his garments" is addressed to the people living at the time of the end—specifically, the Sebat generation—to remind them to be awake and watching for Christ's imminent return. In practical terms it would be foolish to cast aside the Bible's forewarnings and simply not bother to prepare for the coming atomic destruction of the Earth. Spiritually speaking, it would be even more foolish to proceed unprepared to the day of Christ's arrival. In fact, those who will choose to remain indifferent to the Bible's forewarnings concerning the unfolding signs leading up to Christ's return are compared here to a person who, regardless of danger, or of the approach of an enemy, will lay aside his garments and lie down to sleep. Those who select this course will be found spiritually exposed—naked as it were—when Christ arrives unexpectedly, "like a thief."

The Apostle Paul also wrote of Christ's sudden appearance.

> **1** But of the times and the seasons, brethren, ye have no need that I write unto you. **2** For yourselves know perfectly that the day of the Lord so cometh as a thief in the night. **3** For when they shall say, Peace and safety; then sudden destruction cometh upon them, as travail upon a woman with child; and they shall not escape. **4** But ye, brethren, are not in darkness, that that day should overtake you as a thief (1 Thess. 5:1–4).

Christians have known for generations that Christ will return in the latter days to set up His earthly kingdom. Many have also understood that Christ will actually return twice at the end of the age. His first return will be at the sound of the seventh trumpet for the purpose of removing all Christians from the Earth. His second return will occur after the seven last plagues have been fulfilled for the purpose of establishing His promised earthly kingdom of peace. Christ's second return will not overtake Christians as a thief in the night since at the time of the seven last plagues, they will already be with Christ in heaven.

In direct contrast, those who do not know Christ will be unaware of the *inescapable* destruction that will come upon them. In fact, they will be talking about "peace and safety," when the sudden destruction engulfs them. Paul compares the inescapable nature of that destruction to the "travail upon a woman with child." His point is well said since no woman in the middle of delivering a child has ever succeeded in deciding not to have the child after all.

The Apostle Peter's companion account of Christ's return "as a thief in the night" spells out the nature of the plague represented by the contents of the seventh bowl, in unmistakable detail.

> **10** But the day of the Lord will come as a thief in the night; in the which the heavens shall pass away with a great noise, and the elements shall melt with fervent heat, the earth also and the works that are therein shall be burned up (2 Peter 3:10).

In the Greek "the elements shall melt with fervent heat" reads: "and (the) elements burning will be dissolved." This is precisely what happens to the elements during the detonation of a nuclear weapon. In the first moment of the explosion, when the nuclear fusion reaction is initiated, boiling and surging atomic particles reach superstellar temperatures that instantly gasify, or "dissolve," the very elements, or atoms, of the bomb into their more elementary, highly unstable, sub-atomic components.

Another unspeakable air-borne atomic war will engulf the planet on the day Christ returns to reign over the earth. Peter's vivid description of the fantastic power of today's nuclear bombs also contains a personal call for people to be prepared for the Lord's return.

> **11** Seeing then that all these things shall be dissolved, what manner of persons ought ye to be in all holy conversation and godliness, **12** Looking for and hasting unto the coming of the day of God, wherein the heavens being on fire shall be dissolved, and the elements shall melt with fervent heat? (2 Peter 3:11–12).

Once the armies of the nations are assembled in the Middle East "at the place that is called in Hebrew Armageddon," the plague represented by the contents of the seventh bowl will be "poured out into the air."

THE SEVENTH BOWL POURED OUT

17 The seventh angel poured his bowl into the air, and a loud voice came out of the temple, from the throne, saying, "It is done!" (Rev. 16:17, RSV).

The contents of the seventh bowl poured into the air represents an air-borne nuclear exchange in which atomic weapons of mass destruction will descend through the air before they burst with pain upon the heads of the wicked. The Seventh Plague Nuclear War (AWWII) will break out shortly after the armies of the nations gather in the Middle East. The actual Battle of Armageddon will be the final battle of the greater nuclear war unleashed on cities and military bases around the globe. When the atomic smoke clears, there will be radioactive dust and ashes where the world government's capital city once stood.

The voice of God came out of the temple, from the throne, pronouncing "it is done." The meaning is that the destruction of the "beast" is certain and will be accomplished at the time of the pouring out of the seventh bowl into the air.

18 And there were flashes of lightning, voices, peals of thunder, and a great earthquake such as had never been since men were on the earth, so great was that earthquake (Rev. 16:18, RSV). **19** And the great city was divided into three parts, and the cities of the nations fell: and great Babylon came in remembrance before God, to give unto her the cup of the wine of the fierceness of his wrath (Rev. 16:19).

John's account of man's final nuclear holocaust parallels Isaiah's vivid prophecy of this same event (Isaiah 24). Godless and treacherous men will double-cross each other on a grand scale. The climax of their evil will be expressed in the form of brilliant flashes of "nuclear" lightning, earthquakes triggered by massive "earth penetrator" warheads, followed by the mightiest earthquake ever to occur on the planet. When it is over, the cities of the nations will be totally destroyed.

Further, Mystery Babylon will be divided into three parts as a result of the massive earthquake. The reference to "great Babylon came in remembrance before God, to give unto her the cup of the wine of the fierceness of his wrath" parallels Jeremiah

25:26, which states that the King of Sheshach, or Babylon, will drink from the cup of God's "nuclear" wrath, after all the other kingdoms have drunk, and spued, and fallen. Thus, although the world capital will be permitted to practice her evil, seemingly unchecked, God will remember Babylon's evil and give unto her the full seventh bowl of judgment.

The destructive forces unleashed when a one-megaton bomb is detonated a mile above a city illuminates the biblical statement "and the cities of the nations fell." A millisecond into the explosion, the temperature of the fireball (which grows to more than a mile in diameter in less than two seconds) drops from tens of millions of degrees to 540,000 degrees Fahrenheit. As this searing heat descends upon the city it ignites everything flammable, including people, and starts to melt everything else made of metal or glass. About five seconds into the explosion, the shock wave delivers its double punch: overpressures four times normal atmospheric pressure and winds of many hundreds of miles per hour. Unlike a conventional explosive that delivers a swift shock, like a slap, to whatever it hits, the blast wave of a sizable nuclear weapon endures for several seconds. According to the 1977 edition of *The Effects of Nuclear Weapons*, this enduring blast wave "can surround and destroy whole buildings." Within sixty square miles of ground zero any buildings not already flattened and blown away by the ferocity of the winds would be subjected to these crushing overpressure forces. The people inside, along with the furniture and pulverized debris of the collapsing buildings would be swept down onto the streets. This avalanche of people and buildings falling to the streets would fill the streets to a considerable depth in areas containing tall buildings. In this manner the prophesied statement "and the cities of the nations fell" shall come to pass during the final nuclear blowout of the age.

20 And every island fled, and mountains were not found (Rev. 16:20, IGENT).

The combined destruction from AWWII and the unprecedented earthquake will be so great that the very earth itself will be convulsed, and everything will be moved out of its place. In addition to the cities of the nations falling, military and naval bases located on isolated islands in the sea and strategic defense command centers in the midst of remote mountain ranges, will also be included in the list of targets that will be destroyed by atomic warheads.

The sentence "and every island fled, and mountains were not found" compares to the Sixth Seal overview of AWWI— "and every mountain and island were moved out of their places" (Rev. 6:14). This does not mean every island on the planet will be moved over the course of AWWII, but rather, every targeted island hit by an atomic warhead will "flee" or disappear in the face of the overpowering heat and blast forces unleashed by that exploding nuclear weapon. Likewise, "and mountains were not found" means every targeted mountain subjected to the violent forces of a nuclear explosion will not be found when the atomic fire, dust, and smoke clears.

Back in the sixties the feasibility of mountains not being found was unknowingly studied when the U.S. government considered the use of 22 atomic bombs to vaporize part of a mountain that was in the construction path of Interstate 60. The experts felt that all the radioactive fallout would be within a five mile radius, but added that no one could be certain. Fortunately the idea was scrapped due to budget cuts under the Johnson administration. This early study indicates that the future destruction of mountains will be no problem.

A GREAT HAIL STORM

21 And there fell upon men a great hail out of heaven, every stone about the weight of a talent: and men blasphemed God because of the plague of the hail; for the plague thereof was exceeding great (Rev. 16:21).

Only God knows the number and size of the high-powered warheads that the nations will throw at each other in the final nuclear war. Giant hailstones will be a hitherto unparalleled side effect from all the destruction. These hailstones will weigh a little over a hundred pounds apiece. Even more unbelievable than the size of the hail is the fact that the survivors will curse God because of the severity of the hailstorm.

This completes John's prophecy on the final seven judgments of the nations. Notice how the order of the observable features of the destruction contained in the seventh bowl— lightnings, voices, thunders, a great earthquake, and great hail—parallels the seventh trumpet angel's closing statement on the final judgment of the nations: "and there were lightnings, and voices, and thunderings, and an earthquake, and great hail" (Rev. 11:19). This same ordering of destructive effects is important since it indicates the last event of the seventh trumpet epoch and the seventh plague time period are the same event.

The final destruction of the nations and their world government will be the unavoidable outcome of people ignoring God's laws and instruction. Those who will reject Christ and take the mark of the beast will reap the full consequences of that choice during the days of the seven plague judgments. Thus, a life without Christ is one that reaps the self-imposed wrath of God.

23 The Fall of Babylon

The Bible records several pressing circumstances that will drive the events leading up to the fall of "Mystery Babylon." Revelation 16:12 outlines the initial geopolitical situation: a dispute over scarce water supplies in the Euphrates river basin, followed by the mobilization of the armies of "the kings from the east." Isaiah 13 documents a second contributing incident: an Iranian invasion of Iraq.

THE DAY OF THE LORD

1 The burden of Babylon (Isa. 13:1*a*).

6 Wail, for the day of the LORD is near! It will come as destruction from the Almighty. **7** Therefore all hands will fall limp, And every man's heart will melt. **8** And they will be terrified, Pains and anguish will take hold of them; They will writhe like a woman in labor, They will look at one another in astonishment, Their faces aflame. **9** Behold, the day of the LORD is coming, Cruel, with fury and burning anger, To make the land a desolation; And He will exterminate its sinners from it (Isa. 13:6–9, NASB).

"The day of the LORD," twice repeated here, firmly establishes the setting for this prophecy to be during the days of the

465

last atomic war of the nuclear age. The chilling details of the moment of death for those burned alive (their faces literally "aflame") by the scorching thermal pulse of exploding nuclear weapons, removes any lingering doubt.

Isaiah then reviewed the events leading up to the fall of Babylon.

IRAN INVADES IRAQ

> **17** Behold, I will stir up the Medes against them, which shall not regard silver; and as for gold, they shall not delight in it (Isa. 13:17).

(Here, "against them" is a direct reference to Babylon since this prophecy opened with the statement: "The burden of Babylon, which Isaiah the son of Amoz did see," [Isa. 13:1].)

Now inasmuch as AWWII and "the day of the LORD" are the twin themes of the prophetic message leading up to this point in the passage, it follows that the two combatant nations identified here will be bonafide modern nations, residing on the lands of the ancient nations named in the text. Accordingly, since the nations of Iraq and Iran presently appear on the map where the nations of Babylon and Media once held sway, they are the countries to be considered in the continuing analysis of the prophecy.

IRAN'S RELIGIOUS COMMITMENT

Isaiah then proceeded to list two of modern Iran's most striking national characteristics. For example, they "shall not regard silver; and as for gold, they shall not delight in it" is an unmistakable portrait of the Islamic fundamentalist state that emerged out of Ayatollah Khomeini's successful revolutionary take over of the country in the late 1970s. Under Khomeini's religious regime the Iranians rejected Western ways, especially the pursuit of modernization, wealth, and the free-wheeling Western life style silver and gold can buy, in favor of the religious laws and customs outlined by the founder of the Moslem religion, Mohammed the prophet.

The significance of modern Iran's disregard for wealth rests in the fact that her people are willing to sacrifice all their earthly possessions, including their lives, to achieve their national religious goals. This collective national religious resolve (demonstrated in the Iran-Iraq War of the 1980s), means the Iranians will not simply back down when threatened with economic hardship by the world's more economically powerful nations.

In view of the prophesied construction of a grand international capital city within the boundaries of the ancient kingdom of Babylon, the statement "behold, I will stir up the Medes against them" declares that the Iranians will not only attack Iraq during the days leading up to the seventh plague event, but also the world's capital city, residing within Iraq's borders. This future Iranian invasion will immediately present a serious threat to the costly international capital. Even worse, Isaiah's prophecy predicts that the nations will not be able to persuade the Iranians to quit their invasion on the promise of economic gain, since they "shall not regard silver; and as for gold, they shall not delight in it."

Although Isaiah did not spell out precisely how the nations will respond to hordes of Iranians fighting their way into Iraq, it is logical to assume that the fate of the capital city will be one of the reasons that will prompt them to march large armies into the Middle East at the time of the seventh plague event. Isaiah's subsequent description of the Iranian attack certainly underlines the need for an international effort to save the city.

MODERN BOWS OF WAR

18 Their bows also shall dash the young men to pieces; and they shall have no pity on the fruit of the womb; their eye shall not spare children (Isa. 13:18).

The sentence "their bows also shall dash the young men to pieces" could not be a reference to an ancient bow since the bows of Isaiah's day did not kill soldiers by blowing them to bits (which, incidentally, is the equivalent twentieth-century expression for "dash to pieces").

Isaiah did not say the Medes would use ancient bows in the war—only that "their bows" (the future Iranian/Median's bows) would have the unheard of power (in Isaiah's day) "to dash the young men to pieces." Thus, Isaiah called the modern artillery cannon with which the invading Iranian Army was firing high explosive shells into the ranks of Iraqi defenders, a bow, simply because a bow was functionally similar to the modern artillery weapons.

CHILDREN WILL NOT BE SPARED

At first glance the statement— "And they shall have no pity on the fruit of the womb; their eye shall not spare children"— appears to be extraneous. After all, ancient and modern men alike have repeatedly killed men, women, and children, without pity, during the course of battle. However, examination of the original Hebrew word for children—literally "sons"—immediately reveals the importance of the statement. For insertion of the exact word *sons* here identifies the sickening and uniquely Iranian practice, introduced by Ayatollah Khomeini's Revolutionary Army during the 1980's Iran-Iraq War, of depending on human-wave attacks by irregular units to overwhelm the enemy on the battlefield. Iran's irregular units often included large numbers of 12-year-old schoolboys who served as little more than cannon fodder. Thus, the Iranians will also not spare "their own" sons during their invasion of Iraq at the time of the Seventh Last Plague War.

BABYLON'S FINAL FALL

19 And Babylon, the beauty of kingdoms, the glory of the Chaldeans' pride, Will be as when God overthrew Sodom and Gomorrah. **20** It will never be inhabited or lived in from generation to generation; Nor will the Arab pitch his tent there, Nor will shepherds make their flocks lie down there (Isa. 13:19–20, NASB).

This prophesied destruction of Babylon must refer to the downfall of a restored Babylon at the end times. The old city of Babylon was inhabited for several centuries after Cyrus the Great conquered the Kingdom of Babylon in 538 B.C., and Iraq is presently rebuilding ancient Babylon as a tourist attraction. The ancient site of the city, moreover, has been dwelt in from generation to generation. In fact, there are several small, but growing, cities located on the site of Babylon today, including one that retains the ancient name of Babylon. Further, the cities have a large Arab population whose principal occupation is the shepherding of flocks.

In the closing years of the nuclear age, a "Mystery Babylon" will be built that will eventually become the capital city of an all-encompassing world government. That future city will use sorceries, or tricks, realistic lies and convincing magic shows, to deceive the nations into rebelling against the truth presented by God's prophets. But, in order to obtain complete control over the nations, Babylon's rulers and bureaucrats will make the fatal mistake of setting up a systematic procedure to kill God's prophets and the Christians who will oppose their evil regime. These acts of violence against Christ's servants will seal the violent judgment of the city and her inhabitants. That prophesied nuclear destruction will be so complete that the city "will never be inhabited, or lived in from generation to generation; Nor will the Arab pitch his tent there, Nor will shepherds make their flocks lie down there" (Isa. 13:20, NASB).

Revelation 18 also documents the atomic judgment of the "beast's" formidable anti-Christian capital city. John's account provides considerable insight into Babylon's commercial might, its overall violent character and the ostentatious lifestyle of its inhabitants.

> 1 And after these things I saw another angel come down from heaven, having great power; and the earth was lightened with his glory. 2 And he cried mightily with a strong voice, saying, Babylon the Great is fallen, is fallen, and is become the habitation of devils, and the hold of every foul spirit, and a cage of every unclean and hateful bird (Rev. 18:1–2).

After John's previous vision concerning Babylon, a different angel comes down from heaven with more specific details concerning Babylon's overthrow. The description of this angel—"having great power; and the Earth was lightened with his glory"—reveals that God has given him a powerful message concerning Babylon, which will shed more light on its operation and final destruction at the end of the great tribulation.

The text following the angel's proclamation "Babylon the Great is fallen" declares that the desolation of the city will be so complete that no human will ever inhabit the place again. The reference to demons, unclean spirits, and unclean birds dwelling there emphasizes the perpetual uninhabitable condition of the site. Since nuclear fire will destroy the city, the site will remain unpopulated because of the intense long-lived radiation in the area.

> 3 For all nations have drunk of the wine of the wrath of her fornication, and the kings of the earth have committed fornication with her, and the merchants of the earth are waxed rich through the abundance of her delicacies (Rev. 18:3).

The statement that "all nations have drunk of the wine of the wrath of her fornication" identifies the worldwide rebellion against God and acceptance of Babylon's anti-Christian religion as the reason for the utter ruin of the city.

"And the kings of the earth have committed fornication with her" shows that the nations will willingly join Mystery Babylon's rebellion against God. For example, big business will use its influence to get their respective governments to submit to the new international capital's rule because it will be a financially profitable arrangement.

CHRISTIANS ORDERED OUT

> 4 And I heard another voice from heaven, saying, Come out of her, my people, that ye be not partakers of her sins, and that ye receive not of her plagues (Rev. 18:4).

When the world government is first set up it will provide many job opportunities and will not be involved in wholesale slaughter. The international capital will be viewed as an excellent place to work. In time, however, the last beast's goal to eliminate God's people will emerge. Therefore God commands all those who call themselves by His name "to come out of her." Any person living in the world capital will be considered an accomplice in the wholesale murder of innocent people around the globe. The passage also warns that everyone dwelling in Babylon will receive the full force of her plagues and final judgment.

> 5 For her sins have reached unto heaven, and God hath remembered her inquities. 6 Reward her even as she rewarded you, and double unto her double according to her

works: in the cup which she hath filled fill to her double (Rev. 18:5–6).

Although it will appear that Babylon is violating God's laws with impunity, God will eventually judge the city. "For they have sown the wind, and they shall reap the whirlwind" (Hosea 8:7a). Men always reap what they sow and in greater quantity.

FROM GREAT WEALTH TO ASHES

7 How much she hath glorified herself, and lived deliciously, so much torment and sorrow give her: for she saith in her heart, I sit a queen, and am no widow, and shall see no sorrow. 8 Therefore shall her plagues come in one day, death, and mourning, and famine; and she shall be utterly burned with fire: for strong is the Lord God who judgeth her (Rev. 18:7–8).

The international capital's rulers will live in absolute luxury, at the expense of the oppressed of the world. Much of this wealth will be siphoned off by Babylon's computerized central banking system. Exorbitant service charges and the confiscation of the accounts of Christians and other "undesirables" will provide a steady flow of ready cash. Wholesale pilfering of international funds and lavish spending by those running the world government will be the order of the day. The absence of any higher authority to enforce proper fiscal controls will apparently convince the city's inhabitants that nothing could possibly reverse their good fortune.

Yet unavoidably, Babylon's highly visible, outrageous lifestyle will create widespread animosity toward the city. Predictably, as the bureaucracy's insatiable greed grows, so will a determined opposition against the capital. Public outrage will eventually convince the ten most economically powerful nations to put an end to Babylon's destructive and extravagant policies.

THE TIMING OF BABYLON'S FALL

Note here that the decline and fall of Babylon will occur during the period of time referred to as the third woe. (The third woe begins the day Christ removes His people from the Earth and continues through the time of the seven last plagues.) Since the world government's main objective will be to rid itself of the Christian opposition, everyone should be able to live in harmony once Christ removes His followers from the scene. Yet, in a very short time (referred to here in terms of "her plagues will come in one day, death, mourning, and famine") a tremendous power struggle will break out between the ten-nation group and the bureaucrats running the capital. The ten will move with one accord to dismantle the city's authority and strip the bureaucrats of their wealth and power. The ten's final action will be an atomic attack ending in the nuclear obliteration of the city.

BABYLON'S RICHES LAMENTED

9 And the kings of the earth, who have committed fornication and lived deliciously with her, shall bewail her, and lament for her, when they shall see the smoke of her burning, **10** Standing afar off for the fear of her torment, saying, Alas, alas, that great city Babylon, that mighty city! for in one hour is thy judgment come. **11** And the merchants of the earth shall weep and mourn over her; for no man buyeth their merchandise any more: **12** The merchandise of gold, and silver, and precious stones, and of pearls, and fine linen, and purple, and silk, and scarlet, and all thyine wood, and all manner vessels of ivory, and all manner vessels of most precious wood, and of brass, and iron, and marble, **13** And cinnamon, and odours, and ointments, and frankincense, and wine, and oil, and fine flour, and wheat, and beasts, and sheep, and horses, and chariots, and slaves, and souls of men. **14** And the fruits that thy soul lusteth after are departed from thee, and all things which were dainty and goodly are departed from thee, and thou shalt find them no more at all. **15** The merchants of these things, which were made rich by her, shall stand afar off for the fear of her torment, weeping and wailing, **16** And saying, Alas, alas that great city, that was clothed in fine linen, and purple, and scarlet, and decked with gold, and precious stones, and pearls! **17** For in one hour so great riches is come to nought. And every shipmaster, and all the company in ships, and sailors, and as many as trade by sea, stood afar off, **18** And cried when they saw the smoke of her burning, saying, What city is like unto this great city! 19 And they cast dust on their heads, and cried, weeping and wailing, saying, Alas, alas that great city, wherein were made rich all that had ships in the sea by reason of her costliness! for in one hour is she made desolate (Rev. 18:9–19).

This passage itemizes Babylon's overflowing riches and how those who will be connected with her—kings, merchants, shipmasters, and sailors—will grieve their loss of business after the city is destroyed. "What city is like unto this great city!" proclaims that this yet-to-be built world capital will be a show place on a scale of unprecedented proportions. The city will be greater in size, number of buildings, volume of trade, and wealth than any other city in the history of the world.

BABYLON'S ATOMIC OVERTHROW EMPHASIZED

The language of the text emphasizes the magnitude of the nuclear destruction of the city. For instance, the tremendous clouds from "the smoke of her burning" are mentioned twice. John also recorded the great loss felt by kings and sailors at sea who "stood afar off," for fear of the intense radiation in the vicinity of the burning city.

The thrice repeated reference to Babylon's destruction coming in "one hour," serves to underscore the suddenness of the nuclear vaporization of the city. This event will likely take place within 60 minutes.

20 Rejoice over her, thou heaven, and ye holy apostles and prophets; for God hath avenged you on her. 21 And a mighty angel took up a stone like a great millstone, and cast it into the sea, saying, Thus with violence shall that great city Babylon be thrown down, and shall be found no more at all. 22 And the voice of harpers, and musicians, and of pipers, and trumpeters, shall be heard no more at all in thee; and no craftsman, of whatsoever craft he be, shall be found any more in thee; and the sound of a millstone shall be heard no more at all in thee; 23 And the light of a candle shall shine no more at all in thee; and the voice of the bridegroom and of the bride shall be heard no more at all in thee: for thy merchants were the great men of the earth; for by thy sorceries were all nations deceived. 24 And in her was found the blood of prophets, and

of saints, and of all that were slain upon the earth (Rev. 18:20–24).

The clause "a mighty angel took up a stone like a great millstone, and cast it into the sea" pictures the absolute ruin of the city. In other words the city would be as completely destroyed as that stone was covered by the sea's waters, never to be found again. In fact, the angel states that Babylon will be thrown down with such violence that it "shall be found no more at all." In light of today's knowledge of nuclear weapons, it is easy to believe that this city will vanish from the earth in a matter of minutes in the face of a nuclear attack. When the atomic smoke clears, it will be even as God's servants the prophets reported so long ago—there will not be a trace of the place left.

It is hard to imagine that the nations will touch off a second, even more global, nuclear war after the incredible long-term destruction they will be enduring from the First Atomic War. Yet, fear of their neighbors will breed hate. That hate will breed more fear, and more hate, until the insanity of fear and hatred builds to the crescendo of AWWII.

24 The King Returns and Restores Order

The Battle of Armageddon will be the final event of the Seventh Plague Nuclear War (AWWII). Several Bible passages describe how this battle will erupt in the Middle East between the massed armies of the nations. They show God's judgment of the anti-Christian international government culminating at Armageddon where Christ will end man's reign on the Earth.

THE RIPE HARVEST REAPED

> **14** And I looked, and behold a white cloud, and upon the cloud one sat like unto the Son of man, having on his head a golden crown, and in his hand a sharp sickle. **15** And another angel came out of the temple, crying with a loud voice to him that sat on the cloud, Thrust in thy sickle and reap: for the time is come for thee to reap; for the harvest of the earth is ripe. **16** And he that sat on the cloud thrust in his sickle on the earth; and the earth was reaped (Rev. 14:14–16).

This passage opens with a review of Christ's physical return in the air on a white cloud at the sounding of the seventh trumpet. The order to remove, or reap, the good seed sown by Christ and His followers is borne directly from God the Father, by the angel, to Christ the Son. This will be Christ's first return at the end of the age, for the purpose of rescuing Christians from the grasp of the anti-Christian world government. They shall be caught up to meet Him in the air (1 Thess. 4:17).

THE RIPE GRAPES REAPED

17 And another angel came out of the temple which is in heaven, he also having a sharp sickle. **18** And another angel came out from the altar, which had power over fire; and cried with a loud cry to him that had the sharp sickle, saying, Thrust in thy sharp sickle, and gather the clusters of the vine of the earth; for her grapes are fully ripe. **19** And the angel thrust in his sickle into the earth, and gathered the vine of the earth, and cast it into the great winepress of the wrath of God. **20** And the winepress was trodden without the city, and blood came out of the winepress, even unto the horse bridles, by the space of a thousand and six hundred furlongs (Rev. 14:17–20).

This vision represents the destruction meted out to God's enemies at the time of His second return at the end of the age. The ripe grapes represent the wicked who will be cast into the winepress of the wrath of God in the final destruction of the nations and their armies, gathered for the Battle of Armageddon.

"The winepress trodden without the city" notes that the Battle of Armageddon will take place outside the city of Jerusalem. Blood coming out of the winepress "even unto the horse bridles" indicates the magnitude of the great slaughter. "By the space of a thousand and six hundred furlongs" specifies a battlefield covering a space two hundred miles square. This added fact emphasizes the massive size of the army and the extent of the slaughter.

CHRIST'S VICTORIOUS RETURN

Christ's final conquest over the anti-Christian "world government beast" and the armies of the nations at the Battle of Armageddon are described further in Revelation 19.

11 Then I saw heaven opened, and behold, a white horse! He who sat upon it is called Faithful and True, and in righteousness he judges and makes war. **12** His eyes are like a flame of fire, and on his head are many diadems; and he has a name inscribed which no one knows but himself. **13** He is clad in a robe dipped in blood, and the name by which he is called is The Word of God (Rev. 19:11–13, RSV).

In the midst of the Battle of Armageddon Christ will return from heaven with His armies, "and in righteousness" judge and make war against the wickedness of the world. He is not designated here by His usual name but rather by attributes that describe His character and strength. Christ's second return at the end of the age will mark the fulfillment of the prophesied judgment of the "beast" and those who carried out its anti-Christian policies.

14 And the armies of heaven, arrayed in fine linen, white and pure, followed him on white horses. **15** From his mouth issues a sharp sword with which to smite the nations, and he will rule them with a rod of iron; he will tread the wine press of the fury of the wrath of God the Almighty. **16** On his robe and on his thigh he has a name inscribed, King of kings and Lord of lords (Rev. 19:14–16, RSV).

The armies in heaven will follow Christ, the "King of kings and Lord of lords," to witness and rejoice in His victory at the Battle of Armageddon. Note the weapon Christ will employ to smite the nations and their gathered armies: "and out of his mouth goeth a sharp sword." In other words, as He spoke through His Prophets down through the ages concerning the atomic destruction of the nations, so shall the nations be destroyed.

CHRIST'S INVINCIBLE JUST RULE

The next statement "and he will rule them with a rod of iron" declares that Christ will establish His earthly kingdom of peace at the time of the complete overthrow of the nations and their anti-Christian world government. The "rod of iron" symbolically identifies the unbreakable character of the instrument Christ will employ to govern the nations. Since John previously used "a reed like to a staff" (Rev. 11:1, IGENT) to symbolically represent the canon of Scripture (the measuring reed of the church containing the precepts of the Christian faith), the "rod of iron" (literally "an iron staff" in the Greek) represents the character of Christ's future world government, which will be built on the long established precepts of the Christian faith.

Christ will not only base His rule on these precepts, He will also use His power to enforce His just system of government. Thus, the word *iron* is used here to describe the invincible strength of the world government that Christ will set up following AWWII.

MAN'S SELF-INFLICTED JUDGMENT

"He will tread the wine press of the fury of the wrath of God the Almighty" is a figurative declaration that compares the certainty of the vast extent of the slaughter over the course of AWWII to what would happen to grapes in a wine press if "God the Almighty" tread them in the fury of His wrath. Here again John is not suggesting that God will crush man in this coming war, but rather, that the violent destruction of the nations will surely come to pass according to the Word of the Lord.

> 17 Then I saw an angel standing in the sun, and with a loud voice he called to all the birds that fly in mid-heaven, "Come, gather for the great supper of God, 18 to eat the flesh of kings, the flesh of captains, the flesh of mighty men, the flesh of horses and their riders, and the flesh of all men, both free and slave, both small and great." 19 And I saw the beast and the kings of the earth with their armies gathered to make war against him who sits upon the horse and against his army (Rev. 19:17–19, RSV).

A literal interpretation of this text would mean the leaders of the international government and the kings of the Earth, in anticipation of the prophesied return of Christ to set up His earthly kingdom, will make a command level decision to mobolize their armies "to make war against him." The Christian community's well-publicized warnings of the nearness of Christ's Second Coming provide one logical explanation for why the "kings of the earth" would be convinced that Christ was about to return at this particular point in time. The disappearance of the world's Christians at the time of the seventh trumpet Rapture will further emphasize the reality of Christ's imminent arrival. Simple observation of Bible prophecies coming to pass around them may be a contributing factor in the nations' decision to dispatch large armies into the Middle East.

"The beast and the kings of the earth" will fail to carry out whatever plan they devise "to make war against him who sits upon the horse and against his army" at the Battle of Armageddon, since the armies of the nations will actually end up killing each other in keeping with the prophesied atomic destruction of the nations.

THE BEAST AND FALSE PROPHET CAPTURED

> **20** And the beast was captured, and with it the false prophet who in its presence had worked the signs by which he deceived those who had received the mark of the beast and those who worshiped its image. These two were thrown alive into the lake of fire that burns with sulphur. **21** And the rest were slain by the sword of him who sits upon the horse, the sword that issues from his mouth; and all the birds were gorged with their flesh (Rev. 19:20–21, RSV).

The false prophet will be the one who will work "the signs" to "deceive" those who will receive the mark of the beast and worship its image. Through the false prophet's deception, many will believe that the world leader came back to life as a god. The fact that John did not introduce the false prophet, in his initial description of this subject, as the one who will be the master-mind behind this deception, suggests that he may successfully keep his leading role in the matter concealed from the public until the very end. He will not keep his diabolical role hidden from God, however, since John reports that "the beast was captured, and with it the false prophet."

Although Mystery Babylon, along with numerous other cities around the globe, will be destroyed over the course of AWWII, apparently the false prophet and some of the people supporting the world government's policies will survive. However, they will not escape Christ's judgment on everyone who actively participated in the persecution of His Church. The closing statement about the rest being "slain by the sword of him who sits upon the horse" emphasizes the point that no one lending support to, or employed by the murderous anti–Christian international government will escape the death sentence meted out by Christ when He returns.

WORLD LEADER NOT MENTIONED

A legitimate question naturally surfaces here: Why is the charismatic world leader not mentioned in John's account of the final judgment of the anti-Christian forces? Certainly this individual should not be exempt from being cast into the lake of fire along with his accomplice, the false prophet. The answer to this question lies in the fact that the world leader will receive a death wound shortly after coming to power: "and to destruction goeth" (Rev. 17:11). Hence, the charismatic world leader will not be cast into hell along with the false prophet upon Christ's return since he will have been there for quite some time already.

THE JUDGMENT OF REBELLIOUS NATIONS

King David recorded a general description of the judgment of nations that forget God. His remarks provide insight into the high and mighty attitude of those who will touch off AWWII.

> 15 The nations have sunk in the pit which they made; in the net which they hid has their own foot been caught. 16 The LORD has made himself known, he has executed judgment; the wicked are snared in the work of their own hands (Ps. 9:15–16, RSV). 17 The wicked shall be turned into hell, and all the nations that forget God (v. 17).

David pointed out that God makes Himself known by executing judgment against the nations that forget God. That judgment will be carried out by the wicked themselves who will be "snared in the work of their own hands" at the end of the nuclear age.

David noted in the next verse that the nations will finance their expensive weapons systems and military might on the backs of the poor and needy.

> 18 For the needy shall not always be forgotten, and the hope of the poor shall not perish for ever (Ps. 9:18, RSV).

God promises here that His return will mark the end of the nations' long-standing practice of taking the poor and needy's wages to build multi-trillion-dollar war machines. The hopes and dreams of the poor will cease to perish when Christ returns.

> **19** Arise, O LORD! Let not man prevail; let the nations be judged before thee! **20** Put them in fear, O LORD! Let the nations know that they are but men! Selah (Ps. 9:19–20, RSV).

The people who will drive the events leading up to the Battle of Armageddon will actually believe that their advanced weapons of war will prevail over all the laws, instructions, and prophecies that God has established for mankind down through the ages. It will be a case of mortal men becoming evil to the point where they will consider themselves equal to the immortal God who created them in the first place. However, God will not let the nations prevail. The Battle of Armageddon will end abruptly, shortly after the nations start it. When AWWII is over, the prophesied destruction of the nations will be complete. In the end it will be even as it is written; the Captain of the Lord's host will "put them in fear" and will "let the nations know that they are but men!"

The book of Revelation goes on to tell how Satan will be bound a thousand years and not be allowed to deceive the nations during that time of peace. Furthermore, during this coming age of peace, Christ will rule the nations with the aid of those who were His faithful followers on the earth through the ages.

CHRIST'S RESTORATION OF THE EARTH

Considering the magnitude of the destruction that will be wrought by the Initial Atomic War, what on earth will be left for Christ to rule following the Seventh Plague Atomic War? That war will leave the world unfit for plant and animal life. The answer to this question lies in the fact that Jesus Christ is God. Recall that in the beginning God spoke, and a world, teeming with life, and man and woman made in God's image, was created. In the same manner and with the same power and authority, Jesus Christ will restore a burned-out, radioactive planet, called Earth, to life and health.

A detailed description of the restoration of the Earth's dead waters and oceans was shown in a vision to the prophet Ezekiel.

1 Then he brought me back to the door of the house; and behold, water was flowing from under the threshold of the house toward the east, for the house faced east. And the water was flowing down from under, from the right side of the house, from south of the altar. 2 And he brought me out by way of the north gate and led me around on the outside to the outer gate by way of the gate that faces east. And behold, water was trickling from the south side. 3 When the man went out toward the east with a line in his hand, he measured a thousand cubits, and he led me through the water, water reaching the ankles. 4 Again he measured a thousand and led me through the water, water reaching the knees. Again he measured a thousand and led me through the water, water reaching the loins. 5 Again he measured a thousand; and it was a river that I could not ford, for the water had risen, enough water to swim in, a river that could not be forded. 6 And he said to me, "Son of man, have you seen this?" Then he brought me back to the bank of the river. 7 Now when I had returned, behold, on the bank of the river there were very many trees on the one side and on the other. 8 Then he said to me, "These waters go out toward the eastern region and go down into the Arabah; then they go toward the sea, being made to flow into the sea, and the waters of the sea become fresh. 9 And it will come about that every living creature which swarms in every place where the river goes, will live. And there will be very many fish, for these waters go there, and the others become fresh; so everything will live where the river goes" (Ezek. 47:1–9, NASB).

Thus, an incredibly large river of fresh water will flow out of Christ's dwelling place at Jerusalem into the sea. "And it will come about" that the living river of water flowing out of Jerusalem will eventually restore life to the world's oceans. This phenomenal restoration of the seas will remind everyone who survives the tribulation that this same Jesus, who will be reigning at Jerusalem, is the source of all life.

Following the Battle of Armageddon, there will be a widespread recognition of Christ as the promised Savior of the world. Isaiah wrote about the survivors' response to Christ's message of salvation and truth.

> 1 The word that Isaiah the son of Amoz saw concerning Judah and Jerusalem. 2 And it shall come to pass in the last days, that the mountain of the LORD'S house shall be established in the top of the mountains, and shall be exalted above the hills; and all nations shall flow unto it. 3 And many people shall go and say, Come ye, and let us go up to the mountain of the LORD, to the house of the God of Jacob; and he will teach us of his ways, and we will walk in his paths: for out of Zion shall go forth the law, and the word of the LORD from Jerusalem. 4 And he shall judge among the nations, and shall rebuke many people: and they shall beat their swords into plowshares, and their spears into pruninghooks: nation shall not lift up sword against nation, neither shall they learn war any more (Isa. 2:1–4).

Christ will not only usher in a thousand years of peace, but will also restore the balance of nature to Garden of Eden splendor.

> 6 And the wolf will dwell with the lamb, And the leopard will lie down with the kid, And the calf and the young lion and the fatling together; And a little boy will lead them. 7 Also the cow and the bear will graze; Their young will lie down together; And the lion will eat straw like the ox. 8 And the nursing child will play by the hole of the cobra, And the weaned child will put his hand on the viper's den. 9 They will not hurt or destroy in all My holy mountain, For the earth will be full of the knowledge of the Lord As the waters cover the sea (Isa. 11:6–9, NASB).

Isaiah also records the far-reaching effect of Christ's just reign in the following statement.

> 5 No longer will the fool be called noble nor the scoundrel be highly respected (Isa. 32:5, NIV).

Christ will ban all "fools and scoundrels" from positions of authority. This action will make it possible for all people to prosper and live in peace.

THE END IS NEAR

After studying the Bible's prophecies concerning the coming seven trumpet events, one may wonder how soon the First Trumpet Atomic War might occur. According to Zechariah's Sebat connection to Christ's parable of "the fig tree and all the trees," man's first manned space flight "round the earth," on April 12, 1961, identifies both the date to begin the final countdown to the day of Christ's promised return and the generation that "shall not pass away, till all these things be fulfilled." Although the Sebat connection does not immediately pinpoint when AWWI will occur, the fulfillment of the arrival of the Sebat generation does define the present era to be the days when the voice of the first angel is about to trumpet.

Several facts support this position. First, the nuclear weapons technology and missile delivery systems capable of burning up a third of the earth are already in place, poised to attack. Next, the satellite technology needed to fulfill the prophecies foretelling a worldwide Christian evangelistic outreach over those sitting on the earth are in space, ready to do their assigned tasks. The prophecies concerning man's ability to go "to and fro," into and out of earth orbit, compassing the earth, have also been fulfilled in the development of the space shuttle. Then, there is Israel, dwelling safely, in her original land. Also, Red China is growing in importance on the international scene.

Yet, despite these signs, it can also be said without equivocation (at the dawn of the decade of the nineties) that AWWI could not occur any day. The validity of this position rests upon the fact that there must be a widespread awakening of God's people to the coming disaster and their active participation in warning the rest of the world, before AWWI occurs. By biblical precedent, God had Noah warn the wicked concerning the destruction of the earth by a flood before it arrived. Therefore, since Christians serve a God who is "the same yesterday, and today, and forever" (Heb. 13:8), the wicked must be warned before the atomic holocaust occurs.

In light of all these things, it behooves God's people to work while there is still light, for the night cometh when no man can work (John 9:4).

CONCLUSION

The history of the fall of man is a tragedy. We as a people were created in the image of God. We once walked the majestic paths of the Garden of Eden where we freely talked with the King of kings, God the Almighty. Yet we carelessly turned our back on God's instruction and parted company with Him and the paradise He created for us. We were so certain we had a better way to run our lives and the world—so emphatically sure—that we as a race have repeatedly refused to heed His call to return to His instruction.

HERE AM I

1 "I permitted Myself to be sought by those who did not ask for Me; I permitted Myself to be found by those who did not seek Me. I said, 'Here am I, here am I,' To a nation which did not call on My name. **2** I have spread out My hands all day long to a rebellious people, Who walk in the way which is not good, following their own thoughts, **3** A people who continually provoke Me to My face" (Isa. 65:1–3*a*, NASB).

After the nations' fall, the remnant of the human race will find themselves dying on the atomic ash heap of what is left of planet Earth. They never got it right. They never managed to establish lasting peace. Their strategic arms limitations talks between the nations were a dialogue of the deaf that failed completely.

Yet, in spite of the collective rebellion of the human race, God the Father is still standing with outstretched hands all day long saying: "here am I, here am I." God still continues to love the human race and wants what is best for them, which is why God wrote His technological prophecies to the Sebat generation long ago. He is giving today's generation every chance to return to Him by showing us what will be the result of the nations' high-tech arms race and the cumulative sin of the human race.

SEIZE THE TIME REMAINING

Today there is still time to warn the wicked of the error of their way. Christians everywhere need to seize God's prophecies pertaining to the present era and use them to bring men to Christ. The Bible's vivid portraits of nuclear weapons and the destructive wars man will wage with them can be used effectively to accomplish this task. The accuracy of these prophecies indisputably establish the Bible as the ultimate authority on the dark art of nuclear warfare.

Once people are awakened to the grim truth of tomorrow's nuclear wars they are less likely to casually embrace false hopes concerning their future. One false hope is based on the premise that no national leadership would ever use nuclear weapons in a war, knowing they would reap the dreadful expected consequences, even if they won. Yet, history shows that wars have not always been started by normal, well-adjusted leaders.

The Bible warns repeatedly against trusting man's judgment to stave off impending disaster. God's description of man's grandiose plan to end war by constructing an all–encompassing international government after AWWI is a case in point. By anyone's standards, the various powerful groups of nations that will come together to form the Fourth Beast should be able to usher in an era of peace and safety for all nations. It will have the ability to communicate its policies to all people through the universally understood English language—the "mouth of a lion." A common language is certainly a powerful asset for an international government to possess. The feet of a bear law–enforcement division patterned after the sinister methods used to control the Soviet people should be able to effectively ensure peace and safety. The "body of a leopard" Arab states will have the quantities of oil necessary to sustain industrial growth for years to come. A thriving international economy based on ample supplies of reasonably priced Arab oil should keep industry humming and everyone happily employed. The world's ten most influential financial powers will monitor the economies of all nations and will have the authority to enforce necessary adjustments if a nation's economy flounders. This unprecedented financial control over the nations should, in theory, usher in worldwide economic stability and prosperity. Topping off all these assets will be the nation of Red China that will back up the authority of the new international government with the most powerful military force ever assembled on the face of the earth. What an empire it will be! "Who can make war with it?" (Rev. 13:4b, IGENT).

Yet, according to Scripture, man's ultimate effort to heal his wound unto death, suffered when he rebelled against God in the Garden of Eden, will end in a second global nuclear war. Man's future world government will fail completely. It will be the cause of AWWII and the destruction of the nations.

THE ROOT OF MAN'S PROBLEM

In the light of history, why would men still look to government rather than God to bring peace and safety? The answer is found in the Gospel of John.

> **19** And this is the condemnation, that light is come into the world, and men loved darkness rather than light, because their deeds were evil. **20** For every one that doeth evil hateth the light, neither cometh to the light, lest his deeds should be reproved (John 3:19–20).

Jesus noted here that God gave man an irrevocable free will to choose between good and evil, truth and lies, heaven and hell. We all know this to be true. Everyone of us can recall doing something we knew was wrong and displeasing to God. The wicked who refuse to repent of their evil and reject Christ shall be judged along with "all the nations that forget God" (Ps. 9:17). The darkness of hell is the eternal inheritance for those who love evil and refuse to come to the light, lest their deeds should be reproved. The wicked of the Sebat generation will find themselves "snared in the work of their own hands" (Ps. 9:16), literally dying on the atomic ash heap that they alone wrought on planet earth. God never intended any man to come to such an appalling end; but God, being a God of righteousness, will judge the wicked for their evil at the end of the age.

> **1** And after these things I heard a great voice of much people in heaven, saying, Alleluia; Salvation, and glory, and honor, and power, unto the Lord our God: **2** For true and righteous are his judgments: for he hath judged the great whore, which did corrupt the earth with her fornication, and hath avenged the blood of his servants at her hand (Rev. 19:1–2).

God, being just, will judge the world capital and its supporters for persecuting His people.

THE SEAL IS BROKEN

4 But thou, O Daniel, shut up the words, and seal the book,
even to the time of the end (Dan. 12:4*a*).

The seal has been broken. The words of the book are open
to today's generation. The nuclear age has arrived. Daniel's
prophecies to the latter day nations and Zechariah's profound
space-age visions are in plain view for twentieth-century people to inspect. The time of the end is upon us. The book of
Revelation's prophesied events is at the door.

THE U.S. EAGLE'S MISSION

The Sebat generation is headed into the final physical and
spiritual battles of the age. The days directly ahead will be the
most violent ever witnessed by the human race. There is much
work that remains to be done before Christ returns. God's
people need to do the Lord's work now, while there is still time.
One of the messages written to the seven churches in the book
of Revelation exhorts Christians to "be watchful, and
strengthen the things which remain" (Rev. 3:2*a*). One thing
remaining that needs to be strengthened, both spiritually and
physically, is the United States of America. It is the U.S. "eagle"
who will launch a worldwide evangelistic outreach during the
closing days of the nuclear age. U.S. Christians will use God's
space-age prophecies to bring men to the realization that an
all-knowing God is seeking to save lost sinners through the
finished work of Jesus Christ.

MAN'S PRECARIOUS POSITION

In some ways, entering the vastness of space has given man
an underlying feeling of being less earthly. Yet indisputably we
are still very mortal. The space suits, oxygen, and food we bring
along bear witness to our origins. They also betray our fragility
and how perishable we are as a people. Though some have
become caught up in today's fast-paced accomplishments and

have forgotten their personal need for a long-term solution to their short-term longevity, God did not forget. His space-age prophecies bear witness to His personal concern for those in the Sebat generation who have lost their way.

THE STAKES ARE HIGH

One of the purposes of this writing is to open Christians' eyes to the spiritual battle that is being waged for the minds and souls of the Sebat generation. The stakes are high. A man's soul is God-built to last forever. It is important for all Christians to enter the fight for the souls of men; for "faith cometh by hearing, and hearing by the word of God" (Rom. 10:17).

There has been a great falling away among many of today's Christians from the evangelistic efforts of the early church fathers who labored diligently to reach the unsaved in their time. Unfortunately, many of today's Christians spend their time pursuing materialism. They are not aware of God's fresh oil of truth, His message of the hour. They have become indifferent to the lost and dying generation around them.

Fortunately for the lost souls of today's generation, the Captain of the Lord's host did not forget. He has armed today's Christians with the mightiest sword in the universe, God's Word of Truth. Furthermore, He has promised that His space-age prophetic words of truth "shall not return unto Him void, but shall accomplish that which [He] pleases, and it shall prosper in the thing whereto [He] sent it" (Isa. 55:11b).

The Bible warns of a coming time of unprecedented trouble when the majority of the world's billions will be marked for death before their time. The responsibility for this calamity rests on the human race which has sown the wind of rebellion against God. Mankind will unavoidably reap the consequences of this rebellion when they unleash the nuclear whirlwinds of death and judgment at the end of the age. Now is the time for Christians to give God's prophetic word to those who are unaware of the coming destruction.

Today is the day of salvation. Today there is still time for the indifferent, sleeping Christian to wake up and become a factor in building Christ's church. The Captain's marching orders need every Christian's thoughtful response.

19 "Go ye therefore, and teach all nations, baptizing them in the name of the Father, and of the Son, and of the Holy Ghost: (Matt. 28:19). **20** Teaching them to observe all that I have commanded you; and lo, I am with you always, to the close of the age (Matt. 28:20, RSV)."

BIBLIOGRAPHY

Introduction

Time, July 2, 1984.
_____, June 17, 1985.

Chapter 1: Egypt's Wandering Idols

Barnes, Albert. *Barnes' Notes*. Grand Rapids, Mich.: Baker Book House, 1950.

Bio Science, January 1981.

Burns, Edward McNall and Philip Lee Ralph. *World Civilizations*. New York: W. W. Norton & Company, 1955.

Buttrick, George A., ed. *The Interpreter's Bible*. Vol. 5. Nashville: Abingdon Press, 1956.

Environment, May 1981.

Jamieson, Robert, A. R. Fausset, and David Brown. *Commentary on the Whole Bible*. Grand Rapids, Mich.: Zondervan Publishing House, 1945.

Life, February 12, 1971.

National Geographic, October 1963.
_____, May 1965.
_____, May 1966.
_____, May 1969.
_____, May, 1985.

New York Times, May 4, 1975.

Newsweek, March 10, 1986.

The Middle East, January 1988.

The Atlantic Monthly, June 1972.

Time, May 22, 1964.
_____, January 25, 1971.
_____, June 14, 1971.
_____, June 11, 1973.
_____, May 5, 1975.
_____, September 6, 1976.
_____, January 2, 1978.
_____, December 23, 1985.
_____, March 10, 1986.
_____, March 17, 1986.
_____, March 24, 1986.

_____, December 22, 1986.

Chapter 2: Egypt—A Prophetic Hourglass

Barnes, Albert. *Barnes' Notes.* Grand Rapids, Mich.: Baker Book House, 1950.
Buttrick, George A. *The Interpreter's Bible.* Vol. 5. Nashville: Abingdon Press, 1956.
Environment, May 1981.
Halley, Henry H. *Halley's Bible Handbook.* Grand Rapids, Mich.: Zondervan Publishing House, 1976.
Life, June 23, 1967.
_____, February 12, 1971.
National Geographic, May 1985.
_____, May 1965.
Newsweek, September 21, 1970.
_____, January 25, 1971.
Life, Special Edition, "Israel's Swift Victory," 1967.
The Atlantic Monthly, June 1972.
Time, June 30, 1967.
_____, November 11, 1974.
_____, January 2, 1978.
U.S. News & World Report, August 2, 1971.
_____, November 21, 1988.

Chapter 3: Roll Call of the Nations

Barnes, Albert. *Barnes' Notes.* Grand Rapids, Mich.: Baker Book House, 1950.
Ergang, Robert. *Europe Since Waterloo.* Boston: D. C. Heath and Company, Mass., 1954.
Gervasi, Frank. *The Case for Israel.* New York: Viking Press, 1967.
Hall, Walter Phelps and Robert Greenhalgh Albion with the collaboration of Jennie Barnes Pope. *A History of England and the British Empire.* New York: Ginn and Company, 1937.
Hayes, Carlton J. H. *Modern Europe to 1870.* New York: The Macmillian Company, 1953.
Jamieson, Robert, A. R. Fausset, and David Brown. *Commentary on the Whole Bible.* Grand Rapids, Mich.: Zondervan Publishing House.
Lindsey, Hal. *The Late Great Planet Earth.* Grand Rapids, Mich.: Zondervan Publishing House, 1970.
National Geographic, March 1977.

_____, May 1985.
Newsweek, February 1, 1971.
_____, October 4, 1982.
_____, November 1, 1982.
Roberts, Alexander and James Donaldson. Revised by A. Cleveland Coxe. *Ante-Nicene Fathers*. Vol. V, "The writings of the Fathers down to A.D. 325." Grand Rapids, Mich.: WM. B. Eerdman's Publishing Co., 1950–51.
Time, July 14, 1967.
_____, November 11, 1974.
_____, January 19, 1981.
_____, February 9, 1981.
U.S. News & World Report, September 21, 1970.
_____, August 16, 1971.
_____, October 4, 1971.
_____, August 27, 1979.
_____, December 3, 1979.
_____, December 15, 1980.
_____, August 17, 1981.
_____, October 26, 1981.
Wood, L. J., *A Survey of Israel's History*. Grand Rapids, Mich.: Zondervan Publishing House, 1951.

Chapter 4: Russia Invades Israel

Christian Life, May 1975.
Halley, Henry H. *Halley's Bible Handbook*. Grand Rapids, Mich.: Zondervan Publishing House, 1976.
Ironside, H. A. *Expository Notes on Ezekiel the Prophet*. Neptune, N.J.: Loizeaux Brothers, 1949.
Jamieson, Robert, A. R. Fausset, and David Brown. *Commentary on the Whole Bible*. Grand Rapids, Mich.: Zondervan Publishing House
Josephus, Flavius. Whiston, William, trans. *Complete Works of Josephus*. Grand Rapids, Mich.: Kregel Publications, 1963.
Ludwigson, Raymond, *A Survey of Bible Prophecy*. Grand Rapids, Mich.: Zondervan Publishing House, 1951.
Newsweek, November 24, 1975.
_____, June 21, 1982.
_____, September 27, 1982.
_____, October 4, 1982.
_____, September 24, 1984.
_____, June 2, 1986.

Time, June 21, 1971
————, January 17, 1972.
————, October 30, 1972.
————, May 18, 1981.
————, September 24, 1984.
U.S. News and World Report, February 6, 1978.
————, March 22, 1982.
————, September 27, 1982.
————, October 11, 1982.
————, January 10, 1983.
————, August 6, 1984.

Chapter 5: Falling Stars

Barnes, Albert. *Barnes' Notes.* Grand Rapids, Mich.: Baker Book House, 1950.
Glassstone, Samuel and Philip J. Dolan. *The Effects of Nuclear Weapons.* Published jointly by the Department of Defense and the Energy Research and Development Administration, 1977.
National Geographic, May 1987.
Reader's Digest, May 1987.
Schell, Jonathan. *The Fate of the Earth.* New York: Alfred A. Knopf, 1982.
Science Digest, June 1984.
————, March 1985.
Science, December 23, 1983.
Scientific American, August 1984.
The Atlantic, January 1987.
The Atlantic Monthly, November 1984.
Time, May 12, 1986.
U.S. News & World Report, October 18, 1982.
————, March 23, 1987.

Chapter 6: The First Three Trumpets

Discover, August, 1985.
————, December 1987.
Glassstone, Samuel and Philip J. Dolan. *The Effects of Nuclear Weapons.* Published jointly by the Department of Defense and the Energy Research and Development Administration, 1977.
Life, November 1984.
National Geographic Society, May 1972.
Newsweek, October 5, 1981.

_____, July 29, 1985.
_____, May 4, 1987.
Popular Mechanics, April 1987.
Science Digest, March 1985.
Science, December 23, 1983.
Scientific American, May 1983.
_____, August 1984.
Time, February 28, 1972.
U.S. News & World Report, October 18, 1982.
_____, November 28, 1983.
_____, March 5, 1984.

Chapter 7: One Lone Eagle

America, December 5, 1981.
Barnes, Albert. *Barnes' Notes*. Grand Rapids, Mich.: Baker Book House, 1950.
Halley, Henry H. *Halley's Bible Handbook*. Grand Rapids, Mich.: Zondervan Publishing House, 1976.
National Geographic, May 1987.
Newman, Joseph, ed., *Wiring The World*. Washington, D.C.: *U.S. News & World Report* Books, 1971.
Reader's Digest, May 1972.
Science, December 23, 1983.
Scientific American, August 1984.
Time, December 24, 1984.

Chapter 8: The Fifth Trumpet "Nuclear Winter"

Barnes, Albert. *Barnes' Notes*. Grand Rapids, Mich.: Baker Book House, 1950.
Ergang, Robert Ergang. *Europe Since Waterloo*. Boston: D. C. Heath and Company, 1954.
Lang, G. H. *The Histories and Prophecies of Daniel*. London: Paternoster, 1940.
Newsweek, April 12, 1982.
Schell, Jonathan. *The Fate of the Earth*. New York: Alfred A. Knopf, 1982.
Scientific American, August 1984.
The Atlantic Monthly, November 1984.
U.S. News & World Report, December 29, 1980.
_____, January 5, 1981.
_____, March 21, 1983.

Chapter 9: A Biblical View of "The Day After"

America, February 28, 1987.

Barnes, Albert. *Barnes' Notes.* Grand Rapids, Mich.: Baker Book House, 1950.

Datamation, February 1984.

International Combat Arms, May 1988.

Jamieson, Robert, A. R. Fausset, and David Brown. *Commentary on the Whole Bible.* Grand Rapids, Mich.: Zondervan Publishing House, 1945.

Newsweek, June 29, 1981.

_____, October 5, 1981.

_____, April 12, 1982.

Schell, Jonathan. *The Fate of the Earth.* New York: Alfred A. Knopf, 1982.

Science Digest, June 1984.

_____, March 1985.

Science, December 23, 1983.

_____, September 12, 1986.

Scientific American, August 1984.

_____, January 1985.

The Atlantic Monthly, November 1984.

Time, October 11, 1976.

_____, October 6, 1980.

U.S. News & World Report, June 23, 1980.

_____, November 28, 1983.

_____, December 5, 1983.

Chapter 10: Leviathan—The Sea Monster

Aviation Week & Space Technology, December 10, 1984.

Barnes, Albert. *Barnes' Notes.* Grand Rapids, Mich.: Baker Book House, 1950.

Buttrick, George A. *The Interpreter's Bible.* Nashville: Abingdon Press, 1956.

Discover, December 1987.

Life, November 1984.

News & Comment, June 12, 1987.

Scientific American, March 1988.

U.S. News & World Report, March 5, 1984.

_____, December 14, 1987.

Chapter 11:The Captain of the Lord's Host

Halley, Henry H. *Halley's Bible Handbook*. Grand Rapids, Mich.: Zondervan Publishing House, 1976.

Chapter 12:The Sixth Trumpet World War

Barnes, Albert. *Barnes' Notes*. Grand Rapids, Mich.: Baker Book House, 1950.

Jamieson, Robert, A. R. Fausset, and David Brown. *Commentary on the Whole Bible*. Grand Rapids, Mich.: Zondervan Publishing House, 1945.

Lansing State Journal, April 30, 1975.

New York Times, July 6, 1973.

_____, April 13, 1975.

_____, August 15, 1975.

The Middle East, October 1987.

U.S. News & World Report, November 8, 1982.

Chapter 13: The Woman and the Dragon

Burns, Edward McNall and Philip Lee Ralph. *World Civilizations*. New York: W. W. Norton & Company, 1955.

Encyclopaedia Britannica. Vol. VIII, Eleventh Edition. New York: Cambridge University Press, 1910.

Halley, Henry H. *Halley's Bible Handbook*. Grand Rapids, Mich.: Zondervan Publishing House, 1976.

Newsweek, January 31, 1972.

_____, February 21, 1972.

_____, January 22, 1973.

_____, September 27, 1982.

_____, November 22, 1982.

_____, November 29, 1982.

Reader's Digest, July 1982.

_____, April 1983.

Time, November 15, 1971.

_____, January 31, 1972.

_____, February 5, 1979.

_____, February 18, 1980.

_____, March 23, 1981.

U.S. News & World Report, June 21, 1971.

_____, July 17, 1972.

_____, August 7, 1972.
_____, August 3, 1981.

Chapter 14: The Last Beast

Barnes, Albert. *Barnes' Notes.* Grand Rapids, Mich.: Baker Book House, 1950.
Newsweek, May 21, 1973.
_____, September 27, 1982.
_____, November 15, 1982.
Reader's Digest, August 1984.
Time, May 31, 1971.
_____, December 13, 1971.
U.S. News & World Report, February 14, 1972.
_____, August 27, 1979.
_____, February 18, 1985.

Chapter 15: Wake Up!

Jamieson, Robert, A. R. Fausset, and David Brown. *Commentary on the Whole Bible.* Grand Rapids, Mich.: Zondervan Publishing House, 1945.

Chapter 16: The Eye in the Sky

Baron, David. *The Visions & Prophecies of Zechariah.* Grand Rapids, Mich.: Kregel Publications, 1918.
National Geographic, September 1978.
Newman, Joseph Newman, ed. *Wiring The World.* Washington, D. C. *U.S. News & World Report* Books, 1971.
Newsweek, August 7, 1972.
Reader's Digest, May 1972.
The Atlantic Monthly, May 1985.
U.S. News & World Report, January 10, 1972.
_____, May 21, 1973.
_____, July 29, 1974.
_____, March 31, 1975.
_____, September 27, 1976.
_____, April 10, 1978.
_____, June 26, 1978.
_____, May 21, 1979.
_____, July 16, 1979.

_____, March 10, 1980.
_____, June 1, 1981.
_____, November 9, 1981.
_____, April 4, 1983.
_____, May 9, 1983.
_____, December 26, 1983.

Chapter 17: Top Secret

Baron, David. *The Visions & Prophecies of Zechariah.* Grand Rapids, Mich.: Kregel Publications, 1918.

Jamieson, Robert, A. R. Fausset, and David Brown. *Commentary on the Whole Bible.* Grand Rapids, Mich.: Zondervan Publishing House, 1945.

Newsweek, January 9, 1978.
_____, April 27, 1981.
Time, January 12, 1981.
_____, March 2, 1981.
_____, April 27, 1981.
U.S. News & World Report, July 16, 1979.
_____, February 23, 1981.
_____, April 13, 1981.

Chapter 18: The Sebat Generation

Baldwin, Joyce G. *Haggai, Zechariah, Malachi.* Downers Grove, Ill.: Inter Varsity Press, 1972.

Jamieson, Robert, A. R. Fausset, and David Brown. *Commentary on the Whole Bible.* Grand Rapids, Mich.: Zondervan Publishing House, 1945.

U.S. News & World Report, July 4, 1977.

Chapter 19: Mystery Babylon

Josephus, Flavius. William Whiston, trans. *Complete Works of Josephus.* Grand Rapids, Mich.: Kregel Publications, 1963.

Newsweek, September 27, 1971.
_____, October 11, 1971.
_____, June 30, 1980.
_____, April 12, 1982.
_____, May 24, 1982.
Time, July 2, 1979.

U.S. News World Report, June 14, 1982.
_____, April 29, 1985.
_____, November 7, 1988.

Chapter 22: The Seven Last Plagues

"CBS Morning News," January 10, 1984.
Barnes, Albert. *Barnes' Notes*. Grand Rapids, Mich.: Baker Book House, 1950.
Discover, February 1985.
Newsweek, June 12 1972.
_____, November 27, 1972.
_____, July 11, 1988.
Reader's Digest, February 1990.
_____, September 1970.
Schell, Jonathan. *The Fate of the Earth*. New York: Alfred A. Knopf, 1982.
Science, December 23, 1983.
Science Digest, March 1985.
Time, November 8, 1971.
_____, June 13, 1977.
_____, October 19, 1987.
U.S. News & World Report, July 31, 1972.
_____, November 18, 1974.

Chapter 23: The Fall of Babylon

Ludwigson, Raymond. *A Survey of Bible Prophecy*. Grand Rapids, Mich.: Zondervan Publishing House, 1951.
U.S. News World Report, September 15, 1986.
_____, September 25, 1989.

The author would appreciate hearing from you.
If you wish to comment or have questions,
send your remarks to:

TIP
ATTN: Charles W. Miller
P.O. Box 21113
Lansing, MI 48909-1113